U.S.–Japanese Agricultural Trade Relations

U.S.–Japanese Agricultural Trade Relations

edited by
Emery N. Castle *and* Kenzo Hemmi
with Sally A. Skillings

Published by
Resources for the Future, Inc., Washington, D.C.
Distributed by The Johns Hopkins University Press,
Baltimore and London

First published in the United States of America, 1982, by Resources for the Future, Inc., 1755 Massachusetts Avenue, N.W., Washington, D.C. 20036.
Distributed by The Johns Hopkins University Press, Baltimore, Maryland 21218; The Johns Hopkins Press Ltd., London.

First published in Japan, 1982, by the University of Tokyo Press, 7–3–1 Hongo, Bunkyo-ku, Tokyo

Library of Congress Cataloging in Publication Data

Main entry under title:

U.S.–Japanese agricultural trade relations.

   Based on papers presented at a conference held in Tokyo June 1980.
   Includes index.
   1. Produce trade—United States—Congresses.   2. Produce trade—Japan—Congresses.   3.   United   States—Commerce—Japan—Congresses.   4. Japan—Commerce—United States—Congresses.   5. Agriculture and state—United States—Congresses.   6. Agriculture and state—Japan—Congresses.   I. Castle, Emery N.   II. Hemmi, Kenzō, 1923–   .   III.   Skillings, Sally A.   IV. Resources for the Future.
HD9005.U24   1982   382'.41'0952   82-7832
ISBN 0–8018–2815–5   AACR2
ISBN 0–8018–2814–7 (pbk.)

Resources for the Future is a nonprofit organization for research and education in the development, conservation, and use of natural resources and the quality of the environment. It was established in 1952 with the cooperation of the Ford Foundation. Grants for research are accepted from government and private sources only if they meet the conditions of a policy established by the Board of Directors of Resources for the Future. The policy states that RFF shall be solely responsible for the conduct of the research and free to make the research results available to the public. Part of the work of Resources for the Future is carried out by its resident staff; part is supported by grants to universities and other nonprofit organizations. Unless otherwise stated, interpretations and conclusions in RFF publications are those of the authors; the organization takes responsibility for the selection of significant subjects for study, the competence of the researchers, and their freedom of inquiry.

This book is a product of RFF's Renewable Resources Division, Kenneth D. Frederick, director. It was edited by Sally A. Skillings and designed by Elsa B. Williams. The index was prepared by Sydney Schultz. Calligraphy for the jacket is by Hiroko Okahashi Maybury-Lewis.

Contents

Tables

Figures

Preface

In 1978 the Japan Center for International Exchange approached Resources for the Future with, for RFF at least, an unusual proposal. The proposal was for me to chair a group of U.S. scholars who would explore certain aspects of U.S.–Japanese agricultural trade relations in a set of papers. The proposal was unusual in that the efforts of the U.S. scholars were to be coordinated with parallel efforts of a group of Japanese scholars under the chairmanship of Kenzo Hemmi, dean of agriculture at the University of Tokyo; further, the entire scholarly effort was to be integrated with reciprocal visits and discussion between policy makers in the U.S. Congress and the Japanese Diet. At that time I was vice-president and senior fellow at RFF, and after discussing it with President Charles Hitch of RFF and selected staff members, I agreed to undertake the assignment on behalf of the organization.

The primary objective of the entire undertaking, as explained by Mr. Tadashi Yamamoto, director of the Japan Center for International Exchange, was to serve the decision-making process in the two countries. A secondary objective was to develop additional scholarly capacity in both countries for the understanding and analysis of agricultural trade relations. The Japan Center for International Exchange—using grants by the Toyota Motor Company, the Toyota Motor Sales Company, and the Japan–United States Friendship Commission—provided the major funding for the undertaking.

There were no plans at the outset to combine the scholarly work in the two countries in a single volume, but there were plans for a conference of the two groups to facilitate an exchange of findings. Dean Hemmi and I had not met prior to the initiation of the project. Each of us was to choose his scholars, develop his respective outlines, and make the two efforts as complementary as possible through correspondence. When Dean Hemmi saw the U.S. outline, however, he developed a very comparable outline for the Japanese efforts. It became apparent a well-integrated piece of work might result.

In June of 1980 a conference of the authors was held in Tokyo. D. Gale Johnson from the United States and Yujiro Hayami of Japan joined the original group of scholars and also presented papers. Johnson had just completed a manuscript on world food problems and prospects and Hayami one on Japanese agricultural adjustments. Both papers were relevant to U.S.–Japanese trade relations and added significantly to the conference.

At that time, it became apparent that the integration and complementarity of the papers had succeeded beyond our original expectations, and it was decided that an effort should be made to publish the results. I agreed to submit the collected papers to Resources for the Future for consideration as a book.

Thus, Dean Hemmi and I, who had begun the project in the expectation of chairing a small group of scholars in our respective countries on parallel but somewhat loosely coordinated projects, found ourselves working closely together in editing a highly integrated volume. I take this opportunity to recognize Dean Hemmi's professional skill, patience, and wonderful sense of responsibility. What began as a professional association has grown to encompass personal friendship. It has been a genuine privilege to work with him in this undertaking.

Dean Hemmi and I believe the process has produced a book. Efforts of this kind usually result in collections of papers that have substantial duplication, different styles, and gaps in coverage. Although this volume suffers from all of these defects, it is our belief they are minimal when compared with the contribution the volume makes. Dean Hemmi and I have edited each manuscript, and the authors have been exceedingly cooperative in making adjustments. Chapter 1 was written by Dean Hemmi and me after the other chapters were in hand and furnishes the plan of the volume, an overview and summary of the principal findings, and our own conclusions. We believe the volume is a unique treatment of agriculture, agricultural policy, and trade relations of two countries that have great need for mutual understanding. Because the book will be published in both languages (in Japanese by the University of Tokyo Press), scholars and policy makers in each country will have available for the first time data and material on each country viewed in a comparable manner. Some of the Japanese material is available in English for the first time; Dean Hemmi assures me the same is true on the Japanese side.

As noted earlier, the primary purpose of the entire undertaking was to serve decision makers in Japan and the United States. We believe such service already has been and will continue to be rendered. The Japan Center for International Exchange coordinated visits of members of the U.S. Congress and their staffs in Japan as well as visits of Diet members to the United States. Materials from this volume have already been used in numerous ways by policy makers, and I trust such use will continue. The draft papers were supplied to the members of the Japan–U.S. Economic Relations ("wisemen") Group and were cited in recommendations on agricultural trade in their report to the president and prime minister. This volume will also serve the secondary objective of the project—to develop scholarly capacity for the understanding and analysis of agricultural trade relations between the two countries.

Mr. Tadashi Yamamoto of the Japan Center for International Exchange deserves tremendous credit for making the effort possible in the first place and for coordinating it from start to finish. He was ably assisted in the New York office of the center by Mr. Hiroshi Peter Kamura, who was most efficient and always seemed to have the myriad details concerning the project at his fingertips.

Certain individuals within RFF also deserve special mention. Sally Skillings provided expert editorial assistance and helped greatly in making the style of authors of the two countries comparable. Kenneth Frederick served as acting chairman of the RFF Publications Committee for the review of this manuscript.

January 1982   Emery N. Castle
                                                     Washington, D.C.

I

Introduction

1

Overview

Emery N. Castle *and* **Kenzo Hemmi**

Why has the history of agricultural trade relations between the United States and Japan often been so troubled? And what of the future? Even though trade in agricultural commodities is apparently of mutual advantage, unless the issues that have created problems are recognized and defined, future trade relations are likely to be worrisome to both parties. This book is written in the hope that a thorough analysis of the basic complementarities between the two agricultural economies and an understanding of the internal problems of each country will point toward better relations in the future.

The United States has large land areas and large-scale farming. A significant part of its agricultural output is exported, and Japan is a most valuable customer for these exports. In contrast, Japan is an importer of food and its agricultural economy is dominated by small farms. Generally speaking, Japan is a willing importer of U.S. agricultural products and it also wants to be assured of a dependable supply. In addition, the two countries are friends. Both are democracies and both have the same general objectives in the world.

What, then, is the problem? On the surface it would appear that the need for accommodation is so great that, in comparison, any

Emery N. Castle is president of Resources for the Future. Kenzo Hemmi was dean of the Faculty of Agriculture at the University of Tokyo.

1

obstacles which might exist would be insignificant. However, when ones goes beneath the surface, the issues are complicated and need to be recognized by policy makers in both countries. That is what this book is about.

The book has four parts. Part I introduces the issues addressed in this volume, describes the world food situation as a setting for U.S.–Japanese agricultural trade relations, and presents the current policy situation with respect to these relations. Part II discusses agriculture and agricultural policy in Japan and the United States and their interrelationships. Part III shows how agricultural policy in the United States and Japan is made with attention to both similarities and differences. In this connection, the coalitions underlying prevailing agricultural policies are described in detail, thus permitting an assessment of the possibilities of change. Part IV analyzes the interdependence of the two agricultural economies in the belief that future policy development should be based on such knowledge.

Scholars from both countries participated in the preparation of each of the four parts. The reader will find substantial cross-referencing between chapters throughout the book. The writers discovered in a very real way that scholarship, as well as trade, is interdependent.

U.S.–Japanese Trade Relations

Trade between countries occurs in a global context and is never just the result of bilateral negotiation without direct or indirect effect on third parties. Furthermore, the global demand and supply situation for a commodity establishes the general market conditions within which bilateral trade is negotiated, and so it is with food. Accordingly, in chapter 2, D. Gale Johnson provides a description of the world food situation that establishes the context for agricultural trade between the United States and Japan.

In the chapter, Johnson is cautiously optimistic about the world food situation while recognizing that trade relations in the future will undoubtedly be complicated. Despite higher energy prices and disappointing agricultural performance in many parts of the world—notably in parts of Africa and the centrally planned economies—per capita food consumption for the world as a whole increased during the 1970s. Johnson believes that inadequate performance in the production of food usually can be traced to either inadequate consumer income or inappropriate incentive systems. He writes that resource constraints are much less important on a global basis than poverty and institutions.

With the exception of parts of Africa, Johnson believes that the low-income countries gave a remarkable performance in food production during the past decade. Their rate of increase in food production has outstripped that of the higher income countries in a significant way. Relatively, per capita increases are much less, of course, because of population growth. But Johnson notes that one of the real surprises of the past decade has been the decline in birth rates in the more densely populated parts of the world. Although it will be some time before the full impact of this decline is reflected in food produced per capita, there are short-run benefits, and it is a trend lending support to Johnson's cautious optimism.

Johnson analyzes the forces that influence world food trade—a trade that has been growing at approximately twice the rate of food production. The centrally planned economies, especially the Soviet Union and China, have greatly increased their grain imports. In the case of the Soviet Union, these imports were primarily used to increase the production of their livestock industry. Another factor resulting in increased trade has been the greater participation in such trade by the developing countries; some of them have increased their food imports but others have increased their exports. Moreover, these countries are likely to participate in trade as they develop their respective comparative advantages in the international community because it would be uneconomic for all such countries to become self-sufficient in food production. Underlying both of the above trends has been a decline in the real price of grain on a worldwide basis. The application of research results, the development of technology, and the use of advanced management techniques have permitted certain areas of the world to increase grain output under declining cost conditions. It has been to the advantage of these countries to dispose of part of this output elsewhere in the world. In those parts of the world where declining cost conditions do not prevail, it makes economic sense to import rather than produce at higher cost.

But if food trade grows in the future, it will do so in an uncertain world. Food is not traded, of course, in isolation from other commodities, and if trade in food is to flourish, so, too, must trade in other commodities. All trade is much influenced by world politics and global geography. Recent events in the world demonstrate the extent to which trade can be influenced by nations acting in concert (the actions of the Organization of Petroleum Exporting Countries) or by a nation acting alone (the U.S. grain embargo of Russia, and the decision of the centrally planned economies in the early 1970s to enter the world grain market). In fact, one of the results of global economic development is that when measured on a global basis, a relatively small shift in either demand or supply can result in very great changes in quantities traded and in prices on world markets. World markets for many commodities may go from scarcity to glut and back again with blinding speed. Johnson notes that numerous countries solve their own problems of instability by adjusting exports and imports, thus contributing to instability in the world market.

Despite this, Johnson believes that the prospects are favorable for strengthening and expanding trade between the United States and Japan. He further predicts that the real price of grain will continue to decline in international markets, and when this is combined with improvements in the value of the yen relative to the dollar and other currencies, international grain purchases will continue to be a good buy for the Japanese. Johnson obviously believes the United States will continue to export substantial quantities of grain and will have an incentive to continue to supply Japan, currently the largest single purchaser of U.S. foodstuffs.

In chapter 3, James P. Houck presents the basis for agricultural trade between the United States and Japan in terms of both demand and supply, reviews the history of trade relations and negotiations between the two countries, and calculates trade values resulting from multilateral tariff reductions and bindings.[1] He also relates the position that each country takes to the domestic agricultural policy of each country. He notes Japan's understandable concern about great dependence on food imports—a dependence that provides broad public tolerance for high support prices for rice. Although Japan's farmers are quite effective in a political sense (analyzed in detail by Hemmi and Talbot-Kihl in chapters 7 and 8, respectively), the high support price for rice production could not have occurred in the absence of the concern about food self-sufficiency on the part of the population as a whole. Yet the Japanese diet has undergone tremendous transformation in recent years and currently includes livestock products and fruits and vegetables to a much greater extent than was previously the case. This has been made possible by the extraordinary performance of the Japanese economy and the associated per capita income growth which is the basis for the Japanese demand for U.S.-produced

[1] A tariff binding is an agreement not to raise a particular tariff above the existing level.

meat and other livestock products, feed grains, and soybeans. The U.S. policy regarding agricultural exports, then, has special relevance for Japan.

According to Houck, U.S. agricultural export policy has three main elements: (1) the maintenance of competitive prices for world market sale of U.S. products subject to domestic price and income support programs, (2) the expansion of foreign markets through an active and aggressive program of market development and promotion, and (3) the continuation of efforts on a government-to-government basis to reduce tariff barriers. Yet these long-run trends and basic influences can be interrupted by short-run developments that can play havoc with international relations. One such development was the imposition by the United States of an embargo on soybeans and soybean meal in late 1973. Although in fact U.S. soybean exports to Japan were not reduced, the announcement of the embargo, coupled with the entry of the Soviet Union earlier in the decade in the world grain market, raised great concern in Japan about the reliability of its main supplier of foods—the United States. For these reasons and others, Houck notes that barriers to international trade are difficult to deal with internationally because most negotiators are not free to bargain in terms of their own internal food and agricultural policies. Yet the benefits of such negotiations are not insignificant. Apart from their dollar value, they may ensure markets for producers as well as supplies for importers. Houck (in tables 3-8 and 3-9) estimates that the tariff reductions and quota relaxations by Japan resulting from the Kennedy Round (1963–67) and the Tokyo Round (1973–79) amounted to export increases of about 4 percent and 21 percent from base trade values in 1964 and 1976, respectively.

Chapters 4 and 5, by Kuroda and Egaitsu, respectively, should be considered as a unit because they give a remarkably detailed picture of present-day agriculture in Japan and furnish certain data and analysis in English for the first time. From this analysis emerges a picture of the Japanese agricultural economy that is highly relevant to trade relations. Japan has many part-time and small farmers who, at least for some commodities, have high costs of production. But on probing deeper, one becomes impressed by the extent to which this, as well as other features of the Japanese agricultural economy, has been shaped and influenced by government policy and economic development generally. The impressive performance of the Japanese economy since World War II is referred to many times in the following pages and has had a profound impact on Japan's agricultural trade relations.

The performance of the economy generally affected Japan's agriculture directly in two ways. First, as mentioned earlier, it provided an ever expanding market for livestock products, fruits, and vegetables as incomes grew. Second, it provided an ever growing market for labor, which permitted farmers to sell their labor services while continuing to farm part time. But to grasp the problem of farm size in Japan, it is necessary to understand government price supports for rice, land tenure laws, and the persistent, slow rate of inflation.

Egaitsu contributes an interesting analysis of the extent to which inflation has affected asset values in Japan and shows that land holdings have been an effective hedge against inflation in Japan as they have been in the United States. However, differences in credit markets and tenure institutions in the two countries are one explanation of why farm consolidation has occurred so rapidly in one nation but not in the other.

Yet if the complications and subtleties within Japan are confusing to non-Japanese, the agricultural policy of the United States must appear equally complex to the non-American. Gardner (chapter 6) explains what that policy is and how it got that way. A high and growing level of agricultural exports has become increasingly important to the United States, and this trend has greatly influenced agricultural policy in the United States. Not all U.S. agricultural products are exported, of course, and this should be understood as the tapestry of U.S. agricultural policy is studied. Furthermore, export markets for those commodities sold abroad are now viewed from a much longer run point of view than was once the case. No longer is the rest of the world considered a dumping ground for surpluses but rather a collection of actual and potential customers—some more reliable, of course, than others. A high level of agricultural exports also serves many interests within the United States in addition to agricultural producers, and coalitions and linkages exist among these interests. Aside from the obvious commercial interest, agricultural exports help the U.S. balance of payments at a time when U.S. comparative advantage in other areas seems to be slipping. Even though the need for exports provides some discipline for agricultural policy in preventing support prices for exported commodities from getting too far out of line with world prices (as noted first by Houck), Gardner concludes that U.S. support prices have increased the price of wheat. The reason this is possible is the importance of the United States as an exporter in the world wheat market.

Neither can consumers in the United States be ignored if one is to understand U.S. actions. When the world demand–supply situation

causes the price of agricultural commodities to rise rapidly, the political party in power cannot ignore the reaction of consumers who
are also voters. Gardner reviews recent history from this point of view
and puts the temporary embargoes of the mid-1970s in perspective,
including the effects that such embargoes have had on U.S. agricultural policy since that time.

In chapter 7, Kenzo Hemmi presents a remarkably detailed picture
of how political decisions are made on food and agricultural matters
in Japan. He shows the interaction and interdependence among the
Liberal Democratic Party (LDP); the Ministry of Agriculture, Forestry
and Fisheries (MAFF); the Diet; and the rural community. He then
shows how agriculture and food policy is developed by the principal
actors from each of these social groups in the context of prevailing
public opinion. The picture that emerges is that policies are fashioned
on the basis of much compromise and that many of the Japanese
institutions are rooted in conservatism and will be slow to change, but
that change has occurred and will continue to occur. Although there
is accommodation of particular interest groups and reflection of popular concern about particular issues (such as food self-sufficiency),
one comes away with the impression that the nation is not likely to
lose sight of its long-run objectives and enlightened self-interest. On
the other hand, the system is by no means a closed one and there is
opportunity for new development and information to be reflected in
decisions.

Talbot and Kihl contrast the political performance of the United
States and Japan in chapter 8. They contend that agricultural trade
relations between the two nations constitute a subsector process that
is only a partial reflection of their respective political and economic
realities and ideologies. It follows that an understanding of the political power structure within each nation as it is related to food is
necessary for an appreciation of the latitude that can be accorded
negotiators involved in international trade relations. This same point
is made by Houck in chapter 3 and is adopted implicitly by several
of the economists in the volume, most dramatically in chapter 9 by
Yutaka Yoshioka, a Japanese negotiator. Talbot and Kihl believe the
relative abundance of food on the U.S. side could be a key to future
trade relations between the two countries and argue that if U.S. grain
stocks (including soybeans) move to either extreme, there could be
trouble. If surpluses exist, they believe the United States is likely to
push too hard for sales. But if shortages or high prices occur, the
Washington food network is likely to favor the domestic economy.
On the Japanese side, they conclude self-sufficiency considerations

will continue to be important in internal political debate concerning food.

The fourth and final part of the book consists of three chapters, two by Japanese authors and one by a U.S. economist. The three chapters constitute a search for ways the two countries' interdependence can be better managed. These chapters reflect the individual judgment of the writers on the policy issues involved. In chapter 9, Yutaka Yoshioka writes from the perspective of one who has represented Japan in past negotiations. His version of the origin of certain conflicts, the concerns of the Japanese citizen, and agricultural production in Japan is of great importance to anyone wishing to obtain a Japanese view of trade relations. He demonstrates again and again the Japanese concern with food self-sufficiency. A brief quotation captures the strength of this concern:

> Since the war, one of the foremost concerns of the government, regardless of who was in power, has been that of ensuring a dependable supply of food and especially of the principal grains through promotion of domestic production. Whatever the actual results have been, there has never been an administration in power that has not promised greater national self-sufficiency in food as one of its slogans. Furthermore, the opposition parties have never ceased to attack the party in power for being lax in its efforts to increase self-sufficiency. On this general point, therefore, the parties in and out of power have been constantly in accord.

With respect to the soybean embargo, he recognizes that the United States did not, in effect, reduce soybean exports to Japan in 1973. But he then writes:

> Although the public's fears were finally calmed once a supply of soybeans was secured from the American source, the crisis did make people acutely conscious of Japan's dependence on other countries located far beyond the ocean for its food supply—a fact which will not soon be forgotten.

In chapter 10, Yujiro Hayami discusses in a most penetrating way adjustment policies that might be followed by Japanese agriculture in a changing world. It is Hayami's thesis that Japanese agriculture must become competitive with international agriculture and that Japan needs to adopt conscious policies to bring this about. He believes the basic factor limiting Japanese agricultural productivity is small farm size which makes it difficult for Japanese agriculture to make efficient use of modern labor-saving technologies. But he also recognizes the strong attachment for the land held by Japan's small farmers. He believes the dual objectives of greater efficiency and widespread land ownership can be achieved only by activation of the land rental market. This means severing the bond between ownership and cultivation rights. He argues that if this were done, full-time farmers could expand their operations and become competitive internationally. Because many part-time and less efficient farmers produce rice, their disappearance would likely mean greater production of forage and livestock and less of rice. The shift away from rice is essential, Hayami argues, but cannot be accomplished as long as rice is supported by the government at its present levels. Hayami recognizes that an efficient Japanese agriculture would be very different from the large farms of the United States and believes the agriculture of the Netherlands is a more appropriate model for Japan.

Hayami concludes his chapter by distinguishing between food security and food self-sufficiency. In so doing, he analyzes the conditions under which the availability of food might become a problem to Japan. His conclusion is that for Japan, food security can best be achieved by a combination of (a) efficient agriculture, (b) greater use of stockpiles both domestically and internationally, (c) diversification of import sources, (d) a larger livestock industry whose animals can be slaughtered in an emergency, (e) agricultural research, and (f) cooperation with agricultural development efforts in the developing countries to forestall a future food crisis.

Before turning to the final chapter of the book, it is important to note the accomplishments of Japanese agriculture as well as its problems. Since World War II, land reform has been accomplished with the result that ownership of agricultural land is widely dispersed. Because of a booming economy, farm income has been supplemented by substantial nonfarm income, and rural residents are not at an economic disadvantage relative to urban dwellers. The major problem is the one analyzed so effectively by Hayami—small-scale operations and inefficiency. The effects of this inefficiency are manifested in many ways, including the cost to the treasury of maintaining rice prices for domestic rice producers. The food control account in the 1980 budget amounted to 955.6 billion yen, or about 27 percent of the MAFF budget and more than 2 percent of the entire budget of the Japanese government (see chapter 3).

In the final chapter, Sanderson provides an appropriate ending for the book. He reviews major food and agricultural trends in both the United States and Japan, discusses transitional problems, and concludes by outlining implications for U.S.–Japanese agricultural relations. Sanderson's analysis is quite compatible with Hayami's but can be contrasted with Yoshioka's on two points. First, Sanderson believes the Japanese diet will continue to change, and as in the case of other high-income countries, per capita consumption of animal products will eventually approach 40 percent of total caloric intake. Although Yoshioka does not predict future consumption patterns, he quotes nutritional authorities to the effect that the consumption of more animal products by the Japanese is unnecessary for a healthful diet. Yoshioka also questions whether U.S. agriculture is likely to have the same capacity in the future to increase output at reduced real cost as it has had in the past. Sanderson believes there is considerable unrealized capacity in American agriculture and presents data in support of that position.

Pursuit of Common Interests

After one has read all of the chapters in this volume and studied their implications, the question then is: What has been learned that can be used to improve future agricultural trade relations? The remainder of this chapter gives the views of the editors on this question. In it we attempt to identify measures that are implicit in the writings in the volume, or that seem to us to be logical deductions from the findings in the volume. Our views should be considered as supplementary to the many recommendations and conclusions advanced by the individual authors. However, we do not propose to speak for the chapter authors nor do we represent either of our countries in any official capacity. Our thoughts are advanced under three main headings:

1. cooperative U.S.–Japanese measures to improve the world food situation and international trading in food
2. domestic actions that could be taken by each country to improve or minimize difficulties in trade relations
3. steps to improve future agricultural trade negotiations

We believe this volume documents in a most convincing way that continued and, probably, increased agricultural trade is in the interests of both countries. From trade, Japan is able to obtain lower cost food for an increasingly varied diet than would otherwise be the case; and from trade, the United States is provided a market for its agricultural output that is considerably in excess of its domestic needs.

Furthermore, the agricultural economies of the two countries are remarkably complementary: in contrast to Western Europe there is a minimum number of agricultural products that both wish to produce in abundance. Futhermore, trade between the two countries is not limited to agricultural products; they trade in other commodities and products as well.

But beyond their obvious economic interests, the two countries otherwise have much in common. Both are democracies and both have the same general aspirations in the world: both believe the world will become better through peaceful economic development and have rejected armed aggression for themselves, as well as believing such aggression is inappropriate for others in the world.

Our views here are presented in a most rudimentary form. In some cases the following chapters provide great detail on what we are recommending. In such instances, policy proposals could easily be developed from the material in this volume and other readily available information. But for other measures, additional thought and effort would be needed for the development of a detailed policy proposal.

Cooperative U.S.–Japanese measures to improve the world food situation and international trading in food

The editors believe the two nations should consider thoughtfully the world food situation as a basis for developing measures unique to their bilateral situation.

1. The United States and Japan should encourage such multilateral efforts as the World Bank's to improve the world food situation and should together undertake a cooperative program to improve the situation. Although global per capita food consumption and birth rate trends have recently been encouraging, there is still reason for concern. We believe it to be in the long-run interests of both nations to assist with such development. The two nations are in an excellent position to exert such leadership. Agricultural science in both countries is well developed, and there are many public and private institutions in both that are multinational in scope. This joint program should emphasize research and education and have as its objective the development of the comparative advantage of the resources of the low-income countries in the production of food.

2. The United States and Japan should cooperate in measures to minimize year-to-year instability in world food markets. Even though it is beyond the scope of this volume to detail all of the measures that might be taken to accomplish such an objective, certain facts are ob-

vious. Measures have been proposed to create international buffer stocks in grain but they have not been acceptable to all of the nations that would need to cooperate, and multinational efforts should be made to accomplish this objective. Nevertheless, bilateral and national measures can also be taken to increase food stocks when supplies are abundant. The existence of buffer stocks would do much to reassure the Japanese people who are concerned about a dependable food supply.

3. The two countries should cooperate in confronting the powerful wave of protectionism which is sweeping over the world economy. We believe our two countries should approach our agricultural policy and trade issues in conformity with the furtherance of freer trade in the world. Moreover, the expansion of agricultural trade between the United States and Japan should not be viewed in isolation from its effect on world trade in general and nonagricultural commodities and products in particular.

Domestic actions that could be taken by each country to improve or minimize difficulties in future trade relations

By the United States

United States agricultural policy should reflect the reality that one-third of U.S. agricultural output is exported. If this market is to be developed fully, domestic policy cannot increase the prices of agricultural commodities to be sold abroad significantly above world market prices when supplies are short. The needs of good customers must be anticipated and met if they are to remain good customers. In addition, the United States is in an inconsistent position when it argues for free trade on the one hand but maintains protectionist policies with respect to dairy products and beef on the other.

Sanderson (chapter 11) believes that the United States can continue to expand its grain output at decreasing real costs unless a wasteful fuels program based on biomass conversion is undertaken. Johnson (chapter 2) believes that the real price of world grain will continue to decline. Yet there are those who believe that the real economic and environmental costs of additional U.S. agricultural output will increase. We believe that the nature of these trends is very important to future trade relations. We also believe they are not independent of the policies adopted. For example, if Sanderson should prove to be wrong and Johnson correct, the comparative advantage of the United States in grain production will decline even though it could remain a major exporter. Therefore, we believe the United States should favor those policies, including research, that result in more efficient agricultural production. We also believe the United States should avoid basing its agricultural exports on environmentally exploitative farming practices because such output will not be sustainable and will lead to future declines in production.

By Japan

We recommend that Japan approach the objective of food security, a most legitimate and understandable objective, from a more comprehensive and realistic standpoint than that of food self-sufficiency. The latter is an unattainable objective, given Japan's modern industrial state. But food security may be attained by a variety of means many of which are identified by Hayami and Sanderson in this volume. In general, we believe Japan needs to shift production away from rice and develop a more efficient agriculture. The Japanese government seems to believe that extensive and untiring efforts on behalf of structural improvements are the only ways to adapt Japanese agriculture to the world agricultural system but in addition, the Japanese price support program has been based on the principle that the support levels should be sufficiently high to reward existing farmers for their farming activities in spite of their inefficiency. The need to give price incentives to the farmers to improve their farming structure has been neglected. When setting price support levels, the difference in price between the domestic and international markets should be taken into consideration.

Steps to improve agricultural trade negotiations

We believe that future agricultural trade relations between the two countries must be developed in light of the following realities: (a) the international comparative advantage of the two economies, and the heavy dependence of the two countries on export markets and foreign supplies; (b) the need for both governments to maintain a prosperous farm economy, with the farm population obtaining returns comparable to those of the nonfarm population; (c) the significant political influence of the agricultural sector in both countries; and (d) the potential for an agricultural surplus problem in both countries.

We are not persuaded that an elaborate bilateral agricultural trade agreement between the United States and Japan is practical or necessary. If, for example, the volume of trade in soybeans between the United States and Japan were to be fixed, price fluctuations in the remaining world markets would be increased. Such fluctuations would tempt other traders to seek exclusive trade agreements because of the importance of the United States and Japan in the world trade of soy beans, feed grains, and other agricultural products. We do believe, however, there are certain steps which can be taken that will greatly improve relations.

1. In either country, there should be consultation prior to the announcement of a domestic policy change that may affect agricultural trade relations. It is clear that much of the past difficulty has been caused by failure to follow such a practice. For example, the soybean embargo of 1973 did not reduce the export of U.S. soybeans to Japan but it is clear that it had a major impact on Japanese public opinion which, of course, was reflected in the position of the Japanese government. This might have been avoided by appropriate prior consultation that could have made possible better public understanding in Japan of problems in the United States.

2. Each country should recognize the other's position in world food trade. For example, rice is in a surplus situation in Japan and its production is stimulated by government policy, while the United States is a large rice exporter. Given the present Japanese position, should the United States attempt to enter the protected Japanese market, Japanese concern would develop quickly. Conversely, there would be an immediate U.S. reaction if the Japanese were to attempt to dispose of their subsidized rice (even in a form of food aid) on the world market at the expense of U.S. rice exports.

Commitments should be made that the United States will not discriminate against Japan in its exports, and Japan will treat U.S. products fairly in its import program. Current nontariff barriers should not be increased, and strong efforts should be made to eliminate or mitigate them in the long run.

Moreover, there should be mutual recognition of the difference in effect between quantity constraints on the one hand, and import levies or export surcharges on the other. Quantity constraints are disconcerting prospects for a nation like Japan that is heavily dependent on imports for its food supply.

3. Because the two societies are democratic in nature, it is seldom possible to maintain secrecy in the negotiating process. But negotiators should keep in mind the potential effect of the flow of information on public opinion and the feedback effect of that flow on the negotiating process itself. Short-run negotiating progress or the lack thereof should be interpreted for the press in the context of the fundamentals of relations between the two countries and the complementarity of their agricultural economies.

2

The World Food Situation

Developments During the 1970s and Prospects for the 1980s

D. Gale Johnson

The lead sentence in an Associated Press story of November 11, 1979, was: "The Third World is moving toward a massive food shortage that could result in 'economic disaster' within 20 years, a United Nations report says."[1] This gloomy projection was a reporter's interpretation of a report presented to the FAO Council by the director-general of the Food and Agriculture Organization of the United Nations. Fear was expressed that developing countries would require

D. Gale Johnson is Eliakin Hastings Moore Distinguished Service Professor and chairman of the Department of Economics at the University of Chicago. This chapter is included with the permission of the American Enterprise Institute for Public Policy Research of Washington, D.C. Except for minor revisions and extensions, the chapter was published in American Enterprise Institute, *Contemporary Economic Problems, 1980* (Washington, D.C., American Enterprise Institute, 1980), pp. 301–339. Copyright 1980 by the American Enterprise Institute for Public Policy Research

[1] My reading of the report referred to, *Agriculture: Toward 2000*, leaves me with a quite different impression than the newspaper article (*Sunday Sun Times*, 1979) gives. First, the report makes no projections of future events; instead it presents what is likely to occur if recent trends persist and what could be achieved if substantial increases were made in investments in agricultural inputs and research and if appropriate incentives were provided for farmers. To quote from the introduction: "In the study no attempt has been made to forecast or to predict what is likely to happen by the end of the century." Second, there is very little emphasis given to energy. Of course, it is possible that discussion of the report at the conference did emphasize the bleakest possible picture of the future. *Agriculture: Toward 2000* was prepared by the Food and Agriculture Organization of the United Nations and presented at the 20th FAO Conference held in Rome, November 10–29, 1979.

ever increasing grain imports and that the cost of these imports would become a burden that many low-income countries could not bear.

Has the world food situation deteriorated during the 1970s? Have the prices of basic foods increased over time? Are the majority of the world's poor eating less and less as time goes by? If the dire predictions concerning the world's food situation that were so common in 1973 through 1975 had proven to be valid, the answer to each of these questions would be in the affirmative.

But such is not the case. The world food situation has not deteriorated during the 1970s. The prices of basic foodstuffs are low by historical standards. There is no evidence that the world's poor people are eating less well than a decade ago. In fact, on each point the evidence is to the contrary. The 1970s, as did each of the two prior decades, saw an improvement in per capita food supply for the world and in the low-income countries.

In *World Food Problems and Prospects,* published in early 1975, I concluded: "I am cautiously optimistic that the food supply situation of the developing countries will continue to improve over the coming decades. If I had as much confidence in the political process in both the industrial and developing countries as I do in the farmers of the world, I would drop the qualification 'cautiously.' " (p. 81). For the 1970s the cautious optimism was justified. Per capita food supplies in the developing countries improved during the 1970s. However, the improvement was modest and it was far from uniform. In fact, in Africa per capita food production declined during the decade but there were substantial differences within Africa that cannot be attributed primarily to natural conditions.

Supply Keeps Pace with Demand

The general conclusions of *World Food Problems and Prospects* have been borne out by subsequent events. The main conclusions were: (1) grain prices would decline soon (in real terms) to near the levels of the early 1970s; (2) that higher energy prices would not result in substantially higher costs of producing farm products and that adequate supplies of fertilizer would be available; and (3) there would be continuing though small improvement in the per capita availability of food in the low-income countries (Johnson, 1975, chapter 5).

In the mid-1970s the predominant view was that demand was likely to grow more rapidly than supply and that the real prices of food would quite probably increase rather than decrease from the high levels of 1973 and 1974. A number of reasons were given for the expectation that the food supply situation would deteriorate after the early 1970s. These included the assumption that higher energy prices would greatly increase the price of farm inputs, especially fertilizer; that increasing the cultivated area was no longer available as a significant means of increasing the food production; and that the growing use of grain as feed would reduce the food supplies of low-income countries. I shall consider the empirical validity of each of these assumptions before I look at the data on actual changes in per capita food supplies in the world and, particularly, in the low-income countries and in food prices.

Fertilizer prices

After the formation of the Organization of Petroleum Exporting Countries (OPEC), many feared that the sharp increases in the prices of energy would increase the price of fertilizer so much that the use of fertilizer would decline with a significant adverse effect upon food production. "Everyone knows" that fertilizer production is energy intensive and that the several fold increase in prices of energy should result in large increases in the price of fertilizer.

But what in fact has occurred failed to follow this simplistic scenario. In the United States, for example, as 1980 began, the index of the average price paid by farmers for all fertilizer was lower relative to the price index for all farm production items than in the 1967 base period (USDA, 1980a). The difference was not small; as of January 15, 1980, the price index for all production items was 262 while the price index for fertilizer was 222. This meant that relative fertilizer prices had declined by 15 percent between 1967 and the beginning of 1980. Compared to the prices farmers received for their products, the price of fertilizer declined by about 5 percent. These relative price relationships prevailed even though fertilizer prices, which are quite volatile, had increased by 24 percent during 1979. What is perhaps even more remarkable with respect to fertilizer prices paid by farmers is that if one starts the comparisons with 1970, one finds that fertilizer prices paid by farmers increased by just 3 percent more than prices paid for all production items. In 1970 the relative price of fertilizer was the lowest since 1910–14 and, in absolute terms, was 12 percent below 1967. It may also be noted that the farm price of fertilizer at the beginning of 1980 was 9 percent below the absolute (not relative) price reached in 1975.

The experience in the United States has not been unique. In South Korea, for example, the farm price of fertilizer decreased by 10 percent relative to the price index of all production items between 1970 and 1978. In Greece, the relative price of fertilizer declined throughout the 1970s, though this probably reflected a change in governmental pricing policy rather than underlying economic relationships. Fertilizer prices increased at approximately the same rate as all farm production items in Spain, and fertilizer prices increased less than the prices of all production items in the European community during the 1970s (FAO, 1979c, table 114).

How can this price behavior for fertilizer be explained? Several factors may be noted. While energy is an important component of the costs of producing fertilizer, especially nitrogen fertilizers, there has been significant technological progress in fertilizer production during the past fifteen years. In fact, the technological changes that became available for the production of nitrogen fertilizer in the 1960s reduced real costs by about 50 percent. Another factor is that the price farmers pay for fertilizer includes many components in addition to the raw fertilizer—transportation, mixing, marketing, and storage. Finally, a significant part of the world's nitrogen fertilizer output is being produced with low-value natural gas either because of long-term price contracts or of the shifting of nitrogen production to areas where natural gas is still being flared. This shift in the sources of the world's nitrogen fertilizer resulted in closing ammonia and urea producing plants in the United States and Japan in 1977 and 1978.[2]

Arable land

Another fear expressed during the mid-1970s was that the world's supply of arable land had been exhausted and that this source of increased food and agricultural production was no longer available. I do not wish to repeat the refutation of this point made in *World Food Problems and Prospects*. Here I only wish to note that during the past decade the amount of arable land in the world has increased by a little more than 5 percent and by 8 percent in the developing market

[2] (USDA, 1978, p. 22) It is highly likely that in the not too distant future fertilizer prices will increase relative to the prices of all other farm production inputs. Fertilizer prices, especially for nitrogen fertilizer, are highly volatile. But even when recent energy prices are fully reflected in the long-run prices of fertilizer, relative fertilizer prices should be held to an increase of no more than 10 percent compared to 1967. If energy prices increase in real terms, as it seems reasonable to expect, real fertilizer prices will probably increase in the future but almost certainly at a slower rate than real energy prices.

economies. Perhaps even more important was that between 1967 and 1977 the irrigated area in the developing market economies increased from 75.6 million to 94.7 million hectares, an increase of 25 percent. In the heavily populated Far East the absolute increase in irrigated area was almost 13 million hectares and 26 percent (FAO, 1979c, tables 1 and 2).[3]

Feed versus food

The increase in the feed use of grain was frequently cited during the mid-1970s as an important cause of the sharp increase in grain prices after 1972. In other words, livestock were said to be taking more and more food from the relatively poor. It is, of course, in high-income countries that a large fraction of the total grain supply is fed to livestock rather than being consumed directly; in low-income countries relatively little grain is fed to livestock and most of the grain is consumed by people. Some went so far as to argue that affluence constituted a threat to the poor. It is true higher per capita incomes resulted in an increase in the per capita demand for and use of grain, primarily through the increased consumption of meat and milk.

But affluence affects not only demand, but also has an effect upon production. During the decade before 1973 the high-income countries increased grain production more than consumption. Net grain exports from the developed market economies increased from 20 million tons in 1960–62 to 60 million tons in 1972/73 and 1973/74. The centrally planned economies of Eastern Europe did increase grain use more than production during the 1960s and early 1970s. However, if high-income economies are considered as a group, their net exports to low-income countries more than doubled during the period (Johnson, 1975, p. 31).

But developments after 1973 indicate that the use of grain depends upon much more than levels of per capita income. After the sharp increase in grain prices in 1973/74 there was a substantial decline in the use of grain for feed in the United States. In one year grain used as feed declined by 27 percent (USDA, 1977, p. 4). The amount of grain used as feed has not yet returned to the level of 1972/73. The use of grain for feed in the European Community has stabilized since the early 1970s. For all developed market economies, grain used as feed remains at or below the level of 1972/73 (USDA, 1977, 1980c).

[3] In 1977 arable land in the developing market economies was 644 million hectares. The arable land area of the developing market economies of the Far East was 266 million hectares.

And grain exports from the developed market economies increased threefold during the decade.

Grain used for feed has continued to increase in the centrally planned economies, though at a slower rate than during the 1960s. During the 1960s the use of grain for feed grew at an annual rate of 7.1 percent; during the 1970s (as of 1977/78) the rate of growth was 4.1 percent (USDA, 1977).

There was one part of the world in which the rate of growth of grain used for livestock feed was higher in the 1970s than during the 1960s—this was the developing market economies. During the 1960s, use grew at 6.0 percent annually; during the 1970s, at 7.6 percent. As of 1977/78 the feed use of grain accounted for 13 percent of total grain use in such economies. At the beginning of the 1960s feed use of grain was 7 percent of total grain consumption.

Food Supply Changes During the 1970s

It is appropriate to now look at what actually happened to per capita food supplies during the 1970s and, especially, after 1972. For all low-income countries (except centrally planned), per capita food production in 1972 was at the 1961–65 level, a decline from the 1970 index of 106. The recovery from the low 1972 level was rapid, and by 1975 the index of per capita food production stood at 107. Further progress occurred through 1978 by which time the index had increased to 110. However, preliminary indications show a sharp reduction to 106 for 1979. The average index for the last four years of the 1970s was 108.2 compared to 101.2 for the same period a decade earlier. The annual growth in per capita food production for the decade was approximately 0.7 percent. This may seem low, but it was higher than the growth rate for the 1960s and the same as for the entire 1970s.[4]

Viewed in terms of the performance of agriculture, the growth of food production during the 1970s in the low-income countries reflects a remarkable performance. For the decade, food production grew at 3.2 percent annually, compared to 2.0 for the high-income countries. The modest growth in per capita food production was caused by the rapid growth of population.

[4] Data on per capita food production are from USDA, 1974, p. 2, and USDA, 1980b, p. 4.

Imports and food supply

The consumption of food in a given year is generally not the same as the amount of food produced. The supply actually consumed consists of production, changes in stocks, and net trade. We have inadequate data on changes in stocks for the low-income countries. However, if we are interested in average food consumption for a number of years, changes in stocks can have only a limited effect on average consumption. The major source of a difference between food production and food consumption is net trade.[5]

As a group, the low-income countries are net importers of grain. During the 1970s their grain imports increased by 25 million tons to 48 million tons of net imports in 1979/80 (USDA, 1980b). The increase in grain imports would provide about 40 calories per day for more than two billion people. On the basis of an average daily per capita intake of 2,000 calories, the increase in grain imports added 2 percent to the available calories. It is not intended to imply that the increase in grain imports made a major contribution to the improvement of food supplies in the low-income countries but rather to make it quite clear that the increase in per capita food supplies was equal to or greater than the increase in per capita food production during the 1970s.

Increased imports of food are often assumed to be a necessity caused by failure of agricultural production to increase at an appropriate pace. For example, an FAO study recently noted that the developing countries increased their grain imports by more than 50 percent between 1975 and 1979, and this increase portends both increasing dependence upon high-income countries (especially the United States) and increasing difficulties of paying for a rising level of food imports.[6] For many developing countries, increasing food imports may be an efficient use of their resources and a response to rising real incomes and not a signal of imminent or eventual disaster. Associated with the

[5] India has been an exception to the rule that low-income countries have carried minimum stocks of grain. Between 1974 and 1977 India increased grain stocks in the hands of the government from 4 million to 18 million tons. At the end of 1979 grain stocks were estimated to be 19 million tons. India's 1979/80 grain production is projected to be some 18 million tons below the prior year. The drawdown of public stocks will offset a large part of the decline in grain production. See USDA, 1979.

[6] In a discussion of recent trends in world trade in agricultural products in *Agriculture: Toward 2000* (FAO, 1979a) the following was stated: "Every developing region . . . shared in both the downward share of world agricultural exports and the rising share of world agricultural imports . . . A major feature of this deterioration—from the point of view of the developing countries—of trade in agricultural products was the stubborn upward trend in their cereals imports" (p. 12). It was noted that the degree of cereal self-sufficiency declined from 96 percent in 1963 to 92 percent in 1975.

notion that significant food imports are evidence of agricultural failure is the view that most if not all developing countries should be self-sufficient in food.[7]

Often lost sight of in the discussion of food self-sufficiency is that the vast majority of developing countries are net exporters of agricultural products. In 1977 the developing market economies had an excess of $17 billion of agricultural exports over agricultural imports; in terms of percentage the excess of exports over imports was almost 60 percent. If the oil exporters are excluded, the value of agricultural exports was nearly double the value of agricultural imports in 1977 for all other developing market economies (FAO, 1979b, p. 11). The best use of some nation's agricultural resources may be to produce crops for export and import a significant fraction of its food.

It is interesting to note that while concern has been expressed about the increase in grain and food imports by the developing countries, little attention has been given to the even larger increase in the value of agricultural exports by the same group of countries. While food imports of the non-oil developing countries increased at an annual rate of $1.4 billion between 1970 and 1977, the value of their agricultural exports increased by $2.9 billion (FAO, 1979b, p. 11). If one is concerned about rising food imports, why is one not elated by agricultural exports that increase even more rapidly?

Many of the developing countries follow policies that encourage imports, on the one hand, and discourage exports, on the other hand. Many of these countries have overvalued exchange rates; such exchange rates act as subsidies for imports and as taxes on exports. In addition, some developing countries impose export taxes on their major agricultural export products. The significant export surplus for agricultural products achieved by the developing market economies would be even greater if governmental policies were designed to facilitate exports and not to encourage imports in competition with locally produced food and other agricultural products through an overvaluation of currencies.

---

[7] *Agriculture: Toward 2000* is somewhat ambivalent about the merits of self-sufficiency in food and export expansion. For example: "Indeed, the pursuit of the objective of greater self-sufficiency in food is not necessarily inconsistent with a drive toward commodity development aimed at enhancing export earnings. Import substitution for food saves foreign exchange and production for foreign exchange earns foreign exchange. With limited land resources and with the need for foreign exchange earnings—for promoting industrialization and other development efforts—the most profitable use of agricultural resources would depend upon the relative gains from import substitution and export promotion. The individual countries would need to select the right mix of foodstuff production and export crop production, taking into account the relative costs and returns" (FAO, 1979a, p. 189).

Regional variations in food production

It was noted above that during the 1970s, the annual growth of food production per capita in the low-income countries was 0.7 percent. However, there was considerable variation in the increase in per capita food production during the last decade and since 1961–65. Table 2-1 gives production data, total and per capita, for the past six years. Using averages for the past four years, the changes in per capita food production range from a high of 19 percent increase for East Asia to a low of a 9 percent decline in Africa.

The increase in per capita food production in South Asia, which includes 65 percent of the population of the low-income market economies, was only 8 percent between the early 1960s and the late 1970s. Bangladesh actually suffered a decline in per capita food production. The growth of per capita food production in South America was greater during the 1970s than during the 1960s. This was not the case for Central America, which had a slower growth during the 1970s than during the prior decade. However, for the two decades, Central America had a respectable increase of approximately 14 percent. The Caribbean fared badly in both the 1960s and 1970s; except for the Dominican Republic, per capita food production declined in each of the Caribbean countries.

It was noted above that per capita food production declined in Africa during the 1970s. There were, however, a few success stories— the Ivory Coast, Libya, Sudan, Tunisia, and Zambia. Adequate explanations for the sharp differences in production performance are not available, though it is evident that in many cases of poor performance, political instability or deliberate exploitation of agriculture through low output prices were important factors.

Grain prices

Another measure of the supplies of food available to the low-income countries is the price of grain in international markets. If demand were growing more rapidly than supply, as many predicted would occur during the latter half of the 1970s, the real or deflated prices of grain would have increased. Table 2-2 provides data on the U.S. export prices of wheat and corn in 1967 dollars per bushel for the period from 1910 to 1979. The data reveal a long-term downward trend for the real prices of both products. In fact, prices during the late 1970s have been below those that prevailed from 1930 to 1934, during the Great Depression, and significantly below the prices of the late 1930s. Prices in recent years are also lower than during the late 1950s and very near to the low prices of the late 1960s.

TABLE 2-1. SELECTED INDEXES OF WORLD AGRICULTURAL AND FOOD PRODUCTION (EXCLUDING CHINA)
(1961–65 = 100)

Country and region	Total agricultural production						Total food production						Per capita food production					
	1974	1975	1976	1977	1978	1979[a]	1974	1975	1976	1977	1978	1979[a]	1974	1975	1976	1977	1978	1979[a]
Developed countries	129	128	134	137	144	140	131	130	137	139	147	142	118	116	121	123	128	123
United States	117	126	129	136	136	143	122	134	137	143	144	152	109	118	120	124	125	130
Canada	112	127	138	143	146	137	112	128	143	144	148	138	94	106	116	117	118	108
Western Europe	128	125	125	128	136	134	128	125	123	129	136	134	119	115	113	117	124	122
European Community	123	121	118	127	133	132	125	121	118	127	133	132	116	112	109	117	122	121
Eastern Europe	140	137	144	144	149	147	140	137	144	145	150	148	130	128	133	132	136	132
USSR	145	130	153	149	163	144	144	128	153	148	163	142	128	113	133	128	141	121
Japan	110	115	109	118	117	116	111	115	109	118	117	116	97	100	94	101	98	96
Oceania	119	125	124	122	135	129	127	137	138	134	152	142	105	112	111	106	119	110
Republic of South Africa	146	134	135	146	150	142	154	141	143	152	157	148	114	102	100	105	106	98
Developing countries	134	141	144	150	155	154	135	145	149	154	159	158	103	107	108	109	110	106
East Asia	149	156	165	168	171	176	147	155	164	167	170	175	112	116	120	119	119	120
Indonesia	138	140	145	146	157	153	140	142	144	149	161	156	108	107	107	107	114	107
Philippines	146	161	172	173	175	180	147	163	173	175	177	183	107	116	120	118	117	118
Republic of Korea	144	158	170	176	170	187	141	155	167	170	165	181	109	109	125	125	119	129
Thailand	156	162	167	168	181	180	157	167	174	170	182	180	114	118	120	115	121	117

TABLE 2-1. SELECTED INDEXES OF WORLD AGRICULTURAL AND FOOD PRODUCTION (EXCLUDING CHINA) (*Continued*)
(1961–65 = 100)

Country and region	Total agricultural production						Total food production						Per capita food production					
	1974	1975	1976	1977	1978	1979[a]	1974	1975	1976	1977	1978	1979[a]	1974	1975	1976	1977	1978	1979[a]
South Asia	124	138	135	147	154	144	124	140	137	150	157	146	97	107	103	110	113	103
Bangladesh	110	122	114	126	125	123	114	128	118	130	127	124	87	95	85	91	87	83
India	122	139	135	147	156	143	122	140	136	149	158	144	96	108	103	111	115	103
Pakistan	162	155	165	184	178	192	164	161	177	193	190	200	119	114	121	128	123	126
West Asia	144	154	169	166	171	167	141	154	168	166	171	168	104	110	117	112	113	108
Iran	160	179	192	190	199	192	160	183	197	192	203	197	116	129	135	127	130	123
Turkey	136	150	163	164	164	159	131	149	160	161	162	158	99	110	116	114	112	106
Africa	125	128	129	128	131	131	125	130	132	129	133	132	95	96	95	90	91	88
Egypt	118	119	120	118	123	126	125	131	132	129	132	136	95	98	97	92	93	93
Ethiopia	111	107	104	100	95	98	109	100	97	92	88	91	84	75	71	65	61	61
Nigeria	119	121	123	125	126	125	119	122	124	126	127	126	90	89	88	87	85	82
Latin America	138	142	145	152	157	161	145	151	158	163	168	173	108	110	111	112	112	113
Mexico	143	151	148	153	159	162	150	169	165	166	175	180	103	112	105	102	104	103
Argentina	122	123	133	134	149	152	126	127	138	138	155	158	109	108	116	115	127	128
Brazil	150	153	158	170	166	176	164	168	185	193	186	197	121	120	130	131	123	127
World	131	132	138	142	148	145	132	135	141	144	151	147	113	113	117	118	122	118

Source: U.S. Department of Agriculture, Economics, Statistics and Cooperatives Service, *World Agricultural Situation*, WAS-21 (Washington, D.C., January 1980) p. 4.
[a] Preliminary.

TABLE 2-2. UNITED STATES: REAL EXPORT PRICES FOR WHEAT AND
            CORN FOR SELECTED YEARS BETWEEN 1910 AND 1980[a]
($1967 per ton)

Calendar years	Wheat	Corn
1910–1914	100	74
1925–1929	103	76
1930–1934	66	68
1935–1939	79	85
1945–1949	122	94
1950–1954	95	80
1955–1959	69	61
1960	65	53
1961	69	52
1962	70	52
1963	69	56
1964	69	57
1965	62	57
1966	62	56
1967	64	54
1968	60	48
1969	57	48
1970	53	52
1971	54	50
1972	54	46
1973	80	63
1974	110	79
1975	95	76
1976	80	64
1977	58	52
1978	61	50
1979	67	50
1980	66	50

Source: U.S. Department of Commerce, *Statistical Abstract of the United States* (Washington, D.C.)
various issues.

[a] The export prices are export unit values; the price deflator is the U.S. wholesale price index.

These price data indicate that for grains, the supply to the international market has increased somewhat more than demand during
the last seven decades. In fact, compared to the late 1920s, it is an
understatement to say that supply has increased at a "somewhat" faster
rate than demand. The real prices of both wheat and corn have fallen
by approximately a third in a half century. During this time, output
has grown substantially as has, of course, demand. It may be noted
that what were considered to be the very high grain prices in 1974
were less than a tenth higher than average prices for the period 1925–
29 and below the prices that prevailed after World War II. Within
three years after 1974 the real export price for wheat fell by almost

TABLE 2-3. JAPAN: NOMINAL AND REAL IMPORT PRICES FOR CORN,
WHEAT, AND SOYBEANS, 1970–79[a]
(yen per metric ton)

Calendar years	Corn		Wheat		Soybeans		Wholesale price index (1970 = 100)
	Current yen	1970 yen	Current yen	1970 yen	Current yen	1970 yen	
1970	23,986	23,986	24,256	24,256	40,177	40,177	100.0
1971	25,811	26,019	23,221	23,408	45,745	46,114	99.2
1972	19,622	19,622	22,187	22,187	42,761	42,761	100.0
1973	25,611	22,117	44,981	38,844	56,642	48,914	115.8
1974	43,250	28,417	66,610	43,765	78,840	51,800	152.2
1975	44,607	28,448	49,770	31,741	83,507	53,257	156.8
1976	38,892	23,629	43,328	26,323	64,495	39,183	164.6
1977	31,900	19,010	31,087	18,526	81,802	48,749	167.8
1978	24,342	14,888	29,225	17,875	55,405	33,887	163.5
1979	28,636	16,317	40,029	22,808	66,230	37,738	175.5
1980	35,387	17,128	49,145	23,788	67,828	32,831	206.6

Sources: The wholesale price index is from International Financial Statistics, various issues. In the article in FATUS the nominal yen import prices were deflated by the consumer price index for Japan. However, the wholesale price index was used to maintain comparability with the deflation for the United States in table 2-2.

[a] The prices in current yen are the cost, insurance, and freight (c.i.f.) prices at Yokohama and are from FATUS, January/February, 1980, pp. 89–94 and extended by correspondence.

half while the corn price fell by a third. Clearly the world market for grains was not under strong demand pressure during the late 1970s. The prices depicted in table 2-2 prevailed even though the total world trade in grains doubled during the 1970s as did the volume of grain imports by the low-income market economies.

Table 2-3 presents data on the real or deflated import prices for wheat, corn, and soybeans for Japan. The table includes data on the current yen import prices and real or deflated yen prices. I have chosen to deflate using the Japanese wholesale price index, with 1970 as the base. Thus the columns indicated as 1970 yen represent the import prices in real terms as seen by the Japanese importer. The data are presented for 1970 through 1979, reflecting the period of sharp changes in the relative exchange values of the yen and the dollar. These calculations indicate that by the end of the 1970s, the real import cost of corn was 35 percent lower than at the beginning of the decade. The declines in the real import costs of soybeans and wheat were much smaller, namely 6 percent. But for all grains and soybeans together, the real cost of Japanese imports was significantly less in the last years of the 1970s than in 1970. Even if there is some increase in the deflated or real yen costs of grain and soybeans during the 1980s, it is most unlikely that real import costs would increase to the levels of 1970. It can also be noted that if the import costs were deflated by the consumer price index instead of the wholesale price index, the 1979 real import costs of the three products would have been substantially below the 1970 level—45 percent below for corn and 25 percent below for wheat and soybeans.

Malnutrition—How Much?

I have argued that the availability of food in the low-income countries improved during the 1970s as it had during the previous two decades. And as I shall indicate at the end of this paper I have confidence that the 1980s will see further improvement. However, the extent of malnutrition or hunger that exists in the world has not been commented upon. Unfortunately our knowledge is very poor and limited with respect to the number or percentage of people who are inadequately fed, either in the past or today. When knowledge is scanty, estimates can and do vary widely.

Estimates for recent years of the number of people who are malnourished do vary enormously—from the 840 million people estimated by Reutlinger and Selowsky (1976), to the 460 million identified for the World Food Conference, the 400 million estimated by the FAO Fourth World Food Survey, and to a number of much, much lower estimates (World Food Conference, 1974; FAO, 1977).

The [U.S.] Presidential Commission on World Hunger, in its preliminary report issued in December 1979, presented no new estimates of the extent of hunger and malnutrition. It relied upon previous estimates made by FAO and the World Bank, yet one finds in the opening paragraph of the preface the following:

> Widespread hunger is a cruel fact of our time. In 1974, after poor harvests and oil price increases disrupted the international food system, the World Food Conference called on all governments to accept the goal that in ten years' time no child would go to bed hungry, no family would fear for its next day's bread, and no human being's future and capacities would be stunted by malnutrition. *Today, however, the world is even farther from that goal than it was then.* While the good harvests of recent years have prevented widespread famine, the next world food crisis will find the world not much better prepared than it was in 1974. This need not be the case. (Emphasis added)

It is true that in the resolutions of the World Food Conference there was a call for the elimination of hunger within a decade. The elimination of hunger, as defined in the quotation, is an impossibility; it is impossible for the world to completely and fully assure everyone that there will always be enough food all of the time. But nonetheless it is a worthy goal to move toward a reduction of hunger and malnutrition. The sentence that I have emphasized is an astounding sentence to have been produced by a commission appointed by the president of the United States. It is stated as a fact that the world is farther from the goal of reducing hunger and malnutrition than it was in 1974. Not the slightest bit of evidence is presented to back up the statement. It is not even clear what the sentence actually means— Is it that half of the ten years has passed and there has been little improvement? Or is it that conditions are now actually worse with more children going to bed hungry in 1979 than in 1974 and with more families fearing for their next day's bread? Whatever may be intended, most readers will interpret the sentence to say that in 1979 the food situation was even more serious for the world's poor people than it was in 1974 with its poor harvests.

Thomas T. Poleman has viewed the FAO and World Bank estimates referred to above with skepticism, not because he is certain they are wrong but because other evidence does point to significantly lower figures. He cites the results from 101 surveys of children in low-income countries that used body weight to estimate the extent of malnutrition. Severe protein-energy malnutrition was defined as a weight less than 60 percent of a standard, and moderate malnutrition as weight in the 60-to-80 percent range. Using these criteria, the studies showed that 2.3 percent of the children suffered from severe malnutrition and about 19 percent from moderate malnutrition (Poleman, 1979, p. V-8).[8]

[8] The definition of moderate malnutrition as falling in a weight range of 60 to 80 percent of standard weight for age and sex may appear to be a cruel criterion. Two points may be made: First, the standard that is generally used in such studies is an international standard which means that it is the average weight for age and sex from a high-income country such as the United States and not for a particular country or low-income countries generally. Second, living organisms do adjust to their particular environments and especially to their food supply. For example, by the weight standards of Japanese girls in 1974, Japanese girls at age 12 in 1950 would have been suffering from moderate malnutrition. The Japanese girl, age 12 in 1950, weighed just 78 percent as much as the Japanese girl of the same age 24 years later. René Dubos of Rockefeller University interprets the change in the weight and height of Japanese people since World War II as follows: "Thus it is obvious that the pre-war Japanese people had adapted biologically to a low intake of certain nutritional elements (probably protein and fat) by maintaining a small size during youth and throughout life. This biological adaptive state had such profound effects that adult and old Japanese people grown under such conditions do not significantly increase in size even when they adopt the much richer and abundant diet of present days. As in the case of behavioral development, there are probably different types of metabolic development pathways which all may be 'normal' for different environments" (Dubos, 1979, p. 79).

It is generally agreed that if there is malnutrition in a population, the two groups that are most adversely affected are children and pregnant and lactating women. Poleman assumed that either 10 percent or 50 percent of children below five years of age and pregnant and lactating women (approximately double the annual number of births) suffered from malnutrition. The resulting estimate of the vulnerable people at risk in all low-income countries (including China) was 62 million and 309 million. The 50 percent assumption seems extreme, yet it gives figures that are significantly less than the estimates referred to above even though Poleman included China with a quarter of the world's population in his estimates and the others did not (Poleman, 1979, p. V-12).

Erik Eckholm and Frank Record, in a Worldwatch paper, state, "Available population studies show that the severely undernourished, those close to starvation, probably number in the tens rather than the hundreds of millions. While a far cry from the stereotypical notion that 'half the world is starving to death,' this number is still unconscionably large" (Eckholm and Record, 1976, p. 11).

I believe that there is substantial evidence that supports the lower estimates of severely malnourished and the view that the incidence of malnourishment is declining. The very striking increase in life expectancy in the low-income countries since 1950 is worthy of note. For all low-income countries, the increase in life expectancy at birth was from 35 to 40 years in 1950 to 52 years in 1975 (Johnson, 1975, p. 18). Much of the increase in life expectancy has occurred because of a decline in infant mortality, but not all. As Schultz and Ram have shown, life expectancy in the adult years has increased in India to a marked degree in the past three decades (Ram and Schultz, 1979). For example, between 1951 and 1971 male life expectancy at age 20 increased by 8.1 years; at age 40, by 5.4 years and at age 60, by 3.5 years. Life expectancy at birth increased by 14.2 years. In 1971 the average life expectancy for a male at age 20 in India was 41 years, for the same sex and age in the United States in 1919–21, it was 46 years.

The increases in life expectancy in India, whether measured from birth or at other ages, have occurred even though there is, by implication, widespread malnutrition in India according to the estimates made by Reutlinger and Selowsky, or by the Fourth World Food Survey, or which could be inferred from estimates that per capita caloric intake has fallen some 8 to 12 percent below requirements in recent years.

But it is not my intention to engage in a battle of numbers or to claim that the world's poorer people do not face serious problems in obtaining adequate amounts of nutritious food.[9] Instead my objective is to try to measure recent progress or change in per capita food availability and to assess the prospects for improvements in the years ahead. Nor in emphasizing food production and food prices and costs, as I have, am I denying that the primary reason for inadequate nutrition is poverty. In the lower income countries of the world, limited availability of food to purchase is not the reason poor people have inadequate diets. The reason for inadequate diets is insufficient income to buy enough food. But I hasten to add that the majority, perhaps as many as three-fourths, of the poor people in the low-income countries live in rural areas. Thus for many of these people, there is a close and intimate relationship between income, food, and agricultural production. Thus while the primary source of food inadequacy is low income, an important source of low incomes for hundreds of millions is the limited productivity of agriculture. In this situation, many of the measures that will result in increased productivity in agriculture will also increase incomes and the adequacy of diets.

Price Instability

The data in table 2-2 indicate that recent grain export prices are low by comparison with the past. However, the data for the 1970s indicate a high degree of price instability for the decade. I have noted that although there have been some positive changes affecting world food supply and demand during the 1970s, there has been little change with respect to the potential for price instability for grains in international markets and in countries where prices are permitted to vary with international market prices. Was the much greater grain price instability of the 1970s compared to the 1960s caused by greater grain production variability? The evidence clearly supports the conclusion that the source of the increased price instability was not nature but human beings.

In *World Food Problems and Prospects* it was argued that much of the increase in grain prices from 1972 and 1974, and much of the subsequent decline was caused by governmental policies rather than by large production variations (Johnson, 1975, pp. 33–34). The policies

[9] In a section headed "Problems of Nutrition" in *Agriculture: Toward 2000* the obvious truth is stated: "This is an area of relative ignorance, with limited clinical and anthropometrical data" (FAO, 1979a, p. 147). Yet estimates of the number of malnourished continue to be made.

responsible for a major fraction of the upward movement of prices (and the subsequent reductions) were those designed to achieve domestic price stability through varying net international trade. A large fraction of the world's consumption of wheat and other grains occurs in countries that divorce their domestic from their international prices. In other words, numerous countries solve their own problems of instability by imposing that instability upon the rest of the world through varying net trade.

The policies of the European Community, the Soviet Union, Eastern European countries, China, and Japan did not change during the 1970s. Each still maintains a high level of domestic price stability by imposing its internal instability upon the rest of the world. The most notorious example is the Soviet Union, which has highly variable grain production but has attempted to stabilize domestic availability of grain by varying its net imports. The Soviet Union follows a policy of stable prices for livestock products; a production shortfall does not result in higher retail prices in the state stores but in longer queues at the retail markets. The policy decision to maintain retail meat prices constant in current rubles puts a high premium on providing the feed supplies required to keep meat production growing at a reasonably constant rate. To meet this objective when grain production declines requires grain imports.

The shortfalls in Soviet grain production are sometimes greater than can be made up by imports. There is some evidence that part of the shortfall not met by imports is met by stock changes. Since the size of grain stocks is regarded as a state secret in the Soviet Union, changes in grain stocks can only be indirectly inferred. For example, the 1975 grain crop was 55 million tons[10] below the 1974 crop; in 1975/76 Soviet net grain imports were 25 million tons larger than during the prior year; net grain imports in 1979/80 in the absence of the U.S. suspension of grain exports would have been approximately 34 million tons as an offset to a production decline of 58 million tons (USDA, 1980c). To some degree the amount of grain imported is influenced by the capacities of the Soviet ports and transport facilities to move the grain away from the ports. It is probable that the intended 1979/80 level of imports was at or near that capacity and this may also have been true in 1975/76.

Some of the increased instability of international grain prices during the 1970s can be attributed to the monetary disturbances that were so widespread during the decade. The sharp devaluation of the U.S.

[10] All references to tons in this chapter are to metric tons.

dollar relative to the major currencies of Western Europe and Asia during the early 1970s contributed to the increase in dollar prices of grains between 1972 and 1974. The varying rates of inflation and the fluctuating interest rate differentials in the major money markets were reflected in exchange rate variations that had effects upon farm commodity prices. Thus monetary instability was a source of price instability over and above that caused by domestic agricultural policies. It is probable that the 1980s will also see significant monetary instability, contributing to instability of international market prices for grains and other foods.

Because countries that consume well over half of the world's grain stabilize internal grain prices, sharp increases in international market prices such as occurred in 1973 and 1974 cannot be ruled out. In fact, it is not improbable that a similar pattern of price increases could occur during the 1980s. A rather modest decline in world grain production below trend levels could create the potential for similar price changes. Until domestic price policies are changed in many countries, the countries that permit their domestic prices to vary with international market prices will be subjected to significant price instability.

Two Surprises

While I believe that *World Food Problems and Prospects* has stood the test of time very well, in candor I must admit that there have been two significant surprises that affected world food supplies and prices during the 1970s and will have an influence in the years ahead. The two surprises were the sharp decline in birth rates in many low-income countries and the rapid growth of grain imports by the centrally planned economies. In terms of potential long-run effects upon the adequacy of world food supplies, the two surprises are to some degree offsetting.

The declines in birth rates in many developing countries, which have become generally apparent only in recent years, must have started in a number of cases by the mid-1960s. Countries with populations totaling in excess of 2 billion in mid-1977 had estimated declines of birth rates of 15 percent or more between 1960 and 1977 (World Bank, 1979, pp. 160–161). A number of countries had declines of 35 or more percent: Colombia, 35; South Korea, 49; Tunisia, 37; Costa Rica, 40; Chile, 40; Taiwan, 48; Hong Kong, 46; Trinidad and Tobago, 40; Singapore, 50; and China, 39. The declines in population growth rates have so far been very small and will be small for the next decade. Death rates are declining rapidly, too. In Colombia, for example, the crude death rate declined more in percentage terms between 1960 and 1977 than did the crude birth rate. However, the absolute decline in the birth rate (per thousand of population) was substantially greater than the absolute decline of the death rate—16 compared to 6. Consequently, the rate of population growth declined, from 3.0 percent annually for 1960–70 to 2.1 percent for 1970–77.

I do not want to give too much emphasis to the significance of the population growth rate to the long-run adequacy of per capita food supplies. But I believe that a slowing of the population growth rate is important for at least two reasons. First, is that a decline in birth rates results in a transitional benefit—the percentage of the population in the labor force grows and per capita output of both food and all other goods is increased as a result. During the period of decline in birth rates and population growth, there will be an extended time when food output will be affected not at all or very little. Consequently, per capita food availability will increase and if there previously had been sufficient undernutrition to have an adverse effect upon productivity, a positive productivity effect would occur. This is a short-run benefit but one that should not be ignored. Second, a decline in birth rates indicates to me that families now have more control over fertility than they had before and can more nearly fulfill their aspirations than previously.

The second surprise was the rapid increase in grain imports by the centrally planned economies. This growth was in sharp contrast to the general expectation at the World Food Conference in 1974 where the primary concern was the ability of the major grain exporters to provide additional grain exports to meet the growing import demands of the developing market economies. In the periods between 1969/70–71/72 and 1979/80, world grain exports increased by 82 million tons; approximately 60 percent of the increase was accounted for by increased imports of the centrally planned economies.[11] The developing market economies accounted for only 20 percent of the increase in OPEC countries. Grain imports by South Asia, which includes a very large fraction of the world's poorest people, actually declined during the 1970s. The increased imports by the developing countries went to middle-income countries primarily, including the rapidly growing middle-income countries of East Asia.

[11] (USDA, 1980b, p. 41) The projection of world trade in grain, which includes only trade among major countries and regions, has been adjusted to account for the suspension of U.S. grain exports to the Soviet Union.

Without the large increase in grain imports by the centrally planned economies, international grain prices would have been lower during the late 1970s than was in fact the case. World grain trade doubled during the 1970s. Without the large increase in imports by the centrally planned economies, the increase in world grain trade almost certainly would not have been more than half. Of the increase in net grain imports by the centrally planned economies, approximately half was by the Soviet Union, a quarter by other Eastern European countries, and a quarter by China.

The Soviet Union and Eastern Europe

The growth of grain imports by the Soviet Union and Eastern Europe during the 1970s was caused by the demand for livestock feed increasing at a more rapid rate than could be supplied from domestic sources, given the agricultural and food policies of the countries. The growth of grain imports by the Soviet Union was much greater, both relatively and absolutely, during the 1970s than in the Eastern European countries. Eastern Europe doubled grain imports during the decade—from about 8 million tons at the beginning of the decade to 16 million tons at the end. The Soviet Union was a small net exporter of grain at the beginning of the decade—4 million tons on the average for the three years centered in 1970/71. But by 1979/80, it had become the world's largest grain importer by importing about 31 million tons. During the Tenth Five Year Plan (1976 through 1980), net annual grain imports by the Soviet Union were 20 million tons. This compares to annual imports of 11 million tons during the previous Five Year Plan.

It is reasonable to expect further growth in grain imports by the Soviet Union and Eastern Europe in the 1980s. The demand for livestock products will increase as real incomes grow. In the Soviet Union and in several of the European countries, the "meat problem" is made into a serious problem because of a commitment to keep retail prices of meat at a constant level. Thus prices are not permitted to adjust to equate supply and demand. Relatively modest shortfalls of supply result in empty shelves at the butcher shops much of the time and long queues when meat is available. Consequently, the pressure to expand meat production is very great.

As the Soviet Union enters the 1980s it starts from a difficult livestock situation. The short 1979 grain crop and the U.S. suspension of grain sales have resulted in 1980 levels of meat and milk production only slightly greater than in 1975. The rather modest meat production goal for 1980 of 17.3 million tons was missed by nearly 2 million tons and milk production was 10 million tons or 10 percent below the 1980 target. Demand grew by significantly more between 1975 and 1980 than the very modest increases in supply. Consequently even with relatively favorable grain crops, the Soviet Union will require net grain imports averaging at least 20 million tons from 1981 through 1985 to meet the 1980 meat and milk targets, not to speak of the significantly higher 1985 targets. But the 1985 targets for meat and milk are not attainable by that year because of the time required to build livestock herds to the level needed for meat and milk output, 26 and 29 percent, respectively, above the 1980 level.

China

Very little was said about China in *World Food Problems and Prospects.* The reason for the lack of attention was not that China was unimportant; after all, it accounts for approximately a quarter of the world's population. The reason was the lack of reliable information about agriculture and the food supply and even about the size of the population. Population estimates for China for the mid-1970s varied by as much as 100 million. Absolute production figures were generally lacking, and official announcements were in terms of percentage changes from an unknown base.

In July 1979 it was announced in Peking that the population of China was 958,230,000 (*The New York Times,* 1979, p. A9). This figure is significantly greater than the estimates of the United Nations which put the mid-1979 population at less than 900,000,000.[12] The last census figure for China was a population of 590,000,000 in 1953. This means that the annual population growth rate has been 1.9 percent for the past quarter century and greater than generally accepted figures.

While many competent and unbiased Western visitors to China in recent years have returned with optimistic statements concerning food

[12] (FAO, 1979c, p. 66) The 1978 population figure was given as 880 million to which 2 percent may be added to arrive at the 1979 figure. The World Bank estimate for mid-1976 (published in 1978) was 836 million; if this is increased by 6 percent (three years' population growth), it comes to 886 million for the mid-1979 population.

production and its distribution, recent revelations by the Chinese government indicate that the visitors' impressions were misleadingly favorable. The fact that until recently visitors reported seeing no one who gave the appearance of being ill fed may have reflected how easy it is to guide the experiences of short-term visitors in a totalitarian society rather than reality with respect to the food situation.

Recent appraisals of the food situation in China by Chinese officials present a picture that is potentially alarming both to the Chinese and to the world. It was announced on October 6, 1978 in the *People's Daily* (Peking) that "average per capita grain production in 1977 was the same as in 1955—that is, the growth in grain production was only about equal to population growth plus the increase in grain requirements for industry."[13] In the same article it was stated that "except in some better areas, the peasants have a hard life throughout the year. Although production may increase, their income may increase little or not at all. In some areas, incomes have actually declined with the increase of production." A report in the January 20, 1979 issue of *People's Daily* on conditions in Anhwei Province gave the views of a county party secretary who noted that after thirty years of carrying out socialism, "there are many people in the villages who have not enough to eat or enough clothing to keep them warm."[14] Anhwei Province is not an isolated province; its center is approximately 300 miles west of Shanghai. It has been reported that Li Xiannian, a deputy chairman of the Community Party, had stated at a May 1979 conference that 10 percent of China's 950 million people did not have enough to eat.[15] It was reported also that factory workers received a grain ration of 31 pounds per month which was "not enough to sustain hard work." On May 18, 1979, *People's Daily* revealed that begging

[13] The discussion of the food situation in China has been greatly assisted by the writings of Miriam London and Ivan D. London, including a series of articles in *Worldview*, a journal published by the Council of Religion and International Affairs of New York. Articles were included in the following issues: vol. 19 (1976), nos. 5, 6, 7–8, and 12; and vol. 22 (1979), nos. 3, 7–8, and 10.

[14] My daughter Kay Ann Johnson, a political scientist at Hampshire College, knows infinitely more about China than I do. She pointed out to me that Anhwei Province has long been a poor province, with poor soil and variable weather and subject to significant fluctuations in food production. Thus the location of Anhwei Province fairly close to Shanghai has not been enough in either the past or the present to eliminate the impacts of food production variability.

[15] The article by Fox Butterfield in the June 15, 1979 *New York Times* summarizes a report from a Chinese language newspaper in Hong Kong, described as one that "often accurately reflects events in China."

existed in Shanghai. Peasants were identified as among the beggars.[16] But many of the beggars are probably the young people who were sent to the country during the Cultural Revolution and who have now illegally returned to the cities and cannot obtain employment.

The more open approach of the current Chinese government with respect to information supports the view that famine and hunger have not been conquered in China. At least some of the warts are being officially acknowledged. It remains true, of course, that our information concerning agriculture and food in China is less adequate than is our information concerning many other low-income countries. Yet there can be no doubt that we are now in a better position to understand recent and prospective developments than we were a few years ago.

India and China together account for 40 percent of the world's population. A comparison of population and food developments for the past three decades may help to put China's situation in perspective. Until fairly recently it seems safe to say that the general impression was that Chinese agriculture had developed more rapidly during the past three decades than Indian agriculture. The visitors to India, far more numerous than the visitors to China, were ready to accept the impression that Chinese were better fed than Indians. After all, no one could return from India and say that he had seen no one who was underfed or malnourished. But people who in recent years traveled widely in China did say that there was no evidence of poorly fed people or of abject poverty. Since everyone "knows" that famine often visited China before 1940 and that beggars and other poor people were abundantly evident throughout China in the past, obviously

---

[16] An article by Linda Mathews in the *Los Angeles Times*, October 21, 1979, graphically describes similar circumstances: "Beggars in China's drought-plagued Gansu province have been invading restaurants and snatching food from the plates of foreign tourists, according to travelers here (Peking). The report from members of a fifty-person tour organized by Pan American World Airways graphically confirmed earlier suggestions by Chinese officials here that food shortages were occurring this fall in Gansu and Guizhou provinces because of prolonged droughts there. 'Rations are very low in both places,' Zhang Pinghua, vice minister of China's State Agricultural Commission, recently disclosed. 'Large deliveries of grain have been sent in from other parts of the country ... The people have had a hard time.'" The article continues with descriptions of begging, of hungry people stealing food from the plates of tourists, people sleeping in the street, and of small children and teen-agers with running sores. The descriptions were of events that occurred in Lanzhou, a northwestern industrial city of two million population. A further quotation: "For years, the Communist regime claimed that begging and vagrancy vanished after the 1949 Communist revolution. But in recent months, in a surprising wave of candor, the party-controlled media have acknowledged many social problems, including hunger, still persist. Per capita grain rations are now lower than they were twenty years ago, agricultural officials have conceded."

conditions had markedly improved in China after 1949. And conditions probably have improved in the sense that the available supplies
of food are more equitably distributed now than three decades ago.
And recent revelations raise serious questions about how much improvement in terms of increased production has occurred. However,
the brief comparison of agriculture in India and China that will be
made will deal only with aggregate output performance and not with
the allocation of food among individuals and families.

In recent decades per capita production of grains in China has been
approximately 40 percent greater than in India. Thus differences in
economic organization aside, it would not be surprising if the general
physical appearance of Chinese people was somewhat better than that
of Indian people, at least to the casual observer.

How did per capita grain production compare in the past? Any
attempt to answer this question is subject to considerable uncertainty.
Prior to the Communist accession to power in China in 1949, the last
reasonably normal period was the 1930s. And for the 1930s there is
no single series of estimates of grain production that commands firm
respect for its accuracy. In addition, it is not at all clear what the
population of China was during the 1930s. Accepting a Chinese population estimate of 350 million for the period, per capita grain production was approximately 275 kilograms. This compares to an
estimate of 178 kilograms for India for the latter part of the 1930s.[17]
Thus per capita grain production in China may have exceeded that
of India by about 50 percent during the 1930s.

At this date it is impossible to determine with a known degree of
accuracy how much the Chinese per capita grain production exceeded
the Indian level before World War II. We do have reasonably accurate
or, more correctly stated, reasonably consistent grain production series for both China and India since 1949. Table 2-4 presents such
series. The series for India is the official governmental series and
includes pulses as well as grains; the series for China is the U.S.
Department of Agriculture estimates, except paddy rice has been
converted to milled rice, and includes pulses as well as tubers in terms
of their grain equivalent.

The data in table 2-4 indicate that grain production in China did
not grow at a more rapid pace than India's. In neither country was

[17] For a discussion of the limitations of grain production data for China and India,
see Bandyopadhyaya (1976, pp. 12–17). The Chinese and Indian data on grain production lack comparability for several reasons. One is that the Chinese data include
tubers (potatoes and manioc) converted to a grain-equivalent basis. Tubers account for
approximately a tenth of Chinese grain production.

TABLE 2-4. GRAIN PRODUCTION, CHINA AND INDIA, 1949–80
(absolute numbers in million metric tons)

Year	China[a,b]	India[b,c]	China ÷ India (percentage)
1949	92.5	60.7	1.52
1950	107.1	54.9	1.95
1951	115.6	55.5	2.08
1952	132.5	61.7	2.15
1953	134.1	72.2	1.86
1954	137.7	70.6	1.95
1955	149.8	69.2	2.16
1956	156.1	72.3	2.16
1957	157.2	66.5	2.36
1958	170.2	78.7	2.17
1959	139.7	76.7	1.82
1960	126.6	82.2	1.54
1961	137.0	83.0	1.65
1962	149.0	80.3	1.86
1963	157.4	80.7	1.95
1964	171.2	89.3	1.92
1965	171.2	72.3	2.37
1966	184.3	74.2	2.48
1967	198.0	95.1	2.08
1968	184.6	94.0	1.96
1969	188.3	99.5	1.89
1970	204.8	108.4	1.89
1971	208.6	105.2	1.98
1972	204.2	96.5	2.12
1973	212.2	104.7	2.03
1974	224.2	99.8	2.25
1975	229.5	120.8	1.90
1976	231.8	113.0	2.05
1977	229.5	125.0	1.84
1978	236.4	126.0	1.88
1979	243.5	117.2	2.08
1980	231.4	124.2	1.86

Sources: U.S. Department of Agriculture, Economics, Statistics and Cooperatives Service, People's Republic of China, Supplement 6 to WAS-18 (Washington, D.C., June 1979) p. 30; and U.S. Department of Agriculture, Foreign Agricultural Service, Developments in the Grain Sector of Indian Agriculture, FG-15-77 (Washington, D.C., September 1977) p. 6, and FG-25-79 (December 26, 1979) p. 6.

[a] Includes tubers converted to grain equivalent and pulses, but not soybeans.
[b] Rice in terms of milled rice.
[c] Includes pulses (peas and beans).

TABLE 2-5. CHINA AND INDIA: INTERNATIONAL TRADE IN GRAINS,
         1961–79
(million metric tons)

| Year | China | | | India[a] imports |
	Imports	Exports	Net imports	
1960	0.0	1.17	−1.17[b]	5.23
1961	5.56	0.44	5.12	3.61
1962	4.60	0.58	4.02	3.73
1963	5.45	0.64	4.81	4.62
1964	6.31	0.79	5.32	6.38
1965	5.91	0.55	5.36	7.60
1966	5.59	1.26	4.33	10.40
1967	4.94	1.20	3.74	8.74
1968	4.36	0.96	3.40	5.75
1969	3.91	0.80	3.11	3.87
1970	4.63	0.99	3.64	4.21
1971	3.03	0.96	2.07	2.46
1972	4.64	0.90	3.74	0.66
1973	7.68	2.14	5.54	3.69
1974	6.79	1.98	4.81	5.26
1975	3.46	1.44	2.02	7.63
1976	2.06	0.90	1.16	6.49
1977	6.84	1.00	5.84	0.43
1978	9.31	1.37	7.94	0.12
1979	10.87	1.10	9.77	0.02
1980	13.51	1.00	12.51	0.07

Sources: Alva Lewis Erisman, "China: Agriculture in the 1970's," in U.S. Congress, Joint Economic
Committee, China: A Reassessment of the Economy, 94th Cong., 1 sess. (1975) pp. 343–344; U.S.
Department of Agriculture, Foreign Agricultural Service, Developments in the Grain Sector, FG-15-
77 (Washington, D.C., September 1977).
   [a] India had significant exports of grain in the following years: 1971–72, 0.76 million tons; 1976–
77, 1.05 million tons; 1978, 1.1 million tons; 1979, 1.6 million tons; and 1980, 0.66 million tons.
   [b] Net export.

there a significant change in per capita grain production. In both
countries, starting with a three-year average centered in 1953 and,
adjusting roughly for favorable weather in India, ending in 1978,
total grain production increased by a little less than 80 percent.

Table 2-5 presents data on the net grain imports of the two countries. Two things stand out from the data. The first is the great variability of Indian grain imports; the second is the recent sharp increase
in Chinese imports. By comparison with Indian grain imports, Chinese
imports have exhibited a considerable stability. China became a grain
importer only in 1961, as a result of the enormous disaster of the
Great Leap Forward. It has imported grain in every year since. China

has also emerged as the world's third largest grain importer—following Japan and the Soviet Union. India has substantially reduced its grain imports since the mid-1970s and briefly became a net exporter as the decade ended. During calendar year 1978, India exported almost a million tons of wheat to the Soviet Union and Vietnam together.

Together China and India have 40 percent of the world's population and consume approximately a fourth of the world's grain. Production variability in these two countries can have a major impact upon the world's grain situation. Could there be a 10 percent decline in the combined grain production of the two countries? Grain production in India varies by more than 10 percent from year to year in approximately one year out of five. The grain production series for China exhibits relatively little year-to-year variability. There were sharp reductions in production in 1959 and again in 1960 and a small reduction in 1968. But there is no way of knowing if this series represents reality or whether it has been deliberately smoothed to prevent revealing adverse conditions.

China is a large country, which contributes to production stability. Also, a large fraction of its cultivated area is irrigated, which also contributes to stability. Yet one need not be a particularly suspicious soul to believe that there has been more grain production variability than revealed by the series in table 2-4.

There is much that we do not know about the Chinese food situation. What we do know is not without some foreboding for the future. Are the recent increases in grain imports a portent of further increases, say to 20 million tons by the end of the 1980s? Or has China moved to a new and somewhat higher level of grain imports, similar to the fluctuations of around 4 to 6 million tons during the first half of the 1970s? Recent increases in money incomes in China may simply have increased grain consumption to a new and higher level with grain imports being increased to avoid price increases or ration allotments that departed further from the demand level for the majority of families.

The world food situation is clouded by our uncertainty about China's performance in the years ahead. While it is reasonable to assume that China is likely to meet its food needs without extraordinary demands upon the world food economy, there remains the uncertainty of "what if." What if Chinese grain production fell by 20 percent from one year to the next? Could China do as it did in 1959 and accept widespread famine? Or would it no longer be politically possible to permit widespread distress if such distress could be minimized by food imports?

Food Security, Poverty, and Malnutrition

As noted above, the primary reason for inadequate food consumption and the existence of malnutrition in the low-income countries is poverty rather than any lack of food availability. In the world as it is organized today, barring war and civil insurrection, food is available almost anywhere in the world if there is income to purchase it. Such was not always the case. It has only been in the past two centuries that famine was not a potential danger facing the majority of the world's population. Less than a century ago famine was a threat to life for millions in most of Asia and Russia.

The twentieth century has brought a revolutionary change in world food security. Improvements in communication and transportation have brought all but a tiny minority of the world's population into a world food community. Except when governments take action, the world's food supply is now available to virtually anyone anywhere in the world who has the money to pay for food at prices that approach the lowest at which the primary food products (grains) have been available during the past century. The statement that food is now available to anyone "who has the money to pay for it" is not a cynical description of the alternatives available to the poor people of the world. It is a statement that realistically applies to a large and increasing fraction of the world's population, including the majority of the poorest people.

India's per capita income is among the lowest in the world. Yet at the beginning of this decade (1970–71) a large-scale consumption study indicated that more than half of the rural families in the third decile in the income distribution had daily per capita caloric consumption in excess of a reasonable level (2,300 calories); for urban families, half of the families at the 40th percentile in income distribution consumed adequate calories.[18] But even at lower levels of per capita expenditure for all goods and services, there were some families

---

[18] (Shah, 1979, pp. 28–29) The third decile refers to the families with total expenditures falling in the 20th to the 30th percentile; in other words, 20 percent of the families had lower levels of expenditure than did the families in the third decile. The income distribution is assumed to be described by the distribution of total expenditures.

at each expenditure level that had adequate levels of calorie consumption. It was also true that at even the highest expenditure levels, some families consumed few enough calories to be said to have calorie-deficient diets. But the same result is obtained from consumption surveys in the United States.

A possible approach for improving knowledge of the accessibility of poor people to a nutritionally adequate diet would be to determine the minimum cost of such a diet and then estimate what percentage of the world's poor people could afford the cost. However, there are two persuasive arguments against such an approach. One is that there remains considerable doubt about what constitutes a nutritionally adequate diet. The other is that even very poor people have food preferences or tastes that they attempt to satisfy; there is no reason to assume that even very poor people do not wish to obtain some satisfaction from food other than that involved in meeting their physical or biological requirements for food.

C. H. Shah provides strong evidence that at even very low-income levels in India, tastes had a significant role in determining the cost per calorie of food. He found, for example, that families in Kerala spent about 80 percent more per calorie than would have been required for a diet designed to be nutritionally adequate (Shah, 1979, p. 38).

Shah's study also indicated that, at each per capita expenditure level, the families with caloric intakes below what was considered an acceptable level (2,300 calories per day for an adult male) generally obtained a smaller fraction of their calories from grains and pulses—the cheapest sources of calories—than did the families with caloric intakes in excess of the standard. There are at least two important hypotheses that might explain this finding. One is that the calorie standard used is inappropriate in the sense that individual differences in requirements for an active life are so variable that the use of a given standard for all consumers is inappropriate. The other is that poor families are misallocating their food expenditures. The latter hypothesis seems to me to be without supporting evidence. Other data from India show quite clearly that within the category of the lowest cost sources of calories, the grains, low-income families spent significantly less per kilogram of grain than did higher income families. This was true for both urban and rural families (Shah, 1979, p. 38).[19]

[19] Data presented by Shah (1979, pp. 40–41) indicate that for one district in India that the families with the lowest expenditure on food spent approximately 20 percent less per calorie than did the families with a median level of expenditures on food. At each expenditure level, the families that were deemed to be deficient in calories spent more per calorie than did the families not deficient in calories.

Shah draws the following implication from the emergence of food taste as a factor affecting food consumption at poverty levels determined by caloric intakes: ". . . it weakens the claim of calories as a criterion for measuring the extent of poverty. . . . We have already seen that even with rising income there may be a possible increase in the number of persons with calorie intake below the recommended level. While this may not be welcome, it need not be frightening. The improved 'taste' content (which may include increased consumption of even vegetables and fruits and milk, besides pulses), may add to quality of life " (Shah, 1979, p. 24). Most of the estimates of malnutrition referred to earlier were based upon a fixed calorie standard for determining the percentage of the population malnourished. Shah's study indicates such exercises must be interpreted with extreme caution.[20]

Unfortunately the great deal of attention given to food problems during the mid-1970s has resulted in almost no improvement in the factual base for improving our understanding of malnutrition, its causes and extent. True, we know that most malnutrition is associated with low incomes, but we also know that some very poor people are adequately fed while others with equal or higher incomes have less than adequate diets. If we better understood why such differences exist in consumption patterns and what health effects, if any, such differences have, we would be better able to assist those who need it most.

Prospects for the 1980s

Per capita food production in the world and in the developing countries increased during the 1970s. The improvement in the developing

[20] P. V. Sukhatme, a statistician who has devoted much of his career to the study of nutrition, has shown that there is a very large variation in the energy (calorie) needs across individuals and for the same individual from day to day, week to week. "It must be concluded that the daily requirement cannot be assumed to be constant, but that it will vary over time in the same individual, reflecting the fact that the efficiency of utilization of intake varies over time in the same individual, in the same way as it does from individual to individual. Such a result is to be expected since there is considerable evidence that the human possesses a physiological regulatory mechanism which serves to maintain fixed body weight and energy balance over extended periods. Consequently, even as a matter of course, the daily requirement of an individual in health will vary about his true mean requirement within the range of variance typical of the generating mechanism governing energy balance in man, without implying that an individual is undernourished whenever his intake is below the true average requirement and vice versa." (1979, p. 15)

countries was modest over all and in some areas, particularly Africa, per capita food production declined. But the increase achieved in per capita food production during the 1970s represented a continuation of past trends.

There is no significant reason to expect that the 1980s will show less improvement in the per capita food supplies of the low-income countries than in each of the last two decades. The potential for greater improvement clearly exists, though a cautious and realistic view is that during the 1980s, as during the previous two decades, the realization will fall short of the potential. However, as I shall note later, there are some positive factors that may result in a higher rate of growth of per capita food production and consumption in the low-income countries during the 1980s than during the 1970s.

Earlier I considered three reasons that have been emphasized to support a pessimistic view of the outcome of the race between world demand and supply of food. The foreboding factors were higher energy prices, the near disappearance of cultivatable arable land, and the competition between livestock and people for grain. Of these three issues, only higher energy prices merits further discussion. There remains much land that can be brought under cultivation.[21] The presumed competition for grain between livestock and people has always been a false issue. It remains a false issue because the amount of grain produced in the world is as much a function of demand as of supply. If less grain were demanded, less grain would be produced. It is as simple as that. And because it is so simple, an important point is frequently misunderstood or neglected.

Energy

Energy prices will continue to increase in real terms and the real prices of farm inputs using significant amounts of energy will be increased by the higher energy prices. However, the experience of the 1970s shows that there is no simple, one-to-one relationship between the price of energy and the price of an input, such as fertilizer, that has a large energy component. While the index of fertilizer prices paid by U.S. farmers has increased less since 1970 than the index of prices for all farm production items, the index of prices for fuels and oil has increased by about 35 percent more than all production items (USDA, 1980a, various issues). The share of fertilizer, oil, and fuel

---

[21] *Agriculture: Toward 2000* (FAO, 1979a) indicates that the arable land in the low-income countries (excluding China) could increase from 730 million hectares in 1975 to 830 million in 1990 and to 930 million by 2000 (p. 30).

expenditures in total farm production expenses increased between 1970 and 1978, but probably by less than most think. Such expenditures on energy products accounted for 9.1 percent of all production expenditures in 1970 and 11.1 percent in 1978. Preliminary estimates indicate that approximately 11.7 percent of all 1979 farm production expenses were devoted to these energy products.[22]

I do not intend to minimize the importance of energy prices in affecting the costs of producing agricultural products in the United States and other high-income countries. Food and other agricultural products would be lower priced today and output of food would be somewhat greater if energy prices were at their pre-OPEC real levels. But we should not exaggerate the effect of energy prices upon agriculture nor should we assume that farmers can make no adjustment to the higher real prices.

One additional point should be made about energy prices. Energy derived from fossil fuels is a much smaller component of farm production costs in low-income countries than in the United States or Western Europe.[23] Consequently, increased energy prices have had less effect on agriculture in the poor countries than in the United States; and this difference will persist in the years ahead. And we have seen that the effect of higher energy costs on U.S. agriculture has been quite small so far. One indication of this is that real grain prices are now approximately the same as they were a decade ago when energy prices were much lower.

The green revolution

For many people, a look ahead at what the 1980s hold for food supplies in the low-income countries is influenced by their answer to this question: "What happened to the Green Revolution?" Asking this question often implies that the benefits of research leading to the new grain varieties and the cultural practices that were called the Green Revolution were less than had been expected. One reason the question is asked was the unfortunate designation of the new high-yielding varieties of rice and wheat as miracle varieties. The use of

---

[22] These figures do not include expenditures on electricity (USDA, 1979b, pp. 42, 46). The 1979 estimate was made by the writer.

[23] It is estimated that in the low-income countries that agriculture produces approximately 24 percent of the total output of the economies but used only 3.1 percent of all fossil energy consumed in 1975 (FAO, 1979a, p. 233). In the high-income countries agriculture consumes approximately the same amount of fossil energy per unit of output as is true of the economy as a whole.

the term, Green Revolution, also held out the hope of major, yes revolutionary, changes in food supplies. The new varieties represented remarkable achievements but it was unfortunate that they were tagged as revolutionary. One thing that must be learned about research and agriculture—a single revolution is never enough. What is required is a stream of revolutions, each perhaps with rather modest effect but with significant cumulative influence.

The new high-yielding varieties did not have the effects on output that were expected by their most enthusiastic supporters for several reasons. First, the new varieties were well adapted to only part of the areas producing rice and wheat; second, the yield differential between the new and old varieties was significantly smaller under farm than experimental conditions and, third, farmers had to learn how to use the new varieties effectively. This was true specifically in the case of the new rice varieties because such varieties could be used only with irrigation that permitted effective control of water depths. The new rice varieties are short with a stiff straw, characteristics required for the plants to effectively utilize large doses of fertilizer. Many of the irrigation systems in South and Southeast Asia do not provide effective control of water levels. On the other hand, since most wheat irrigation is done with tube wells in South Asia, there has been much wider adoption of the new varieties of wheat than of rice. In India in 1976/77, 35 percent of all rice was sown with the new varieties while more than 70 percent of the wheat area was sown with new varieties. The doubling of wheat yields and the trebling of wheat output in India would have been impossible without the new wheat varieties.

Hybrid corn

When hybrid corn was first introduced in the 1930s, the general methods of cultivating and producing corn had been unchanged for several decades. Little or no fertilizer was used on corn. In this setting the yield advantage of hybrid corn over the traditional (open pollinated) varieties was approximately 15 percent. In years of average weather, the national average corn yield prior to the introduction of hybrids was 1.5 tons per hectare (25 bushels per acre). Thus hybrid corn would have increased average yield by about 0.22 tons per hectare (less than 4 bushels per acre). In the Corn Belt of the United States, where yields were higher than the national average and hybrids were first introduced, the absolute yield advantage of the hybrids was on the order of 0.3 tons per hectare (5 bushels per acre). But as noted above, corn yields are now 6.2 tons per hectare (100 bushels per acre) with average weather. Hybrid corn has been an important contributor to the quadrupling of yield over the past four or five decades. But there were many other changes that made the recent yields possible—fertilizer, herbicides (weed killers), insecticides, more plants per unit of land. In addition, today's hybrids are very, very different from the hybrids of forty years ago or even twenty years ago. Increasingly corn hybrids are adapted to the climatic and soil and moisture conditions of quite small areas and some part of the yield increases in the last decade or two was caused by such increased adaptation of hybrid seeds.

I have emphasized increasing corn yields that occurred following the introduction of the first of the miracle varieties, namely hybrid corn. Had research and development on hybrid corn been halted in the 1930s, or the 1940s or the 1950s or as of yesterday, opportunities for further yield increases and lowered production costs would have been lost. Research investment must be continuous; no one development by itself is enough to make a significant contribution to expanding food production. How much better fed the people of the developing countries will be by the end of this decade will depend, in part, on research investments made in recent years and investments that will be made by the mid-1980s.

Grain yield trends

The 1970s saw repeated references to the possibility, if not the probability, that the growth rate of grain yields was declining in the world. The feeling of unease was buttressed for many by grain yields in the United States, especially corn, in 1975 and 1976 and, to a lesser degree in 1977, that were below prior peak yield levels. Thus some concluded that grain yields in the United States were slowing down and perhaps might have reached their peak levels.

However, research undertaken at the University of Illinois has shown that the tapering off of corn yield growth after 1974, at least in Illinois, was caused by climatic factors. After account was taken of the climatic effects, there was no evidence of a slowing down of the growth of yields of corn or soybeans. For the period 1950–76 the inclusion of weather variables in the analysis increased the annual rate of growth of corn yields from 0.182 metric tons per year to 0.207 metric tons per year (2.96 bushels per acre per year to 3.37 bushels per acre per year). The inclusion of weather variables increased the annual trend by approximately 14 percent, a significant change (Swanson and Hyankori, 1979). In 1978 and 1979, weather variables influencing corn production were more favorable than in 1975 and 1976, and U.S. corn yields increased substantially, reaching an average yield of 109 bushels per acre (6.7 tons per hectare) in 1979; this was between 9 and 10 percent in excess of the trend level of corn yields for that year. In other words, the trend level of corn output in 1979 was 6.95 billion bushels (177 million tons) rather than the actual amount of 7.8 billion bushels (197 million tons). But even at the trend level of yield, output in 1979 would have been 2.1 billion bushels more than the 1965 output on the same area.

Agricultural policies

At the beginning of this section I indicated that there were some positive factors that might result in a higher rate of growth of per capita food production and consumption in the low-income countries in the 1980s than during the 1970s. One of the positive developments has been a modest improvement in the terms of trade facing agriculture since the mid-1970s.[24]

Prior to 1975 most developing countries held down the price of at least one important food crop and protected farm input-producing industries, such as the fertilizer industry. While there remain numerous examples of exploitation of farmers for the presumed benefit of consumers or input-producing sectors, many developing countries now have support and purchase prices for major farm crops that are in excess of world market prices. Agricultural exports are still often burdened by an overvalued currency, such as is true in Argentina and was true until very recently in Brazil. The probable improvement in the structure of incentives facing farmers in the low-income countries will have a positive effect on the growth of agricultural output.[25] Unfortunately, incentives can be modified quickly and in a fashion adverse to agriculture.

Agricultural research

During the past two decades there has been a major growth in the expenditures for agricultural research on the problems of increasing

[24] *Agriculture: Toward 2000* (FAO, 1979a) includes an entire chapter (chapter 11) on agricultural price policies. This FAO publication is much more explicitly critical of the past and current agricultural pricing policies of the low-income countries than were the documents prepared for the World Food Conference.

[25] For a discussion of the effects of incentives and of distortions of those incentives upon agricultural development, see Schultz (1978).

farm production in the low-income countries. In the fifteen years between 1959 and 1974, expenditures on agricultural research in the major developing regions (Latin America, Africa, and Asia) increased from $228 million to $957 million (1971 constant U.S. dollars). This increase occurred both in the international agricultural research centers and in the research institutions of the low-income countries. As a share of an increasing world expenditure on agricultural research, the expenditures in the three low-income regions increased from 17 percent in 1959 to 25 percent in 1974.[26] Since there is a lag of five to ten years between research investment and actual application on farms, most of the effects of the increased investments made after 1973 have still not been felt.

Irrigation

Earlier it was noted that during the past decade there has been a substantial increase in the irrigated area in low-income countries. Much of the increase in irrigation has occurred in the densely populated regions of the world, principally Asia. Current rates of investment in irrigation in South and Southeast Asia are high by historical standards. Irrigation, whether new projects or improvements of existing systems, is capital intensive. This is an investment area where the availability of foreign capital may be important in improving per capita food availability. A report of the Trilateral Commission indicated that it would require more than $50 billion (1975 purchasing power) of investment to provide the irrigation expansion and improvements in South and Southeast Asia required for a doubling of rice production by the early 1990s (Colombo, Johnson, and Shishido, 1978). Approximately a third of the required investment could come from sources within the region.

Income growth

Two other factors will have a positive effect on per capita food consumption by the end of the 1980s. One of these is the continued growth of per capita income in the developing countries. The World Bank projects the annual growth of per capita gross domestic product

[26] (Evenson, 1978, p. 224) The reader interested in further exploration of the potential contributions of agricultural research to improving food production and nutrition may wish to pursue that interest by consulting the following: *World Food and Nutrition Study: The Potential Contributions of Research*, written by a steering committee of the U.S. National Academy of Sciences (1977); and Sterling Wortman and Ralph W. Cummings, Jr., *To Feed This World: The Challenge and the Strategy* (1978). At the end of each chapter in the latter there is an excellent classified bibliography.

of the low-income (per capita income of less than $300) developing countries during the 1980s at 2.7 percent (World Bank, 1979, p. 13). The middle-income developing economies are projected to have a significantly higher growth rate of 3.4 percent. The population (as of 1976) of the low-income developing countries was 1,193 million and of the middle-income countries, 1,037 million. An income growth rate of 2.7 annually means a 30.5 percent growth in income level in a decade. Such a growth of income would, on the average, call forth at least a 15 percent increase per capita in real food expenditures for low-income persons. If this growth in demand for food is reasonably well distributed among all segments of the population, the growth will go a substantial distance toward reducing both severe and moderate malnutrition in the low-income countries.

Slower population growth

The other factor is the potential decline in the rate of population growth in many low-income countries. As noted earlier, the decline in the rate of population growth will not significantly alleviate the world's food deficiencies during the 1980s. A slowing down of population growth has two effects on per capita food supply—a larger fraction of the population is in the working ages during the transition period to a lower rate of population growth and there are fewer people eating from a given food supply after some period of time. These effects will not be large during most of the 1980s, though they will be of modest significance. The difference in a decade between 2.3 and 2.1 percent annual growth rates is a little less than 2 percent for the total population. The two growth rates are those for India for the 1960s and from 1970 to 1977. If there is a further decline in the population growth rate for the 1980s to 1.9 percent, a further 2 percent lower total population would result by 1990. These differences appear to be small, but compared to annual per capita increases in food consumption of 0.5 or 0.6 percent, the effects on per capita food consumption of a 2 percent difference in population size would increase the growth of consumption by a third. It is by small and additive improvement that the nutrition of the world's poorest people will be improved during the rest of the century.

Oil import costs for developing countries

The general tenor of my evaluation of prospects for improvements in per capita food production is quite positive. Earlier I noted that rising energy prices have so far not been a significant factor in inhibiting the growth of food production, in either the high-income or the developing countries. In fact, the real price of fertilizer has not increased over the past decade.

But there is another aspect of the much higher oil prices that is of concern to many. While it may be true that the increased oil prices have had no differential adverse effects upon agriculture, the sharp increase in oil prices faced by the non-oil producing developing countries has resulted in a loss of real income for those economies. It is estimated that in 1980 the oil import bill for the non-oil producing developing countries was 58 billion; in 1975, after the first round of OPEC price increases, such countries had an oil import bill of $22 billion. These countries had a large deficit in their current accounts with the rest of the world in 1980 of $61 billion.[27]

But it is very important to understand the great differences between the low-income and middle-income developing countries with respect to their dependence upon imported oil. The low-income developing countries are those with per capita gross national products of less than $360, while the middle-income developing countries have per capita gross national products of more than $360. The average for the low-income developing countries in 1980 was $168 (in 1977 U.S. dollars) and $1,275 for the middle-income developing countries (World Bank, 1980). The low-income developing countries are not heavily dependent upon imported oil. The estimated oil import bill for the low-income developing countries in 1980 was only $3.3 billion and less than 2 percent of their gross national product. The World Bank projections indicate that these countries may import the same quantity of oil in 1985 as in 1980, namely 0.3 million barrels per day. Thus even with a projected increase in nominal oil prices of more than 60 percent, the oil import bill of this group of low-income countries might increase to about $6 billion by 1985. The import bill projected for 1980 would be less than 3 percent of projected gross national product.

Implications for U.S.–Japanese Agricultural Relations

My discussion of the world food situation has been primarily from the viewpoint of the low-income countries of the world. However, there are certain implications that are worth noting for U.S.–Japanese

[27] The estimates and projections of the oil imports and gross national products of the non-oil importing low-income and middle-income developing countries are from (World Bank, 1980, pp. 6–13). For the middle-income developing countries the oil import bill in 1980 was approximately 6 percent of gross national product in 1980.

agricultural trade relations. On the whole, I consider the prospects as favorable for the strengthening and expansion of agricultural trade relations between the two countries.

The first and most important point is that the available evidence points toward a continuation of the gradual decline in the real dollar prices of grain in international markets for the decade of the 1980s. Growth in output of grain and other primary foods should be at approximately the same rate as growth in demand. The second point is that international market prices for grains and other farm products during the 1980s will be at least as unstable as during the 1970s. Given the current policies of governments, it is most unlikely that there will be a return to the very stable prices of the 1950s and 1960s. The major food exporters are now following price policies that permit significant price fluctuations. No country seems willing to hold substantial stocks of grain. Given the efforts made by countries that consume a large fraction of the world's grain to stabilize domestic prices, international market prices will be very unstable in the years ahead.

Finally, if Japan's competitive position in world markets continues to grow as it has since World War II and the Japanese yen continues to increase in value compared to the dollar and other major currencies, the real cost of grain imports in terms of yen could decline significantly during the 1980s. In other words, to acquire a ton of grain will require less of Japanese domestic resources as the decade progresses than is true at the present time, or was true during the 1970s. During the 1970s, the increased value of the yen in terms of the dollar resulted in a fall in the real yen price of imported grain and soybeans. It seems very probable that this trend will continue during the 1980s.

Concluding Comments

It is common in the discussion of the potential growth of food production to emphasize the restraints imposed by nature—the finite limits of our natural resources and the vagaries of climate. It is easy to paint a gloomy picture of the future of the world if you accept the view that our supplies of fossil energy will be exhausted in some finite period, that erosion will destroy a large part of the land used for crops, and that future scientific discoveries will be increasingly less relevant to increasing food production.

If there is an enemy that will prevent improving the nutrition of the world's poor people, it consists of human beings and not nature.

Humankind, not nature, will be the primary factor in determining the rate of growth of food production in the rest of this century. Nature is often niggardly and at times terribly cruel. But we now know enough about what is required to expand food production that we should no longer blame our failures upon nature.

When I say that human beings, not nature, will impose the greatest barriers to the potential expansion of food production, I am not referring to the consequences of the acts of farmers, traders, processors, or suppliers, but to human beings as they function in the political process. If policies are adopted that permit appropriate incentives for farmers, provide them access to supplies at reasonable prices, and permit farmers to sell at the best possible prices, the growth of production will be favored. And if policies are followed that encourage research on problems of the agriculture of the low-income countries, all will gain. The mistakes of the past have been costly. One can hope that the next decade will see fewer such mistakes.

References

Bandyopadhyaya, Kalyani. 1976. *Agricultural Development in China and India: A Comparative Study* (New Delhi, Wiley Eastern, Limited).

Colombo, Umberto, D. Gale Johnson, and Toshio Shishido. 1978. *Reducing Malnutrition in Developing Countries: Increasing Rice Production in South and Southeast Asia* (New York, The Trilateral Commission).

Dubos, René. 1979. "The Intellectual Basis of Nutritional Science and Practice," in Marilyn Chou and David P. Harmon, eds., *Critical Food Issues of the Eighties* (New York, Pergamon).

Eckholm, Erik, and Frank Record. 1976. *The Two Faces of Malnutrition*, Worldwatch Paper 9 (Washington, D.C., Worldwatch).

Evenson, Robert. 1978. "The Organization of Research to Improve Crops and Animals in Low-Income Countries," in Theodore W. Schultz, ed., *Distortion of Agricultural Incentives* (Bloomington, Ind., Indiana University Press).

FAO. *See* U.N. Food and Agriculture Organization.

Johnson, D. Gale. 1975. *World Food Problems and Prospects* (Washington, D.C., American Enterprise Institute).

National Academy of Sciences. 1977. *World Food and Nutrition Study: The Potential Contributions of Research* (Washington, D.C., NAS).

The New York Times. 1979. July 5.

Poleman, Thomas T. 1978. *Quantifying the Nutrition Situation in Developing Countries*, Cornell Agricultural Economics Staff Paper No. 79-33 (Ithaca, N.Y., Cornell University).

Presidential Commission on World Hunger. 1979. *Preliminary Report of the Presidential Commission on World Hunger* (Washington, D.C.).

Ram, Rati, and Theodore W. Schultz. 1979. "Life Span, Health, Savings and Productivity," *Economic Development and Cultural Development* vol. 27, no. 3 (April), pp. 329–421.

Reutlinger, Shlomo, and Marcelo Selowsky. 1976. *Malnutrition and Poverty,* World Bank Staff Occasional Paper 23 (Washington, D.C.).

Schultz, Theodore W. 1978. *Distortions of Agricultural Incentives* (Bloomington, Ind., Indiana University Press).

Shah, C. H. 1979. *Food Preferences and Nutrition: A Perspective on Poverty,* Presidential Address, Indian Society of Agricultural Economics (Bangalore, December 18).

Sukhatme, P. V. 1979. *Malnutrition and Poverty,* Ninth Lal Bahadur Shastri Memorial Lecture, Indian Agricultural Research Institute (New Delhi, January 29).

Sunday Sun-Times (Chicago). 1979. November 11.

Swanson, Earl R., and James C. Hyankori. 1979. "Influence of Weather and Technology on Corn and Soybean Yield Trends," *Agricultural Meteorology* vol. 20 (1979).

U.N. Food and Agriculture Organization. 1977. *Fourth World Food Survey,* Statistical Series 11 (Rome).

————. 1979a. *Agriculture: Toward 2000* (Rome).

————. 1979b. *FAO Commodity Review and Outlook: 1977–79* (Rome).

————. 1979c. *FAO Production Yearbook* vol. 32 (Rome).

UN World Food Conference. 1974. *Assessment of the World Food Situation, Present and Future,* E/CONF. 65/3 (New York).

USDA. 1974. U.S. Department of Agriculture, Economic Research Service. *The World Food Situation and Prospects to 1985,* Foreign Agricultural Economic Report No. 98 (Washington, D.C.).

————. 1977. U.S. Department of Agriculture, Foreign Agricultural Service. *World Consumption of Grain and Livestock Feed,* FG-14-77 (Washington, D.C.).

————. 1978. U.S. Department of Agriculture, Economics, Statistics, and Cooperatives Service. *1979 Fertilizer Situation* (Washington, D.C.).

————. 1979a. U.S. Department of Agriculture, Foreign Agricultural Service. *India: Grain Situation Update,* FG-25-79 (Washington, D.C.).

————. 1979b. U.S. Department of Agriculture, Economics, Statistics, and Cooperatives Service. Farm Income Statistics, *Statistics Bulletin No. 627* (October).

————. 1980a. U.S. Department of Agriculture, Economics, Statistics, and Cooperatives Service. *Agricultural Prices* (Washington, D.C.).

————. 1980b. U.S. Department of Agriculture, Economics, Statistics, and Cooperatives Service. *World Agricultural Situation,* WAS–21 (Washington, D.C.).

————. 1980c. U.S. Department of Agriculture, Foreign Agricultural Service. *Foreign Agricultural Circular—Grains,* FG-2-80 (Washington, D.C.).

———. 1980d. U.S. Department of Agriculture, Foreign Agricultural Service. *Foreign Agricultural Circular—Grains,* FG-4-80 (Washington, D.C.).

World Bank. 1980. *World Development Report* (Washington, D.C., World Bank).

———. 1979. *World Development Report* (Washington, D.C., World Bank).

Wortman, Sterling, and Ralph W. Cummings, Jr. 1978. *To Feed This World: The Challenge and the Strategy* (Baltimore, The Johns Hopkins University Press).

3

Agreements and Policy in U.S.–Japanese Agricultural Trade

James P. Houck

The international trade of the United States and Japan results mainly from differing relative endowments of labor, land, and capital. Japan is densely populated with a land area about as large as California and nearly six times the population. The Japanese people, highly skilled and industrious, have at their disposal an up-to-date technically sophisticated industrial plant. With these characteristics, virtually no abundant raw materials, and limited amounts of arable land, Japan's pattern of international economic comparative advantage is clear. Japan should import raw materials and agricultural commodities and export finished goods, both consumer products and manufactured intermediate products.

The United States, on the other hand, has an abundant endowment of rich agricultural land and an efficient farm production sector. This, along with high per-hour labor costs throughout the economy, a relatively older industrial plant, lagging productivity, high per capita incomes, and much less overall economic dependence on foreign trade than Japan, creates the general export–import pattern of the United States. The United States is a net exporter of agricultural commodities

James P. Houck is professor, Department of Agriculture and Applied Economics, at the University of Minnesota. Helpful comments were offered by Bruce Gardner, Susan Hale, Yujiro Hayami, Kenzo Hemmi, Anne Price, and Mary Ryan.

TABLE 3-1. A PROFILE OF U.S.–JAPANESE COMMODITY TRADE, 1978

Item	U.S. exports to Japan	Japanese exports to United States
	(————percent of total————)	
Food and agricultural products	33	a
Industrial supplies	39	20
Capital goods	18	20
Automotive products	1	33
Consumer goods	6	25
Other	3	2
Total	100	100
Value (billion $U.S.)	$12.9	$24.5

Source: U.S. Department of Commerce, Bureau of the Census, Highlights of U.S. Export and Import Trade (FT 990) (Washington, D.C., 1979).
a Less than 1 percent.

and tends to be a net importer of manufactured consumer goods, some raw and semifinished industrial materials, and, of course, huge amounts of crude oil.

This rather simple view of comparative advantage does not capture the complexity of international trade in its many dimensions for either nation. For example, the United States exports much more than agricultural products and raw materials even though it is currently a net importer of many nonagricultural goods. In fact, nonagricultural exports amounted to about 80 percent of the U.S. total export trade in 1977–78. Much of this is high-technology capital goods and machinery, including computers and electronic gear.[1]

Nevertheless, this rather elementary view of comparative advantage and trade does capture the bilateral trade flow fairly well. Agricultural and raw material exports flow from the United States to Japan, and consumer products and manufactured goods flow from Japan to the United States, as shown in table 3-1. This chapter focuses on the large agricultural component in that table, with particular emphasis on the recent trade agreements and policy issues that have jointly concerned decision makers in these two nations. To set the stage for an evaluation of recent agreements, a sketch of basic agricultural trade and policy conditions between the two countries is in the following sections of this chapter.

[1] Unless otherwise indicated, the data used in this chapter are drawn from official publications of the U.S. Department of Agriculture, U.S. Department of Commerce, and the Japan Ministry of Agriculture, Forestry and Fisheries.

Agricultural Trade

United States–Japanese agricultural trade results from the interaction of powerful economic forces and strong political drives that occasionally work at cross-purposes. To assess this agricultural trade flow, it is important to at least summarize the changes in Japanese food demand and the role of farm and food policies as they affect trade. Then mutual dependence and the evolution of major commodity trade flows can be examined.

Food demand change in Japan

From the U.S. viewpoint, the growth of income and industrial production in Japan has been crucial to the growth of American farm exports to that nation. Income growth and rising living standards have wrenched food demand away from the traditional rice and fish diet toward more Westernized reliance on meat and other livestock products (see Egaitsu, Yoshioka, and Sanderson in this volume). Similarly, the growth in nonfarm employment and industrial output has reduced the supply of potential farm labor. Thus, a lower and more rapidly declining degree of food self-sufficiency has emerged than otherwise would have occurred in the postwar period.

Real per capita income has increased steadily since the mid-1950s at annual rates averaging 8 to 9 percent. With income elasticities of demand for meat and livestock products averaging about +1.0, the yearly income-related increase in demand for these products is obvious (see Sanderson in this volume). On the other hand, estimated income elasticities for cereals are very low, close to zero (Bale and Greenshields, 1977). Consequently, the Japanese diet is changing in a marked way, as shown in table 3-2.

Notice that meat and livestock product consumption has increased four and one-half times since 1960 along with a doubling of fats and oils intake. Starch consumption (mainly cereals) has fallen 26 percent on a per-capita calorie basis. Moreover, this fundamental dietary shift has been accompanied by a 9 percent increase in average daily caloric intake. Accompanying these changes, self-sufficiency rates for all major food product classes have fallen, with the notable exception of rice. Japan is now more dependent than ever on imports of nonrice food grains, feed grains, pulses, fruits, vegetables, dairy products, eggs, and meat, according to Yoshioka, in this volume. Meanwhile, Japan's agricultural working population has been reduced by half,

TABLE 3-2. PERCENTAGES OF DAILY PER PERSON CALORIC INTAKE
FROM VARIOUS FOOD CLASSES IN JAPAN, 1960 AND 1977
(percentage)

Item	1960	1977	
Starch	69	51	(21)
Fish	6	4	(2)
Meat and livestock products	2	11	(33)
Fats and oils	6	12	(16)
Other[a]	17	22	(28)
Total	100	100	(100)
For reference:			
Calories per day	2,290	2,490	(3,370)

Note: Comparable U.S. data are in parentheses.

Sources: Yutaka Yoshioka, *Food and Agriculture in Japan*, About Japan Series, no. 23 (Tokyo, Foreign Press Center); Japanese Ministry of Agriculture, Forestry and Fisheries, *Statistical Yearbook, 1977–78* (Tokyo, 1979) p. 497; U.S. Department of Agriculture, *Agricultural Statistics* (Washington, D.C., 1975) pp. 553–554.

[a] Fruits, vegetables, sugar, etc.

and domestic agricultural output as a proportion of the net domestic product has fallen from 10 percent in 1960 to 5 percent in 1977.

Policy regime: Japan

To the outside observer, Japan's agricultural and food policy seems to exhibit three, interlocked foundation stones—(1) rice, (2) self-sufficiency, and (3) the political power of the farmer.[2] Each has important implications for agricultural trade with the world in general and the United States in particular.

In 1977, rice accounted for 39 percent of farm income, 32 percent of the caloric intake of the nation's people, and close to 10 percent of total food expenditures. Rice prices at the farm are supported well above world prices and even higher than equivalent wholesale levels inside Japan. This can occur because farm-to-wholesale rice trade is in the hands of a government monopoly, the Japanese Food Agency, which also controls all food grain imports and exports.

The high support level for rice naturally has far-reaching effects on all of Japan's agriculture. Rice is planted on about 48 percent of

[2] These three subjects are recurring themes throughout this volume. More detailed discussions of rice policy are in chapter 5 by Egaitsu and chapter 10 by Hayami; of self-sufficiency in chapter 4 by Kuroda, chapter 7 by Hemmi, chapter 9 by Yoshioka, and chapter 10 by Hayami; and of farmers' political power in chapter 7 by Hemmi and chapter 8 by Talbot and Kihl.

cultivated cropland. So the direct farm income effect of the rice support policy is very strong. In addition, land and other resources to be used for producing alternative crops and livestock must somehow be attracted away from rice production. Even agricultural resources not well suited to rice will reflect, through indirect competition with those that are, the artificially high returns sustained by the rice price guarantees. Hence, the effects of the high rice price spread throughout agriculture and the food system creating pressures for import protection throughout the farm economy.

The rice policy is clearly part of Japan's strong commitment to as much food and raw material self-sufficiency as is practicable, given economic and political realities. Bitter past experiences foster this commitment despite the heavy dependence of the modern Japanese economy on all manner of foreign raw materials. Self-sufficiency is a dominant political and social theme that simply cannot be denied in Japan's trade policy.

The data in table 3-3 show estimates of Japan's current degree of self-sufficiency in major foods and feeds. Notice that, with the exception of sugar, self-sufficiency is very high in commodities for *direct* consumption. However, it is less than 10 percent for several key feed and food ingredients. Almost no major food or agricultural product groups display an intermediate level of self-sufficiency, of as much as 40 to 60 percent. This obvious dichotomy is a reflection of how food self-sufficiency objectives are met by the Japanese economy.

Even though self-sufficiency is declining, its rather high level and broad distribution among food commodities suggest a rather protective agricultural policy for a nation with high population density and only 15 percent of its land suitable for farming. Farms on this thin agricultural base average only 1.2 hectares in size with about 87 percent classified as part-time operations. Only 2 percent are larger than 3.0 hectares. Moreover, Japanese consumers devote an average 33 percent of their living expenditures to food compared with about 18 percent in the United States.

Much of the pressure for protective policies on behalf of Japan's 4.8 million farm households, at the general expense of 109 million consumers and taxpayers, can be traced to special characteristics of the nation's political life as it relates to agriculture. Other chapters in this volume deal with this topic in detail. Here, it is sufficient to say that, by any standard, Japanese farmers are well organized and well situated for political action. With the generally reliable support of the powerful Ministry of Agriculture, Forestry and Fisheries, various farm and commodity organizations press for and obtain economic protec-

TABLE 3-3. FOOD SELF-SUFFICIENCY IN JAPAN, 1977
(percentage)

| | Degree of Japan's self-sufficiency | |
Item	1960	1977
Rice	102	100
Vegetables	100	98
Fish	101	97
Eggs	108	97
Milk	89	87
Meat	86	77
Fruits	84	85
Sugar	10	18
Feed grains	66	7
Wheat	39	4
Soybeans	28	3
All foods	90	70

Sources: Japanese Ministry of Agriculture, Forestry and Fisheries, *Statistical Yearbook 1977–78* (Tokyo, 1979) pp. 496–497; Fred H. Sanderson, *Japan's Food Prospects and Policies* (Washington, D.C., The Brookings Institution, 1978) p. 29; U.S. Department of Agriculture, *Foreign Agriculture* vol. 13, no. 40 (October 6, 1975) p. 9.

tion on a broad front, including trade. An important reason for their success is the crucial role played by agricultural interests within the Liberal Democratic Party (LDP) (see Hemmi in this volume). The LDP has been in power continually since 1948. Nearly all government agencies and lobbying groups are firmly connected with it. The party draws much strength from two important constituencies, big business and rural districts. As with many other industrial nations, the voting districts in Japan are apportioned so that the rural vote is overrepresented in national elections. Hence, the LDP is heavily influenced by Japanese farm interests, especially in recent years as the relative political strength of the LDP has waned.

Policy regime: United States

It is beyond this chapter's scope to discuss the complex agricultural policy of the United States or the full range of economic and political issues that affect the general flow of U.S.–Japanese trade. This can be found in Gardner's chapter in this volume. This section, however, contains some ideas about the role of U.S. agricultural trade policy as it affects this flow.

One thing is certain: the agricultural trade policy of the U.S. government has little effect on the rather small flow of agricultural trade from Japan to the United States. Japan never has been a significant source of U.S. agricultural imports. In 1978, only 0.6 percent of all U.S. agricultural imports came from Japan (USDA, *Foreign Agricultural Trade*, various issues). Practically all of this $88.6 million total is specialty food products and highly processed nonfood items. (These products often encounter complex and conflicting standards imposed by individual states.) United States policy on agricultural trade with Japan is fundamentally concerned with the maintenance and expansion of agricultural exports. Its effect on imports can be safely ignored. Despite occasional short-term deviations, such as the 1973 curtailment of soybean exports, the main thrust is expansionary.

Japan is the leading single national buyer of U.S. agricultural exports, and has held first or second place annually since the 1950s. Therefore, the overall U.S. policy concerning agricultural exports always has specific relevance for the Japanese market. Today, there are three principal elements in this policy. The first is to maintain competitive prices for world-market sales of those U.S. products that are subject to domestic price and income support programs. These products include several of special importance to Japan: wheat, feed grains, soybeans, and cotton. Together, these commodities have accounted for most of the two-nation trade, averaging 74 percent of the total in 1977 and 1978 and 89 percent as far back as 1952 and 1953. Bruce Gardner in chapter 6 of this volume discusses the nature of these programs and how they are now geared to minimize interference with export sales.

The second element in U.S. trade policy is to expand foreign markets through an active and aggressive program of market development and promotion. Much of this work is a joint undertaking by the Foreign Agricultural Service of the U.S. Department of Agriculture and designated commodity groups from U.S. private trade. The network of agricultural counselors and attachés, located in major embassies around the world, including Tokyo, is crucial in organizing and directing this work as well as giving it official status within the web of commercial and diplomatic relations between the governments. The network's objective is to create or encourage a commercial climate within which trade can expand, given existing official policy and regulatory constraints of both sides. Another objective is to lobby for reductions in trade restrictions of all types, official and unofficial. Chapter 8 in this volume, by Talbot and Kihl, describes these market development and trade promotion projects more fully.

The third main thrust of U.S. agricultural trade policy, also important for the Japanese market, is the continuing organized effort on a government-to-government basis to reduce trade barriers. This involves (1) continual efforts to secure favorable, market-expanding interpretations of existing import policies and regulations and (2) the conduct of formal trade negotiations within the existing system of international agencies. Periodic multilateral negotiations have been conducted for over thirty years within the General Agreement on Tariffs and Trade (GATT). Recent unsuccessful wheat agreement talks and other negotiations have been held under the auspices of the United Nations Conference on Trade and Development (UNCTAD). Discussion of these negotiations and their results forms a major part of the balance of this chapter.

Mutual dependence

The United States and Japan are locked together in mutual dependence upon the vast flow of agricultural commodities between the two nations. In the first instance, the United States depends heavily on the Japanese market for a large share of its foreign sales that are so vital to farm and agribusiness income. In a similar fashion, despite some efforts to diversify its sources, Japan depends critically on the United States for a major share of its imports of food, feed, and agricultural raw materials.

Japan has been the leading agricultural customer of the United States for many years. In 1978, shipments to Japan accounted for 15 percent of total U.S. farm exports. Table 3-4 is a ranking of major agricultural commodities and commodity groups for which Japan is

TABLE 3-4. RANK AND EXPORT SHARE OF MAJOR U.S. AGRICULTURAL EXPORTS TO JAPAN, 1978

Exported item	Japan's rank among all buyers	Sales to Japan as percentage of total exports of indicated products
Meats and meat products	1	33
Wheat and flour	2	10
Feed grains	1	20
Fruits and vegetables	2	15
Oilseeds and products	2	14
Tobacco	1	20
Cotton	2	19
All agricultural products	1	15

Source: U.S. Department of Agriculture, Economics and Statistics Service, U.S. Foreign Agricultural Trade, Statistical Report, Calendar Year 1975 (Washington, D.C., 1976) various tables.

a leading buyer. It also shows Japan's market share from the U.S. viewpoint.

Table 3-5 shows a comparative profile of U.S. agricultural exports to Japan, first in 1952–53 and again in 1977–78. It is clear that the evolution in the commodity mix over the past twenty-five years reflects the rapidly growing importance of meat and livestock products in the Japanese diet. Notice the relative expansion in imports of meat, feed grains, and soybeans, all of which directly or indirectly relate to live-stock production or consumption. These changes have occurred as a result of underlying economic forces. No major or decisive change in Japan's agricultural production and trade policy has occurred.

The relative decline in the importance of wheat reflects both the high degree of self-sufficiency in food grains (mainly rice) achieved by Japan's farm and food policy and the static nature of food grain demand. The decline in cotton's comparative position over this twenty-five-year period is caused, among other things, by the rapid growth in competitive textile manufacturing and exports by Japan's southeast Asian neighbors, especially South Korea, Hong Kong, and Taiwan.

The other side of the mutual dependence phenomenon is Japan's heavy reliance on imports from the United States for its food and fiber requirements. Despite various efforts to diversify its sources of farm product imports, Japan has been growing slowly more dependent upon the United States, as is evident in table 3-6. The evolution

TABLE 3-5. PROFILE OF U.S. AGRICULTURAL EXPORTS TO JAPAN, ANNUAL AVERAGES, 1952–53 AND 1977–78
(percentage)

Exported item	1952–53	1977–78
Meat and other livestock products	4	13
Wheat and flour	23	10
Feed grains	18	28
Soybeans	9	23
Other fats, oils, and oilseed products	3	3
Cotton	39	13
Fruits and vegetables	1	5
Other products	3	5
Total	100	100
In millions of $U.S.	$422	$3,967

Source: U.S. Department of Agriculture, Economics and Statistic Service, *U.S. Foreign Agricultural Trade, Statistical Report* (Washington, D.C.) various annual summaries.

of the Japanese diet toward more meat and livestock products has fostered this growing dependence. No other nation or region in the world has the same ability as the United States to produce feed grains and protein-rich oilseeds. Moreover, the falling relative value of the U.S. dollar has kept the comparative yen price of these commodities at bargain levels throughout most of the 1970s.

Table 3-7 illustrates the overwhelming U.S. share in many of the markets for products which are growing in relative importance in Japan's farm trade picture. These include soybeans, corn, and other feed grains and feedstuffs.

TABLE 3-6. U.S. SHARE OF JAPAN'S IMPORTS OF ALL AGRICULTURAL
           PRODUCTS, SELECTED YEARS BETWEEN 1954 AND 1977
(percentage)

Year	U.S. share of all Japanese agricultural imports
1954	30
1964	31
1972	34
1975	36
1976	38
1977	37

Sources: Hughes H. Spurlock, *Trends and Developments in Japan's Economy Affecting the Market for U.S. Farm Products*, Report No. 10 (Washington, D.C., U.S. Department of Agriculture, Economic Research Service, 1964) pp. 37, 74; U.S. Department of Agriculture, Economics, Statistics and Cooperatives Service, *Foreign Agricultural Trade of United States* (Washington, D.C.) various issues.

TABLE 3-7. U.S. SHARE OF JAPAN'S IMPORTS OF SELECTED
           AGRICULTURAL COMMODITIES, 1977
(percentage)

Item	U.S. share of Japan's imports
Soybeans	95
Soybean meal	75
Corn	82
Sorghum	47
Alfalfa meal	56
Live cattle	96
Cattle hides	83
Wheat	59
Citrus fruit	95

Source: U.S. Department of Agriculture, Economics, Statistics and Cooperatives Service, *Foreign Agricultural Trade of United States* (Washington, D.C., April 1978) pp. 20–26.

Multilateral Trade Negotiations: The Setting

Because of the reliance of the United States and Japan upon each other in both agricultural and nonagricultural trade, it is useful to look at how the results of recent trade negotiations affect agricultural trade flows. Both Japan and the United States are members (contracting parties) of GATT. The United States was a charter member at GATT's 1947 inception. Japan acceded to the agreement in 1955.

A cornerstone of GATT is the "most favored nation" principle which requires nondiscrimination among trading parties in the application of tariffs (Curzon, 1965). Similarly, any new trading privilege or trade barrier relaxation accorded by one nation to another is to be immediately available for similar products from any other contracting party. This concept, together with the commitment by members of GATT to undertake periodic multilateral trade negotiations, has made the formal negotiating rounds of GATT significant in the evolution of trade policy between Japan and the United States.

The two most recent rounds of negotiations involving the United States, Japan, and other nations were the Kennedy Round (1963–67) and the recently completed Tokyo Round (1973–79). Each stretched over several years. The five previous rounds were each comparatively short because they dealt almost exclusively with tariff cuts and bindings. It was with the Kennedy Round that nontariff trade barriers, so important in agricultural trade policy, were first systematically discussed with a view toward possible negotiation.

Under negotiating procedures that have evolved in GATT since 1947, multilateral tariff and trade concessions for individual commodities or industrial sectors occur only when two or more of the leading trading nations in the relevant products are able to agree on the main lines of a settlement. Then other interested parties can join in and, by their participation, come to an agreement on a multilateral package in which all GATT members may share.

In both the Tokyo Round and the Kennedy Round, United States, Japan, and the European Community occupied center stage in agricultural negotiations. (Though quite important in the Kennedy Round, the United Kingdom is now submerged within the European Community Group of Nine.) Other important nations in the inner circle, next to the "big three," are Canada, Mexico, Brazil, Argentina, and Australia. These few nations form the pool from which pairs and other combinations must be drawn for any significant agricultural dealing to occur. Each, including the United States and Japan, has a complex domestic agricultural policy that has severely restricted its ability to negotiate broadly on agricultural trade. In addition, a historical tendency to treat agricultural negotiations in a separate package, largely isolated from industrial agreements, adds even more rigidity to this picture. This tendency was broken in the Japanese–U.S. agreements of the Tokyo Round.

Barriers to agricultural trade have been extremely difficult to negotiate internationally. Any relaxation toward more liberal trade usually undermines national farm or food policies by making them either more costly or administratively difficult to operate. Furthermore, most nations, including Japan and the United States, are unwilling to negotiate the terms of their own, *internal* agricultural policy. Although imperfect and inconsistent everywhere, existing agricultural policies and programs have been slowly and painfully constructed. They are not altered or put aside lightly. It is in this context that the objectives and agricultural results of the Kennedy and Tokyo rounds are examined and evaluated. It is clear that from the viewpoint of "new" trade created, the agreements reached in the Kennedy and Tokyo rounds were modest indeed. Yet to look only at trade expansion is to take a rather narrow view. The negotiating process itself permits a healthful airing of viewpoints, problems, and positions that otherwise might remain obscure. Achieving an agreement, however modest in scope, does reassert continuing political support by the signatories in an open and multilateral system of world trade. Therefore, agreements such as those reached in the Kennedy and Tokyo rounds help to smooth out trade relations between major trading partners such as Japan and the United States and hold protectionist forces at bay.

The Kennedy Round: 1963–67

During the Kennedy Round, official statements were continually advanced about the crucial importance of agricultural agreements to the United States. For instance, John Schnittker (1970) quotes from a 1963 speech by Christian A. Herter, the U.S. chief negotiator for the Kennedy Round. "It is, of course, the firm position of my government that negotiations must include agricultural products. This means that my government will not be prepared to conclude the negotiations until equitable tariff and trade arrangements have been developed for agricultural products" (p. 8). Yet major breakthroughs in agricultural trade negotiations simply did not materialize in the Kennedy Round. Those familiar with its history know that the major parties, especially the United States and the Group of Six from the European Community were too far apart and too inflexible within their own domestic farm policy constraints to maneuver toward anything new.

General results

At the 1967 conclusion of the Kennedy Round, the political commitment by the United States for a substantive agricultural agreement was deemed satisfied in two main ways (USDA, 1967). First, an international grains arrangement was signed. As an outgrowth of previous international wheat agreements, it contained a food aid convention and an ill-fated, price-fixing trade convention for wheat. Second, a series of tariff cuts and bindings was concluded for agricultural products whose trade coverage value, at that time, was $866 million for U.S. exports and $860 million for imports. Incidentally, at 1978–79 price levels, these trade values approximate $2.0 billion. In comparison, the trade coverage values of the agricultural agreements of the 1973–79 Tokyo Round approximate $4.0 billion.

Japan played a rather passive negotiating role in the Kennedy Round. Most of the political fireworks and negotiating confrontations occurred between the United States and the European Community, many of these over agricultural matters. Yet, Japan joined the International Grains Arrangement of 1967 as a full signatory, agreeing to contribute the value of 5.0 percent of 4.5 million metric tons pledged annually to the food aid convention by participating nations (USDA, 1967a). Further, United States and Japan reached a significant *bilateral* agreement on agricultural tariff cuts and bindings which was then available to all GATT members.

U.S.–Japanese agreement

The Kennedy Round settlement involved U.S. agricultural products exported to Japan whose 1964 trade value was $240.4 million.[3] In these terms, it was the second most important agricultural tariff and trade agreement in the round, exceeded only by the $279.1 million package between the United States and the European Community. Thus, the U.S.–Japanese settlement accounted for 28 percent of the total trade coverage in the U.S. agricultural export portion of the Kennedy Round. Of this total, $19.3 million reflected tariff bindings

---

[3] Trade value data for 1964 were used by the office of the U.S. special trade representative for negotiating and reporting purposes.

by Japan on a variety of products, the most important of which were prepared animal feeds. The balance, $221.1 million, reflected the trade coverage value of approximately ninety items whose existing tariffs were cut an average of 53 percent by Japan. Of the ninety items included in this tariff-cutting package, soybeans represented 64 percent of its total coverage value. Soybean tariffs were reduced from 13 percent ad valorem to the equivalent of 5 or 6 percent.

Compared with the annual value of U.S.–Japanese agricultural trade, the Kennedy Round agreements were relatively modest. They covered only 31 percent of the 1964 value of total farm trade. No specific tariff or nontariff agreements were reached on basic commodities like wheat or feed grains, central to or highly competitive with Japanese agriculture.

The analytical method shown in appendix 3-A at the back of this chapter was used to estimate the value of "new" U.S. agricultural exports to Japan resulting from the Kennedy Round tariff reductions. These estimates are presented in table 3-8. The total new trade estimate of $8 million per year is about 3 percent of the base trade value of the affected items and only about 1 percent of total 1964 agricultural trade from the United States to Japan. These new trade estimates are the *annual* value of additional U.S. exports to Japan as a specific and direct result of the negotiated tariff cuts.

In the Kennedy Round, Japan made no specific concessions on several items of expressed interest to the United States. These included tobacco, soybean meal, oranges and grapefruit, honey, and chicken. However, Japan did offer to consider raising quotas on some of these items.

For its part, the United States made tariff concessions on about $20 million worth of agricultural products supplied by Japan. About half

TABLE 3-8. KENNEDY ROUND: SUMMARY OF ANNUAL U.S.
AGRICULTURAL EXPORT INCREASES TO JAPAN
UNDER FULL TARIFF REDUCTIONS AS NEGOTIATED
(million $U.S.)

Item	Base trade value 1964	Estimated new value	Change
Soybeans	154	157	+3
Safflower seeds	22	23	+1
Tallow (beef)	28	29	+1
Lard	6	7	+1
Others	11	13	+2
Total	221	229	+8

of the total value was accounted for by canned mandarin oranges. Other items, all specialty products, included frog meat, soy sauce, rice wine, and dried mushrooms.

The Tokyo Round: 1973–79

The seventy-nine-month Tokyo Round, concluded in April 1979, was the lengthiest formal trade negotiation in GATT history (GATT, 1979). The objectives of this round were set out in the Tokyo Declaration of September 1973 that formally opened the negotiations (U.S. Congress, 1975). Finance ministers of over 100 nations drafted this charter, setting the tone for subsequent deliberations.

From the outset, agriculture again was viewed by the United States as a critical area. As with the Kennedy Round, the official U.S. stance, reiterated time and again by Ambassador Robert Strauss and his negotiating team, was that no overall settlement was possible unless agricultural trade was significantly benefited. This stance was buttressed by similar language in the Trade Act of 1974 authorizing U.S. participation (U.S. Congress, 1975).

The format

The ninety-eight-nation Trade Negotiations Committee of GATT assumed overall responsibility for the groups and working units actually conducting the negotiations. The principal groups and themes for negotiating were set out in the Tokyo Declaration (GATT, 1979). Major efforts focused on:

- tariffs
- nontariff measures
- agriculture
- tropical products
- safeguards
- the GATT framework

Tariffs

Tariff reduction has been the traditional core of all GATT negotiations. It has always been the most visible sign of success or failure in any particular round. A central goal adopted for the Tokyo Round was a multilateral series of tariff agreements both to lower duties and to harmonize them among nations. Harmonization implies that higher tariffs would be cut relatively more than lower tariffs. Agreed-upon general formulas were adopted for this purpose and applied mainly in industrial goods sectors.

Nontariff measures (NTMs)

Emphasis on nontariff barriers was given concrete status within the Tokyo Round. The NTM negotiations were separated into five subgroup categories:

1. quantitative restrictions—mainly quotas and licensing procedures
2. subsidies and countervailing duties—procedures to deal with "dumping" *via* export subsidies and consequent retaliation by both importers and other competing exporters
3. technical barriers—mainly product standards, labeling and packaging restrictions, statements of origin, and the like, applied to restrict trade
4. customs issues—primarily involving consistent product valuation procedures for tariff purposes
5. government procurement—procedures to regularize and open up government purchasing to allow international sellers better access to government contracts

Agriculture

Along with the NTM emphasis, agricultural trade was identified separately in order to provide a negotiating basis for whatever commodity agreements might be proposed. Subgroups were identified for grains (primarily coarse grains), meat, and dairy products. Negotiations for an international wheat agreement, ultimately unsuccessful, proceeded in parallel fashion first within the International Wheat Council and later under the auspices of UNCTAD.

Tropical products

The Tokyo Declaration also singled out tropical products in order to highlight the importance of such products to the developing nations and to deal with such products separately since they are not heavily competitive with domestic agriculture in the United States, Japan, and Europe. Moreover, some concrete concessions for tariff cuts on tropical products appeared early in the round suggesting that a separate grouping for these agreements would be sensible within the overall negotiating context.

Safeguards

This negotiating group was identified to improve the mechanisms by which nations impose trade restrictions or withdraw prior concessions when competing domestic industries are severely injured by sudden or unexpected changes in imports. Prompt, orderly procedures for phasing out safeguard actions also were to be emphasized. (No final safeguard agreement was reached in the Tokyo Round.)

GATT framework

This was a catch-all category for review and revision of the general agreement itself to make it more suitable to modern conditions, better able to accommodate trade problems of developing countries, a better mechanism for managing trade conflicts, and an improved vehicle to speed up and clarify dispute settlements.

The Downing Street Summit

By May 1977, negotiations had faltered, and many governments were questioning whether to continue. A meeting in London of heads of state was called to assess the matter. It was dubbed the Downing Street Summit and included the newly elected U.S. president, Jimmy Carter. Ambassador Alan Wolfe, formerly U.S. Deputy Special Trade Representative for Trade Negotiations, later wrote of this meeting:

> Two people stood out in particular on that occasion. Prime Minister Fukuda of Japan and our President [Carter]. Fukuda was the only one of the world leaders who had sufficient seniority to have been present at the London Economic Conference in the early 1930s. He recalled for the group that the conference had ended in failure. . . . And the Prime Minister noted that following that failure at cooperation, there ensued the depression and within it lay the seeds of the second World War. He was absolutely determined that that would never occur again. (1979, p. 2)

With renewed commitments to success and a new U.S. negotiating team led by Ambassador Robert Strauss, the Tokyo Round resumed for a further two years. At the close of the negotiations in April 1979, a series of agreements was struck that would affect U.S.–Japanese agricultural trade both directly and indirectly. With the passage of implementing legislation in July 1979 and official administration acceptance in December 1979, the participation of the United States in these agreements was assured. As with the Kennedy Round, specific agricultural agreements were very difficult to arrange, and the final results were modest.

Agreements important to U.S.–Japanese agricultural trade

The Tokyo Round agreements that directly affect agricultural trade can be visualized in three categories. First are the specific tariff and import quota concessions similar to those of previous rounds. These were achieved within the traditional, bilateral, "offer and request" framework. They are available to all signatories under the "most favored nation" principle. Second are the behavioral codes, the most important for agricultural trade being the "export subsidies/countervailing duty" code and the "standards" code. The former seeks to tighten international responsibility and restraint regarding export subsidies and tariff retaliation. The latter is designed to reduce the use of various standards, certification, and product testing as trade barriers. Third are international consultative agreements for dairy products, beef, and general agricultural policy. These latter agreements have no substantive economic provisions.

Tariff bindings

Tokyo Round tariff bindings by Japan cover some fourteen items of interest to the United States whose 1976 base trade value was $809 million.[4] (A tariff binding is an agreement not to raise a particular tariff above the existing level.) Although these bindings are scattered over a number of products, the zero tariff binding on soybeans alone accounted for $770 million, or 95 percent of this total. It is impossible to calculate or predict the value of this kind of trade concession. Most observers feel that a similar duty-free binding on soybeans obtained from the European Common Market during the 1962 Dillon Round has been at least partially responsible for the huge growth of soybean exports to that market. Given the relatively low level of per capita meat consumption in Japan and its high income elasticity, the duty-free binding on soybeans could easily become the most valuable concession granted by Japan to the United States in the Tokyo Round.

No tariff bindings on agricultural items of interest to Japan were offered by the United States in the Tokyo Round.

[4] Trade figures for 1976 were used by the office of the U.S. special trade representative for negotiating and reporting purposes. The specific Tokyo Round tariff and quota agreements discussed and analyzed in this part of the paper are taken from unpublished memoranda of the special trade representative's office.

Tariff cuts

Excluding bound items, the value of tariff reductions offered by Japan in the bilateral package averaged 35 percent, across the board, and covered approximately 150 agricultural items.[5] In this analysis, tariff reductions are assumed to exert downward pressure on retail and wholesale prices inside Japan. The economic value of any tariff reduction occurs because the total market for a general product line expands *and* because the market share of an imported item grows because of its relative price reduction. The analyses in this section focus on the total negotiated tariff reductions, without considering the intermediate staging that will occur in their actual application. The method, described in appendix 3-A, is the same as for the Kennedy Round.

Table 3-9 contains the results of calculations of the annual trade effects of the negotiated tariff changes. As with the Kennedy Round, they are to be viewed as approximations indicating relative magnitudes; they are not predictions because they attempt to isolate the pure effect of the tariff changes. Moreover, they are lower bounds on estimated change since no Japanese supply responses to the tariff-induced price changes were calculated.

Almost 40 percent of the estimated annual trade increase is concentrated in the pork market. This calculation assumes that imported pork will actually fall in relative price because of the negotiated settlement. However, Japanese imports of pork are subject to charges which resemble variable import duties. Consequently, this part of the calculation will be void if the relative price of imported pork is not permitted to decrease inside Japan. Agricultural trade values increase by an estimated $88 million per year, or about 20 percent of the base value of the covered items. Without pork, the $53 million increase represents 18 percent of the base value of covered items.

The U.S.–Japanese settlement contained no U.S. tariff cuts on agricultural items of specific export interest to Japan.

Quota increases

The U.S.–Japanese package contained import quota relaxation by Japan for four commodities in which the United States has a sizable, direct interest and which are directly competitive with Japanese products: high-quality beef, oranges, orange juice, and grapefruit juice.[6] Table 3-10 presents the current quotas for these products, the full

[5] See footnote 4.

[6] See footnote 4.

TABLE 3-9. TOKYO ROUND: SUMMARY OF U.S. AGRICULTURAL TRADE
INCREASES TO JAPAN UNDER FULL TARIFF REDUCTIONS
AS NEGOTIATED

(million $U.S.)

Item	Base trade value 1976	Estimated new value	Change
Fruits and vegetables	168	197	+29
Poultry	16	29	+13
Livestock products			
Pork	150	185	+35[a]
Tallow	40	42	+2
Offals	14	15	+1
Horsemeat	4	5	+1
Grain and feed	4	5	+1
Seeds	3	4	+1
Cottonseed oil	7	9	+2
Others	38	41	+3
Total	444	532	+88

[a] Tentative upper bound estimate subject to Japanese policy decisions on floor and ceiling prices for pork.

TABLE 3-10. TOKYO ROUND: U.S.–JAPANESE QUOTA AGREEMENTS;
SUMMARY OF CHANGES AND ESTIMATED ANNUAL TRADE
VALUE

Item	Original quota	New quota	Change	Annual value of change (million dollars)
	(————million lbs————)			
Beef	37.0	67.9	+30.9	77.3[a]
Oranges	99.2	180.8	+81.6	24.5[b]
Orange and grapefruit juice	8.8	27.6	+18.7	21.5[c]
Total				123.3

[a] Calculated at $2.50/lb.
[b] Calculated at 30¢/lb.
[c] Calculated at $1.15/lb.

relaxation implied in the settlement, and the estimated annual trade value of the quota increases. These calculations assume that the new, larger quotas are entirely filled by imports from the United States. These quota adjustments reflect changes in significant nontariff barriers. Their precedent-setting value should not be neglected despite relatively small dollar amounts. Although difficult to achieve, they may presage further quota relaxation by Japan and other U.S. trading partners.

Summary

The estimated annual value of tariff and quota adjustments by Japan amount to as much as $211 million in 1976 dollars. To this must be added unknown but possibly large future values of (1) the tariff bindings achieved, especially on soybeans, and (2) the precedent-setting value of import quota changes. The *new* trade values represent 6 percent of 1976 agricultural exports from the United States to Japan. From the U.S. agricultural viewpoint, the Tokyo Round yielded substantially more trade gains, in relative terms, than the Kennedy Round. The main reason for this gain is the quota relaxations by Japan in response to intense negotiating pressures not present during the Kennedy Round when U.S.–European Community relations dominated the scene. Elsewhere, the author has argued that, in total, the Tokyo Round yielded agricultural trade concessions worth $460 million annually to the United States in *new* trade (Houck, 1979). Hence, the U.S.–Japanese agreement represents about 46 percent of this total.

The new codes and consultative agreements

As signatories to the Tokyo Round agreements, the United States and Japan will be influenced by several new multilateral codes and agreements. The various behavioral codes do not provide highly specific guidelines or detailed rules of conduct. These may emerge as experience accumulates and as precedents are established through individual cases brought before GATT. At this time, it is impossible to make a prediction or analysis of their effect on trade. The specifics of the codes are described in detail elsewhere and are not repeated here (U.S. Congress, 1979; GATT, 1979). The two codes that may be of some relevance to U.S.–Japanese agricultural trade are the standards code and the export subsidy/countervailing duty code.

The new standards code does not attempt to set product standards or prescribe specific guidelines for standard setting. Nor does it provide any nation with veto power over the health, safety, and other standards of another nation. The code's objective is to make the standards-setting process more transparent and open than ever before. It also encourages nations to use existing international standards and standard-setting bodies. In addition, this code establishes international procedures through GATT by which signatories may complain of code violations by others, obtain reviews of their complaints, and, in validated cases of violation, take retaliating action. Occasionally, U.S.–Japanese agricultural trade relations have been marked by disputes over health or safety standards of the type encompassed by this code.

It is possible that such future disputes will fall within this code's purview.

Without doubt, the new subsidy/countervailing duty code is the one of most importance to U.S. agriculture although not necessarily in relation to Japan. As framed in the Tokyo Round, this code attempts to meet head on a major nontariff distortion to trade—the export subsidy. The code imposes a flat prohibition of export subsidies on nonprimary products and primary mineral products. It recognizes and permits export subsidies (and certain domestic subsidies affecting trade) for agricultural products under limiting conditions which are rather imprecisely defined at the moment. If export subsidies *not* meeting these conditions are applied, affected importers and competing exporters may retaliate with countervailing duties or other measures, if they can show direct injury to domestic industry.

This new code describes the nature of various export subsidies more fully than previous GATT documents. In particular, it provides that nations should not use subsidies to displace exports of others or significantly undercut prices in foreign markets. The specific language of the code is very carefully balanced so as to be acceptable to a wide spectrum of nations and interests. As a result, it is sufficiently vague so that only experience and legal precedent can establish its ultimate strength.

It is possible that trade disputes covered by this code and involving the United States and Japan could arise in one or two ways. For instance, if Japan began to export rice to Asian markets on a commercial basis, the United States could argue plausibly that such trade reflected a large export subsidy and was, therefore, prohibited under the code. This would follow because of the difference between the high internal farm-level support price for rice and much lower prices on international markets. As another example, suppose that a competing wheat or feed grain exporter attempted to capture a larger share of the Japanese market by means of an export subsidy. Such behavior might be challenged successfully under this code.

The three consultative agreements negotiated within the Tokyo Round provide for regular meetings of signatories on an official level to exchange information and to discuss trade and policy matters about bovine meats, dairy products, and farm and food policies generally. The procedural rules under which dairy and meat trade matters are presented for discussion and under which recommendations may be made to member governments make it unlikely that controversial issues will be settled within the agreements or that strong recommendations will be forwarded to governments. The wide international diversity of views about both commodity agreements and about the coordination of *domestic* agricultural and food policies limits these three agreements to relatively innocuous consulting forums.

Their strength will be to provide a generally nonadversarial setting in which current and potential trade problems, induced by political and economic changes, can be aired and information exchanged. No specific economic evaluation can be made yet for these agreements, but their existence will not add any disruptive elements to world agricultural trade and may help nations to avoid or manage future conflicts. Of the two commodity agreements, it is likely that the meat agreement will be of the most joint interest to the United States and Japan, with the United States seeking to encourage further meat imports by Japan.

A Bilateral Accord: The Butz-Abe Understanding

The tumultuous international economic environment of the early 1970s provided the background for a high-level conference and a subsequent document of "understanding" between the U.S. Secretary of Agriculture, Earl Butz, and the Japanese Minister of Agriculture and Forestry, Shintaro Abe. The letter of understanding, signed in November 1975, sought to bolster the stability of U.S.–Japanese agricultural trade relations by setting minimum annual quantities of wheat, feed grains, and soybeans that the United States would supply to Japan in 1976, 1977, and 1978. The approximate amounts were 3 million metric tons of wheat, 3 million tons of soybeans, and 8 million tons of feed grains (Coyle, 1978).

There seem to have been three major events or episodes leading up to this bilateral undertaking. First was the well-known export trade embargo on soybeans and soybean meal imposed by the United States in late 1973. This worldwide cut-off hit the Japanese market severely and, along with several other international events, dramatized Japan's vulnerability to sudden disruptions in food and raw material imports. Second was the emergence of the Soviet Union as both a large grain importer and a potentially erratic force in international grain markets. In some years, the Soviet Union competes directly and indirectly with Japan for grain supplies from the world's major exporters. A third, related development was the signing of a five-year bilateral grain supply agreement between the United States and the USSR in October 1975. This agreement, designed to add stability to the U.S.–USSR grain trade, assured the Soviets access to specific minimum levels of grain supplies annually from the United States. Taken together, these events made it important for Japan to achieve some concrete agricultural trade assurances from its largest supplier.

From the U.S. point of view, the Butz-Abe understanding served to reaffirm the basic expansionary philosophy of agricultural export policy, to attempt to offset the loss of Japan's confidence in our reliability as a supplier of agricultural products, and to head off a major new Japanese effort to seek alternative sources of international supplies.

With the exception of feed grains shipments in 1976, the targets were all exceeded over the three-year life of the understanding. This likely would have been the case even without the understanding. The agreement has not been renewed in a formal sense, but recent diplomatic trade consultations suggest that the basic objectives of the earlier understanding are still relevant in U.S.–Japanese agricultural trade relations.

Farm Exports and U.S. Foreign Policy in 1980

On January 4, 1980, President Carter suspended deliveries to the Soviet Union of all agricultural products above the levels required in the five-year bilateral grain agreement mentioned earlier. This partial export embargo was a response to the Soviet invasion of Afghanistan. The immediate effect was to disrupt some existing sales contracts and displace export authorizations totaling about 17 million metric tons of U.S. wheat and feed grains. The embargo continued throughout the Carter administration and was lifted by President Reagan on April 24, 1981. However, the long-run economic and political implications of this maneuver are still unfolding (Anthony and coauthors, 1980).

Although U.S.–Japanese trade relations were not directly affected, it is fair to argue that this sales suspension, taken for foreign policy and national security reasons, was disturbing to business people and political leaders in Japan—even though political relations with the United States are solid and friendly. At the very least, it dramatically illustrates that trade in food and strategic materials is a political weapon that may be employed when serious confrontations occur in foreign policy. In today's highly volatile political environment, any other view would be a mistake, even though it is difficult to design interventions that do not extract heavy economic costs from the nations imposing them. Such maneuvers, actual or threatened, add additional risk and uncertainty to agricultural trade and trade policy among all nations.

In many importing nations, including Japan, supporters of additional food and feed self-sufficiency positions will find their cases strengthened. Moreover, it is plausible to predict that, in the wake of the U.S.–Soviet sales suspension, the Japanese government will seek some new, formal assurance of U.S. export commitments along the lines of the earlier bilateral Butz-Abe understanding—or perhaps something more binding. Also, some Japanese observers have recently suggested that Japan purchase and hold some of the displaced grain in the United States as a food reserve. These inventories would be held in U.S. facilities but would be under the ultimate and assured control of the Japanese government. At this time, no public action has been taken on either possibility.

Concluding Comments

Looking ahead, it is hard to predict anything but expansion in U.S.– Japanese agricultural trade and a continuation of the current trends in its commodity composition. This expansion probably will occur even if no changes occur in the agricultural and trade policies of either nation or if no further trade agreements either bilateral or multilateral are signed. It is clearly in the best overall economic interest of both nations to expand agricultural trade on a long-term basis. The trade agreements and accommodations that have been fashioned over the past twenty-five to thirty years have fostered expansion in a modest way.

No one can predict the direction and extent of year-to-year fluctuations in this trade flow caused by precipitous and uncertain acts of human beings and nature. However, the pace and form of the general evolution in U.S.–Japanese agricultural trade will hinge on the net outcome of perhaps five major economic and political forces:

1. Changes in consumer tastes, the growth rate of per capita real income in Japan, and the extent to which they are translated into demand for meat, other livestock products, and a more varied diet generally.
2. The trends in the economic and political strength of Japan's farmers and others committed to food self-sufficiency who are willing to wage political battles in its behalf.

3. The strength of continuing efforts to reduce the bilateral imbalance of *total* U.S.–Japanese trade by inducing Japan to import
   more agricultural products from the United States than it otherwise might wish.
4. The continual U.S. drive to expand farm exports in an orderly
   way for balance-of-payments reasons and to sustain domestic
   farm and agribusiness income.
5. The willingness of the United States to guarantee long-term,
   stable customers like Japan assured annual supplies of food and
   agricultural raw materials even in troubled times.

Other factors like shifting currency values, differential inflation
rates, bad weather, and political upheavals almost anywhere in the
world may override and obscure these fundamental forces in any
given year or two. However, unless a major, unpredicted economic
depression or armed conflict occurs, these five trends will shape the
trade values, trade policies, negotiations, and mutual agreements that
emerge in the 1980s.

Appendix 3-A

Method Used to Calculate New Trade Values Resulting from Tariff Changes

The method used to calculate new trade values resulting from tariff changes comes from partial equilibrium analysis. For any given product, let

$$I = C - S \tag{1}$$

where I = volume of imports
C = volume of domestic consumption
S = volume of domestic production

Then if P is the domestic price observed at the import level

$$\frac{\partial I}{\partial P} = \frac{\partial C}{\partial P} - \frac{\partial S}{\partial P} \tag{2}$$

Then by making appropriate multiplications and divisions, equation (2) can be restated in a general elasticity form as follows

$$\frac{\partial I}{\partial P} \cdot \frac{P}{I} = \left[\frac{\partial C}{\partial P} \cdot \frac{P}{C} \right] \frac{C}{I} - \left[\frac{\partial S}{\partial P} \cdot \frac{P}{S} \right] \frac{S}{I} \tag{3}$$

or

$$E_I = E_D (C/I) - E_S(S/I) \tag{4}$$

where E_I = price elasticity of import demand
E_D = price elasticity of domestic demand
E_S = price elasticity of domestic supply

For purposes of this analysis, E_S was taken to be equal to zero in all cases. This rules out specific consideration of domestic supply re-

84

sponse or stock adjustments to changed prices as tariffs change. Thus

$$E_I = E_D(C/I) \tag{5}$$

The import demand elasticity is the domestic demand elasticity (obtained from various empirical research studies) weighted by the ratio of consumption to imports, this ratio being greater than or equal to 1.0.

Finally, the percentage change in imports ($\% \Delta I$) was calculated as

$$(\% \Delta I) = E_I(\% \Delta P) \tag{6}$$

where ($\% \Delta P$) is the estimated percentage change in domestic price as the result of a specified tariff change. This estimate is then applied to base trade value figures on the plausible assumptions that the tariff cuts will not alter world prices and that the United States maintains its share of all markets. This generates an annual "new trade" value. The annual value of quota changes was estimated by assuming that new specific quotas would be filled at world prices by U.S. suppliers. Both tariff and quota analyses focus on the full adjustments as negotiated without considering any intermediate staging.

Results from these calculations must be viewed as approximations; they are not "predictions" because they attempt to isolate the pure effect of negotiated tariff and quota changes. Moreover, they are lower bounds on estimated change since no domestic supply responses to induced price changes entered into the calculations.

A graphic illustration of this procedure is contained in figure 3-A-1. Panel A of figure 3-A-1 is the domestic market of a country granting a tariff cut to all international suppliers of a given product; the domestic demand curve for the product is D and the completely inelastic domestic supply curve is S. Panel B is the international market for this product; ED is the nation's excess demand curve, formed as the horizontal difference between D and S (Panel A) at various prices. The world price is WP, to which the original tariff, T, is added, resulting in a domestic price of $WP + T$.

When the tariff is removed, the domestic price falls to WP, and the price-quantity equilibrium moves down the domestic demand curve (D) from b to c and down the excess demand curve (ED) from e to f. The shaded area in Panel B is the international value of new trade generated by the tariff cut. This value can then be apportioned to supplying nations on the basis of historical market shares. An import quota increase can be evaluated in much the same way. Assume that a binding quota is relaxed from M to N on the horizontal axis of Panel

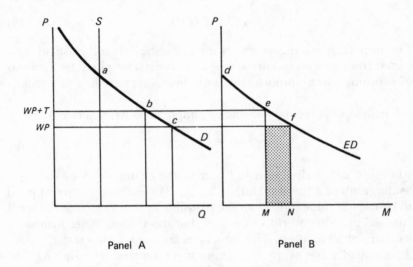

Panel A   Panel B

Figure 3-A-1.

B. When *WP* prevails on the international market, the shaded area measures the new trade value.

References

Anthony, W., W. Cochrane, M. Christiansen, R. Dahl, M. Ryan, and G. Schuh. 1980. *The Partial Suspension of Grain Sales to the USSR: An Interim Analysis,* Agr. Extension Misc. Publ. 103 (Minneapolis, Minn., University of Minnesota).

Bale, Malcolm, and Bruce L. Greenshields. 1977. *Japan: Production and Imports of Food—An Analysis of the Welfare Cost of Protection.* U.S. Department of Agriculture, Economic Research Service, Foreign Agricultural Economic Report No. 141 (November).

Coyle, William. 1978. "The Butz-Abe Understanding, 1975–78." Mimeo. (Washington, D.C., U.S. Department of Agriculture).

Curzon, Gerard. 1965. *Multilateral Commercial Diplomacy: GATT and Its Impact on Commercial Policies and Techniques* (London, Michael Joseph).

"Determination Regarding the Multilateral Trade Negotiations." 1979. *Federal Register,* vol. 44, no. 244 (December 18), pp. 75781–75784.

General Agreement on Tariffs and Trade (GATT). 1979. *The Tokyo Round of Multilateral Trade Negotiations*. Report by the Director General (Geneva, GATT).

Houck, James P. 1979. *MTN Studies (2): The Tokyo/Geneva Round; Its Relation to U.S. Agriculture*, Committee Print 96-12, Senate Committee on Finance, 96 Cong. 1 sess. (June).

Japanese Ministry of Agriculture, Forestry and Fisheries. 1979. *Statistical Yearbook 1977–78* (Tokyo).

Sanderson, Fred H. 1978. *Japan's Food Prospects and Policies* (Washington, D.C., The Brookings Institution).

Schnittker, John. 1970. "Statement Before Sub-Committee on Foreign Economic Policy, Joint Economic Committee of Congress." Mimeo. (March 19).

Spurlock, Hughes H. 1964. *Trends and Developments in Japan's Economy Affecting the Market for U.S. Farm Products*, Rep. No. 10 (Washington, D.C., U.S. Department of Agriculture, Economic Research Service, May).

U.S. Congress. 1975. *Background and Status of the Multilateral Trade Negotiations*. Committee Print 94-5, House Subcommittee on Trade of the Committee on Ways and Means, 94 Cong. 1 sess. (February 4).

———. 1979. *Agreements Reached in the Tokyo Round of the Multilateral Trade Negotiations*. House Rept. 96-153, Part I, 96 Cong. 1 sess. (June).

USDA. Various issues. U.S. Department of Agriculture, Economics, Statistics, and Cooperatives Service. *Foreign Agricultural Trade of the United States* (Washington, D.C., various monthly issues and annual summaries).

———. 1967a. U.S. Department of Agriculture, Foreign Agricultural Service. *International Grains Arrangement*, FAS-M-195 (Washington, D.C., November).

———. 1967b. U.S. Department of Agriculture, Foreign Agricultural Service. *Report on the Agricultural Trade Negotiations of the Kennedy Round*, FAS-M-193 (Washington, D.C.).

Wolfe, Alan M. 1979. "The Tokyo Round: What It Did and Did Not Do." Speech given at the University of Minnesota Spring Hill Center, Minneapolis, Minn., September 30.

Yoshioka, Yutaka. *Food and Agriculture in Japan*. 1979. About Japan Series no. 23 (Tokyo, Japan Foreign Press Center).

II

Agriculture and
Agricultural Policy in
Japan and the United States

4

The Present State of Agriculture in Japan

Yoshimi Kuroda

Since World War II, especially during the 1960s through the early 1970s, Japanese agriculture experienced dramatic changes. These changes occurred not only in food consumption but also in agricultural production. In the process, a number of issues emerged. They surround economic growth and changes in food consumption patterns; economic growth and changes in the patterns of agricultural production; and an increased dependence on food imports. The objective of this chapter is to investigate in detail these major issues.

Postwar Economic Growth and Changes in Food Consumption

The changes in Japanese food consumption that occurred during the postwar years can be shown by examining changes in consumption expenditures for foods and changes in the quantities of foods consumed. In addition, some estimates of income and price elasticities of food demand are examined to give a quantitative basis to the findings.

Yoshimi Kuroda is a lecturer in economics at the University of Tsukuba.

Increases in food consumption expenditures[1]

The Japanese economy as a whole has experienced very rapid progress during the last two decades, especially after the introduction of the Doubling Income Policy in 1960. During these two decades, the gross national product (GNP) measured in 1970 prices increased from 26 trillion yen in 1960 to 105 trillion yen in 1977, as shown in table 4-A-1 in the appendix at the back of this chapter. This increase in real GNP implied an annual rate of growth of almost 9 percent. The per capita real GNP also showed a rapid increase, from 274,000 yen in 1960 to 923,000 yen in 1977, which implied a 7.5 percent annual rate of growth for the period 1960–77.

What happened to consumption expenditures on food during the postwar years? Table 4-A-2 presents the consumption expenditures per month of an average household in cities with a population of more than 50,000 persons for the period 1955–77. The table shows the following:

First, family size decreased from five persons to four during the period. This was probably because of a trend away from the extended family system during those years.

Second, the share of expenditures on food in total expenditures for an average household (that is, the Engel coefficient) decreased fairly rapidly from 47 percent in 1955 to 31 percent in 1977. The value of the Engel coefficient during the 1970s, 31 to 34 percent, is fairly comparable to those in other developed countries, although the share of expenditures on starchy food was much higher in Japan (Namiki, 1973).

Third, the shares of expenditures on housing, fuels and light, and clothing were fairly stable from 1960 through 1977, while those on miscellaneous items increased at a rapid pace for the same period. The latter may have been caused by a rapid increase in expenditures on education, health, entertainment, and transportation during the postwar years.

An examination of food expenditures for an average household in a little more detailed fashion offers a different picture. Table 4-A-3 gives both the nominal and real food expenditures per person per month of an average household for the period 1965–77. The nominal expenditure on food per person per month was obtained by dividing the total food expenditure by the number of persons per household reported in table 4-A-2. This was then deflated by the consumer price

---

[1] We use alternately the terms income elasticity and (total) expenditure elasticity as equal on the assumption that total expenditure is a constant proportion of total income.

index for food (with 1975 calendar year prices being unity), yielding the real expenditure on food per person per month.

The nominal expenditure on food per person per month increased from about 5,000 yen in 1965 to 16,000 yen in 1977, almost a 300 percent increase. However, the food expenditure per person per month in terms of 1970 constant prices increased by only 1,600 yen from 1965 to 1970, but after 1970 it seems to have reached a plateau at 13,000 yen.

There are at least two possible reasons for this phenomenon. One is that in terms of value, the food consumption of an average household may have reached a saturation point during the 1970s, although, as is well known, the pattern of Japanese food consumption has been Westernized during the postwar years. The other reason is that an average household had been spending relatively less money on food in order to meet increased expenditures on education, health care, entertainment, and transportation, as well as savings. The second reason deserves more careful analysis.

Table 4-A-4 presents changes in the shares of expenditures on various foods consumed by an average household per month over the period 1955–77. According to this table, the expenditure share of staple food decreased from 37 percent in 1955 to 14.3 percent in 1977, whereas the shares of "subsidiary" foods and luxury foods increased steadily over the same period.

More careful examination of the changes in these shares shows a different pattern before and after 1973. On the one hand, during the period 1955–73, the share of staple food in total food expenditures decreased very rapidly, while the shares of subsidiary and luxury foods increased at a fairly steady pace. On the other hand, for the period 1973–77, none of the three shares showed conspicuous changes. In other words, in terms of expenditures, the food consumption pattern of an average household seems to have reached an equilibrium after 1973. Also, according to table 4-A-4, almost the same tendency exists for each item within the three categories. Nonetheless, at least three remarkable changes should be noted here.

First, the expenditure share of rice decreased from 28.3 percent in 1955 to 9.3 percent in 1977. Second, the expenditure share of meats, milk, and eggs increased from 10 percent in 1955 to 18 to 19 percent in 1977. Finally, the share of expenditures on restaurant meals, that is, "meals away from home," increased dramatically over this period, from 4 percent in 1955 to 12 percent in 1977. From these findings, we may infer that the food consumption pattern of the Japanese has been Westernized by reducing expenditures on starchy food and increasing expenditures on protective foods (foods high in proteins and vitamins), as well as by eating meals in restaurants.

Increases in consumption of protective foods

So far we have examined changes in Japanese food consumption patterns during the postwar years in terms of expenditures. Because how much is spent on a commodity is a function of the price and the quantity of that commodity, there are in general two factors that change expenditures for that commodity: changes in the price, changes in the quantity (or changes in both).

Although there are no data available for investigating changes in quantities of foodstuffs consumed by an average Japanese during the period 1955–77, there are the MAFF annual reports on "quantities of per capita food supplies" for the period 1955–77. Data from these appear in table 4-A-5. Assuming that this set of data reflects the quantities of foodstuffs consumed, changes in the food consumption patterns of an average Japanese during the postwar years can be analyzed in terms of quantities.

First, according to table 4-A-5, the quantity of rice consumed by an average Japanese decreased consistently from 105 kilograms in 1955 to 83 kilograms in in 1977. Also, the consumption of potatoes and sweet potatoes decreased over the same period. In other words, in terms of quantity, the consumption of starchy foodstuffs decreased during the postwar years.

Next, in terms of quantity, the per capita consumption of protective foods such as meats, milk, eggs, vegetables, and fruits increased from 1955 to 1977. In particular, increases in consumption of pork, chicken, and milk and milk products were remarkable during this period. Caused mainly by increases in consumption of pork and chicken, the total consumption of meats per capita increased from 3.3 kilograms in 1955 to 20.3 kilograms in 1977.

Still, the per capita consumption of beef increased only slowly from the level of 1.1 kilograms in 1955 to 3.0 kilograms in 1977. It is clear from table 4-A-5 that the consumption of meats as a whole in terms of quantity does not seem to have reached a plateau, contrary to the finding in terms of expenditures in table 4-A-4. However, the consumption of chicken eggs seems to have stabilized, and that of whale meat begun decreasing after 1965.

The above findings can be confirmed by examining how an average Japanese increased his caloric intake (as well as his intake of protein and fat) through changing his food consumption patterns (see table 4-A-6). The table reports the supplies of food per person per day for the period 1955–77. According to the table, the total caloric intake per day of an average Japanese increased from approximately 2,200 in 1955 to 2,500 in 1977. At the same time, the patterns of intake changed drastically during this period; that is, the shares of cereals, potatoes and sweet potatoes, and pulses in the total caloric intake decreased steadily over time, although that of cereals was still the largest (46 percent in 1977).

On the other hand, the number of calories from vegetables, fruits, meats, eggs, milk and milk products, sugar, and oil and fats increased very consistently over the 1955–77 period. The share of these foods in the total caloric intake per day by an average Japanese changed from 18 percent in 1955 to 44 percent in 1977. A similar tendency can be observed in the cases of protein and fat during the same period.

At this point, it may be useful to compare Japanese food consumption patterns with those in other countries in order to gain an international perspective. Table 4-A-7 presents the quantities of food and caloric intake per person per day in various countries, including developing countries (DCs) and less developed countries (LDCs) in the early 1970s. By examining the figures in table 4-A-7, one can note several remarkable differences in the patterns of food consumption between Japan and other countries.

First, although the level of consumption of cereals by an average Japanese decreased fairly rapidly during the postwar years, it was still high compared with those in Western countries in the early 1970s. We should add, however, that the total amount of cereals, potatoes, and starches consumed was almost the same in Japan and the Western countries.

Second, the level of consumption of meats by the Japanese was considerably below that of Westerners in the early 1970s, being only one-eighth to one-fourth that of Westerners. Furthermore, the per capita consumption of milk and milk products in Japan was also very low in the early 1970s compared with that in Western countries. As in the case of meat consumption, the level of consumption of milk and milk products of an average Japanese was only 10 to 25 percent of that of Westerners.

Third, compared with Western countries, the level of vegetable consumption in Japan was fairly high in the early 1970s, except for Italy. Nonetheless, although it increased substantially during the postwar years, fruit consumption in Japan was still fairly low compared with that in Western countries.

Finally, reflecting the above major differences in food consumption patterns between Japan and the Western countries, the total caloric intake per day of an average Japanese (2,500 calories) was much lower than that of an average Westerner (about 3,200 calories) in the early 1970s. It was almost the same level as in Venezuela, Syria, and Korea, each of which has a much lower GNP per capita than Japan.

By noting that the level of caloric intake per person seems to have a strong positive correlation with the level of per capita income, it can be inferred that the Japanese will increase their caloric intake as the level of per capita income rises. It is apparent from the facts earlier in this section that this increase in the level of caloric intake will have been caused mainly by increased consumption of meats, milk and milk products, vegetables, and fruits, as can be seen from the fact that meats, vegetables, and fruits have relatively larger expenditure elasticities than do cereals and other foods (table 4-A-8). This is true even though the level of expenditure elasticity of each food has been decreasing over time as per capita income grew.

Other important factors affecting food consumption are the relative price levels of foods and their price elasticities. Table 4-A-9 gives the levels of prices of various foods in Tokyo compared with those in the capital cities in six Western countries in 1977. The table shows clearly that the levels of prices of all foods except eggs are higher in Japan than in the six Western countries. This is especially true of beef, which in Japan is three to nine times as high as that in the six Western countries, while the price levels of pork and chicken meat in Japan are only 1.3 to 3.0 times those in Western countries. These high beef prices could have been the major reason that the consumption of beef in Japan did not increase as rapidly as pork and chicken during the last two decades, as observed in table 4-A-5 (1.1 kilograms per person per year in 1955 to only 3.0 kilograms in 1977). Thus, if the price levels of meats, milk, and milk products could be lowered in the future, the levels of consumption of these foods would be much higher.

To confirm this reasoning, however, it is necessary to examine the price elasticities of these foods. Table 4-A-10 shows income and price elasticities of various foods as estimated by Yuize (1966) for the period 1956–62. Although these estimates are for a period in the past, they offer a general picture of food consumption in Japan during the postwar period. At this point we will discuss price elasticities, since income elasticities were already discussed earlier in this section.

Restaurant meals showed the highest price elasticity (− 3.1 in absolute terms),[2] while the second highest elasticity was for milk and

[2] Price elasticities will be discussed in absolute terms.

to 110

eggs (-1.7) during the period 1956–62. The price elasticity of meats was -0.8 during the same period. Finally, the price elasticities of other foods ranged roughly from -0.5 to -0.9.

The price elasticity of meats, -0.8, may be considered as a weighted average of the price elasticities of beef, pork, chicken, and other meats. This implies that the individual price elasticities of these items may be smaller than, equal to, or larger than -0.8. For example, according to some estimates for recent years, the price elasticity of beef in the intermediate-to-long run is about -1.5.[3] This implies that if the price level of beef is lowered to half of the present level (which is still much higher than the levels in Western countries), the level of consumption demand for beef will become close to three times as high as the present level of consumption of beef (Hayami, 1978).

If one assumes the price elasticities of other items of foods given in table 4-A-10 are valid at the present time, a 50-percent decrease in the price levels of those foods will lead to more than a 50-percent increase in the quantity taken from the market of those foods except dried fish and seaweeds, and beverages. For these foods, the quantity taken will increase less than 50 percent.

The possibility of lowering the price levels of foods can be seen only by investigating the conditions on the production side.

Postwar Economic Growth and Changes in Agricultural Production

While postwar economic growth has changed the patterns of food consumption of the Japanese, it also has altered the pattern of agricultural production. The objective of this section is to show how agricultural production in Japan has changed and to evaluate those changes from an economic point of view.

The most important changes will be discussed in order: (1) the relative decline of labor productivity and workers in agriculture, (2) the selective expansion of agricultural production, (3) the decrease in the level of land utilization, (4) rapid labor migration and agricultural mechanization, (5) the increase in energy inputs to agricultural production, and (6) changes in the agricultural budget.

---

[3] The author does not have information on individual price elasticities of pork, chicken, and other meats at present.

Relative decline in labor productivity and number of workers

Japanese agriculture experienced a fairly rapid growth during the postwar years, especially from 1951 to 1973. The annual rate of growth of agricultural production in real terms for the 1951–77 period was almost 3 percent, as shown in table 4-A-11. At the same time, a large number of agricultural workers migrated to nonagricultural sectors to meet the greatly increased demand for labor in those sectors. Thus, real agricultural production per worker increased even more rapidly than did total real agricultural production during the 1951–77 period.

On the other hand, in real terms, the production of nonagricultural sectors grew dramatically during this period, although there was a rapid decline after the "oil shock" in 1973. In table 4-A-11, manufacturing is shown as an example of how rapidly nonagricultural sectors grew during the postwar years. The annual growth rate of total real production in the manufacturing sector was 11.7 percent, while that of production per worker was 8.8 percent for the 1951–77 period. Both rates were much higher than the corresponding rates for the agricultural sector. This has been the major reason that the comparative productivity of agriculture has remained very low during the postwar years (see table 4-A-12). And this low productivity of agriculture is considered to have been one of the most important agricultural problems in the postwar years.

Another important aspect of the decline in agriculture during the postwar years is that the number of agricultural workers decreased rapidly from 15.4 million in 1953 to 5.7 million in 1977, only 37 percent of the level in 1953 (see table 4-A-13). The annual rate of decrease during the 1953–77 period was 4.3 percent. Because of this rapid decrease, the share of the number of agricultural workers in the number of total workers declined from 42 percent in 1953 to 12 percent in 1977.

In contrast, the numbers of workers in the secondary and tertiary sectors have grown rapidly to meet the increased demand for labor caused by rapid economic growth over this period. The major part of this increase in the demand for labor in the nonagricultural sectors has been met by migrants from the agricultural sector.

Indeed, it was not difficult for migrants from rural areas to find fairly attractive jobs in city areas until 1973. After the oil price rises in 1973, however, the number of workers in the secondary sector seems to have started decreasing, while that in the tertiary sector continued to increase even after 1973, although at a slower pace than before 1973. If this pattern continues in the future, it will be much more difficult for agricultural migrants to find jobs, especially in the secondary sector, than before 1973.

Selective expansion of agricultural production

As seen earlier, real agricultural production in Japan has grown at a fairly high annual rate (3 percent for the 1951–77 period), although its comparative status declined in the economy as a whole during the postwar years. But how has Japanese agriculture increased production during the postwar years?

Table 4-A-14 shows the changes in the shares of production of various agricultural products in total agricultural production in terms of value for the period 1960–77. Among several remarkable changes that the table shows, one of the most conspicuous changes in the patterns of agricultural production is that the share represented by crop production has been decreasing, while livestock has been increasing. The production of wheat and barley, beans, and potatoes and sweet potatoes decreased dramatically, while the production of rice reduced its share by 9 percentage points during the period 1960–77. However, the share represented by vegetables, fruits, and industrial crops increased over the same period. The increase for vegetables has been remarkable.

On the other hand, the production of pork, chicken meat, and eggs, and milk and milk products increased their shares by more than 50 percent over the 1960 levels during the 1960–77 period. The production of beef cattle increased its share by only a small amount, however.

Changes in the shares of production of agricultural products given in table 4-A-14 were in terms of value. The next question is: What has happened to the level of physical production of various agricultural products during the postwar years? Table 4-A-15 presents indexes of physical production of several agricultural products for the period 1955–77. This table shows that the physical production of wheat and barley, beans, and potatoes and sweet potatoes decreased dramatically during the 1955–77 period. At the same time, the levels of physical production of vegetables, fruits, and livestock products increased fairly rapidly for the same period. These changes may be regarded as a reflection of the changes in food consumption patterns of the Japanese during the postwar years, as observed earlier.

Decrease in the level of land utilization

Land is one of the most important inputs to agricultural production. During the last two decades, not only has the total cultivated land area declined, but the total planted area also decreased consistently (see table 4-A-16). The total cultivated area was 6.1 million hectares in 1960, but it decreased to only 5.5 million hectares in 1977.

In contrast, the total planted area decreased from 8.1 million hectares in 1960 to 5.7 in 1977. The rate of decrease of the total planted area was greater than that of the total cultivated area. This implies that the level of land utilization declined over the last two decades. It was 134 percent in 1960, but only 104 percent in 1977. This means that double-cropping was still popular in the early 1960s, but in the 1970s farmers utilized their lands only once during a crop year. This low utilization of land may have been caused by a shortage of labor resulting from the rapid migration of farm workers to nonagricultural sectors during the postwar years. This point will be discussed in more detail later in this section.

What has caused the decrease in cultivated land during the postwar years? Table 4-A-17 reports the areas of expansion and destruction of paddy and upland fields annually for the period 1960–78. Although there was some expansion of cultivated land area every year, the area of destruction was always larger during this period. The destruction of paddy and upland farm fields has been caused by urbanization and conversion of cultivated land to forests. Because of the rapid growth of nonagricultural sectors, urbanization required a large amount of land for increased construction of factories, roads, and residential areas during the last two decades, especially in the 1960s. The increase in area of cultivated land through reclamation was almost completely offset by the area of farmland destroyed for these purposes.

Another important factor in the decrease in total cultivated land area was the conversion of cultivated land to forests. These probably involved marginal upland fields. The major reason for this may have been the shortage of labor to take care of crops planted on such lands.

The conversion of cultivated land to industrial uses such as factories, roads, and residential areas has caused another important problem in Japanese agriculture; that is, prices of lands skyrocketed during the last two decades as can be clearly observed in table 4-A-18. The average prices of paddy and upland increased dramatically during the last two decades, with the annual rates of increase being 17 and 20 percent, respectively; increases in urban areas led the way, with the annual rates of price increase being approximately 27 percent per year for the period 1960–78. Even in rural areas, the prices of land rose at annual rates of between 12 and 19 percent. Although the annual rates of increase in land prices decreased in the 1970s, the rates were still greater than 10 percent.

This rapid increase in land prices has led farmers to keep their land as an asset and has strongly restricted movements of land among farm households. In addition, the Agricultural Land Act, established immediately after World War II, has also restricted farmers from selling their lands freely. Thus, although a great number of agricultural workers has migrated to nonagricultural sectors, the total number of farm households has not decreased as rapidly as the number of agricultural workers. Because of this slow decrease in the total number of farm households, the cultivated land area of an average farm household has changed only slightly during the postwar years: from 1.0 hectares in 1950 to only 1.2 hectares in 1977, as shown in table 4-A-19.

According to table 4-A-19, the numbers of small-scale farm households with under 1.5 hectares of land steadily decreased during the 1950–77 period, while those of large-scale farm households with more than 2 hectares increased consistently, but by only a small absolute number. This group probably would have increased its numbers much more had land prices not risen so rapidly and had the Agricultural Land Act not restricted farmers' freedom in selling and renting their land.

Instead, a great number of farm households became part-time farm households during the postwar years. According to table 4-A-20, the total number of farm households decreased annually by one percent on average during the 1953–77 period. However, the number of full-time farm households decreased very rapidly, at an annual rate of 5.8 percent. In 1953, the share of full-time farm households of the total number of farm households was 41 percent, in contrast to only 13 percent in 1977. On the other hand, the number of part-time farm households has increased steadily during the postwar years. As a result, by 1977, almost nine out of ten farm households were part-time.

Part-time farm households can be classified into class A and class B. Class A part-time farm households are those whose on-farm income is larger than their off-farm income, while class B part-time farm households are those whose off-farm income is larger than their on-farm income. In table 4-A-20, it can be clearly seen that the number of class B part-time farm households has increased rapidly during the postwar years, amounting to 67 percent of the total in 1977. This implies that for seven farm households out of ten, farming was only a supplemental job by the late 1970s. This is why part-time farmers are often called "laborers with lands." This tendency seems to have been increasing over time.

Furthermore, the rapid labor migration from agricultural to non-agricultural sectors during the postwar years has entailed a rapid exodus of a large number of heads of families and first sons from rural areas. Consequently, farms have been taken care of mainly by old and female labor in such farm households. This may, in turn, have been a factor explaining the decline of land utilization in spite of rapid mechanization of agriculture in the postwar years.

Rapid labor migration and farm mechanization

As we have seen earlier in this section, many agricultural workers migrated to nonagricultural sectors during the postwar years. The annual rate of decrease in the agricultural labor force for the period 1953–77 was as high as 4.3 percent, although declining to 3 percent after 1973 (table 4-A-13). This rapid decrease in the agricultural labor force has been caused by the continuously strong demand for labor in nonagricultural sectors during the postwar years—a demand which in turn has increased farm wage rates significantly, as shown in table 4-A-21. On the other hand, the price level of farm machinery did not rise as fast as the farm wage rates, mainly because of technological progress in the industrial sectors.

This change in the relative price of labor and machinery resulted in the rapid mechanization of farming even on small-scale farms in the postwar years. According to table 4-A-22, an average farm household decreased its labor input from 4,174 hours per year in 1957 to only 2,148 hours in 1977. On the other hand, it increased the machinery input drastically for the same period, from 67 hours in 1955 to 301 hours in 1977. Labor hours per 10 ares declined from 430 in 1957 to 188 in 1977, while machinery hours per 10 ares increased from 7 to 26 over this same period.

Table 4-A-23 presents changes in the numbers of major agricultural implements during the 1955–77 period. It is clear from the table that during the 1960s agricultural mechanization occurred mostly on small-scale farms, as represented by the rapid increase in the number of walking-type cultivators. However, in the 1970s a larger scale mechanization occurred as represented by a drastic increase in the number of driving-type tractors.

One could ask, does this high degree of mechanization of agricultural production pay on such small-scale farms? To date, there are very few empirical studies that give a clear answer to this question, although an increase in quasi-rented cultivation (*ukeoi kosaku*) of recent years may give a hint. That is, those farmers who rent lands generally farm on a large scale. And they usually possess large-scale farm machinery. We may therefore infer that large-scale farmers have not only been increasing their total output through cultivating rented lands in addition to their own, but have also been trying to use their machinery as much as possible in order to equalize the marginal productivity of machinery capital to the marginal cost of machinery use.

Increases in farm operating costs

In the postwar period changes have also occurred in the operating costs of farms. Table 4-A-24 presents changes in gross agricultural product, total operating costs, and farm income of an average farm household over the period 1957–77. It is very clear from the table that although the gross agricultural product of an average farm household increased very rapidly over this period, the increase in total operating costs was even faster. As a result, farm income increased more slowly than did gross agricultural output and total operating costs.

This can be captured more clearly by looking at changes in the ratio of either farm income or total operating costs to gross agricultural product over the 1957–77 period. The share of the total operating costs of the gross agricultural output of an average farm household was 36 percent in 1957. But it rose to 50 percent in 1977. Actually, it reached a peak in 1970 (48.4 percent) and then declined to 45 percent in 1975. However, it again increased, to 50 percent in 1977.

Total operating costs of a farm household are composed of a number of items, as shown in table 4-A-25, which gives the change in the share of each item in the total operating costs during the 1957–77 period. There are a number of distinctive features here.

First, the share of the wage bill for hired labor decreased in a secular fashion. It was only 2 percent of the total operating costs in 1977, although it was 6 percent in 1957. This was mainly because of the difficulty of hiring agricultural workers since they were able to find better jobs in nonagricultural sectors, and partly because of agricultural mechanization, which has been substituted for labor.

Second, fertilizer costs decreased their share very rapidly over time, from 24 percent in 1957 to 11 percent in 1977, with the lowest being in 1973. Notwithstanding, it seems to have started increasing again after 1973, mainly caused by the increased price of chemical fertilizers, as shown in table 4-A-26.

Third, the share of feed costs has been growing steadily, reflecting an increase in the production of livestock products during the postwar years. Considering the strong likelihood of a steady increase in the consumption of livestock products in the future, the production of such products, and hence the expenditure on feeds, will also increase in the future.

Fourth, the shares of costs of machinery-associated inputs such as machinery itself, fuels and light, automobiles, and rentals for machinery increased consistently over the period from 1957 through 1977. This has been caused by the rapid mechanization of agriculture during the postwar years. In addition, the share of expenditures on agrichemicals increased over the same period. These inputs, together with chemical fertilizers, are all strongly related to increases in oil prices, especially after 1973, as clearly shown in table 4-A-26.

In sum, increases in the expenditures on feeds and energy-related inputs have been responsible for the remarkable rise in total operating costs of an average farm household during the postwar years.

Changes in the agricultural budget

At this point, it may be useful to examine what the Japanese government has done for agriculture during the postwar years. According to table 4-A-27, the total agricultural budget amounted to about 8 percent of the total government budget in 1960. Then, the share increased to 11 percent in the early 1970s but declined to about 8 percent in 1978, or about the 1960 level.

How was the agricultural budget spent during this period? In 1960, 61 percent of it was for agricultural production, but this percentage decreased to 33 in the early 1970s. After 1973, however, the budget for agricultural production purposes again began to increase. As a result, it became 55.4 percent of the total agricultural budget in 1978. In this category, major expenditures have been for selective expansion of agricultural production and increases in productivity. Of the latter, the major expenditure has been for infrastructural improvements in agricultural production.

Another important item of government expenditure has been for price and income policies for agricultural production. As a share in the total agricultural budget, such spending increased from 26 percent in 1960 to 49 percent in 1975, although the share decreased to 30 percent in 1978. Although it is not clear from the table, expenditures for this item probably have been mainly for the rice price support program.

In contrast, only 3 to 6 percent of the total agricultural budget was spent on improving the structure of agriculture during the last two decades. Those improvements that were made were directed basically at enlarging the size of farmland, particularly that of full-time farm households. What the government did, however, has been limited only to improving soils and irrigation and drainage systems and consolidating scattered pieces of land. It did not do much to improve the present structure of small-scale farming.

Increased Dependence on Food Imports

Thus far we have seen changes in food consumption patterns and changes in the production pattern of agriculture in postwar Japanese agriculture. Above all, one of the most remarkable changes has been increased dependence on importation of agricultural products.

Increases in food imports and decreases in the rate of self-sufficiency

Table 4-A-28 is a balance sheet of selected foods for the period from 1955 through 1977. According to the table, the total quantity of cereals domestically produced decreased from 17 million tons in 1955 to 14 million in 1977. This decrease was caused by rapid decline in the production of wheat, barley, and beardless barley.

On the other hand, the total amount of cereals imported rose fairly rapidly for the same period in order to meet the increase in cereal consumption. The major foods responsible for this increase were wheat, barley, maize, and soybeans. Most of the barley and maize and about 10 to 15 percent of the wheat are used as feeds for animal husbandry, which has been growing rapidly during the postwar years.

Because of this rapid increase in the importation of cereals, the total amount of domestically available supplies of cereals increased from 19 million tons in 1955 to 34 million in 1977. Furthermore, owing to the decrease in the total domestic production of cereals, the self-sufficiency rate of cereals as a whole declined rapidly from a level of 88 percent in 1955 to only 40 percent in 1977.

This rapid decrease in the self-sufficiency rate of all cereals was mainly caused by a drastic decrease in the domestic production of wheat, barley, and maize. The rates were only 4, 7, and 0.1 percent, respectively, in 1977. However, more rice has been produced domestically than there is demand for. This has been caused mainly by the now infamous price support policy for rice production, which is looked upon as a kind of income, or "security," policy by the Japanese government.

On the other hand, the major reasons for the decrease in the domestic production of wheat, barley, and maize may have been (1) the lack of a favorable price support and (2) the free trade policy for these products during the postwar years. Almost the same reasons may apply to the drastic decrease in the self-sufficiency rate of soybean production (only 3 percent in 1977).

What about meats? The domestic production of meats increased very rapidly during the last two decades. It was only 356,000 tons in 1955, but rose to 2.6 million tons by 1977. But domestic production was not able to meet the increased demand for meats, and as a result, imports of meat rapidly increased, especially after 1960. With the strong demand for meats, imports are expected to grow to a higher level in the future.

For example, domestic production of beef has not increased as rapidly as that of pork and chicken, although it has been protected from being freely traded until the present. One of the major reasons for this relatively slow growth in beef production in Japan may have been the shortage of land for pastures.

In contrast, consumption of beef increased faster than domestic production over the 1955–77 period, although the rate of increase in beef consumption was not as rapid as that of pork and chicken meat for this period. This may have been caused mainly by high beef prices, as shown in table 4-A-29. According to the table, in 1977, the price level of beef in Japan was about twice that of pork and almost three times that of chicken.[4]

Changes in the status of agricultural trade within the total foreign trade of the Japanese economy for the period 1965 through 1978 can be seen in table 4-A-30. The value of exports of agricultural products was very small during this period, about 2 percent of the total value of exports in 1965, declining to only 0.5 percent in 1978. On the other hand, the value of imported agricultural products was about 35 percent of the value of total imports in 1965. Subsequently, however, the relative share decreased to 17 percent in 1978 mainly because imports of industrial raw materials and final products increased much faster than agricultural imports.

Nonetheless, the value of agricultural imports jumped from 1.5 trillion yen in 1970 to 3.3 trillion in 1975 and 2.8 trillion in 1978. This may have been caused by rapid increases not only in the quantities but also in the prices of wheat, maize, soybeans, and other foods since the 1972 food shortage, as shown in table 4-A-31. In spite of these increases in prices of imported foods, however, the share of agricultural imports in the total value of imports decreased from 1970

---

[4] Although table 4-A-29 gives prices of major meats in Tokyo, a very similar tendency is observed in other major cities in Japan.

to 1978 as seen above. This may have been mainly because the prices of industrial raw materials, especially oil, increased faster than the prices of foodstuffs during this period.

Japan as a major food importer

During the last two decades, Japan became one of the most important food-importing countries in the world. To put this in perspective, let us first examine the present state of world agricultural production and exports.

Table 4-A-32 shows the production and export of major agricultural products in the world during the 1965–77 period. From this, one can see that the production of major agricultural products increased steadily over the period. The annual rates of growth of production of wheat, rice, barley, and maize were 3 to 4 percent, while the production of soybeans and oranges grew more than 5 percent per year. During the same time, however, the production of beef and pork increased relatively slowly.

The export of maize and soybeans grew very rapidly from 1965 to 1977, with the annual rates of growth being 7.1 and 9.1 percent, respectively. Furthermore, the export of beef and pork also increased fairly rapidly, although in absolute quantity terms, it was still small.

On the other hand, the export of wheat, rice, and barley did not grow as fast as that of maize, soybeans, beef, and pork. Nonetheless, the export of the former has been steadily growing since 1965. This may have been a reflection of a steady demand for wheat, rice, and barley as staple foodstuffs in the world. It is a well-known fact that there are many developed and developing countries in the world that have to depend to a large extent on importation of these staple foodstuffs. Therefore, it can be expected that worldwide production and export of wheat, rice, and barley will grow steadily in the future.

Japan has been playing an important role in this world food trade, as table 4-A-33 shows. It has been increasing its share of total cereal imports in the world throughout the postwar years. The share was 6.5 percent in 1960; in 1977, it was 13.4 percent. The total quantity of cereals imported increased from 4.4 million tons in 1960 to 22.1 million tons in 1977, indicating slightly more than a 400-percent increase within seventeen years.[5]

---

[5] The corresponding figures from table 4-A-28 are 4.5 and 22.7 million tons. These figures are for the fiscal year, that is, from April 1 to March 31 in the next year; the figures in table 4-A-33 are for the calendar year.

This was especially true for maize, sugar, and soybeans, whose imports increased dramatically over the 1960–77 period. As a share of world imports these products came to more than 10 percent for this period. In particular, those of maize and soybeans were more than 20 percent in the early 1970s, although they declined slightly after 1973. As for wheat, the total quantity imported by Japan increased from 2.7 million tons in 1960 to 5.7 million tons in 1977, indicating more than a 200-percent increase. During this period, the share of Japanese wheat imports in world wheat imports was consistently about 8 percent.

As seen in table 4-A-28, Japan has rapidly increased her degree of dependence on imports of basic agricultural products. We may expect that she will even increase her dependence on imported foodstuffs unless the present structure of agricultural production in Japan changes substantially in the future.

At this point, it may be useful to look at the major exporting countries of those agricultural products on which Japan has been and will be dependent.

In table 4-A-34, the three most important exporting countries of wheat, maize, soybeans, and beef are given for the period 1960–1977. According to this table, the United States has enjoyed the most important position in the export of wheat, maize, and soybeans during this period. She provided 33 to 46 percent of world wheat exports in 1970 and 1975, respectively. Her export shares of maize and soybeans were even higher than that of wheat. They were as large as 65 to 81 percent in the late 1970s.

The other major exporting countries have been Canada and Australia for wheat; Argentina and South Africa for maize; and Brazil, Paraguay, and Argentina for soybeans. On the other hand, Australia, Ireland, and New Zealand have been the top three beef-exporting countries.

As is clear in table 4-A-34, the concentration of exports of each of these agricultural products by the top three countries has been great and seems to have been increasing. For example, the United States, Brazil, and Argentina were responsible for 97 percent of the world's soybean exports in 1977.

Summary

In this chapter, we have investigated the major trends in Japanese agriculture during the postwar years. We have looked not only at changes in the patterns of consumption and production of agricultural products, but also at increases in dependence on imports of agricultural products during the postwar years. The main points are summarized as follows.

As per capita income has rapidly grown during the postwar years, especially after 1960 when the Doubling Income Policy was introduced, food consumption in Japan has been Westernized to a large extent. That is, the consumption of protective foods such as livestock products, vegetables, and fruits has increased very rapidly. In contrast, the consumption of starchy foodstuffs such as rice, barley, beardless barley, potatoes, and sweet potatoes has declined rapidly during the postwar years.

Although the Japanese food consumption pattern may not be completely Westernized because of differences in culture between Japan and Western countries, it is still very likely that Japanese will consume more protective foods and less starchy foods in the future. The domestic production of livestock products, vegetables, and fruits has dramatically increased, reflecting these changes in food consumption patterns during the postwar years. However, because of the strong demand for labor by nonagricultural sectors resulting from rapid economic growth, a great number of agricultural workers, including even heads of families and first sons, has migrated to nonagricultural sectors. This, in turn, has been associated with a rapid mechanization of agriculture during the postwar years.

Nonetheless, the number of farm households has not decreased as much as the number of agricultural workers has during the postwar years. Indeed, migration of labor has proceeded in such a way as to increase the number of part-time farm households. Many of these part-time farm households have kept their lands as an asset mainly because of the drastic increase in land prices. This high level of land prices, together with the Agricultural Land Act established right after World War II, has strongly restricted land movements. All these factors have maintained a system of small-scale farms.

In addition, the shortage of labor on farms caused by rapid migration and the price support policy for rice have led a great many farm households, especially part-time farm households, to produce only rice. This has resulted in a surplus of rice as well as in a low level of land utilization since the war.

Furthermore, total operating costs on an average farm household have been increasing more rapidly than total agricultural production. As a result, farm income as a percentage of the value of total production, has been decreasing. The increase in total operating costs has been due mainly to the price increases of energy-associated inputs such as chemical fertilizers, agrichemicals, fuels and light, and machinery, as well as feeds.

On the other hand, a large part of the agricultural budget of the Japanese government has been spent on a program of selective expansion of agricultural products and on a price support program for rice production. However, the budget for improving the structure of agricultural production has been only a small part of the total agricultural budget.

There has been a rapid increase in the import of basic foods such as wheat, maize, and soybeans as well as animal meats to meet increased demand. As a result, Japan has become one of the most important food-importing countries in the world. A steady increase in demand for food in the future is probable even with lower rates of economic growth. And the degree of dependence on imports of various foods will increase still more in the future.

References

Hayami, Yujiro. 1978. "Nosanbutsu Jiyuka no Sekkei" (A Design for Free Trade of Agricultural Products), *Kikan Gendai Keizai* vol. 31, pp. 62–79.
Namiki, Masayoshi. 1973. "Engel Keisu no Kokusaiteki Hyojunka" (International Standardization of the Engel Coefficient), *Nogyo Sogo Kenkyu* vol. 27, no. 4, pp. 31–60.
Yuize, Yashuhiko. 1966. "Shokuryo Juyo no Susei Koka" (Trend Effects of Food Demand) *Nogyo Sogo Kenkyu* vol. 20, no. 1, pp. 57–114.

Appendix 4-A

Data on Japanese Agriculture in the Post–World War II Period

TABLE 4-A-1. JAPAN: POPULATION, GNP, AND GNP PER CAPITA, 1960–77

Year	Population (million persons)	GNP at 1970 prices (10 billion yen)	GNP per capita at 1970 prices (1,000 yen)
1960	93.4	25,576	274
1965	98.3	41,177	419
1970	104.7	73,435	702
1973	109.1	93,009	852
1975	111.9	93,841	838
1977	114.2	105,363	923
Percentage annual growth rate			
1960–73	1.2	10.4	9.2
1973–77	1.2	3.2	2.0
1960–77	1.2	8.7	7.5

Source: Keizai Kikaku Cho (Japan Bureau of Economic Planning), *Keizai Yoran* (Abstract of Economic Statistics) (Tokyo, 1979) pp. 2–3, 33.

111

TABLE 4-A-2. JAPAN: CONSUMPTION EXPENDITURES OF AN AVERAGE HOUSEHOLD, 1955–77
(yen per month)

Year	Persons per household	Earners per household	Total	Living expenditures				
				Food	Housing	Fuels & light	Clothing	Misc.
1955	4.84	1.55	23,211 (100.0)	10,896 (46.9)	1,331 (5.7)	1,216 (5.2)	2,717 (11.7)	7,056 (30.4)
1960	4.51	1.65	31,276 (100.0)	13,000 (41.6)	2,790 (8.9)	1,597 (5.1)	3,755 (12.0)	10,134 (32.4)
1965	4.24	1.66	51,832 (100.0)	19,738 (38.1)	4,787 (9.2)	2,317 (4.5)	5,916 (11.4)	19,073 (36.8)
1970	3.95	1.60	82,792 (100.0)	28,307 (34.2)	8,864 (10.7)	3,168 (3.8)	8,968 (10.8)	33,484 (40.4)
1973	3.88	1.58	116,431 (100.0)	37,257 (32.0)	12,519 (10.8)	4,212 (3.6)	13,404 (11.5)	49,039 (42.1)
1975	3.86	1.54	160,475 (100.0)	51,916 (32.4)	15,645 (9.7)	6,439 (4.0)	16,828 (10.5)	69,647 (43.4)
1977	3.78	1.48	193,742 (100.0)	60,123 (31.0)	18,393 (9.5)	8,018 (4.1)	19,512 (10.1)	87,696 (45.3)

Notes: The figures are for an average household in all cities with more than 50,000 persons. Numbers in parentheses are percentages.
Source: Sorifu Tokei Kyoku (Bureau of Statistics, Office of the Prime Minister), Kakei Chosa Nenpo (Annual Report on the Family and Expenditure Survey) (Tokyo, 1965, 1970, and 1977).

TABLE 4-A-3. JAPAN: PER CAPITA FOOD EXPENDITURES OF AN
AVERAGE HOUSEHOLD, 1965–77
(absolute numbers in yen per month)

Year	Consumer price index for food[a]	Per capita food expenditure	
		Nominal	Real
1965	42.2	4,655	11,031
1970	56.5	7,166	12,683
1973	73.9	9,602	12,994
1975	102.4[b]	13,450	13,135
1977	117.3	15,906	12,890

Sources: For the consumer price index of food, the data were taken from Sorifu Tokei Kyoku
(Bureau of Statistics, Office of the Prime Minister), *Kouri Bukka Tokei Chosa* (Survey Statistics of
Retail Prices) (Tokyo, 1979) p. 55. The per capita food expenditure was calculated by dividing the
food expenditure by the number of persons per household (table 4-A-2).
[a] 1975 calendar year = 100.
[b] For fiscal year 1975.

TABLE 4-A-4. JAPAN: SHARES OF EXPENDITURES ON VARIOUS FOODS CONSUMED BY AN AVERAGE HOUSEHOLD PER MONTH, 1955–77

Food	1955	1960	1965	1970	1973	1975	1977
Total food expenditure (yen/month)	10,891	13,000	19,738	28,307	37,257	51,916	60,123
Total food expenditure (%)	100.0	100.0	100.0	100.0	100.0	100.0	100.0
Staple food (%)	37.1	29.5	22.0	16.2	13.8	13.9	14.3
Rice	28.3	24.8	17.1	12.1	9.4	9.0	9.3
Barley and other cereals	2.9	0.6	0.1	0.05	—	—	—
Bread	3.2	2.3	2.3	2.0	2.0	2.4	2.6
Others	2.7	1.8	2.5	2.0	2.4	2.5	2.4
Subsidiary food (%)	44.6	48.1	51.6	52.7	54.0	54.4	53.4
Fresh fish	7.2	6.9	7.1	7.9	7.8	8.6	8.7
Dried fish	2.7	2.8	2.6	3.2	3.6	3.5	3.6
Meats	10.0[a]	7.0	9.4	10.7	12.2	12.2	12.2
Milk and eggs	—	7.0	8.5	7.7	6.6	6.6	5.9
Vegetables	7.6	7.5	8.2	9.0	8.9	8.4	8.4
Seaweeds	1.9	1.9	1.8	1.7	1.6	1.4	1.3
Processed food	7.7	8.3	8.5	7.9	8.6	8.8	8.9
Seasonings	7.5	6.5	5.6	4.6	4.7	4.9	4.4
Luxury food (%)	14.6	16.0	18.9	21.3	21.1	20.6	20.0
Cakes	6.0	5.4	5.8	5.7	5.6	5.9	5.6
Fruits	3.6	4.2	5.5	6.3	6.3	5.8	5.3
Liqueurs	3.6	4.1	4.4	4.8	4.5	4.4	4.4
Refreshing drinks	1.4	2.3	3.2	4.5	4.7	4.5	4.7
Restaurant meals (%)	3.8	6.4	7.4	9.8	11.1	11.1	12.2

Notes: Figures are for an average household in all cities with more than 50,000 persons. Totals do not always add to 100 because of rounding.
Source: Sorifu Tokei Kyoku (Bureau of Statistics, Office of the Prime Minister), Kakei Chosa Nenpo (Annual Report on the Family and Expenditure Survey) (Tokyo, various years).
[a] Figure includes meats, milk, and eggs.

TABLE 4-A-5. JAPAN: PER CAPITA FOOD SUPPLIES, 1955–77
(kilograms per year)

Food	1955	1960	1965	1970	1973	1975	1977	Ratio 1977/55	Percentage annual growth rate 1955–77
Cereals	149.9	149.5	145.2	128.5	124.6	122.1	117.9	0.8	−1.1
Rice	105.3	114.3	111.7	95.1	91.1	88.1	83.4	0.8	−1.1
Wheat	25.1	25.8	29.0	30.8	31.0	31.5	31.8	1.3	1.1
Potatoes & sweet potatoes	48.7	34.0	22.8	16.2	16.2	16.0	17.4	0.4	−4.8
Starches	3.6	6.8	8.3	8.2	7.8	7.5	9.2	2.6	4.4
Pulses	9.3	10.2	9.8	9.7	9.8	9.3	8.7	0.9	−0.3
Vegetables	67.9	86.3	109.6	115.6	112.3	111.0	115.5	1.7	2.4
Fruits	14.6	25.3	28.5	37.6	43.7	43.0	41.4[a]	2.8[a]	4.9
Meats	3.3	4.9	9.0	13.1	16.2	17.9	20.3[a]	6.2[a]	8.6
Beef	1.1	1.2	1.5	2.0	2.3	2.6	3.0	2.7	4.7
Pork	0.8	1.2	3.1	4.7	6.4	7.3	8.3	10.4	11.2
Chicken	0.3	0.4	1.6	3.8	5.0	5.3	6.5	21.7	15.0
Other meats	0.2	0.5	0.7	1.1	1.4	1.8	1.8	9.0	10.5
Whale	0.9	1.6	2.1	1.5	1.1	0.9	0.7	0.8	−1.1
Hen eggs	3.4	4.8	8.8	14.8	14.5	14.0	14.4	4.2	6.8
Cow milk & milk products	12.0	25.6	37.4	50.1	52.8	53.3	57.0	4.8	7.3
Fish & shellfish	20.1	25.4	29.2	32.1	34.3	34.9	34.1	1.7	2.4
Sugar	12.3	14.9	18.8	26.8	28.2	25.1	26.2	2.1	3.5
Oils & fats	2.7	4.3	6.8	9.5	11.1	11.4	11.9	4.4	7.0
Vegetable	N.A.	N.A.	5.1	7.3	8.7	9.2	9.9	1.9[b]	5.7[b]
Animal	N.A.	N.A.	1.7	2.2	2.4	2.2	2.0	1.2[b]	1.4[b]

Note: N.A. = Not available.
Source: Norinsuisarisho (Ministry of Agriculture, Forestry and Fisheries), *Norinsuisansho Tokeihyo* (Statistical Yearbook of the Ministry of Agriculture, Forestry and Fisheries) (Tokyo, various years).
[a] Figures are preliminary.
[b] For 1965–77.

TABLE 4-A-6. JAPAN: FOOD SUPPLIES PER PERSON PER DAY, 1955-77 (protein and fat supplies in grams per day)

Food	1955 Calories	1955 Protein	1955 Fat	1960 Calories	1960 Protein	1960 Fat	1965 Calories	1965 Protein	1965 Fat	1970 Calories	1970 Protein	1970 Fat	1973 Calories	1973 Protein	1973 Fat	1975 Calories	1975 Protein	1975 Fat	1977 Calories	1977 Protein	1977 Fat
Cereals	1,406.7	31.9	4.5	1,403.1	30.7	4.3	1,399.7	28.5	3.6	1,237.7	25.8	3.2	1,201.1	25.2	3.1	1,174.5	24.7	3.0	1,136.7	24.1	2.9
Rice	986.6	19.4	2.3	1,057.6	19.8	2.5	1,075.7	19.1	2.5	914.3	16.2	2.1	876.0	15.5	2.0	844.4	14.9	1.9	801.9	14.2	1.8
Wheat	236.8	7.4	1.4	243.4	8.2	1.4	281.9	8.2	1.0	298.5	8.9	1.0	300.9	9.1	1.0	305.3	9.3	1.0	309.1	9.4	1.0
Others	184.3	5.1	0.8	102.1	2.7	0.4	142.3	1.2	0.1	24.9	0.7	0.1	19.8	0.2	0.1	20.3	0.2	0.1	20.9	0.2	0.1
Potatoes & sweet potatoes	137.2	1.9	0.2	90.5	1.5	0.1	57.0	1.1	0.0	38.8	0.7	0.0	39.2	0.8	0.1	38.7	0.8	0.1	41.8	0.8	0.1
Starches	32.7	0.0	0.0	62.4	0.0	0.0	76.4	0.0	0.0	75.7	0.0	0.0	73.6	0.0	0.0	69.5	0.0	0.0	85.2	0.0	0.0
Pulses	94.5	7.0	3.0	108.0	8.0	4.0	102.2	7.7	3.8	103.4	7.9	4.1	103.9	7.9	4.1	99.1	7.6	4.1	92.7	7.1	3.7
Vegetables	52.5	2.8	0.2	69.5	3.5	0.7	89.4	4.3	0.6	93.3	4.5	0.6	88.2	4.3	0.6	86.6	4.4	0.6	90.6	4.6	0.6
Fruits	17.2	0.2	0.1	29.9	0.4	0.2	38.4	0.5	0.3	52.3	0.8	0.4	60.5	0.9	0.5	58.0	0.9	0.4	56.9	0.9	0.5
Meats	12.7	1.9	0.5	19.3	2.8	0.9	54.4	4.6	3.8	78.0	6.7	5.4	99.4	8.4	7.0	102.9	8.7	7.3	126.9	10.3	9.1
Hen eggs	14.0	1.2	1.0	20.2	1.7	1.5	37.8	3.1	2.7	63.1	5.1	4.5	61.8	5.0	4.4	59.8	4.9	4.3	61.7	5.0	4.4
Cow milk & milk products	19.4	1.0	1.0	41.4	2.1	2.2	60.7	3.0	3.4	80.9	4.0	4.5	85.5	4.2	4.8	86.0	4.2	4.8	92.2	4.5	5.2
Fish & shellfish	63.6	10.2	2.4	76.6	12.7	2.7	90.0	15.1	2.7	92.2	16.0	2.5	98.7	17.0	2.8	99.3	17.1	2.7	100.8	17.1	3.0
Sugar	132.9	0.0	0.0	161.5	0.0	0.0	196.8	0.0	0.0	281.6	0.0	0.0	297.5	0.0	0.0	274.3	0.0	0.0	275.4	0.0	0.0
Oils & fats	67.5	0.0	7.5	106.4	0.0	11.8	168.6	0.0	19.0	228.7	0.0	25.8	270.7	0.0	30.5	276.6	0.0	31.2	288.8	0.0	32.6
Misc.	102.1	5.9	0.9	111.6	5.6	0.8	112.2	5.6	0.8	142.8	7.3	0.8	132.8	6.3	0.9	114.8	5.9	0.9	139.6	5.8	0.8
Total	2,153.0	64.1	21.4	2,300.4	69.0	29.2	2,474.6	73.5	40.8	2,471.2	76.9	51.9	2,525.5	79.4	58.8	2,467.2	78.8	59.4	2,489.6	79.5	62.9

Note: Numbers are based on table 4-A-5.

Source: Norinsuisansho (Ministry of Agriculture, Forestry and Fisheries), *Norinsuisansho Tokeihyo* (Statistical Yearbook of the Ministry of Agriculture, Forestry and Fisheries) (Tokyo, various years).

TABLE 4-A-7. QUANTITIES OF FOOD SUPPLIES AND CALORIC INTAKE PER PERSON PER DAY IN SELECTED COUNTRIES

Country	Year	Cereals	Potatoes & starches	Sugar	Pulses	Vege-tables	Fruits	Meats	Eggs	Fish & shellfish	Milk & milk products	Fats & oils	Caloric intake (cal./day)	GNP per capita (dollars)
						grams per day								
Denmark	1973	177	211	141	7	136	164	172	29	107	948	77	3,229	6,660
France	1973	202	255	109	14	316	220	251	35	46	848	50	3,178	6,274
W. Germany	1973	185	255	110	10	193	333	234	47	25	764	54	3,215	7,101
Italy	1973	379	105	92	24	420	303	181	32	27	601	58	3,370	3,148
Netherlands	1973	183	223	138	8	239	312	179	31	33	739	66	3,143	5,916
U.K.	1973	199	276	138	15	181	136	199	40	22	910	45	3,126	4,131
Canada	1973	182	192	149	26	178	211	261	36	18	858	48	3,177	6,800
U.S.	1973	175	120	154	19	260	191	396	46	20	700	63	3,311	7,464
Argentina	1969	259	298	97	9	217	264	335	18	6	338	51	3,160	1,810
Brazil	1970	272	537	128	81	40	150	84	11	7	195	18	2,820	924
Venezuela	1970	252	409	99	27	36	114	99	16	13	221	27	2,430	2,252
Egypt	1968/69	565	28	44	24	288	199	31	4	4	135	19	2,770	262
Israel	1969/70	304	107	107	30	331	410	155	62	18	403	42	2,990	3,886
Syria	1964–66	459	25	46	24	156	354	31	5	2	152	32	2,450	537
India	1969/70	384	48	49	53	10	48	4	1	3	116	10	1,990	146
Japan	1973	340	65	77	27	307	119	47	40	94	144	30	2,522	4,455
Korea	1973	606	103	21	23	186	42	25	11	76	5	6	2,634	488
Ethiopia	1970	403	82	10	67	24	14	55	7	N.A.	66	11	1,980	104
Australia	1972	216	134	149	4	190	210	298	34	15	888	38	3,048	6,483
New Zealand	1974	208	152	113	10	244	233	328	49	15	1,076	20	3,245	4,122

Note: N.A. = Not available.
Sources: Norinsuisansho (Ministry of Agriculture, Forestry and Fisheries), *Shokuryo Kanri Tokei*; (Statistical Yearbook of Food Balances), 1978; UN Food and Agriculture Organization, *Gross Domestic Product, Private Consumption Expenditure and Agricultural GDP at 1975 Constant Prices Historical Series, 1960–1975, and Projections, 1975–1990,* ESC/ACP/WD.76/2 Rev. (New York, 1977).

TABLE 4-A-8. JAPAN: EXPENDITURE ELASTICITIES OF VARIOUS FOODS
             1965–77

Food	1965	1970	1973	1975	1977
Total food	0.73	0.66	0.65	0.51	0.58
Staple food	0.41	0.41	0.44	0.39	0.42
Rice	0.34	0.35	0.39	0.35	0.38
Wheat, barley, & other cereals	−0.56	−0.06	−0.19	0.28	0.28
Bread	0.88	0.74	0.65	0.55	0.59
Noodles & others	0.52	0.47	0.47	0.36	0.39
Subsidiary food	N.A.	0.68	0.66	0.46	0.58
Fresh fish & shellfish	0.82	0.70	0.66	0.46	0.64
Dried fish & shellfish	0.77	0.64	0.68	0.52	0.66
Meats	1.12	0.94	0.87	0.60	0.78
Milk & milk products and eggs	0.87	0.65	0.56	0.42	0.39
Vegetables	0.78	0.70	0.64	0.45	0.55
Dried groceries	0.64	0.53	0.45	0.39	0.50
Processed food	0.61	0.55	0.57	0.37	0.43
Dressings	0.54	0.47	0.48	0.38	0.44
Luxury food	N.A.	0.63	0.61	0.54	0.52
Cakes	0.86	0.69	0.66	0.55	0.54
Fruits	0.92	0.72	0.68	0.55	0.67
Alcohol	0.50	0.50	0.55	0.53	0.42
Fresh beverages	0.87	0.56	0.54	0.51	0.42
Restaurant meals	1.10	1.04	0.97	0.90	0.89

Notes: For 1965, figures are for all cities with more than 50,000 persons. For 1970–77, figures are for Japan as a whole. N.A. = Not available.

Source: Sorifu Tokei Kyoku (Bureau of Statistics, Office of the Prime Minister), *Kakei Chosa Hokoku* (Annual Report on the Family and Expenditure Survey) (Tokyo, various years).

TABLE 4-A-9. RATIO OF PRICES IN TOKYO TO THOSE IN SIX WESTERN CITIES, 1977[a]

City	Beef (sirloin without bone)	Pork (chops)	Chicken meat (broiler)	Chicken eggs	Butter	Milk	Bread	Rice
Washington, D.C.	7.2	1.6	3.0	1.5	1.7	1.8	1.1	1.7
Canberra	8.7	1.9	1.5	1.0	2.6	2.0	1.3	1.6
London	4.9	2.0	2.1	1.3	2.6	2.5	2.0	1.4
Paris	4.6	N.A.	1.7	0.8	1.4	2.3	1.1	1.1
Bonn	3.3	1.3	1.6	0.9	1.6	2.0	1.6	0.7
Rome	4.2	1.6	1.3	0.9	1.4	2.1	1.7	1.0

Note: N.A. = Not available.

Source: Yujiro Hayami "Nosanbutsu Jiyuka no Sekkei" (A Design for Free Trade of Agricultural Products) *Kikan Gendai Keizai* vol. 31, pp. 62–79.

[a] Based on the exchange rates at the time of the survey.

TABLE 4-A-10. INCOME AND PRICE ELASTICITIES OF VARIOUS FOODS FOR HOUSEHOLDS IN ALL CITIES IN JAPAN

Food	Time series			Cross-sectional income elasticity
	Income elasticity	Price elasticity	Growth rate (percent)	
Total food	0.61	−1.42	0.9	0.47
Fish & shellfish	0.52	−0.97	0.5	0.44
Meats	1.77	−0.84	5.0	0.96
Milk & eggs	1.27	−1.74	2.4	0.88
Vegetables	0.34	−0.54	−1.1	0.52
Dried fish & seaweeds	1.41	−0.17	5.9	0.46
Processed food	0.72	−0.75	3.0	0.23
Dressings	0.37	−0.75	0.3	0.32
Cakes & fruits	0.95	−0.64	1.4	0.72
Beverages	2.19	−0.46	7.1	1.03
Restaurant meals	1.54	−3.06	2.6	1.11
Alcohol	1.20	−0.70	3.3	0.66

Notes: The time period for estimation is 1956–1962. The figures for cross-sectional income elasticities are based on laborers' households in all cities in 1960. Data for all estimates are from *Kakei Chosa Nenpo* (Annual Report on the Family and Expenditure Survey) published by the Bureau of Statistics, Office of the Prime Minister.

Source: Yasuhiko Yuize, "Shokuryo Juyo no Susei Koka" (Trend Effects of Food Demand) *Nogyo Sogo Kenkyu* vol. 20, no. 1, pp. 57–114.

TABLE 4-A-11. JAPAN: INDEXES OF REAL PRODUCTION, NUMBERS OF WORKERS, AND PRODUCTION PER WORKER IN AGRICULTURE AND MANUFACTURING, 1951–77
(1950–52 = 100)

Year	Agriculture			Manufacturing		
	Production	Workers	Production per worker	Production	Workers	Production per worker
1951	97.5	97.8	99.7	107.7	98.7	109.1
1955	124.5	102.8	121.1	170.6	116.6	146.3
1960	133.3	90.4	147.5	403.2	147.8	272.8
1965	149.2	74.1	201.3	683.3	180.2	379.2
1970	167.7	61.3	273.6	1,506.0	213.0	707.0
1973	192.2	48.1	399.6	1,948.8	222.4	876.3
1975	198.9	45.0	442.0	1,665.6	207.5	802.7
1977	207.1	42.8	483.9	1,927.7	206.6	933.1
Percentage annual growth rate						
1951–60	3.5	–0.9	4.4	15.8	4.6	11.2
1960–73	2.9	–5.0	7.9	12.9	3.1	9.8
1973–77	1.9	–2.9	4.8	–0.3	–1.9	1.6
1951–77	2.9	–3.2	6.1	11.7	2.9	8.8

Note: Annual growth rates were computed by the following formula: $a(1 + g)^n = b$ where a = the index number of the initial year, b = the index number of the last year, n = the number of years covered, and g = the rate of growth.

Sources: Norinsuisansho (Ministry of Agriculture, Forestry and Fisheries), *Nogyo no Doko ni kansuru Nenji Hokoku* (Annual Report on Changes in Agriculture) (Tokyo, 1961) p. 33; Norinsuisansho (Ministry of Agriculture, Forestry and Fisheries), *Nogyo Hakusho Fuzoku Tokeihyo* (Statistics from the Agricultural White Book) (Tokyo, various years).

TABLE 4-A-12. JAPAN: COMPARATIVE PRODUCTIVITY OF
AGRICULTURE, 1960–77

Year	Net production per gainfully employed worker		Agricultural productivity as percent of nonagricultural productivity
	Agriculture[a] (1,000 yen)	Nonagriculture[a] (1,000 yen)	
1960	96	379	25.3
1965	186	666	28.1
1970	337	1,360	24.8
1973	625	1,963	31.8
1975	854	2,573	33.2
1977	897	3,103	28.9

Source: Norinsuisansho (Ministry of Agriculture, Forestry and Fisheries), *Nogyo Hakusho Fuzoku Tokeihyo* (Subsidiary Statistics from the Agricultural White Book) (Tokyo, 1978) p. 14.
[a] Numbers are in nominal terms.

TABLE 4-A-13. JAPAN: NUMBERS OF WORKERS IN PRIMARY, SECONDARY, AND TERTIARY SECTORS, 1953–77
(absolute numbers in 1,000 persons)

Year	Total (2)+(4)+(6) (1)	Primary		Secondary		Tertiary
		Subtotal (2)	Agriculture (3)	Subtotal (4)	Manufacturing (5)	(6)
1953	39,270	16,540	15,400	9,440	7,230	13,290
1955	41,520	16,460	15,410	10,100	7,790	14,960
1960	44,650	13,270	11,960	12,630	9,590	18,730
1965	47,540	11,000	9,810	15,240	11,680	21,290
1970	51,080	8,750	8,110	17,990	13,820	24,280
1973	52,480	7,050	6,360	19,230	14,430	26,200
1975	52,120	6,610	5,960	18,410	13,460	27,100
1977	53,310	6,340	5,660	18,580	13,400	28,390
Percentage annual growth rate						
1953–60	1.9	– 3.2	– 2.9	4.2	4.1	5.0
1960–73	1.3	– 5.0	– 5.0	3.3	3.2	2.6
1973–77	0.4	– 2.7	– 3.0	– 0.9	– 1.9	2.0
1953–77	1.3	– 4.1	– 4.3	2.9	2.6	3.2

Note: For the computation of annual growth rate, see table 4-A-11.
Sources: Sorifu Tokei-Kyoku (Bureau of Statistics, Office of the Prime Minister), *Rodo Ryoku Chosa Kaisan Kekka Hokoku* (Revised Report on the Labor Force Survey) (Tokyo, 1966 and 1971); Norinsuisansho (Ministry of Agriculture, Forestry and Fisheries), *Pokketo Norinsuisan Tokei* (Pocket-size Statistical Yearbook of the Ministry of Agriculture, Forestry and Fisheries) (Tokyo, 1979) p. 23.

TABLE 4-A-14. JAPAN: SHARES OF PRODUCTION OF VARIOUS AGRICULTURAL PRODUCTS IN TOTAL AGRICULTURAL PRODUCTION, 1960–77

(percentage)

Products	1960	1965	1970	1975	1977	1977 as ratio of 1960
Total agricultural production	100.0	100.0	100.0	100.0	100.0	100.0
Total crops	80.4	76.0	73.4	71.8	72.1	0.90
Rice	47.6	43.1	37.9	38.3	39.0	0.82
Wheat & barley	5.6	3.0	1.0	0.6	0.8	0.14
Beans	2.6	1.6	1.2	0.8	0.9	0.35
Potatoes & sweet potatoes	3.0	2.5	1.7	1.4	1.4	0.47
Vegetables	8.3	11.8	15.8	16.2	14.9	1.80
Fruits	6.1	6.6	8.5	7.1	7.0	1.15
Industrial crops	4.4	4.8	4.4	4.3	5.1	1.16
Sericulture	3.0	2.3	2.7	1.6	1.5	0.50
Total animal husbandry	15.1	20.9	23.2	25.9	25.7	1.70
Beef cattle	2.3	2.4	2.1	2.7	2.6	1.13
Milk cows	2.6[a]	4.6	6.1	6.3	7.0	1.52[b]
Pigs	2.9	4.4	5.4	8.1	7.6	2.62
Chickens	5.2	8.7	8.9	8.3	8.0	1.54

Note: Numbers do not always add to 100 because of rounding.
Source: Norinsuisansho (Ministry of Agriculture, Forestry and Fisheries), Nogyo Hakusho Fuzoku Tokeihyo (Subsidiary Statistics from the Agricultural White Book) (Tokyo, various years).
[a] Milk only.
[b] For 1965–77.

TABLE 4-A-15. JAPAN: INDEXES OF PHYSICAL PRODUCTION OF AGRICULTURAL PRODUCTS, 1955–77 (1975 = 100)

Products	1955	1960	1965	1970	1973	1975	1977	1977÷1955
Total agric. production	68.5	75.8	84.7	95.3	96.8	100.0	104.8	1.5
Total crops	87.3	93.2	92.2	95.8	96.0	100.0	101.9	1.2
Rice	93.9	97.5	94.4	96.6	92.2	100.0	100.0	1.1
Wheat & barley	758.2	695.0	481.0	208.8	87.7	100.0	95.5	0.1
Beans	223.7	243.2	167.9	137.9	133.0	100.0	101.5	0.5
Potatoes & sweet potatoes	206.8	181.7	168.3	121.4	101.1	100.0	108.7	0.5
Vegetables	56.9	70.3	81.3	96.7	101.2	100.0	105.4	1.9
Fruits	26.6	46.1	56.4	81.4	96.7	100.0	102.8	3.9
Industrial crops	88.2	87.6	109.7	96.7	102.7	100.0	105.8	1.2
Sericulture	122.9	121.1	115.3	122.4	118.6	100.0	87.0	0.7
Total animal husbandry	23.6	33.7	61.9	91.6	97.4	100.0	113.5	4.8
Milk cows	32.1	58.0	81.6	117.5	101.6	100.0	106.3	3.3
Meat cattle	N.A.	3.9	28.5	69.6	94.2	100.0	105.1	1.6[a]
Pigs	13.5	23.4	56.5	90.7	105.3	100.0	120.5	8.9
Broilers	N.A.	3.9	28.5	69.6	94.2	100.0	122.7	31.5[a]
Hen eggs	25.3	35.7	67.1	99.3	101.2	100.0	105.4	4.2
Fresh milk	20.5	38.6	65.2	95.3	97.7	100.0	116.7	5.7

Note: N.A. = Not available.
Source: Norinsuisansho (Ministry of Agriculture, Forestry and Fisheries), *Nogyo Hakusho Fuzoku Tokeihyo* (Subsidiary Statistics from the Agricultural White Book) (Tokyo, various years).
[a] For 1960–77.

TABLE 4-A-16. JAPAN: CULTIVATED AND PLANTED LAND AREA, 1960–77
(absolute numbers in 1,000 hectares)

| Year | Cultivated land area | Paddy field | Upland field | | | | | Planted land area | Land utilization (percent) |
			Total	Ordinary field	Orchard	Pasture			
1960	6,071	3,381	2,690	N.A.	N.A.	N.A.		8,129	133.9
1965	6,004	3,391	2,614	1,948	526	140		7,430	123.8
1970	5,796	3,415	2,381	1,495	600	286		6,311	108.9
1973	5,647	3,274	2,373	1,310	632	431		5,663	100.3
1975	5,572	3,171	2,402	1,289	628	485		5,755	103.3
1977	5,515	3,133	2,382	1,248	604	530		5,707	103.5

Note: N.A. = Not available.
Source: Norinsuisansho (Ministry of Agriculture, Forestry and Fisheries), *Nogyo Hakusho Fuzoku Tokeihyo* (Subsidiary Statistics from the Agricultural White Book) (Tokyo, 1979) p. 28.

TABLE 4-A-17. JAPAN: EXPANSION AND DESTRUCTION OF PADDY AND UPLAND FIELDS, 1960–78
(absolute numbers in 1,000 hectares)

Year	Expansion			Destruction					Net increase (1) − (2)
	Total (1)	Reclamations	Restoration	Total (2)	Natural disaster	Total	Non-natural destruction		
							Factory, roads, residence	Forest	
1960	29.3	19.2	9.9	34.3	10.5	23.7	N.A.	N.A.	−5.0
1965	33.4	31.6	2.0	69.9	1.1	69.0	31.2	35.7	−36.5
1970	49.8	47.4	2.5	103.0	2.0	100.9	52.0	46.8	−53.2
1973	51.8	47.8	3.9	88.1	1.2	87.1	48.7	34.5	−36.3
1975	46.2	44.9	1.4	89.0	0.5	88.7	29.2	56.6	−42.8
1978	33.7	32.7	1.0	57.0	1.1	55.9	23.9	32.0	−23.3

Note: N.A. = Not available.
Source: Norinsuisansho (Ministry of Agriculture, Forestry and Fisheries), *Nogyo Hakusho Fuzoku Tokeihyo* (Subsidiary Statistics from the Agricultural White Book) (Tokyo, 1979) p. 30.

TABLE 4-A-18. JAPAN: PRICES OF FARM LAND, 1960-77
(absolute numbers in 1,000 yen per 10 ares)[a]

| | All Japan | | Urban areas | | Rural areas | | | | | | | |
| | | | | | Flat areas | | Quasi-flat areas | | Quasi-mountain areas | | Mountain areas | |
Year	Paddy	Upland	Paddy	Upland	Paddy	Upland	Paddy	Upland	Paddy	Upland	Paddy	Upland
1960	198	129	343	340	194	143	202	136	188	110	171	91
1965	343	281	1,870	1,999	322	292	321	278	329	248	228	146
1970	1,022	914	6,686	7,420	1,163	946	1,102	1,020	831	662	472	366
1973	1,885	1,809	15,800	16,987	1,883	1,727	1,874	1,830	1,345	1,196	700	545
1975	2,818	2,653	21,300	23,044	3,082	2,941	2,729	2,556	2,065	1,795	1,001	769
1978	3,424	3,242	26,101	28,348	3,428	3,116	3,254	3,012	2,440	2,076	1,226	946
					Percentage annual growth rate							
1960–73	18.9	22.5	34.3	35.1	17.5	21.1	18.7	22.1	16.3	20.1	11.5	14.8
1973–78	12.7	12.4	10.6	10.8	12.7	12.5	11.7	10.5	12.7	11.7	11.9	11.7
1960–78	17.2	19.6	27.2	27.9	17.3	18.7	16.7	18.8	15.3	17.7	11.6	13.9

Notes: Prices are for medium-quality paddy and upland fields. For the computation of annual growth rate, see table 4–A–11.
Source: Norinsuisansho (Ministry of Agriculture, Forestry and Fisheries), *Nogyo Hakusho Fuzoku Tokeihyo* (Subsidiary Statistics from the Agricultural White Book) (Tokyo, various years).
[a]10 ares = 0.1 hectare.

TABLE 4-A-19. JAPAN: NUMBER OF FARM HOUSEHOLDS BY SIZE CLASSES, 1950–77
(1,000 households)

Year	less than 0.3 ha	0.3–0.5 ha	0.5–1.0 ha	1.0–1.5 ha	1.5–2.0 ha	2.0–2.5 ha	2.5–3.0 ha	3.0 ha and over	Total	Cultivated land area per farm household (ha)
					Size of farm					
1950	1,429	1,032	1,952	945	363	176	—	27	5,931	1.01
1955	1,268	1,006	1,995	981	376	132	48	30	5,806	1.04
1960	1,266	991	1,907	1,001	404	147	54	36	5,823	1.04
1965	1,131	954	1,762	945	407	156	59	41	5,466	1.10
1970	1,106	910	1,619	875	407	172	72	63	5,236	1.11
1975	1,119	865	1,436	727	349	162	74	76	4,819	1.16
1977	1,911		1,416	710	340	162	80	90	4,709	1.17

Note: Dashes = Not applicable.
Sources: For 1950, 1955, and 1960, Norinsho (Ministry of Agriculture and Forestry), *1960 Sekai Noringyo Census* (1960 World Census of Agriculture and Forestry) (Tokyo). For 1965 and 1970, Norinsho (Ministry of Agriculture and Forestry), *1970 Sekai Noringyo Census* (1970 World Census of Agriculture and Forestry) (Tokyo). For 1975 and 1977, Norinsuisansho (Ministry of Agriculture, Forestry and Fisheries), *Nogyo Chosa* (Agricultural Survey) (Tokyo, 1978).

TABLE 4-A-20. JAPAN: FULL-TIME AND PART-TIME FARM HOUSEHOLDS, 1953–77
(absolute numbers in 1,000 households)

Year	Total (1) = (2) + (3)		Full-time		Part-time					
					Total		Class A[a]		Class B[b]	
	Number	Share (%) (1)	Number	Share (%) (2)	Number	Share (%) (3)	Number	Share (%) (4)	Number	Share (%) (5)
1953	6,142	100.0	2,511	41.0	3,632	59.0	2,232	36.3	1,400	22.8
1955	6,043	100.0	2,105	34.9	3,938	65.2	2,275	37.6	1,663	27.5
1960	6,056	100.0	2,078	34.3	3,979	65.7	2,036	33.6	1,942	32.1
1965	5,806	100.0	1,242	21.4	4,564	78.6	2,008	34.6	2,556	44.0
1970	5,342	100.0	832	15.6	4,510	84.4	1,802	33.7	2,709	50.7
1973	5,100	100.0	675	13.2	4,425	86.8	1,303	25.5	3,122	61.3
1975	4,953	100.0	616	12.4	4,337	87.6	1,259	25.4	3,078	62.2
1977	4,835	100.0	643	13.3	4,192	86.7	931	19.3	3,261	67.4
Percentage annual growth rate										
1953–60	–0.2		–2.7		0.7		–1.3		4.8	
1960–73	–1.3		–9.0		0.8		–3.5		3.7	
1973–77	–1.3		–1.2		–1.4		–2.6		1.1	
1953–77	–1.0		–5.8		0.6		–3.7		3.6	

Source: Norinsuisansho (Ministry of Agriculture, Forestry and Fisheries), *Norinsuisansho Tokeihyo* (Statistical Yearbook of the Ministry of Agriculture, Forestry and Fisheries) (Tokyo, various years).
^a On-farm income is larger than off-farm income.
^b Off-farm income is larger than on-farm income.

TABLE 4-A-21. JAPAN: AGRICULTURAL WAGE RATES, 1951–77

Year	Wage Rate[a]		Index		Ratio of Females to Males
	Male (yen/day)	Female (yen/day)	Male (1951 = 100)	Female (1951 = 100)	
1951	213	165	100.0	100.0	0.77
1955	301	239	141.3	144.8	0.80
1960	382	314	179.3	190.3	0.82
1965	853	688	400.5	416.9	0.81
1970	1,611	1,263	756.3	765.5	0.78
1973	2,412	1,901	1,132.4	1,152.1	0.79
1975	3,640	2,867	1,708.9	1,737.6	0.79
1977	4,441	3,403	2,084.9	2,062.4	0.77

Source: Norinsuisansho (Ministry of Agriculture, Forestry and Fisheries), *Noson Bukka Chingin Chosa Hokokusho* (Survey Report on Prices and Wage Rates in Farm Villages) (Tokyo, various years).
[a] Wage rates are for temporary hired labor.

TABLE 4-A-22. JAPAN: LABOR AND MACHINERY INPUTS TO AN AVERAGE FARM HOUSEHOLD, 1957–77

Year	Labor input (————	Machinery input ——hours per year———	Animal input ————)	Cultivated land area (ares)	Labor hours per 10 ares	Machinery hours per 10 ares
1957	4,174	67	110	97.1	430	7
1960	3,971	105	97	99.0	401	11
1965	2,987	175	21	103.2	289	17
1970	2,661	245	4	108.7	245	23
1973	2,323	216	1	109.4	212	20
1975	2,245	224	0	113.1	198	20
1977	2,148	301	0	114.5	188	26

Note: 10 ares = 0.1 hectare.

Source: Norinsuisansho (Ministry of Agriculture, Forestry and Fisheries), *Noka Keizai Chosa Hokoku* (Report on the Economic Survey of Farm Households) (Tokyo, various years).

TABLE 4-A-23. JAPAN: MAJOR AGRICULTURAL IMPLEMENTS ON FARMS INDIVIDUALLY AND JOINTLY OWNED BY FARM HOUSEHOLDS, 1955–77

(thousands)

Year	Power cultivator & tractor		Power sprayer	Power duster	Power rice planter	Reaper & binder	Combine & auto-thresher	Dryer for rice, wheat, and barley	Truck
	Walking type	Driving type							
1955	63	0	58	12	0	0	0	0	46
1960	517	0	263	143	0	0	0	0	103
1965	2,156	39[a]	494	206	0	0	0	1,073[a]	378
1971	3,201	267	1,149	1,251	77	0	84	1,616	1,015
1973	3,312	291	1,214	1,306	248	920	158	1,719	1,130
1974	3,374	339	1,253	1,381	434	1,129	217	1,771	1,199
1977	3,182	832	1,382	1,679	1,247	1,579	525	1,777	1,373

Source: Norinsuisansho (Ministry of Agriculture, Forestry and Fisheries), *Norinsuisansho Tokeihyo* (Statistical Yearbook of Ministry of Agriculture, Forestry and Fisheries) (Tokyo, various years).
[a]1966.

TABLE 4-A-24. JAPAN: GROSS AGRICULTURAL PRODUCT, TOTAL OPERATING COSTS, AND FARM INCOME, 1957–77

Item	1957	1960	1965	1970	1973	1975	1977	1977/1955
(1) Gross agricultural product (¥1,000)	299	353	639	985	1,411	2,081	2,332	7.8
(2) Total operating costs (¥1,000)	107	134	274	477	669	935	1,159	10.8
(3) Farm income (1)−(2) (¥1,000)	192	219	365	508	742	1,146	1,173	6.1
Ratio (3)/(1) (percent)	64.2	62.0	57.1	51.6	52.6	55.1	50.3	0.8
Ratio (2)/(1) (percent)	35.8	38.0	42.9	48.4	47.4	44.9	49.7	1.4

Source: Norinsuisansho (Ministry of Agriculture, Forestry and Fisheries), *Noka Keizai Chosa Hokoku* (Report on the Economic Survey of Farm Households) (Tokyo, various years).

TABLE 4-A-25. JAPAN: SHARES OF AGRICULTURAL OPERATING COSTS OF AN AVERAGE FARM HOUSEHOLD, 1957–77. (percentage)

Costs	1957	1960	1965	1970	1973	1975	1977
Total operating costs	100.0	100.0	100.0	100.0	100.0	100.0	100.0
Wages for hired labor	5.9	5.2	3.6	3.0	2.3	2.2	1.9
Plants and cocoons	4.2	3.7	3.6	3.8	4.0	3.8	3.8
Animals	6.7	7.9	6.7	6.4	5.5	4.8	6.2
Fertilizers	24.3	19.9	12.8	9.9	8.9	10.7	10.6
Feeds	14.9	17.6	24.9	24.1	25.8	23.2	21.3
Agrichemicals	3.1	3.6	4.1	4.5	4.8	5.9	6.1
Other current inputs	3.2	3.6 }	4.3	4.9	6.7	5.8	5.8
Raw materials	0.8	0.7					
Fuels and light	2.1	2.6	3.3	3.3	2.8	3.6	3.4
Machinery	15.1	16.8	19.2	23.0	16.1	15.1	16.7
Automobiles	0	0	0	0	6.3	6.6	6.9
Farm buildings	9.9	8.5	8.2	8.5	6.8	6.7	6.1
Machinery rentals	4.2	4.6	4.3	4.5	5.8	7.1	6.8
Land improvements	2.2	2.5	2.0	2.3	2.3	2.3	2.3
Land rent	1.0	0.9	0.8	0.9	0.9	1.4	1.4
Other	2.4	1.9	1.2	0.9	1.0	0.9	0.8

Note: Items such as plants, animals, machinery, automobiles, and farm buildings include depreciation.
Source: Norinsuisansho (Ministry of Agriculture, Forestry and Fisheries), *Noka Keizai Chosa Hokoku* (Report on the Economic Survey of Farm Households) (Tokyo, various years).

TABLE 4-A-26. JAPAN: PRICE INDEXES OF MAJOR AGRICULTURAL INPUTS, 1952–77 (1960 = 100)

Year	Total agricultural inputs excl. labor	Fertilizer	Feed	Agrichemicals	Fuels & light	Machinery
1952	99.1	126.9	101.8	152.8	94.8	78.0
1955	98.8	116.8	104.9	126.5	101.6	89.5
1960	100.0	100.0	100.0	100.0	100.0	100.0
1965	115.8	104.2	112.4	90.9	115.1	102.5
1970	136.5	108.2	119.2	87.9	123.8	112.5
1973	185.9	133.1	158.9	95.2	156.9	135.5
1975	247.4	223.7	205.1	133.3	247.8	181.5
1977	264.8	237.6	207.1	141.8	276.3	190.5
			Percentage annual growth			
1952–60	0.1	−3.0	−0.2	−5.4	0.7	3.1
1960–73	4.9	2.2	3.6	−0.4	3.5	2.4
1973–77	9.2	15.6	6.8	3.1	15.2	8.9
1952–77	4.0	2.5	2.9	−0.3	4.4	3.6

Source: Norinsuisansho (Ministry of Agriculture, Forestry and Fisheries), *Noson Bukka Chingin Chosa Hokokusho* (Survey Report on Prices and Wage Rates in Farm Villages) (Tokyo, various years).

135

TABLE 4-A-27. JAPAN'S AGRICULTURAL BUDGET, 1960–77
(absolute numbers in billion yen)

Item	1960 Budget	1960 Share (%)	1965 Budget	1965 Share (%)	1970 Budget	1970 Share (%)	1973 Budget	1973 Share (%)	1975 Budget	1975 Share (%)	1978 Budget	1978 Share (%)
Total national budget	1,765		3,744		8,213		15,273		20,837		34,440	
Total agricultural budget	139	100.0	346	100.0	885	100.0	1,645	100.0	2,000	100.0	2,662	100.0
Percentage share in the total national budget		(7.9)		(9.2)		(10.8)		(10.8)		(9.6)		(7.7)
Production measures	85	61.2	162	46.8	295	33.3	541	32.9	796	39.8	1,474	55.4
Selective expansion	8	5.8	8	2.3	20	2.3	50	3.0	184	9.2	425	16.0
Increases in production & productivity	46	33.1	106	30.6	212	24.0	371	22.6	454	22.7	857	32.2
Improvements in production infrastructure	39	28.1	90	26.0	181	20.5	330	20.1	394	19.7	748	28.1
Development & extension of agricultural technologies	6	4.3	14	4.0	29	3.3	36	2.2	60	3.0	109	4.1
Disaster measures	35	25.2	48	13.9	63	7.1	120	7.3	158	7.9	192	7.2
Improvements in agricultural structure	4	3.1	20	5.8	34	3.8	63	3.8	77	3.9	153	5.7
Promotion of improvements in agricultural structure	—	—	16	4.6	22	2.5	34	2.1	41	2.1	71	2.7
Fund for modernization of agriculture	—	—	3	0.9	6	0.7	9	0.5	12	0.6	17	0.6

136

Measures for prices, marketing, and income	36	25.9	140	40.5	417	47.1	737	44.8	982	49.1	797	29.9
Price stabilization and rationalization of distribution	32	23.0	129	37.3	394	44.5	644	39.1	862	43.1	740	27.8
Improvements in distribution system of fresh agricultural products	—	—	—	—	3	0.3	8	0.5	15	0.8	13	0.5
Promotion of demand for agricultural products & processes	4	2.9	6	1.7	13	1.5	20	1.2	21	1.1	22	0.8
Rationalization of production & distribution of agricultural inputs	1	0.7	4	1.2	4	0.5	65	4.0	79	4.0	16	0.6
Others	14	10.1	24	6.9	57	6.4	101	6.1	145	7.3	239	9.0
Regulation of rice production	—	—	—	—	82	9.3	203	12.3	—	—	—	—

Note: Dashes = Not applicable.
Source: Norinsuisansho (Ministry of Agriculture, Forestry and Fisheries), *Nogyo Hakusho Fuzoku Tokeihyo* (Subsidiary Statistics from the Agricultural White Book) (Tokyo, various years).

TABLE 4-A-28. JAPAN: DOMESTIC SUPPLY, CONSUMPTION, AND IMPORTATION OF FOODS, AND SELF-SUFFICIENCY RATES, 1955–77

(absolute numbers in 1,000 metric tons)

Food	Year	Domestic production (1)	Foreign trade		Changes in inventory (4)	Domestically available supply (1)+(2)−(3)−(4) (5)	Self-sufficiency rate (percent) (6)
			Import (2)	Export (3)			
Total cereals	1955	16,686	4,603	7	+2,274	19,008	88
	1960	17,101	4,500	48	+873	20,680	83
	1965	15,208	10,410	88	+848	24,682	62
	1970	13,858	15,803	835	−415	28,989	48
	1975	13,693	19,422	36	+1,513	31,566	43
	1977	13,585	22,709	104	+2,391	33,799	40
	1977/55	0.81	4.93	—	—	1.8	—
Rice	1955	12,385	1,290	—	+2,400	11,275	110
	1960	12,858	219	—	+459	12,618	102
	1965	12,409	1,052	—	+468	12,993	96
	1970	12,689	15	785	−281	11,948	106
	1975	13,165	29	—	+1,228	11,964	110
	1977	13,095	71	—	+1,583	11,483	114
	1977/55	1.1	0.06	—	—	1.02	—
Wheat	1955	1,468	2,238	6	+82	3,618	41
	1960	1,531	2,660	47	+179	3,965	39
	1965	1,287	3,532	88	+100	4,631	28
	1970	478	4,621	46	−159	5,207	9
	1975	241	5,715	34	+44	5,578	4
	1977	236	5,662	4	+133	5,761	4
	1977/55	0.16	2.52	—	—	1.59	—

Barley						
1955	1,148	681	—	−35	1,863	62
1960	1,206	30	—	+70	1,165	104
1965	721	512	—	−38	1,271	57
1970	418	1,072	—	+15	1,474	28
1975	174	2,117	0	+141	2,150	8
1977	167	2,238	—	+94	2,311	7
1977/55	0.15	3.29	—	—	1.24	—
Beardless barley						
1955	1,260	—	—	−184	1,444	87
1960	1,095	—	—	+119	976	112
1965	513	—	—	+96	417	123
1970	155	—	—	−57	211	73
1975	47	—	0	+2	45	104
1977	39	—	—	−2	41	95
1977/55	0.31	—	—	0.01	0.28	—
Other cereals[a]						
1955	425	394	—	+11	808	53
1960	411	1,591	—	+46	1,956	21
1965	278	5,314	—	+222	5,370	5
1970	122	10,095	—	+67	10,149	1
1975	14	11,561	0	−47	7,629	0.2
1977	8	14,738	—	+597	8,724	0.1
1977/55	0.02	37.41	—	—	10.80	—
Soybeans						
1955	507	767	—	+39	1,235	41
1960	418	1,081	—	−18	1,517	28
1965	230	1,847	—	+47	2,030	11
1970	126	3,244	0	+89	3,281	4
1975	126	3,334	0	−42	3,502	4
1977	111	3,602	—	−21	3,734	3
1977/55	0.22	4.70	—	—	3.02	—

(Continued)

TABLE 4-A-28. JAPAN: DOMESTIC SUPPLY, CONSUMPTION, AND IMPORTATION OF FOODS, AND SELF-SUFFICIENCY RATES, 1955–77 (*Continued*)

Food	Year	Domestic production (1)	Foreign trade		Changes in inventory (4)	Domestically available supply (1) + (2) − (3) − (4) (5)	Self-sufficiency rate (percent) (6)
			Import (2)	Export (3)			
Meats[b]	1955	356	1	0	0	357	100
	1960	376	6	0	0	382	98
	1965	1,016	118	34	0	1,100	92
	1970	1,626	220	15	0	1,831	89
	1975	2,056	728	3	+79	2,702	76
	1977	2,552	769	3	−11	3,329	77
	1977/55	7.17	769.0	—	—	9.32	—
Beef	1955	135	1	0	0	136	99
	1960	141	6	0	0	147	96
	1965	190	11	0	0	201	95
	1970	265	33	0	0	298	89
	1975	327	91	0	+11	407	80
	1977	371	132	0	+6	497	75
	1977/55	2.75	132.0	—	—	3.65	—

Note: Dashes = Not applicable.
Source: Norinsuisansho (Ministry of Agriculture, Forestry and Fisheries), *Shokuryo Kanri Tokei.*
[a] Only maize after 1975.
[b] Includes whale meat.

TABLE 4-A-29. RETAIL PRICES OF MAJOR MEATS IN TOKYO, 1955-77
(absolute numbers in yen per 100 grams)

Year	Beef	Pork	Chicken	Beef/Pork (percentage)	Beef/Chicken (percentage)
1955	45	50	44	0.90	1.02
1960	55	64	48	0.86	1.15
1965	85	75	72	1.13	1.18
1970	137	91	77	1.51	1.78
1973	198	112	80	1.77	2.48
1975	271	155	99	1.75	2.74
1977	315	159	113	1.98	2.79

Notes: Numbers are in current prices. Prices of beef and pork are for medium quality.

Source: Norinsuisansho (Ministry of Agriculture, Forestry and Fisheries), *Norinsuisansho Tokeikyo* (Statistical Yearbook of the Ministry of Agriculture, Forestry and Fisheries) (Tokyo, various years).

TABLE 4-A-30. JAPAN: EXPORT AND IMPORT OF AGRICULTURAL
PRODUCTS, 1965-77
(absolute numbers in 10 billion yen)

Item	1965	1970	1975	1978	1978/ 1965 (ratio)
Exports					
Total	3,043	6,954	16,545	20,556	6.8
Agriculture, forestry, & fisheries products	217	316	308	333	1.5
Percentage of total exports	64	140	115	112	1.8
Agriculture, forestry, & fisheries products	7.1	4.5	1.9	1.6	0.2
Agricultural products only	2.1	2.0	0.7	0.5	0.2
Imports					
Total	2,941	6,797	17,170	16,727	5.7
Agriculture, forestry, & fisheries products	1,243	2,250	4,639	4,498	3.6
Percentage of total imports	1,018	1,511	3,326	2,822	2.8
Agriculture, forestry, & fisheries products	42.3	33.1	27.0	26.9	0.6
Agricultural products only	34.6	22.2	19.4	16.9	0.5
Balance					
Total exports − total imports	102	157	−625	3,829	37.5
Exports of agriculture, forestry, and fishery products − imports of agriculture, forestry, and fisheries	−1,026	−1,934	−4,331	−4,165	4.1
Exports of agricultural products only − imports of agricultural products only	−954	−1,372	−3,211	−2,710	2.8

Source: Norinsuisansho (Ministry of Agriculture, Forestry and Fisheries), *Norinsuisan Tokei Geppo* (Monthly Statistics of Agriculture, Forestry, and Fisheries) (Tokyo, various years).

TABLE 4-A-31. PRICES OF WHEAT, MAIZE, AND SOYBEANS, 1970–78
(CHICAGO MARKET PRICES)

	Wheat		Maize		Soybeans	
Year	$/Bushel	Index	$/Bushel	Index	$/Bushel	Index
1970	1.57	100	1.35	100	2.75	100
1971	1.63	104	1.37	101	3.16	115
1972	1.80	115	1.28	95	3.46	126
1973	3.58	228	2.11	156	6.86	249
1974	4.86	310	3.19	236	6.84	249
1975	3.65	232	2.93	217	5.57	203
1976	3.22	205	2.72	201	5.81	211
1977	2.53	161	2.31	171	7.22	263
1978	3.21	204	2.35	174	5.68	239

Source: Norinsuisansho (Ministry of Agriculture, Forestry and Fisheries, Nogyo Hakusho Fuzoku Tokeihyo (Subsidiary Statistics from the Agricultural White Book) (Tokyo, 1979) p. 70.

TABLE 4-A-32. WORLD AGRICULTURAL PRODUCTION AND EXPORTS,
             1965–77
(absolute numbers in million tons)

Food	1965	1970	1975	1977	Annual rate of growth (percentage)
Wheat					
Production	267.4	318.4	354.7	386.6	3.1
Exports	50.1	50.2	67.3	66.0	2.3
Exports as % of production	18.7	15.8	19.0	17.1	
Rice					
Production	171.2	205.9	239.9	244.5	2.9
Exports	8.1	8.0	7.8	10.8	2.4
Exports as % of production	4.7	3.9	3.2	4.4	
Barley					
Production	106.3	139.6	150.0	173.1	4.1
Exports	8.1	10.4	12.5	12.8	2.9
Exports as % of production	7.6	7.4	8.3	7.4	
Maize					
Production	227.8	261.3	324.3	349.7	3.6
Exports	25.1	29.2	51.3	57.1	7.1
Exports as % of production	11.0	11.2	15.8	16.3	
Soybeans					
Production	36.4	46.5	69.7	77.5	6.5
Exports	7.0	12.6	16.5	20.0	9.1
Exports as % of production	19.1	27.1	23.6	25.8	
Beef					
Production	33.1	40.3	44.3	46.2	2.8
Exports	1.5	2.1	2.4	2.9	5.6
Exports as % of production	4.4	5.1	5.3	6.3	
Pork					
Production	31.5	37.1	42.5	43.8	2.6
Exports	0.4	0.7	1.0	1.1	8.8
Exports as % of production	1.4	1.9	2.4	2.5	
Mutton					
Production	6.0	7.1	5.5	5.6	−0.6
Exports	0.6	0.7	0.7	0.8	2.4
Exports as % of production	9.3	10.2	12.2	14.4	
Oranges					
Production	21.7	30.3	39.9	40.1	5.3
Exports	3.7	4.3	5.1	5.4	3.2
Exports as % of production	16.8	14.3	12.8	13.5	

Sources: UN Food and Agriculture Organization, *Production Yearbook* (Rome, various years); UN Food and Agriculture Organization, *Trade Yearbook* (Rome, various years).

TABLE 4-A-33. SHARES OF JAPAN IN WORLD AGRICULTURAL IMPORT
              TRADE, 1960–77
(absolute numbers in 1,000 metric tons)

Food	1960	1965	1970	1973	1975	1977
Total cereals						
World	67,231	102,164	112,102	158,845	156,433	165,456
Japan	4,362	10,262	15,578	18,608	18,848	22,112
Japan as %						
of world	6.5	10.0	13.9	11.7	12.0	13.4
Wheat						
World	31,563	55,707	54,943	77,826	72,705	72,408
Japan	2,678	3,653	4,685	5,386	5,654	5,676
Japan as %						
of world	8.5	6.6	8.5	6.9	7.8	7.8
Maize						
World	12,123	23,774	29,042	47,049	51,621	56,407
Japan	1,354	3,434	6,018	7,771	7,470	9,068
Japan as %						
of World	11.2	14.4	20.7	16.5	14.5	16.1
Bananas						
World	4,142	4,685	5,602	6.350	6,288	6,541
Japan	42	358	844	931	894	825
Japan as %						
of world	1.0	7.6	15.1	14.7	14.2	12.6
Sugar						
World	16,760	18,794	22,144	23,400	22,242	27,867
Japan	1,251	1,696	2,376	2,368	2,466	2,701
Japan as %						
of world	7.5	9.0	10.7	10.1	11.1	9.7
Soybeans						
World	118	6,626	12,234	14,718	16,314	19,662
Japan	0.08	1,847	3,244	3,635	3,334	3,602
Japan as %						
of world	0.06	27.9	26.5	24.7	20.4	18.3

Source: UN Food and Agriculture Organization, Trade Yearbook (Rome, various years).

TABLE 4-A-34. MAJOR EXPORTERS OF WHEAT, MAIZE, SOYBEANS, AND BEEF, 1960–77

	1960				1965			
	Wheat	Maize	Soybeans	Beef	Wheat	Maize	Soybeans	Beef
First (percent)	U.S. 41.2	U.S. 47.2	U.S. 47.4	Australia 19.6	U.S. 34.9	U.S. 60.6	U.S. 70.3	Australia 21.9
Second (percent)	Canada 19.8	Argentina 21.6	W. Germany 18.6	New Zealand 10.3	Canada 22.6	Argentina 11.2	Brazil 3.7	New Zealand 8.2
Third (percent)	Australia 7.4	South Africa 4.8	Canada 15.9	Ireland 4.9	Australia 11.5	South Africa 1.3	Paraguay 0.1	Ireland 3.7
Total of the three (percent)	68.4	73.6	81.9	34.8	69.0	73.1	74.1	33.8
World total (1,000 metric tons)	100.0 33,369	100.0 11,897	100.0 1,110	100.0 973	100.0 56,354	100.0 25,028	100.0 2,801	100.0 1,467

(Continued)

TABLE 4-A-34 MAJOR EXPORTERS OF WHEAT, MAIZE, SOYBEANS, AND BEEF, 1960–77 (Continued)

	1970				1975			
	Wheat	Maize	Soybeans	Beef	Wheat	Maize	Soybeans	Beef
First (percent)	U.S. 33.4	U.S. 48.9	U.S. 68.0	Australia 11.7	U.S. 46.0	U.S. 65.3	U.S. 75.9	Australia 37.4
Second (percent)	Canada 20.1	Argentina 17.8	Brazil 9.8	New Zealand 6.3	Canada 16.4	Argentina 7.6	Brazil 20.3	Ireland 24.3
Third (percent)	Australia 12.8	South Africa 0.9	Paraguay 0.5	Ireland 5.0	Australia 11.7	South Africa 6.3	Paraguay 0.6	New Zealand 17.3
Total of the three (percent)	66.3	67.6	78.3	23.0	74.1	79.2	96.8	79.0
World total (1,000 metric tons)	100.0 57,145	100.0 29,432	100.0 5,380	100.0 2,808	100.0 67,337	100.0 51,285	100.0 16,459	100.0 1,114

TABLE 4-A-34 MAJOR EXPORTERS OF WHEAT, MAIZE, SOYBEANS, AND BEEF, 1960–77 (Continued)

	1976				1977			
	Wheat	Maize	Soybeans	Beef	Wheat	Maize	Soybeans	Beef
First (percent)	U.S. 42.4	U.S. 71.6	U.S. 77.6	Australia 44.7	U.S. 36.1	U.S. 70.9	U.S. 81.0	Australia 42.7
Second (percent)	Canada 16.9	Argentina 5.0	Brazil 18.4	New Zealand 18.6	Canada 21.6	Argentina 9.6	Brazil 12.9	Ireland 17.7
Third (percent)	Australia 12.1	Netherlands 4.0	Paraguay 1.1	Ireland 14.6	Australia 12.0	South Africa 3.3	Argentina 3.1	New Zealand 17.4
Total of the three (percent)	71.4	80.6	97.1	77.9	69.7	83.8	97.0	77.8
World total	100.0	100.0	100.0	100.0	100.0	100.0	100.0	100.0
(1,000 metric tons)	62,557	61,993	19,753	1,230	65,981	57,122	19,996	1,482

Source: UN Food and Agriculture Organization, Trade Yearbook (Rome, various years).

147

5

Japanese Agricultural Policy

Present Problems and Their Historical Background

Fumio Egaitsu

Japan's agricultural policy needs to address several extremely difficult tasks. Three major problems are pressing for solutions. The first is the overproduction of rice. Rice is Japan's most important agricultural product, accounting for approximately 40 percent of total agricultural production in 1975. Excess supply of rice began to appear from about 1968, and even though a policy of restricting supplies by means of large public subsidies to farmers was applied, the problem has persisted. Tendencies to overproduce have also appeared in products such as milk, mandarin oranges, and vegetables.

The second problem is the improper and inefficient use of farmland. While Japan has a surplus in certain agricultural products, it imports a great deal of wheat, soybeans, and feed grains. Self-sufficiency in grain has declined from 83 to 43 percent between 1960 and 1975.

Much of its farmland has been either poorly utilized or transferred to other uses, with the cropping ratio declining significantly. According to the *Sakumotsu Tokei* (Statistical Yearbook of Crops and Farmland), the total acreage of farmland has decreased from 6.07 million hectares in 1960 to 5.77 million in 1975, and the cropping rate, which

---

Fumio Egaitsu is an associate professor in the Faculty of Agriculture at the University of Tokyo.

rose to a peak of 130 percent in 1960, declined to a mere 100 percent in 1975.[1]

The third problem is the high cost of agricultural production. Although there are some exceptions such as pork and broilers, which are dependent upon imported feed grains, the cost of domestic agricultural production is high by international standards, resulting in relatively high consumer prices for agricultural products.

The three problems are linked to structural changes in the agricultural sector, the most important characteristic of which is the increase in the number of class B part-time farmers.[2] For these farmers, agriculture is no longer their major economic pursuit, but has become a supplemental occupation. In general, the major labor resources of their households are utilized in the nonagricultural sector, and agriculture has become less important as a source of family income. Such farmers lack the motivation to develop ways to reduce production costs and improve profitability through technological innovation.

According to the Census of Agriculture, the percentage of class B part-time farmers was 25.7 percent in 1960; but it rose to 61.7 percent in 1975 and 70 percent in 1980. Even though these farmers have their economic base in the nonagricultural sector, they use 50 percent of the total farmland in Japan. Furthermore, the productivity of their land is remarkably low compared with full-time farmers.

The increase in the number of class B part-time farmers results from a combination of postwar socioeconomic development, agricultural policy, and other factors. The following sections will detail the postwar history of Japan's agricultural policy and explain why and how it caused the increase in the number of class B part-time farmers and, in turn, resulted in the three problems. Solutions are also suggested.

Although agricultural policy may be evaluated from various points of view, in this chapter the evaluation of the effect of a policy will be based upon five points: (1) price, (2) production, (3) farm household income, (4) food consumption, and (5) agricultural structure. The term, "agricultural structure," refers to how the productive force of agriculture is constituted in terms of land ownership, size of farms, productivity, responsiveness to demand, and the like. Long-term levels of both prices and production of agricultural products, as well as of farmers' income are all influenced by the structure of agriculture.

[1] The cropping rate is the percentage that acreage cropped is of the acreage farmed. The planting of more than one crop per year makes it possible for the cropping rate to exceed 100.

[2] A statistical term that means the type of farm household whose dominant income is of off-farm origin.

Historical Background

The period of food shortage, 1945 to 1955

POLICY TASKS.   The principal objective of Japan's agricultural policy from 1945 to 1955 was to secure staple food supplies, an extremely difficult task to accomplish because fertilizer and agricultural machinery had been destroyed by the war at the same time that population was increasing rapidly with the repatriation of military personnel and colonists. The vivid memory of starvation conditions during this period has profoundly influenced Japan's agricultural policy to the present time.

The second objective was to introduce and implement land reform. Prewar Japanese agriculture had been characterized by a landlord–tenant relationship with a tinge of feudalism; landlords had lost their role in the development of agricultural production, with some of them residing off of their lands. It was thus considered necessary to transfer the ownership of farmland to the hands of those who cultivate it in order to improve productivity and to make the society more democratic.

The third task was to provide employment for the large number of people who had lost their jobs because of Japan's defeat in the war. With industrial facilities devastated, only agriculture could employ the domestic labor force, which had increased drastically. The total number of persons employed in agriculture, which was 13 million in 1935, reached 16 million in 1950, although it was to decrease rapidly later on with the recovery in industrial production.

POLICY MEASURES.   The major policy measure taken during this period was direct legal control. Even though state control of staple food existed before the war, government control, particularly during this period, and especially the first half, was enforced rigidly under the Staple Food Control Act. Enacted in 1942, the law was intended "to control food and to carry out the adjustment of supply and demand and prices and also to control distribution in order to secure food for people and to ensure stability in [the] national economy."[3]

The law had within its scope total state control of the distribution of major foods such as rice, wheat, and potatoes; that is, official prices were set by the government, the government purchased food from producers, and the government distributed it to consumers. Of course

[3] Staple Food Control Act, Article 1.

there was some black marketeering even at that time; but it is difficult to ascertain its scale quantitatively. At any rate, the distribution of staple food was mainly conducted by the state until 1950.

With improvement in the food situation, however, distribution control was gradually relaxed. Rationing of potatoes was terminated in 1950, followed by wheat in 1952. At present, the government still purchases and sells rice and wheat, although for different reasons.

An important feature of the Staple Food Control Act is the provision that the prices at which government purchases from producers and the prices at which it sells to consumers are to follow principles independent of each other. That is, the law provides that the government purchase prices "are to be determined for the purpose of securing reproduction of rice by taking into consideration the cost of production, prices and other economic conditions,"[4] and sale prices "are to be determined for the purpose of stabilizing the consumer's budget by taking into consideration the cost of living, prices and other economic conditions."[5] Of course, even under such provisions, the purchase prices and the sale prices are not necessarily determined completely independently of each other. But it is certain that these provisions constitute one of the causes for the present excess supply of rice.

The objective of the land reform was completely realized during the occupation. This resulted in 1.7 million hectares of land being purchased by the government and sold to the tenants of that land. The purchase prices turned out to be extremely low because of the galloping inflation, resulting in an advantageous situation for the tenants. As a result of the land reform, tenant land, which had accounted for nearly 50 percent of total farmland, contracted to 9 percent with almost all cultivators becoming owner-operators.

The legal measure for implementing the land reform was the Agricultural Land Law of 1952, the purpose of which was to facilitate and protect the ownership of farmland by cultivators, "recognizing that it is most appropriate for farmland to be owned by the cultivator."[6]

Among other things, the law provided for:

1. transfer of ownership and tenant rights to farmland on an approval basis, with ownership granted only to those cultivators of more than 0.3 but less than 3 hectares

[4] Ibid., Article 3.
[5] Ibid., Article 4.
[6] Agricultural Land Law, Article 1.

2. prohibition of land ownership by nonresident landowners (resident landowners were also to be prohibited from owning tenant land exceeding 1 hectare.)

3. rent to be paid in fixed amounts in money and its maximum to be prescribed by ordinance

The reason the Agricultural Land Law limited the size of farmland ownership to at least 0.3 hectares but less than 3 hectares was that it was considered to be the cultivable limit for family labor in view of labor productivity at that time. As a result of the land reform, the average size of farms and farmland ownership became approximately 1 hectare, the Agricultural Land Law became very effective, and the results were almost immediately apparent.

Furthermore, emergency agricultural land development works were carried out to increase food production and to absorb excess population in agriculture. Such reclamation projects were intended to cultivate virgin soil for settlement by providing public subsidies and low-interest, long-term loans. The Emergency Five-Year Agricultural Land Development Plan listed as its objectives development of agricultural land of 1,550,000 hectares, reclamation by drainage of 100,000 hectares, and the settlement of 1 million households (Norinsuisansho, 1972a).

EVALUATION OF THE POLICY.   The occupation authorities played a major role in implementing agricultural policy during this period. The prices of staple food such as rice were invariably kept low. Evaluating the level of controlled prices is not simple and many factors should be considered. However, black markets existed with black market prices at levels above the official prices during this period (see table 5-1).

Government price control resulted in income transfers from producers, but that income was not necessarily transferred directly to the consumer. During this period, the cost of food was a major item in consumers' expenditures, and low food prices meant low wages. Thus, it may be said that the final effect of low agricultural prices during this period was to facilitate capital accumulation in the industrial sector.

Despite the low prices, agricultural production increased. This was partly because of the rapid recovery of fertilizer production, although the most important cause was the production incentive provided by land ownership. The opportunity to capture the economic rent accruing to land was a most important stimulus to production.

TABLE 5-1. JAPAN: GOVERNMENT PURCHASING PRICE, BLACK MARKET
PRICE, AND COST OF PRODUCTION OF RICE, 1946–56
(ratio)

Year	Government price ÷ cost of production (1)	Government price ÷ black market price (2)
1946	1.07	0.123
1947	1.27	0.199
1948	1.36	0.272
1949	0.87	0.322
1950	1.55	0.630
1952	1.68	0.755
1954	1.53	0.716
1956	1.64	0.896

Source: Ichiro Kato and Kusuhiko Sakamoto, eds., Sengo Nosei no Tenkai Katei (Postwar Development of Japanese Agricultural Policy) (Tokyo, Noseichosa-Iinkai, 1967) p. 142.

Despite low agricultural prices, the standard of living of farmers during this period was by no means lower than that of urban workers, even though it is difficult to compare standards of living during the period of confusion after the war on the basis of statistical data. However, according to a 1949 study conducted by Kazushi Okawa, from the standpoint of urban workers, the standard of living of farmers was 5 to 14 percent lower, while from the standpoint of farmers, the standard of living of urban workers was 10 to 18 percent lower (Okawa, 1953). There was a large surplus of labor in the Japanese economy as a whole during this period. The standard of living of both urban workers and farmers was close to minimum subsistence level.

Agricultural land development policy did not reach its planned goal by far. It was responsible for development of only 430,000 hectares and settlement of 200,000 households with a population of 620,000 between 1946 and 1951. Food production, in separate terms of rice, increased by 450,000 tons through land development in 1951 (Norinsuisansho, 1972a). The policy was more effective in absorbing the excess population than in increasing food production. The majority of those forced to settle on land of extremely low productivity ultimately abandoned farming after suffering severe hardships.

The food shortage was ameliorated by the importation of grains financed by the Government Appropriation for Relief in Occupied Areas Fund (GARIOA) and the Economic Rehabilitation in Occupied Areas Fund (EROA). Rice imports increased from 550,000 tons in 1946 (equal to about 10 percent of domestic production) to 1,650,000 tons in 1947, and 1,870,000 tons in 1948. By 1950, the food shortage was almost completely resolved (Norinsuisansho, 1972b).

Finally, the impact of agricultural policy on agricultural structure during this period was marked by the establishment of the small owner-operator system. Six million farmers born out of the land reform and the agricultural land development policy managed farmland averaging 1 hectare as owner-farmers. Although this size corresponded to labor productivity at that time, it was to play a restrictive role later. The restrictions imposed by the Agricultural Land Law on land transactions were later relaxed by revisions of the law. In reality, however, the size of farms resulting from the land reform has remained the same.

This system of farms averaging 1 hectare in size brought about two major problems by the end of this period: stagnant labor productivity in agriculture and a differential in income between the agricultural and nonagricultural sectors. These two problems were the reasons for the enactment of the Agricultural Basic Law and induced a shift in agricultural policy during the next period.

The period of rapid economic growth, 1955 to 1970

The ten year period from 1960 to 1970 is normally regarded as the period of rapid economic growth of the Japanese economy. There were equally significant changes in agricultural policy as the decade became the so-called age of Basic Law Administration with the enactment of the Agricultural Basic Law in 1961. In any case, the period from 1955 to 1959 was indeed the preliminary stage for the decade which followed, both in terms of the development of the Japanese economy and in terms of agricultural policy. The Agricultural Basic Law was enacted to clarify the problems of agricultural policy as well as to provide an approach to their solution.

POLICY TASKS. The national economy, which had been recovering from the devastation of the war, more or less regained a long-term growth trend in 1955, and with it, problems in agricultural policy underwent marked changes. First of all, the expansion of the nonagricultural sector increased the demand for factors of production, including the labor force, thus rapidly raising the opportunity cost of agricultural labor. The low marginal productivity of the enormous labor force that had hitherto been employed in the agricultural sector (because of the necessity for self-sufficiency in food and the lack of employment opportunities in the nonagricultural sector) began to be questioned during this period. The rate of increase of labor productivity in the agricultural sector lagged behind the nonagricultural sector. As a result of the rapid increase in both income and standard of living in urban areas, the income level of farmers fell below that of urban workers, whereas prices of agricultural products increased in relative terms. Disguised unemployment, or "overoccupation," of the agricultural labor force was thus revealed as a problem.[7]

Side by side with the development of the nonagricultural sector within Japan, the international economic environment underwent a marked change. The world's food supply and demand became characterized by excess supply, and the necessity for self-sufficiency in staple food decreased. The cost of self-sufficiency in food thus began to be compared with imported food prices. The efficiency of production of Japanese agriculture began to be viewed not only in terms of the marginal productivity differential with the domestic nonagricultural sector, but also from the viewpoint of comparative costs of production on an international basis.

The rise in the level of national income diversified the demand for agricultural products with relatively greater emphasis being given by consumers to vegetables, fruits, and livestock products. This diversification of demand, which germinated during the 1955 to 1960 period, developed much more rapidly later.

In this setting, the new tasks for agricultural policy were three in number. The first was to correct the income differential between the agricultural and nonagricultural sectors. It is no easy task to compare the income levels of the two sectors with statistical accuracy, even though farm income was clearly below nonfarm income at the beginning of the period. That such an income differential is a welfare problem is evidenced by the differential in the standard of living. Statistically, it is difficult to adjust the many factors controlling the standard of living in such a way that they can be compared between urban and rural areas. Table 5-2 shows consumption expenditure per family member as one such indicator. It should be noted that the national average of agricultural household expenses per head was only 70 percent of that of urban workers' households in 1960. The prospect of the permanent existence of such a differential in the standard of living was a major problem in economic welfare, and it was appropriate that agricultural policy address the problem.

The second task was to increase the marginal productivity of agricultural labor. Although relatively low marginal productivity is closely

[7] Underemployment in this agricultural sector was widely studied by Kazushi Okawa (1953).

TABLE 5-2. JAPAN: ANNUAL EXPENDITURE PER FAMILY MEMBER, FARM
AND NONFARM HOUSEHOLDS
(absolute figures in 1,000 yen)

Year	Farm household (national average) (1)	Nonfarm household (inhabitants of cities with over 50,000 population) (2)	(1) ÷ (2) × 100
1960	60.7	85.7	70.8
1961	68.9	97.6	70.6
1962	78.2	108.9	71.8
1963	88.8	124.3	71.4
1964	101.2	135.4	74.7
1965	115.5	147.3	78.4
1966	130.8	162.3	80.6
1967	156.0	179.4	87.0
1968	177.4	199.9	88.7
1969	207.6	225.4	92.1
1970	236.8	255.7	92.6
1971	267.9	280.0	95.7
1972	311.5	308.1	101.1
1973	380.5	367.3	103.6
1974	467.6	454.0	103.0
1975	546.4	513.5	106.4
1976	600.3	569.5	105.4
1977	667.1	612.6	108.9
1978	709.8	657.8	107.9

Source: Norinsuisansho (Ministry of Agriculture, Forestry and Fisheries), Nogyo Hakusho (Whitepaper on Agriculture) (Tokyo, each year).

related to income differentials, the issue here was efficient allocation
of the factors of production and was different from the income distribution problem that was a problem of welfare.

As a result of the rapid improvement in labor productivity in the
nonagricultural sector, wage rates increased, and this in turn caused
a rise in product prices in the agricultural sector where the rate of
productivity increase was low. Table 5-3 shows that the price of agricultural products during this period began to exceed international
prices. The task of improving labor productivity was equivalent to the
task of lowering prices of agricultural products.

The third task was to alter the composition of agricultural products
in response to the diversifying demand. As the Engel's coefficient fell
from 1960 onward, the ratio of staple food to total food consumption

TABLE 5-3. JAPAN: PRICES OF DOMESTIC AND IMPORTED
AGRICULTURAL PRODUCTS, 1935-78

	Ratio of domestic producers' prices to import[a] prices						Exchange rate (yen/dollar)
Year	Rice	Wheat	Soybeans	Butter	Beef	Pork	
1935	200	102	121	175	—	—	3.5
1951	85	69	66	222	—	—	360
1955	113	130	149	178	—	—	360
1960	134	150	158	173	144	133	360
1964	167	182	169	162	—	—	360
1970	298	209	207	239	156	119	360
1975	264	166	167	215	242	135	308
1978	404	446	354	382	247	108	201

Note: Dashes = not applicable.
Sources: 1935–55: Noringyogyo Kihonmondai Chosajimukyoku, *Nogyo no Kihoumondai to Kihon-taisaku—Kaisetsu Ban* (Tokyo, Norin Tokei Kyokai, 1960); 1960–78: *Nogyo Hakusho* (Whitepaper on Agriculture) each year; exchange rates: The Bank of Japan, *Economic Statistics Annual* (Tokyo, each year).
[a] Cost, insurance, and freight (c.i.f.) prices.

decreased, while meat and other items increased in relative weight. It was thus extremely important for agricultural policy, which had hitherto had as its primary objective the expansion of rice production as the staple food, to respond to such a shift in demand (Noringyogyo, 1960).

POLICY MEASURES.   The Agricultural Basic Law enacted in 1961 listed as its main objectives the correction of productivity differentials be-tween agricultural workers and those engaged in other industries (article 1). To achieve these objectives, article 2 listed three policy measures: (1) the selective expansion policy, (2) the structural improvement policy, and (3) the price policy. In addition, article 4 of the law provided that it was the responsibility of the government to take necessary legislative and financial measures to implement these objectives. The agricultural policy followed during this period was according to these objectives of the Agricultural Basic Law, hence the term Basic Law Administration given to the period.

During this period, the emphasis in policy measures shifted from legislation to financial expenditures, and in many cases the measures were accomplishing objectives by using the mechanism of the market economy. Nevertheless, various laws enacted during the previous period, particularly the Staple Food Control Act and the Agricultural Land Law, remained in force, albeit in somewhat revised forms, and exerted a strong influence.

The fundamental measure conceived under the Basic Law Administration was the structural improvement policy. This policy was intended to (1) expand farm size in order to raise the capital–labor ratio in agriculture through reallocation of farm labor into nonagricultural sectors and (2) consolidate land ownership. This policy was designed to bring about an increase in labor productivity responsive to wage rate increases and to reduce the cost of production as well as to attain income parity. It was thought, moreover, that the expansion of farm size would increase the ability to shift supply patterns in response to changes in market conditions.

First of all, the structural improvement policy instituted viable farms as an objective, and necessary legislative and financial measures were adopted to bring this about. A viable farm was defined as a "family farm of such a scale that those members of the family of a normal composition engaged in agriculture may be almost completely employed while attaining normal efficiency, thereby securing such income as to lead to a level of living comparable to that of those engaged in other industries" (according to article 14 of the Agricultural Basic Law). The standard acreage of such a viable farm was considered to be between 1.5 and 2.5 hectares.

Three policy measures adopted to foster viable farms may be mentioned: a structural improvement project, land improvement projects, and financing at low rates. The structural improvement projects were to provide subsidies for the modernization of farmland and farm roads as the basis of agricultural production and also for investments in collective production facilities. These projects have been carried out in 5,851 areas with public expenditures totalling ¥580,000,000.

Because of its very nature it was difficult for individual farms to carry out the land improvement project. Accordingly, as table 5-4

TABLE 5-4. JAPAN: COMPOSITION OF INVESTMENT IN FARMLAND, 1960–78

Year	Total investment (100 mil. yen)	Farm households' own funds (———————	Loans percent———	Subsidies ————)
1960	1,082	14.5	24.2	60.7
1965	2,254	11.9	20.3	67.8
1970	4,068	8.7	20.3	70.9
1975	8,726	2.4	20.9	76.7
1978	15,409	1.0	19.3	79.7

Source: Norinsuisansho (Ministry of Agriculture, Forestry and Fisheries), *Nogyo to Noka no Shakai Kanjo* (Social Account of Agriculture and Farm Households) (Tokyo, each year).

shows, in almost all cases, it was carried out in the form of a state, prefectural, or organizational enterprise. Under the provisions of the Land Improvement Law of 1949, the approval by more than two-thirds of the local farmers concerned was necessary, and subsidies were often provided.

Land consolidation gradually increased from 1960 onward, taking the place of investments in reclamation, irrigation, and drainage for the primary objective of increasing paddy rice production.

As structural and land improvements were in some way joint or public projects, they were assisted by long-term, low-interest loans and subsidies. Investments in agricultural machinery and other fixed capital assets of individual farmers were also assisted by financing at low rates with government subsidies. The funds were provided mainly by the Agricultural Modernization Fund System (Nogyo Kindaika Shikin Seido), based on deposits with the agricultural cooperatives, and the Agriculture, Forestry and Fisheries Fund System (Noringyo-gyo Shinkin Seido), based on the funds of the Fund Operation Department of the Ministry of Finance, which made advances through the Agriculture, Forestry and Fisheries Financial Corporation. These subsidized finances are shown in table 5-5.

The structural improvement policy assisted investments in agricultural fixed capital (including land improvement) by subsidies, and thereby fostered commercially viable farms; its direct objective was to improve productivity.

In contrast, the selective expansion policy was designed to respond to the diversification of food demand. The policy was to determine the objectives of agricultural production on the basis of a long-term outlook of demand and to disburse production subsidies to stimulate production in the required direction.

In the policy, Long-term Outlook of Supply and Demand for Agricultural Products, instituted in 1961, it was considered desirable to expand livestock production by approximately three times and fruit production by two times during the following decade, and various promotional measures such as bounties were to be adopted. In contrast, it was forecast that the demand for rice as the staple food would decrease gradually.

The outlook for a clear import policy apparently did not exist in 1961. As a result, it was determined that Japan would import grains other than rice, and the supply of livestock and fruit production was to be met by fostering domestic production. An *ex post* evaluation of this result would be that it did, in effect, protect rice as a staple food and treated livestock and fruit as infant industries.

TABLE 5-5. JAPAN: AGRICULTURAL FIXED CAPITAL FORMATION[a] AND SUBSIDIZED FINANCE, 1960–78

Year	Agricultural fixed capital formation (———100 mil. yen———) (1)	Subsidized finance (2)	(2) ÷ (1) (percentage) (3)	Agriculture-related capital formation (———100 mil. yen———) (4)	Subsidies in (4) (5)	(5) ÷ (4) (percentage) (6)
1960	2,095	310	14.8	138	103	74.6
1965	4,709	790	16.8	347	200	57.6
1970	9,547	1,208	12.7	948	442	46.6
1975	15,412	3,052	19.8	1,794	882	49.2
1978	16,558	6,732	40.7	n.a.	n.a.	n.a.

Note: Agriculture-related investment includes investments on community agricultural facilities through the Agricultural Restructuring Program. Method of estimation was changed in 1978. In 1978, (4) was included in (1).

Source: Norinsuisansho (Ministry of Agriculture, Forestry and Fisheries), *Nogyo to Noka no Shakai Kanjo* (Social Account of Agriculture and Farm Households) (Tokyo, each year).

[a] Excluding land.

The price policy had as its direct objectives the achievement of an equal and stable farm income. In addition to direct state control of distribution in the case of rice, various policy measures were adopted under the price policy, such as: the deficit payment system for milk for processing, soybeans, and rape seeds; government intervention in the market for beef and pork; and the stability fund system for vegetables. Nevertheless, control of the distribution of rice and wheat under the Staple Food Management Law continued to occupy the most important role in agricultural policy of this period.

Table 5-6 shows the agricultural budget and its composition as it appears in the general government accounts. Subsidies for irrigation and land improvement investment formed the largest item in 1960; but the relative weight of price policy expenditure gradually increased thereafter, forming the largest item of public expenditure almost every year.

Under the Staple Food Control Special Account, the rice account has shown substantial deficits (table 5-7). The deficit in the Staple Food Control Special Account occurred because, as has been described, the Staple Food Control Act stipulated that the government purchase prices from producers and sale prices to consumers be determined by independent principles. Between 1946 and 1951, official government purchase prices were determined by a parity formula based on the standard years 1934 through 1936. The parity index was calculated by official prices set far below free (black) market prices. As a result, the parity index for the rice price also greatly decreased. This discrepancy was rectified in 1950 when parity began to be calculated in terms of market prices. Nonetheless, in terms of commodity price parity, changes in the cost of rice production were undervalued because the productivity increase in the rice sector was relatively low, resulting in a disequilibrium of income.

It was not until 1960 that a price calculation based on a clear presentation of income equilibrium was implemented. According to this method, for those farmers whose yield per hectare is below average by one standard deviation, a method known as the "cost of production and income compensation" method is used to adjust the rice price and make the rice producers' income comparable to those of other industries. This method was used to ratify the low rate of productivity increase.

EVALUATION OF THE POLICY.   The agricultural policy of this period may be evaluated in terms of its three objectives, that is, income parity, response to demand, and improvement in productivity. The first was

TABLE 5-6. JAPAN: COMPOSITION OF THE AGRICULTURE-RELATED BUDGET, 1946–78

Year	Expansion of selective agricultural production	Irrigation and land improvement	Fixed capital formation for the improvement of agricultural structure	Price support, distribution, and income policies	R & D	Others	Total (100 mil. yen)
	(——————————————————————————— percent ———————————————————————————)						
1946	1.0	14.0	3.0	67.5	1.9	12.6	100
1947	1.1	20.0	10.6	41.3	3.3	23.7	156
1948	2.7	29.4	18.0	9.0	4.1	36.8	245
1949	1.2	7.2	4.1	69.5	1.6	16.4	957
1950	2.1	15.8	4.3	46.3	2.4	29.1	714
1951	2.6	14.8	1.5	37.7	1.6	41.8	949
1952	3.1	16.7	0.8	39.8	2.5	37.1	1,265
1953	2.8	17.5	0.8	23.6	2.2	53.1	1,501
1954	3.8	26.1	1.0	1.2	3.9	64.0	938
1955	4.8	28.6	1.3	11.5	3.6	50.2	797
1956	3.5	33.4	3.2	7.4	7.3	45.2	739
1957	2.5	26.0	4.0	32.6	5.3	29.6	1,023
1958	3.0	33.9	4.8	3.4	5.7	49.2	858
1959	3.3	35.6	4.9	10.4	6.3	39.5	922
1960	2.4	28.1	3.2	26.1	4.6	35.6	1,386
1961	2.3	23.9	4.3	38.9	3.9	26.7	1,961
1962	2.4	26.5	6.8	36.9	4.2	23.2	2,112
1963	2.3	25.9	8.8	33.7	3.9	25.4	2,537

TABLE 5-6. JAPAN: COMPOSITION OF THE AGRICULTURE-RELATED BUDGET, 1946–78 (Continued)

Year	Expansion of selective agricultural production	Irrigation and land improvement	Fixed capital formation for the improvement of agricultural structure	Price support, distribution, and income policies	R & D	Others	Total (100 mil. yen)
			—percent—			—)	
1964	2.3	25.2	9.0	38.4	4.3	20.8	2,997
1965	2.4	26.7	5.9	40.4	4.0	20.6	3,459
1966	3.0	22.5	5.8	46.7	3.2	18.8	4,887
1967	2.3	24.0	4.9	48.4	3.3	17.1	5,454
1968	2.4	22.9	5.1	49.1	3.4	17.1	6,079
1969	2.3	22.0	4.5	49.8	3.0	18.4	7,371
1970	11.5	20.5	3.9	47.1	3.2	13.8	8,851
1971	21.0	23.5	4.0	34.7	3.2	14.2	10,083
1972	19.6	25.6	4.1	32.0	3.0	15.7	12,167
1973	15.4	20.1	3.8	44.8	2.4	13.5	16,448
1974	12.7	16.7	3.2	51.3	2.4	13.7	20,088
1975	9.2	19.7	3.9	49.0	2.9	15.3	20,000
1976	8.0	20.2	4.3	44.4	3.2	19.9	21,675
1977	8.8	26.5	4.9	37.1	4.1	18.6	23,213
1978	16.0	28.1	5.7	29.9	4.1	16.2	26,624

Sources: 1946–59: Norin-sho-Daijinkanbo (Ministry of Agriculture, Forestry and Fisheries, Minister's Secretariat), Norin-gyosei-shi (History of Agricultural and Forestry Administration), vol. 9, 1972. 1960–78: Norinsuisansho (Ministry of Agriculture, Forestry and Fisheries), Nogyo Hakusho (Whitepaper on Agriculture) (Tokyo, each year).

TABLE 5-7. JAPAN: SHARE OF RICE IN TOTAL GOVERNMENT
EXPENDITURES FOR PRICE SUPPORTS, 1960–78

Year	Total expenditure (100 mil. yen) (1)	Deficit in rice price support account (100 mil. yen) (2)	(2) ÷ (1) (percent) (3)
1960	362	281	77.6
1961	762	504	66.1
1962	779	529	67.9
1963	855	886	103.6
1964	1,152	1,229	106.6
1965	1,396	1,335	95.6
1966	2,282	2,234	97.9
1967	2,641	2,423	91.7
1968	2,985	2,683	89.8
1969	3,842	3,479	90.1
1970	4,169	3,608	86.5
1971	3,414	4,461	130.7
1972	3,891	4,273	109.8
1973	7,371	5,261	71.4
1974	10,318	6,077	58.9
1975	9,818	7,088	72.2
1976	9,630	7,408	76.9
1977	8,607	7,469	86.8
1978	7,966	7,432	93.3

Source: Norinsuisansho (Ministry of Agriculture, Forestry and Fisheries), Nogyo Hakusho
(Whitepaper on Agriculture) (Tokyo, each year).

achieved successfully, while the second was partially successful, and
the third a complete failure.

The failure to achieve the second policy objective was, needless to
say, apparent from the excess rice production and was closely related
to the failure of the third policy objective, which resulted in a large
number of class B part-time farmers. The success of the income equilibrium policy was shown in table 5-2. As to the response to demand,
the rapid increase in the production of fruits and livestock products
may be regarded as a success. It is, however, the unsuccessful areas
of past agricultural policy that are really important in considering
present agricultural policy.

Let us now evaluate the effect of the policy on rice prices. Academic
opinion is divided about whether the present rice prices are high or
low (Tokiwa, 1978). This is a problem of criterion. Japanese rice prices
are markedly higher than the international prices; in fact two or three
times the import prices, according to table 5-3. We attempt to show
that rice prices are also high when viewed from a domestic standpoint.

One such criterion for examining the effect of the policy on domestic rice prices is free market prices, but so far they have been strongly influenced by the government in Japan and cannot be used as the criterion. Accordingly, the only other criterion is the cost of production, and here opinions are divided.

The cost of production of rice is available in two ways. One is based on the difference in yield per hectare, which often just reflects the fertility of the farmland. The other is based on the difference in the size of rice-producing farms—a difference that reflects types of machinery used and the working hours required per hectare. When considering the former, there emerges the argument that present rice prices are low because areas actually planted in rice include pieces of land of markedly low fertility for which rice prices do not cover the cost of production.

The second way to get at the cost of production is by considering the difference in the size of farms. It should perhaps be the criterion for evaluating the effect of the policy on the prices of rice, because what is important for the individual farm are the income and expenditure of the farm as a whole, and this is subject to a cost of production of the farm based on the average yield. Table 5-8 shows the distribution of production costs in this sense. The types of agricultural machinery that could be used were limited in 1960, and as a result, the distribution of production cost by scale was not particularly marked; it became much more dispersed in 1975.

It may be said that the present prices of rice are more or less at an appropriate level in relation to the average cost of production of the existing rice-growing farm, the average size of which is only 0.8 hectares. Still, attention should be paid to the fact that there exists a size of farm which can supply rice at much lower prices even at the present level of technology. That size is attainable if the structural improvement policy turns out to be successful. In this sense, the present price of rice is clearly higher than it should be.

In the 1950s, Japan's agriculture was predominantly subject to constant returns to scale (Tsuchiya, 1955; Kuroda and Yotopoulos, 1978). Later, by contrast, economies of scale began to prevail and, at present, increasing returns to scale are predominant in almost every agricultural sector. Accordingly, unit cost of production is a decreasing function of farm size.

The high level of rice prices is interfering with the farmland concentration necessary for viable farming, and as a result, the high average cost of production is maintained. The prices of rice, stable at a high level, have kept small farmers in the cultivation of rice. Al-

TABLE 5-8. JAPAN: COST OF RICE PRODUCTION BY FARM SIZE,
1960 AND 1975

Farm size (ha per farm)	Total production cost per 150 kg of rice (yen)	Worker hrs. per ha of land	Total cost (index)	Worker hrs. (index)
		1960		
0.0–0.3	6,136	19.68	100.0	100.0
0.3–0.5	6,482	19.75	105.6	100.3
0.5–1.0	6,284	18.13	102.4	92.1
1.0–1.5	5,891	16.92	96.0	85.9
1.5–2.0	5,630	16.36	91.7	83.1
2.0–3.0	5,623	15.56	91.6	79.0
3.0–	5,319	14.13	86.6	71.7
		1975		
0.0–0.3	31,188	11.57	100.0	100.0
0.3–0.5	28,995	10.78	93.0	93.2
0.5–1.0	26,153	9.46	83.9	81.8
1.0–1.5	23,270	8.27	74.6	71.5
1.5–2.0	20,788	7.00	66.6	60.5
2.0–3.0	18,898	6.59	60.6	57.0
3.0–	18,648	5.54	59.8	47.9

Source: Norinsuisansho (Ministry of Agriculture, Forestry and Fisheries), *Kome Seisan-hi Chosa* (Survey of Rice Production Cost) (Tokyo, each year).

though such prices are not the only reason for small farms, they are an important influence.

Although only rice prices have so far been discussed, prices of wheat, soybeans, and beef—also objects of the price policy—were invariably maintained at a level higher than world prices. The only exception was pork, with prices close to the international level as shown in table 5-3. This was because pork production depended on imported grains and because pig farming does not require concentration of land.

Because the price policy covered 60 to 70 percent of all agricultural products, agricultural prices were, as a whole, greatly influenced by the policy, especially by the rice price policy. The agricultural price index did not show any marked difference in the movements of different categories (table 5-9).[8]

[8] Farmers have shifted their production to rice and other products that are subject to the price program and have decreased supply of other products. For example, the production of feed grains has completely disappeared so that their prices are not included in the price index shown in table 5-9. Consequently, the price index shown

The effect of the agricultural policy on production varied considerably from crop to crop. Overproduction appeared in rice, mandarin oranges, and milk; but not for the same reasons. With regard to rice, if the consumer's prices were lowered, increases in quantity consumed then could not be expected in view of the small price elasticity. As the income elasticity was in fact negative, it was absolute overproduction.

In the case of the demand for mandarin oranges, both price elasticity and income elasticity are estimated to be fairly high. Overproduction implies that the demand prices are low compared with the average cost of production. Mandarin oranges were first regarded as the selective expansion crop, and the earning capacity was relatively high.

The income elasticity of demand for milk and dairy products is estimated to be about 0.5 and the price elasticity close to -2.0. Because the consumption is markedly small compared with Western countries, the quantity consumed in the market may be expected to increase considerably with a change in the pattern of consumption. Accordingly, any overproduction should be regarded as temporary and relative to the level of the average cost of production. Needless to say, the overproduction of mandarin oranges and milk is related to whatever import policy is decided on for the future.[9]

Wheat and soybeans represent those crops whose domestic production has been destroyed almost entirely by their low profitability. The rise in their prices was not sufficient to cover the rise in cost of production, so the increasing demand was met by imports.

Although meat production increased rapidly, it is largely dependent on imported feed grains. As a result of the rapid increase in imports of wheat, soybeans, and feed grains, the self-sufficiency ratio of grains fell markedly.

Despite the high prices of agricultural products, the level of food consumption rose rapidly. With Engel's coefficient falling steadily, it is difficult to think that agricultural prices during this period were pressing the consumer's household. This was because the income level

---

in column (4) of that table mainly reflects the prices of those kinds of products that are physically unimportable, for example, vegetables. Furthermore, column (4) includes the prices of the products that are not directly subject to government price supports but are subject to import restrictions, for example, mandarin oranges. These are the main reasons that there is not much difference between the price indexes in table 5-9.

[9] See Norinsuisansho Daijinkanbo (1977) about elasticities of demand.

TABLE 5-9. JAPAN: EFFECTS OF PRICE PROGRAM, 1960–78
(1975 = 100)

Year	Price index of domestic agricultural products subject to price program (1)	Group A (2)	Group B (3)	Price index of domestic agricultural products excluding (1) (4)
1960	27.8	27.1	30.2	29.1
1961	29.1	28.5	31.2	33.3
1962	32.2	31.0	35.0	36.3
1963	34.7	33.5	39.2	38.2
1964	37.0	37.7	35.2	39.2
1965	40.8	41.3	39.6	44.1
1966	44.4	44.9	43.0	46.6
1967	48.7	48.7	48.8	50.5
1968	51.1	51.5	50.3	48.8
1969	52.1	52.3	51.8	56.0
1970	52.8	52.8	52.7	58.7
1971	55.8	55.1	57.5	56.8
1972	58.6	57.4	61.4	60.4
1973	67.7	66.3	71.4	80.5
1974	86.6	87.4	84.7	91.3
1975	100.0	100.0	100.0	100.0
1976	105.6	105.8	105.2	112.1
1977	110.1	112.2	106.8	107.7
1978	112.5	114.9	108.6	114.0

Note: Group A includes rice, wheat, and tobacco; group B includes sweet potatoes (for processing), potatoes, soybeans, beets, sugarcane, cocoons, milk, pork, and beef.

Source: Norinsuisansho (Ministry of Agriculture, Forestry and Fisheries), Noson Bukka Chingin Tokei (Statistical Yearbook of Rural Prices and Wages) (Tokyo, each year).

of the consumer rose at a surprisingly fast pace (see Kuroda in this volume).

The most serious defect of the Basic Law Administration was its failure to improve the structure of agriculture. As table 5-10 shows, viable farms accounted for less than 10 percent of the total number of farm households, even in 1975. An overwhelmingly large number of farmers were class B part-time farmers dependent upon nonagricultural income. They did not dispose of their land and continued farming as a pursuit secondary to their main jobs. Such farms had high costs of production and generally were not responsive to changes in market conditions and technology.

The increase in the number of class B part-time farmers contributed to the equilibrium between household incomes of farmers and in-

TABLE 5-10. JAPAN: SHARES OF VIABLE FARM HOUSEHOLDS AMONG
ALL FARM HOUSEHOLDS, 1960–78
(percentage)

Year	Number of households (1)	Gross agricultural production (2)	Cultivated land (3)	Full-time farmers (4)	Agricultural fixed capital (5)
1960	8.6	23	24	16	19
1965	9.1	27	22	21	18
1970	6.6	25	18	19	19
1975	9.2	36	28	30	27
1978	8.9	39	29	32	32

Source: Norinsuisansho (Ministry of Agriculture, Forestry and Fisheries), Nogyo Hakusho (Whitepaper on Agriculture) (Tokyo, each year).

dustrial workers. Productivity of class B part-time farmers in the agricultural sector is extremely low, as shown in table 5-11. However, because of their high income level in the nonagricultural sector, the average level of their earned income is in fact higher than that of full-time or class A part-time farmers. Thus, income equilibrium, which was one of the tasks of the Basic Law Administration, was achieved by an increase in the number of class B part-time farmers, not by a decrease in the number of farmers or by an increase in the percentage of viable farms, as was expected at the start of the administration.

There are two major reasons why farmland did not become more concentrated. One was agricultural policy and the other was rapid economic growth accompanied by inflation. Two points should be mentioned about the agricultural policy: (1) those provisions made under the Agricultural Land Law restricting the mobility and leasing of land (because of apprehensions about the revival of the landlord system) were maintained in their original form even though the circumstances were completely different; and (2) government purchase prices of rice under the Staple Food Control Act were kept at a level that could well cover the production cost of small-scale rice cultivation of under 1 hectare.

Table 5-12 gives some basic figures concerning the rapid economic growth. What merits special attention here is that while wages and prices rose drastically, the interest rate was fixed at the level of about 8 percent, but the average rate of interest on borrowings by farmers was about 6 percent.

TABLE 5-11. JAPAN: FARM HOUSEHOLD ECONOMY BY TYPES, 1961–78

Year and type of farmer	Cultivated land (ha/farm) (1)	Agricultural income (1,000 yen/ha) (2)	Agricultural income per on-farm laborer (yen/hour) (3)	Off-farm income per off-farm laborer (yen/hour) (4)	Disposable income per family member (1,000 yen/worker) (5)	On-farm income as percent of total income (6)	Percent of total agric. production sold (7)	Percent of males in total on-farm labor (8)	Percent of rice in total agricultural production (9)
1961									
I	1.33	264	73	99	78.9	83.1	78.1	52.2	43.8
II	1.20	257	74	62	80.4	67.5	74.6	49.9	47.9
III	0.52	205	50	106	91.3	21.1	53.2	40.2	51.9
1965									
I	1.64	458	143	117	135.4	86.8	84.8	52.6	36.8
II	1.33	452	156	102	140.1	69.1	82.0	50.4	45.8
III	0.56	305	106	177	154.3	20.1	63.5	40.9	53.0
1970									
I	1.92	528	216	299	261.8	85.7	87.6	52.3	28.9
II	1.65	608	251	200	283.1	68.4	86.3	51.2	39.5
III	0.67	362	149	341	317.1	15.7	73.5	41.3	51.6
1975									
I	2.14	1,140	551	626	740.4	87.4	92.5	53.5	25.1
II	1.97	1,316	683	504	759.5	68.8	91.8	51.7	37.2
III	0.68	805	413	815	800.5	14.9	79.5	44.3	55.7
1978									
I	2.27	1,260	666	746	913.1	87.0	92.7	54.0	20.6
II	2.08	1,508	799	640	964.3	67.0	93.0	53.1	34.4
III	0.74	770	451	1,027	1,007.8	12.4	82.6	45.7	56.8

Notes: I = Full-time farmer. II = Class A part-time farmer. III = Class B part-time farmer.
Source: Norinsuisansho (Ministry of Agriculture, Forestry and Fisheries), *Noka no Keitaibetsu ni Mita Noka-keizai* (Economic Survey of Farm Households by Type of Farmers) (Tokyo, each year).

TABLE 5-12. ECONOMIC GROWTH AND INFLATION IN JAPAN,
             1955–59 TO 1975–78
(percentage)

Years	Growth rate of real GNP (1)	Growth rate of CPI (2)	Growth rate of wages (3)	Growth rate of prices of agri- cultural products (4)	Interest rate[a] (5)
1955–59	7.3	0.9	5.3	0.0	8.49
1960–64	11.7	5.4	9.8	7.1	8.01
1965–69	11.2	5.5	12.3	7.3	7.49
1970–74	6.5	10.9	19.1	10.9	7.72
1975–78	5.1	8.3	10.4	6.5	7.30

Sources: Keizai-Kikaku-cho (Economic Planning Agency), Kokumin Keizai Keisan Nenpo (Annual Report on National Accounts); Norinsuisansho (Ministry of Agriculture, Forestry and Fisheries), Noson Bukka Chingin Tokei (Statistical Yearbook of Rural Prices and Wages); The Bank of Japan, Economic Statistics Annual.

[a] Interest rate = National average of interest rates for loans from banks.

When the rate of interest is fixed artificially in inflationary times, a bias emerges in the price ratio of fixed factors of production. Let us say

wage rate is W_0 and the rate of increase w
interest rate i
price of fixed capital goods P_0
durable years of fixed capital goods T

Then, the ratio of the cost W for employing labor force L for T years to the acquisition cost P_0K of fixed capital goods K may be expressed in terms of the discounted present value as below

$$W/P_0K = W_0L/P_0K \sum_{t=1}^{T} [(1+w)/(1+i)]^{t-1}$$

If the rate of interest is fixed irrespective of inflation, the capital cost P_0K is relatively low compared with the wage cost W. Based on that evaluation, the capital–labor ratio K/L turns capital intensive. This is what should be called a technical bias caused by inflation (Egaitsu, 1978). Furthermore, when land is considered as a kind of fixed asset, and because its durable years are infinite, if earnings from land are

R_0 and the rate of increase r, economic valuation Q of land without considering risks may be

$$Q = R_0 \sum_{t=1}^{\infty} \left(\frac{1 + r}{1 + i} \right)^t$$

Thus, if r is larger than i, Q will be infinite. In fact, as long as r is close to i, Q must be much larger than capitalization R_0/i of R_0. Increase in land valuation Q increases the demand price of land; but it hampers land transactions. It is because, unlike the case of ordinary fixed capital, the availability of borrowing is limited by the ability of the borrower to pay higher prices. Table 5-13 shows the trends in land prices and earnings.

Arguments are divided on how much of a farmer's income can be imputed to the land. For our purposes, the price of land has been calculated as the capitalization of the annual flow of revenue, based on the premise that all income is imputed to the land. This, of course, overestimates the economic value of land. In reality, the actual price of land accounted for 70 to 80 percent of calculated land prices in the first half of the 1960s. However, actual land prices began to exceed calculated land prices in the 1970s and have increased two- or three-fold in recent years. The price of farmland is so high that it cannot be explained by the agricultural income from land. It can only be explained by inflation and the expectation of inflation.

Table 5-14 shows transfers in ownership of farmlands. Annually, transfer of land ownership accounts for only 1 percent of total lands

TABLE 5-13. LAND PRICE AND PRODUCTIVITY IN JAPAN,
1960–64 TO 1975–78

Year	Paddy land price	Dry land price	Agricultural income per unit of land (—1,000 yen per ha	Capitalization of (3) ——)	(1) ÷ (4)
	(1)	(2)	(3)	(4)	(5)
1960–64	2,640	2,080	274	3,428	0.77
1965–69	5,280	4,480	453	6,064	0.87
1970–74	16,710	15,600	611	7,883	2.12
1975–78	24,840	29,280	1,679	14,411	1.72

Sources: Zenkoku-Ngogyo-Kaigisho (The National Chamber of Agriculture) Den-hata Baibai Kakaku (Purchase/Sales Price of Farm Land) (Tokyo, each year). Norinsuisansho (Ministry of Agriculture, Forestry and Fisheries), Noka Keizai Chosa (Economic Survey of Farm Households) (Tokyo, each year).

TABLE 5-14. TRANSFER OF FARMLAND IN JAPAN, 1955–78
(thousand hectares)

Year	Transfer of ownership with compensation (1)	Creation of right to lease (2)	Cancellation of right to lease (3)
1955	39.1	4.0	20.0
1960	56.7	2.7	18.4
1967	73.9	2.5	12.3
1970	71.2	1.8	9.0
1975	47.6	6.3	5.7
1978	42.1	9.4	4.1

Sources: 1955–75: Isao Kajii, Tochiseisaku to Nogyo (Land Policy and Agriculture) (Tokyo, Ie-no-Hikari-Kyokai, 1978); 1978: Norinsuisansho (Ministry of Agriculture, Forestry and Fisheries), Nochi-Ido-Jittai-Chosa (Survey of the Transfer of Farmland) (Tokyo).

on the average. The high prices of farmland as well as the expectation of even higher prices in the future inhibit the transfer of land.

In many cases, the renting or leasing of farmland involved secret landlord–tenant relationships in violation of the Agricultural Land Law, a law that was primarily designed to protect cultivators from the revival of exploitation by landlords. Under this law, the tenant rights of the cultivator are strongly protected. Therefore, these cases show the behavior of landowners who did not wish to form formal lender–borrower relationships based on the Agricultural Land Law. Table 5-14 shows only the transfer of ownership based on the Agricultural Land Law. It is very difficult to confirm statistically how much should be labelled as illicit tenancy, but it is clear that this has increased in recent years.

Because of the reasons given above, Japanese agriculture during this period was not able to use land effectively and became strongly biased toward the use of other forms of fixed capital. Consequently, greenhouse farming, pig farming, and poultry farming developed rapidly; the size of grain-growing farms was not enlarged enough; and the intensity of land use fell. During the process of rapid economic growth, farm size did not expand commensurately, a factor associated with the extremely high cost of agricultural production. In addition, the rice price skyrocketed compared to international prices because the increasing cost of production was incorporated into established rice price policy. With respect to wheat and soybeans, production fell drastically because the price could not sufficiently compensate for the increase in cost of production. Thus, as noted at the beginning, the three problems of Japan's agriculture emerged.

Present Problems and Policy

Problems

As mentioned at the beginning, the problems facing Japanese agriculture at present—such as overproduction of rice, a decrease in
self-sufficiency in grain, a fall in the intensity of farmland use, and
the high cost of agricultural production—are invariably linked to the
increase in the number of farmers who lack risk-bearing entrepre-
neurship and dynamic responsiveness to changes in market conditions. The large numbers of class B part-time farmers who emerged
because land could not be concentrated in viable farms are less concerned about using their land effectively by responding quickly to
changes in market demand for agricultural products or reducing the
cost of production by introducing new technology. This is because of
the relative economic insignificance of agricultural income for them.

Table 5-11, which appeared earlier in the chapter, shows the economic characteristics of the types of farm households. Land utilization
by class B part-time farmers is small, and the major labor force consists
of women. However, disposable income per family of this type is
higher than for full-time farmers or class A part-time farmers. This
is made possible by income earned from off-farm employment for
which wages are about equal to the average wage of industry as a
whole. Agricultural income accounted for only 12 percent of gross
income of class B part-time farm households in 1978. But agricultural
production is by no means undertaken only for self-consumption,
because over 80 percent of the products are marketed, and most of
this is rice.

Both full-time and class A part-time farmers are gradually reducing
their ratios of rice production in response to changes in demand. In
contrast to this, class B part-time farmers are more and more inclined
to rely only on production of rice. This is because distribution of rice
is under governmental control; there is no marketing problem and
there is no risk because prices are officially guaranteed. Thus, one of
the reasons for overproduction of rice can definitely be attributed to
the increasing number of class B part-time farmers.

Next, let us consider the land utilization ratio of the farmers classified by type of farming—full-time or part-time.[10] The difference in

---

[10] Farmers are divided into two groups. One includes full-time and class A part-time
rmers, and the other consists of class B part-time farmers. There are definite dif-
ences between them which are based on the fact that the former earn their main
sehold income in agriculture and the latter do not. (See also Kuroda in this volume.)

agricultural production per hectare of farmland was only about 20 percent between full-time and class B part-time farmers in 1961; the difference expanded to 63 percent in 1978. It may be clear from the above that the class B part-time farmers are inefficiently utilizing farmland as a factor of production. Table 5-11 shows that agricultural production per hectare of farmland of full-time farmers is lower than that of class A part-time farmers. This is because those aged farmers who retired from their off-farm jobs are now included in the category of full-time farmers. According to the 1980 Census of Agriculture, such aged, full-time farmers are about 33.3 percent of all full-time farmers. The economic characteristics of these aged full-time farmers must be nearly the same as those of class B part-time farmers, but they are included in the class of full-time farmers for the purposes of the Economic Survey of Farm Households.

No statistics are available on production costs among class B part-time farmers, but in view of the small size of their farms, economies of scale are not applicable. Judging from this and other factors discussed thus far, it is almost certain that their costs of production are higher than those of full-time farmers. The high cost of production is compensated for by the government's rice price policy.

These class B part-time farms accounted for 70 percent of the total number of farms in 1975, owning 50 percent of the total farmland. It is clear from the above that the various problems confronting Japan's agriculture today are linked to class B part-time farmers.

To solve these problems it is necessary to reduce the number of class B part-time farmers and to foster viable farms by transferring farmland into the hands of full-time farmers. For such structural improvement to take place, there must be changes in the general economic situation (such as a decline in the rate of inflation) as well as changes in agricultural policy. The above analysis shows that the improper rice price policy and the outdated Agricultural Land Law are two important changes to be made.

Policy

It was about 1970 when Japanese agricultural policy began to move toward the solution of the problems that had appeared during the period of the Basic Law Administration and rapid economic growth. The Agricultural Land Law was revised in that year in order to concentrate farmland, and the Rice Cultivation Diversion Measure was initiated to cope with the overproduction problem in rice. Although nearly a decade has elapsed since then, during which confusion caused by the oil crisis has occurred, it must be said that basically the problems of agricultural policy have not changed. This shows that the fundamental means of solving these extremely difficult problems have not yet been worked out.

It has already been mentioned that these problems are all linked to structural change, that is, the increase in the number of class B part-time farmers. In fact, such structural change has advanced further in the last ten years. The rapid inflation caused by the oil crisis and the failure of the land policy brought about a marked rise in land prices in general, making the concentration of farmland in viable farms even more difficult. Although the Rice Cultivation Diversion Measure was carried out as a five-year program from 1971, it stopped short of a mere temporary solution of the overproduction of rice. Accordingly, the Measure for the Reorganization of the Use of Paddy Fields was adopted in 1978 as a ten-year program.

The difficulty in solving the problem of overproduction of rice lies in the fact that it is not only a socioeconomic problem, but also a technical one. It does not go too far to say that Japanese farmers have been concentrating on rice cultivation since the beginning of history, not to speak of the period of food shortage after the war. Moreover, technical developments in agriculture have overwhelmingly centered around rice. What is more important is the fact that approximately 50 percent of all farmland is in paddy fields suitable only for rice cultivation.

Although the Basic Law Administration foresaw in the long term an overproduction of rice, it failed to prevent it in its actual policy implementation. The government purchase prices of rice from the producer were kept at a high level, and land improvement investments, 70 percent of which were dependent on public financing, were made principally to increase the rice production of paddy fields. Perhaps this should be regarded as an error of judgment resulting from the "inertia" produced by the period of rice shortage, which was far too long.

The Measure for the Reorganization of the Use of Paddy Fields, which is aimed directly at the solution of the excess rice problem, consists of two policy measures. One is to determine the areas to be diverted from rice to other crops and to allocate them to individual producers. Although the total area necessary for diversion can be determined on the basis of a demand and supply forecast, allocating to individual producers constitutes a problem. The process is complex: it is neither a purely economic choice nor a purely administrative location; it is a mixture of both. The process begins with the allocation from the government to prefectures, then from prefectures to municipalities, and finally, from municipalities to individual producers. This allocation is based on the area for diversion and the upper-limit quantity of government purchases.

The second measure aimed at the solution of the rice problem is the provision of incentive payments per unit area prescribed for each diversion crop for those who carry out diversion. The incentive payment is determined according to the supply and demand for each crop. For instance, 55,000 yen per 0.1 hectare is to be paid for major diversion crops such as wheat, soybeans, and forage crops.

Table 5-15 demonstrates the problem of overproduction of rice. Although the total diverted area was just over 400,000 hectares in 1978, a total of nearly 800,000 is expected to be required from a long-term point of view. The financial burden of incentive pay for diversion amounted to 260 billion yen in 1978, accounting for 10 percent of the general account budget relating to agriculture. If similar subsidies are to be paid out for diversion areas totalling 800,000 hectares, it will amount to at least 500 billion yen.

As far as allocation of diversion area and public expenditure in the form of diversion incentive pay are concerned, the Measure for the Reorganization of the Use of Paddy Fields has only a supplementary relationship to the problem of fostering viable farms through the concentration of farmland. Moreover, although it is accompanied by economic incentives through diversion payments, administrative allocation of diversion areas is by no means desirable from the viewpoint of efficient resource allocation. The microeconomic problem of the allocation of resources is best solved if it is left to individual producers. No government can solve it better than the competitive market.

Except for public subsidies for rice cultivation diversion, the structure of agricultural finance remains unchanged (see table 5-6). The largest item of expenditure is related to the price support policy, and occupies 30 to 40 percent of the total. A slight decrease in this proportion was brought about because financial expenditure to sustain the rice price was reallocated as subsidies for diversion to nonrice crops. Public subsidies for land improvement projects continue to occupy a 25 percent share, while 5 percent goes for structural improvement.

With the realization that concentrated farmland ownership is difficult in face of the upsurge in land prices, the agricultural administration formulated two measures. One was the Law for the Improvement of Agricultural Development Areas, enacted in 1969. This was a legislative measure to restrict the diversion of farmland to other

TABLE 5-15. JAPAN: OVERPRODUCTION OF RICE, 1960–78

Year	Production (1)	Consumption (2)	Government stock in October (3)	Diverted area (4)	Planted area (5)	Government expenditures (100 mil. yen) (6)
		—1,000 mil. tons—		—1,000 ha—		
1960	12,858	12,618	440	—	3,142	—
1965	12,409	12,993	52	—	3,123	—
1970	12,686	11,948	7,202	—	2,836	818
1971	10,887	11,859	5,891	540	2,695	1,840
1972	11,897	11,948	3,074	567	2,640	2,029
1973	12,149	12,078	1,477	563	2,620	2,027
1974	12,292	12,033	615	313	2,724	1,279
1975	13,165	11,964	1,142	264	2,764	928
1976	11,772	11,819	2,641	195	2,779	759
1977	13,095	11,483	3,675	211	2,757	924
1978	12,589	11,364	5,722	437	2,516	2,606

Note: Dashes = Not applicable.
Source: Norinsuisansho (Ministry of Agriculture, Forestry and Fisheries), *Syokuryo-Kanri-Tokei-Nempo* (Statistical Yearbook on Food Control) (Tokyo, each year).

uses by adopting the zoning of agricultural areas (like the zoning of urban areas under the City Planning Law) so that the increase in farmland prices could be checked.

The second measure was intended to realize the concentration of farmland in viable farms through leasing. This policy is intended to concentrate farmland by decreasing the degree of tenant right protection, signifying a marked change in agricultural policy as stated in the Agricultural Land Law. It must be added that as a structural improvement policy, it is based on a distinctly different principle from that of the Agricultural Basic Law-oriented policy. Structural improvement policy based on this approach has been tried in various forms since 1970, and several legal measures were also introduced to relax restrictions under the Agricultural Land Law. Nonetheless, decisive legal change finally occurred when the Law for the Promotion of Farmland Utilization was enacted in 1980 and the later revision of the Agricultural Land Law.

In 1975, the Law for the Improvement of Agricultural Development Areas was revised. At the same time, a farmland utilization promotion project was introduced to bypass the issue of farmland mobility without enforcement of the Agricultural Land Law. The Law for the Promotion of Farmland Utilization is an expanded version of the above project. With respect to the three-year or five-year short-term lease, municipal communities are to act as a medium to carry out the project on a planned basis. Leasing based on this approach is not subject to restrictions under the Agricultural Land Law.

Changes in the Agricultural Land Law include two elements: First, the cultivators' tenant rights to the land are diluted so that apprehensions on the part of the owners will be reduced. Second, regions, including municipal communities, will promote the consolidation of farmland as a whole. Even though it is clear that leasing of high-priced land cannot take place without mutual trust between the lessor and the lessee, the Law for the Promotion of Farmland Utilization attempts to reinforce such trust by giving it a legal basis. This policy has only just begun. Whether or not it can reconcile fears on the part of the owners and lessees remains to be seen.

Today Japan's agricultural policy is confronted with the most difficult problems since 1960. The overproduction of rice and high land prices are both products of a long historical process, and the social and technical foundations that produced these problems have not yet disappeared. A long transitional period will be required to divert paddy fields to farmland suitable for upland crops and to develop and extend the cultivation techniques for wheat and forage crops. To divert land which is valued at more than 30 million yen per hectare from the hands of class B part-time farmers totalling more than 4 million to full-time farmers numbering just 500,000 is a task that will perhaps require a complete new policy measure. Still, unless Japan succeeds in achieving the objective, its 5.5 million hectares of farmland may not be used efficiently and other valuable domestic resources will not be put to their best use.

References

Egaitsu, Fumio. 1978. "Noka no Nogyo Toshi" (Investment Behavior of the Farm Household) in Yuzuru Kato and Fumio Egaitsu, eds., *Inflation to Nihon Nogyo* (Inflation and Japanese Agriculture) (Tokyo, Tokyo University Press).

Kuroda, Yoshimi, and Pan A. Yotopoulos. 1978. "A Microeconomic Analysis of the Production Behavior of the Farm Household in Japan: A Profit Function Approach," *Keizai Kenkyu* (The Economic Review) vol. 29, no. 2 (April).

Noringyogyo Kihonmondai Chosajimukyoku. 1960 (Secretariat for Research on Fundamental Problems of Agriculture, Forestry and Fisheries) *Nogyo no Kihoumondai to Kihontaisaku Kihontaisaku Kaisetsu Ban* (Fundamental Problems and Policy Measures of Agriculture) (Tokyo, Norin Tokei Kyokai).

Norinsuisansho. Various years. (Ministry of Agriculture, Forestry and Fisheries) *Sakumotsu Tokei* (Statistical Yearbook of Crops and Farmland) (Tokyo, various years).

———. 1980 (Ministry of Agriculture, Forestry and Fisheries) *Nosanbutsu No Jyuyo to Kyokyu no Choki Mitooshi* (Long-term Projection of the Demand and Supply of Agricultural Products) (Tokyo).

Norinsuisansho Daijinkanbo. 1977 (Minister of Agriculture, Forestry and Fisheries' Secretariat) *Shokuryo Jyuyo Bunseki* (Analysis of Demand for Food) (Tokyo).

———. 1972a. (Minister of Agriculture, Forestry and Fisheries' Secretariat) *Norin Gyoseishi* (History of the Agricultural and Forestry Administration, volume 6) (Tokyo).

———. 1972b. (Minister of Agriculture, Forestry and Fisheries' Secretariat) *Norin Gyoseishi* (History of the Agricultural and Forestry Administration, volume 8) (Tokyo).

wa Kazushi, ed. 1960. *Kajosyugyo to Nihon Nogyo* (Underemployment and apanese Agriculture) (Tokyo, Syunjyu-sya).

———. 1953. *Seikatsu Suijun no Sokutei* (Measurement of the Standard of Living) (Tokyo, Iwanami Shoten).

Tokiwa, Masaji. 1978. *Nosanbutsu Kabaku Seisaku* (Agricultural Price Policy) (Tokyo, Ienohikari Kyokai).

Tsuchiya, Keizo. 1955. "Nogyo ni Okeru Seisan Kansu no Kenkyu" (A Study of Agricultural Production Functions), *Nogyo Sogo Kenkyu* (Quarterly Journal of Agricultural Economy) vol. 9, no. 1 (January).

6

The Economics of U.S. Agricultural Policy

Bruce Gardner

Scope and Context

U.S. agricultural policy is best understood with reference to two general goals, which will be labeled "economic" and "political." The economic goal is to maximize the economic well-being of the nation as a whole. In the context of a market economy like that of the United States, it justifies government action and intervention in markets when markets fail to promote the general well-being. The political goal is to achieve and retain political office. It is a reason for market intervention in pursuit of votes.

Ideally, the political process could be viewed as a means by which economically optimal programs are attained; then the two goals would not conflict. In the actual U.S. situation, the goals do conflict; the current set of programs is not economically optimal. In the last analysis, this conclusion is a value judgment, but it is a very widely shared judgment. Indeed, not even the governmental officials most powerful matters of food and agricultural policy claim that the existing set programs is optimal. This is not to say that the programs are all ctionable, or worse than no programs at all, from the point of view

e Gardner is professor of agricultural and resource economics at the University land.

of promoting the nation's economic interests. It is to say that in the future there will continue to be substantial change in agricultural policy in pursuit of both economic and political goals.

In recent years there have been increasing calls for a unified U.S. food and agricultural policy that would integrate and coordinate governmental interventions. Recent interventions have covered an extremely broad spectrum from the resource level (for example, federal sponsorship of research and extension; policy concerning farmland, labor, credit, environmental and other resource issues) through commodity market management (the traditional focus of agricultural policy) to the retail food level (for example, policies addressed to health and safety of foods, food aid to the poor, and sporadic attempts at food price controls). A unified treatment of all these areas is not about to occur, but there is increased awareness that policy in the different areas should not be developed autonomously.

Despite the range of governmental action, it would be misleading to regard the agricultural economy as basically government directed, or as a kind of public utility. Food and agriculture in the United States remain essentially private, market-centered activities. Farmers' production decisions, production practices, kinds of food products sold (including their ingredients and marketing techniques employed), as well as the prices paid and received at all levels from resource prices through food prices, are basically the result of individual or corporate choice in a market context. To a large degree, farm prices and producer incomes remain market determined. Policy serves to put certain constraints on the range of market prices, production practices, and a few other regulated activities; but on the whole, the U.S. agricultural economy is moved predominantly by market forces.

While policy in such areas as food additives, the environment, and the regulation of price discovery (in farm and wholesale food product markets) is the subject of much current controversy, the traditional areas of farm commodity programs are of greatest importance for present purposes. It is on these programs, and their international ramifications, that this paper focuses. Table 6-1 shows the annual government payments to farmers under all the main programs. In either industry-aggregate or per capita terms, the past five years (1973–78) show less governmental activity in real terms than any other five-year period, except the years immediately following World War II.

However, the amount of government payments can be a misleading indicator of the degree of government involvement in commodity markets, primarily because supply control and government purchases of commodities to support market prices do not show up in these

TABLE 6-1. U.S. GOVERNMENT PAYMENTS TO FARMERS
($1972)

Year	Billion dollars	Dollars/farm population	Percent of net farm income	Percent of farm household income
1934	1.6	49	0.15	0.08
1935	2.0	63	0.11	0.07
1936	1.0	31	0.06	0.04
1937	1.1	36	0.06	0.04
1938	1.5	49	0.10	0.06
1939	2.7	86	0.17	0.10
1940	2.5	81	0.16	0.10
1941	1.7	57	0.08	0.05
1942	1.8	64	0.07	0.05
1943	1.7	65	0.05	0.04
1944	2.0	81	0.07	0.05
1945	1.9	76	0.06	0.04
1946	1.7	68	0.05	0.04
1947	0.6	24	0.02	0.02
1948	0.5	20	0.01	0.01
1949	0.4	15	0.01	0.01
1950	0.5	23	0.02	0.01
1951	0.5	23	0.02	0.01
1952	0.5	22	0.02	0.01
1953	0.4	18	0.02	0.01
1954	0.4	23	0.02	0.01
1955	0.4	20	0.02	0.01
1956	0.9	47	0.05	0.03
1957	1.6	89	0.09	0.06
1958	1.6	96	0.08	0.06
1959	1.0	61	0.06	0.04
1960	1.0	65	0.06	0.04
1961	2.2	146	0.12	0.08
1962	2.5	173	0.14	0.09
1963	2.4	165	0.06	0.04
1964	3.0	232	0.21	0.11
1965	3.3	268	0.19	0.11
1966	4.3	368	0.24	0.14
1967	3.9	358	0.25	0.14
1968	4.2	401	0.29	0.15
1969	4.4	424	0.27	0.14
1970	4.1	419	0.27	0.14
1971	3.3	348	0.22	0.11
1972	4.0	412	0.21	0.12
1973	2.4	248	0.08	0.05
1974	0.4	47	0.02	0.01
1975	0.6	69	0.03	0.02
1976	0.5	62	0.04	0.02
1977	1.1	146	0.09	0.04
1978	1.5	180	0.09	0.04

Sources: Computed from data in U.S. Department of Agriculture, *Farm Income Statistics*, Statistical Bulletin No. 627 (Washington, D.C., October 1979); and Council of Economic Advisors, *Economic Report of the President* (Washington, D.C., GPO).

data. For example, government's role from 1948 to 1955 is under-
stated in the table because in that period governmental commodity
acquisition was an important price support mechanism. In the post-
1972 period, however, supply control and government purchases also
have been less extensively used.

Not only has the market orientation of U.S. agricultural commodity
policy increased in recent years, but many commodities have traditionally been free from massive intervention. For an overall view of
major commodities affected by farm programs, see table 6-2. The
table indicates that, counting cattle as an essentially free-market com-

TABLE 6-2. MAJOR PROGRAMS BY COMMODITY
(billion dollars)

Commodity	Farm value 1978	Nature of program
Cattle	28.1	• Import restraints
Feed grains	16.0	• Deficiency payments, price supports, voluntary acreage restraints, storage incentives
Dairy products	12.7	• Price supports, classified pricing, import controls
Soybeans	11.1	• No effective program[a]
Hogs	7.7	• No program
Hay	7.1	• No program
Poultry and eggs	7.8	• No program
Wheat	4.8	• Deficiency payments, price supports, mandatory acreage set-asides, storage incentives, grazing payments
Cotton	3.9	• Deficiency payments, price supports
Tobacco	2.5	• Acreage/marketing controls, price supports
Rice	1.0	• Deficiency payments, price supports, storage incentives
Sugar beets and cane	1.1	• Import levies
Peanuts	0.8	• Price supports, acreage limitations
Top six vegetables and fruits (potatoes, tomatoes, grapes, apples, lettuce, oranges)	5.7	• Essentially free market, but some import restraints and marketing orders

Sources: U.S. Department of Agriculture, Agricultural Statistics, 1979 (Washington, D.C., 1979);
and U.S. Department of Agriculture, Farm Income Statistics, Statistical Bulletin No. 627 (Washington,
D.C., October 1979).

[a] There is a support price for soybeans but it is so far below current and prospective market
prices as to be meaningless.

modity, no effective farm program exists for $68 billion or just over half of the $112 billion of commodities that make up the great bulk of U.S. agricultural production (USDA, 1979a).

It should be noted, however, that the table includes only explicitly price-making programs. Regulatory powers pertaining to broad classes of activity—such as executive branch authority pertaining to export embargoes, inspection and grading of products, taxation, environmental protection, wage and occupational safety rules, food quality and safety regulation, special provisions for cooperatives, regulation of credit and transportation—are all omitted. So the United States has not after all attained a farm sector that would be entirely pleasing to Adam Smith.

Behind the political sources of agricultural policy lie objective and perceived economic conditions that call for governmental intervention. Less than 4 percent of the U.S. population live on the 2.3 million U.S. farms (USDA, 1979c). It is customary to attribute their political muscle to overrepresentation of the less populated states in the Senate and the presidential electoral college, and to peculiarities of the congressional legislative process, particularly the dominance of the committees on agriculture (and perhaps even more important, the committees that appropriate funds to carry out legislation) by Southern-state representatives of agricultural interests. However, in the last fifteen years there has been substantial reform of the congressional committee system. The survival of legislation favoring farm interests despite these reforms emphasizes a fact not as widely recognized as it should be; namely, that farm interests could not command the political strength necessary to enact legislation favorable to them without some support, or at least lack of opposition, from nonfarm people.

This support has many roots and branches, but three perceptions about it seem of primary importance. The *first* is the belief that farmers are in some sense an economically hard-pressed, if not deprived group. Apparently the most potent statements by politicians in support of farm programs are those that invoke the spectre of widespread bankruptcy in the absence of action. The *second* important perception is that a principal reason for farmers' economic position is their relatively disadvantaged position in the marketplace—the firms from which farmers buy and to which they sell have a degree of market power which farmers lack utterly. This perception lends support to the idea that economic justice would be promoted by redistributing income to farmers by means of price supports or measures to increase farmers' bargaining power. The *third* perception is that in the absence of governmental intervention there would be an intolerable degree of instability in the commodity markets, adversely affecting not only farmers but also consumers of food and fiber.

Given this policy environment, it is possible that the 1980s will see changes in the perception of facts, particularly with regard to the first item listed, that will make a substantial difference in policy. For evidence is increasing that farmers today are in no sense an economically deprived class. In 1978, the estimated average income of farm operators was $23,300 (USDA, 1979c). This figure equals, or perhaps slightly exceeds, comparable incomes in the nonfarm sector. There are of course many farm families with lower incomes, and many below the poverty line. But poor farm residents are negligible participants in the commercial markets for farm products. It has been the case for many years that the poverty that exists in agriculture cannot practicably be remedied through price support or other commodity-oriented farm programs. Although having less than one-quarter of the farm population, commercial farms with $40,000 or more in annual sales produce about three-fourths of U.S. farm output. The mean income of this category of farmers in 1978 was $39,700, of which $8,100 was from off-farm sources. For the smallest farms, with less than $2,500 in sales, mean income was $18,900, of which $17,200, or 91 percent, was from off-farm sources, principally nonagricultural employment (USDA, 1979a).

Not only do commercial farmers have generally comfortable income levels, but they are in addition owners of net worth in agricultural assets well beyond the wealth ownership of the nonfarm population. In 1978, the farm operators with $40,000 or more in annual sales had an average of $700,000 in assets and $150,000 in debt for an average proprietor's equity (net worth) of $550,000 (USDA, 1979d).

At the same time, the great expense of the physical plant necessary for commercial farming creates difficulty for young persons entering agriculture—a difficulty that is aggravated by the substantial inflation premium in interest rates. A farmer who borrows half the funds necessary to buy a farm will be likely to find the current returns from land at best barely covering interest costs. Although these costs are expected to be offset by asset-price appreciation over the longer term, current cash-flow difficulties can be a burden. Nonetheless, cash-flow problems are similar to the problem of rural poverty in not being amenable to solution by means of traditional commodity-program approaches.

Let us turn to the second public perception conducive to governmental intervention in favor of farmers' commercial interests, the idea that farmers are unfairly treated in the marketplace. The realization that commercial farmers cannot be characterized as an economically deprived class may dampen this perception, but it is possible that farmers have a case for intervention even if their incomes are not low. For it could be that the rate of return on investment in farming is low relative to nonagricultural investments. Nonetheless, recent attempts to estimate rates of return in agriculture, for example Hottel and Evans (1980), find average rates of return in agriculture higher over the past ten to fifteen years than the rates of return earned by investors in U.S. common stocks or bonds, or by most publicly held nonfarm corporations.

Governmental intervention may nonetheless be justified to counteract the market power of large corporations in agriculture and food marketing. But while the policy remedies may involve antitrust or regulatory action in agricultural business enterprises, there is no apparent reason to utilize commodity programs of the traditional kinds in this area.

The issue of instability has been heightened by the commodity price gyrations of the 1970s. These events gave a new impetus to policies such as grain stockpiling programs and U.S. participation in international trade and commodity agreements. Still, the extent to which such policies promote the interests of U.S. farmers is a matter of some dispute, and the steps taken to date seem to have had only modest stabilizing effects (discussed further below).

Despite the preceding considerations, which suggest a factual basis for expecting less governmental activity that is narrowly in pursuit of farmers' commercial interests, programs of this type continue to be important. They are especially important, in the present context, in that they influence heavily the environment for international commerce in agricultural commodities.

The commodity programs that are most important for the U.S. farm sector, for U.S. international relations in general, and for U.S.–Japanese trade in particular are the programs that regulate the U.S. grain markets. Not only are the products affected most important in the international arena, but in addition, programs for the grains tend to set the tone for U.S. farm policy as a whole, both domestically and internationally. There are also lessons to be learned from other commodity areas where trade issues are intertwined with domestic policy: livestock and meat (primarily beef), dairy, sugar, and certain specialty products. The specialty products include citrus fruits and nuts produced or marketed by cooperatives under marketing orders. The relevance of marketing orders to international trade arises from a tendency to segment markets into a higher-priced fresh market that is predominantly domestic and lower-priced processing outlets that often involve exports.

Economics and Politics of Current Programs

Grains: Main policy instruments

There are three important features of current U.S. grain programs: some of their provisions are only recently established, they are complex, and they are constantly changing. All three contribute to making it very difficult to provide a simple economic analysis of these programs that one can have much confidence in, or whose relevance will endure for more than a few years.

The legislation authorizing the current (1980) programs for the major field crops (grains and cotton) is the Food and Agriculture Act of 1977. Even before the first crops were produced under the act in 1978, however, the programs were significantly altered by the Emergency Agriculture Act of 1978, a response to political pressure brought to bear by the American Agriculture Movement in early 1978. Further changes were made in the Agricultural Adjustment Act of 1980, enacted in March 1980. The 1981 crops will be the last produced under the 1977 act. The (Republican) Reagan administration will have the opportunity to make its mark in new legislation.

The 1977 act contains substantial evolutionary changes from preceding legislation. The Agriculture and Consumer Protection Act of 1973 and the Rice Production Act of 1975 established programs similar in most major respects, but except for rice, these programs had not been tested because of the strength of the grain markets. If history is a guide, despite its sharp differences from the Carter administration, the Reagan administration will not result in dramatic changes in farm policy, but in continued evolutionary development.

Although important differences exist among the programs for the five principal grains (wheat, rice, corn, sorghum, and barley), the basic structure of governmental regulation is the same for all of them. This structure is especially notable in that it establishes separate policy instruments for attaining the political and economic goals of farm policy. In this respect, probably the single most important feature of the 1977 act, continued from the 1973 act and earlier legislation, is the establishment of *two different regulated prices* for most of the major crops: one a guaranteed "target" price to producers, the other a "loan rate" at which the market price is supported via Commodity Credit

Corporation (CCC) loans and purchases. The importance of the existence of two separate prices is that it allows separation of the goal of farm income support from the goal of commodity price stabilization. One can, for example, guarantee prices to farmers substantially above world grain market prices, yet maintain U.S. market prices low enough to promote exports. Ideally, it might be hoped that the political capabilities of producers to extract transfers from the U.S. Treasury would be used in increasing target prices, while allowing markets to clear without the imposition of the uneconomic stockpiles, attempts to control production, and export subsidies that characterized pre-1972 farm programs.

Target price and deficiency payments

The mechanism for guaranteeing the target price is a "deficiency" payment to farmers of an amount equal to the difference between the target price and the higher of the U.S. average market price received by farmers or the loan rate. Because most farmers sell their crops at some price other than the U.S. average price, and because the U.S. average farm price may be below the loan rate (as it was for wheat throughout the summer of 1977), the "guarantee" is not exactly the target price either for any individual or for all farmers as a group. Nonetheless, the essence of the program is to ensure program participants of a minimum level of producer receipts per unit of quantity produced.

The results are depicted schematically in figure 6-1. With no program, the farmer's price would be P_o, a price judged on economic or political criteria to be too low. A program is desired to guarantee producer price P_p instead. However, supporting the market price at P_p would result in excess supply equal to the distance AB. Such excess supplies accumulated in U.S. government hands in very large quantities during the 1950s and 1960s. This experience led to the adoption of the deficiency-payment approach in the 1973 and 1977 acts. The guarantee of P_p induces producers to undertake production of quantity Q_p. This quantity is then sold through the usual market channels, resulting in a market price of P_c. It is this price that is built into the consumer cost of agricultural products. Thus, producers receive more for their efforts and consumers pay less for food. The net gain above opportunity costs for producers is the hatched area P_oP_pBE. The net gain to consumers is the hatched area P_oP_cED. The gains are not costless, however, in that the taxpayer must finance deficiency payments equal to area P_cP_pBD.

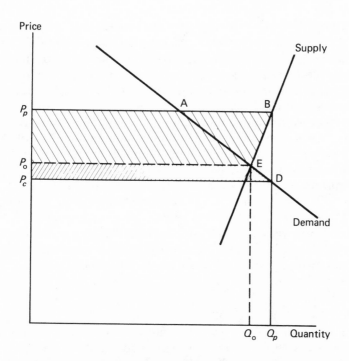

Figure 6-1. Schematic effect of target price on producer and
market price.

Market price floor

Target prices do nothing to support market prices and indeed tend
to drive them down by encouraging production. The 1977 act recognizes to an extent not incorporated in previous legislation that market prices for the major crops are essentially world prices, and that
therefore one cannot support U.S. prices for exported commodities
without either large excess supply at the support price or else some
form of export subsidy. Because the use of export subsidies to maintain a relatively high domestic price seems to have become politically
disreputable since the Soviet purchases of 1972, and because the adverse consequences of past large excess supplies at high support prices
are by now a lesson well learned, the 1977 act treads lightly on market
support prices.

The 1977 act maintains the concept of a market price floor and
does so through the traditional mechanism of the loan rate, the price
which farmers may receive as a "nonrecourse loan" from the Com-

modity Credit Corporation. The loan is "nonrecourse" in the sense that the CCC must accept grain at the loan rate to pay off CCC loans. Consequently, grain will be delivered to the CCC whenever the market price falls below the loan level by more than the transportation and handling costs of putting grain under loan. The loan program imposes a market price floor.

A market price floor added to a target price or deficiency payment program does not add appreciably to producers' returns. Its role has more to do with the economic management of commodity markets. For example, in the case depicted in figure 6-1 it might be desired to maintain the market price at P_o while paying producers P_p. This goal can be attained by imposing *both* a target price of P_p and a loan rate of P_o. The result is that Q_p is produced and Q_o consumed, the difference being added to CCC stocks. Thus, under the 1977 act, a market support price's main role is to govern stockpiling of commodities as insurance against future random variation in production and export demand.

Storage and stabilization programs

Under traditional CCC loan programs for purposes of supporting market prices, the CCC acquires stocks of commodities delivered to pay off nonrecourse loans. The release of these stocks had never been developed as part of a comprehensive price stabilization program. Stocks of various commodities have been released at 105 to 115 percent of the loan rate, or at the discretion of the secretary of agriculture. The 1977 act provides a framework for more systematic specification of policy instruments in market management (in addition to the loan rate). These include: payments for commodity storage by farmers, specified "trigger prices" at which payments cease, and subsidies for the construction of on-farm storage. The specification of these policy variables has been changed a few times in the period since the 1977 act became law, and they add up to a rather complex program. Its basic intention is to have grain held by producers in a farmer-owned reserve, yet at the same time to give the government some control over the size of stocks.

Acreage restraints

Although the policy instruments so far discussed would appear sufficient for both farm income support and for price stabilization, programs to restrain production also exist. Such programs can be used in farm income support, for example, by regulating the quantity produced to the point that supply equals demand at point A in figure

6-1. This approach is in fact used in the United States for tobacco. In the case of grains, however, wheat producers rejected the production-control approach in a watershed referendum in 1963, that led to the evolutionary development resulting in the 1977 act. Both the Nixon-Ford (in 1973–76) and the Carter administrations indicated a belief that production restraints, as implemented by programs to idle productive cropland, were unnecessarily wasteful.

Nonetheless, two outcomes of 1977 act programs are encouraging the use of supply restraints. First, even if below long-run trend prices, target prices increase price expectations by eliminating low-price outcomes and thus tend to promote overproduction. Thus, in figure 6-1 a supply control program to bring production back to Q_o instead of Q_p is attractive. Second, the large deficiency payments that low market prices may engender can be reduced by reducing production. In figure 6-1 there would be zero U.S. Treasury payments to achieve the producer price of P_p if production controls put the market at point A. Given the current strong interest in reducing the federal budget deficit, restraining production is an irresistible alternative. The production-restraining mechanism in current grain programs is inducement to set aside cropland acreage, that is, to allocate productive cropland to less productive soil-conserving uses. In addition, the Agricultural Adjustment Act of 1980 establishes a lower target price for production beyond normal yield on "normal crop acreage" (NCA) established for each farm by the U.S. Department of Agriculture. For example, the 1980 wheat target price falls from $3.63 per bushel on NCA to $3.08 for "excess" production.

In summary, it should be noted that the preceding discussion of policy instruments, although already somewhat complex, is greatly simplified. The types of instruments used, and their interaction, vary greatly from one commodity to another. And all involve complications not mentioned yet. Still, the essence of current U.S. programs for the major crops can be encapsulated in three primary sets of policy instruments, each with its own role. They are: (1) target price and deficiency payments—to support farm income; (2) loan rates, storage payments, and release prices—to provide price stabilization; (3) acreage set-asides—to reduce excess supplies and deficiency payments.

Grains: Economic effects of current programs

To spell out more precisely the national and international consequences of the current programs, it is necessary to consider the actual supply–demand situation in the United States as well as the specific provisions of the programs. This section concentrates on wheat as representative of the food grains, and corn and soybeans as representative of feed crops.

The analytical issues bring out the difficulty of making firm judgments about program effects. Furthermore, a full assessment of the consequences of policy require counterfactual analysis—attempting to ascertain what would have been the case under alternative policy regimes. Not enough is known about the U.S. agricultural economy to permit making firm quantitative counterfactual judgments. Nonetheless, plausible estimates can be made on many issues in qualitative terms, and sometimes quantitatively. That is, we can feel confident of the direction of the effect of many programs on food prices, farmers' incomes, trade flows, and other variables. And in some instances plausible estimates in terms of dollars have been made by agricultural economists.

Wheat

The target price for wheat for the 1980 crop was $133.22 per metric ton ($3.63 per bushel).[1] The loan rate, which puts a floor under the market price, was $91.85 per ton. The average market price received by farmers for 1979 wheat was about $140 per ton, above both support prices (USDA, 1980). Prices received by U.S. farmers in the 1970s have been volatile, and have moved roughly in proportion to world trading prices. Following a drawdown of carryover stocks to the minimum necessary to maintain flows through the marketing system ("pipeline" stocks) and extremely favorable prices for producers in 1973–75, the 1976 and 1977 wheat crops were large enough to generate a substantial price decline. Measured in 1978 dollars, the real farm price of wheat fell from $227 per ton in the 1973 crop year to $91 per ton in the 1977 crop year.[2] Note that the 1973 price is well above the current target price and that the depressed 1977 price is still above the current market floor price, in real terms. This low support price is the reason for saying that the current program is market oriented—CCC loans will not hold market prices above plausible open-market levels in the years immediately ahead.

[1] Quantity units used in this chapter are metric tons, with prices in dollars per metric ton. However, prices are also quoted in bushels, following U.S. practice. There are 36.74 bushels of wheat in a metric ton. An idiosyncrasy of the U.S. bushel is that a bushel of wheat weighs more than a bushel of some other grains; for example, there are 39.37 bushels of corn in a metric ton.

[2] The 1977 crop year for wheat runs from June 1, 1977, to May 31, 1978. June 1 is an arbitrary date at which new-crop winter wheat is beginning to be extensively harvested, although some is harvested in May in Texas, and northern spring wheat is not fully harvested until September.

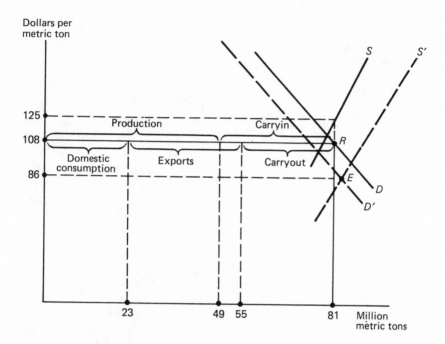

Figure 6-2. The U.S. wheat market in 1978–79.

The overall situation as of the 1978 crop year is depicted in figure 6-2. The total supply available was 49 million metric tons of production plus 32 million tons in beginning stocks (or "carryin" stocks). The disposition of this wheat was: U.S. domestic consumption, 23 million tons; exports, 32 million tons; and ending (or "carryout") stocks, 26 million tons. The total demand that cleared the market at the $108 average price was 81 million tons (USDA, 1979c).

In analyzing the effect of the wheat program in the context of figure 6-2, it is first necessary to consider the supply function. The program does not simply move us along the supply curve S. Indeed, we cannot even assume that a point on the program-constrained supply curve is given by the target price and actual output.[3] The reason consists of two complications in the wheat program that have not yet been considered.

First, producers do not receive payments on the full amount of production. The secretary of agriculture annually determines an "al-

---

[3] Even apart from the fact that actual production is often significantly different from intended production because of the random element in yields. Actually, U.S. 1978 yields seem to have been about on trend.

location factor," which is multiplied by a producer's program production (acreage planted for harvest multiplied by the program yield, determined by the producer's local Agricultural Stabilization and Conservation Service (ASCS) committee) before calculating payments. The allocation factor represents the secretary's judgment of the ratio of actual production "needs"; for example, if 65 million tons is judged to be needed for purposes of consumption, exports, and additions to carryover stocks, and actual production is 75 million tons, then the allocation factor is 65 ÷ 75 = .867. Suppose that a producer's program production is 500 metric tons, with a difference between the target price and the market price of $125 − 108 = $17; then his deficiency payment will not be 500 tons × $17 per ton = $8,500, but instead will be $8,500 × .867 = $7,369. Therefore the effective price guarantee is not the target price of $125, but rather $108 + .867($17) = $122.74 per ton.

The second complication is that the set-aside program, which shifts the supply curve, works by conditioning eligibility for deficiency payments on holding one acre out of production for each five planted for harvest. The ratio 1:5 is called a 20 percent set-aside. This is the figure that has applied to 1978 and 1979 wheat. The set-aside acreage must lie fallow or be used in one of a few specified low-value activities. Consequently, the incentive price for growing wheat is not the target price because each added acre involves the requirement to set aside one-fifth of one acre.

The overall production incentives caused by the target price and set-aside programs together may be analyzed as follows. The expected marginal revenue from an additional bushel of wheat *in the absence* of a program, or for a nonparticipant, is the expected market price P (which may be the loan rate). The expected marginal revenue *for a participant* is P plus two additional elements. First is the expected deficiency payment, which is the target price, PT, minus the expected market price multiplied by the allocation factor, the fraction of additional production expected to be covered. The target price element is always positive and would therefore induce additional production in the absence of controls. The incentive exists even if the expected market price is greater than the target price, because the target price eliminates some potential low-price outcomes that producers would otherwise take into account. Second, there are the controls in the form of a set-aside as a requisite for payments. The expected marginal revenue for participants must therefore be reduced by the fraction of acreage set aside (γ) times the difference between the expected price of wheat and the comparable expected marginal returns from the best use of set-aside land.

Putting these elements together, the marginal revenue for a participating wheat grower is

$$MR = P + \alpha(PT - P) - \gamma(P - \tilde{P})$$
$$= (1 - \alpha - \gamma)P + \alpha PT + \gamma\tilde{P}$$

where γ is the set-aside ratio, α is the allocation factor, and $\tilde{P}$ is the net value of set-aside wheat land in permitted uses. For 1978 wheat, $\gamma = .20$; $\alpha = .96$, and let us assume $\tilde{P} = 0$. Then we have

$$MR = (1 - .96 - .2) \, \$108 + (.96) \, \$125$$
$$= \$112.72 \text{ per metric ton}$$

Thus, the producer price expectation under the program is nearer the market price than the target price. The calculation, however, is quite conjectural, especially the value for $\tilde{P}$, and varies from one producer to the next. This is the reason it is difficult to specify the location of the supply function S. With universal participation in set-asides, S' would be expected to be shifted by about 20 percent. But universal participation is not to be expected. And those who do participate may be able to choose substantially poorer land for set-asides so that production does not decline by as much as acreage.[4] As a matter of fact, 1978 U.S. wheat acreage harvested was down 14.5 percent from the preceding year (when the 1977 act was not in effect), while 1978 production was down 11.5 percent (USDA, 1980).

Difficult as it may be to believe, the preceding discussion is a considerable simplification of the supply side incentives facing wheat producers in 1978. First, the 1977 act also contained a provision for disaster payments, essentially subsidized insurance against crop failure, whose benefits were contingent upon participation in set-asides. Second, there was a voluntary acreage reduction program that made $\alpha = 1.0$ for some producers. Third, there was a payment to producers who chose to graze cattle on winter wheat rather than harvest it for

[4] These considerations about incentives have concerned expanded wheat production along the same underlying supply function that would exist in the absence of any program. However, production control schemes based on acreage are usually expected to generate incentives for increased yield—use of more fertilizer, denser planting, and so forth, to increase production from given acreage. This incentive is reduced but not eliminated, in the 1977 act by the limitation of payments to "normal" production per acre. The effectiveness of the limitation to normal yields depends on the Agricultural Stabilization and Conservation Service actually using average yields for program purposes and not, for example, eliminating the exceptionally dry years. And even a strict average-yield criterion for program yield would still not eliminate the incentive to increase expected yield. The reason is that while there is no deficiency-payment reward to above-average yields, there is still a deficiency-payment loss to below-average yields. There is increased reason to attempt to ensure at least an average yield, that is, to use more pesticides and in fact to set a target yield above normal yield.

grain. Fourth, there were tie-ins between wheat and the programs for other grains and cotton. Fifth, the price guarantee reduced the variability of returns as well as increasing the expected return, and this should have increased production by risk-averse producers. These complications make it still more difficult to specify the location of S and S' in figure 6-2.

On the demand side, there is a better base point to work from in that the wheat supply of 81 million metric tons did in fact clear the market at $108 per ton. The question is how demand was shifted from a no-program situation. It is likely that demand would have declined in the absence of the programs, primarily because of the loan rate and the farmer-owned reserves. Although the loan rate is well below the 1978–79 market price, it provides insurance against drastic future price declines. This increases the demand for carryover stocks. So do the payments to producers for keeping grain in the extended CCC loan program. In the absence of the program, more wheat would have to clear the current consumption and export market, hence depressing price.

The net result of all the preceding considerations is that in the absence of the programs, the supply of U.S. wheat would shift to the right, and the demand for U.S. wheat would shift to the left. The income of wheat producers would fall considerably. The complexities of the programs are such that it is not possible to be precise about *how much* supply and demand would shift. The most likely scenario seems to be on the order of D' and S' as shown in figure 6-2. The wheat programs hold supply somewhat below and producer prices substantially above the levels they would otherwise have. More important for international considerations, U.S. wheat programs are probably increasing market (consumer and export) wheat prices—the current restrained equilibrium being at point R in figure 6-2, with the no-program equilibrium at a point like E. The exact results depend on the supply and demand shifts and on their elasticities, neither of which is well established empirically. The relevant elasticity of demand for U.S. wheat is probably quite high because of the importance of the export market. Econometric estimates range from $-.15$ (Taylor and Talpaz, 1979) to -6.0 or more (Grennes, Johnson, and Thursby, 1977), depending on the length of run and model specification. The estimates that seem most pertinent to the present context—total demand (the sum of domestic use, exports, and private stock demand) in a year-to-year adjustment period—indicate an elasticity of demand of about $-.66$ (Gardner, 1979, p. 124). The available work on the supply side suggests an elasticity of supply of U.S wheat of about 0.3

for a one-year period of adjustment. The overall picture in figure 6-2 suggests a U.S. wheat price falling to perhaps $90 per ton under 1978–79 conditions without the 1977 act programs. Therefore, the program elements together caused roughly a 15 percent increase in market price and a 20 percent ($1.0 billion) increase in producer gross receipts. In an independent estimate, Robinson (1979) suggests that 1978 wheat prices were increased 50 to 60 cents per bushel, or 16 to 20 percent, by the programs.

The assertion that U.S. wheat programs are raising *market* prices may be surprising. Because there are no significant distortions between U.S. and world trade prices (that is, off-shore prices, not landed, duty-paid prices in any particular country), a higher U.S. price means a higher world price. Yet a target price and deficiency payment program as sketched in figure 6-1 *lowers* market price. In an international context, such a program shifts the supply of U.S. exports to the right and can therefore be regarded as a *de facto* export subsidy. However, the assertion implied in figure 6-2 is that the set-asides and stockpiling programs have more than offset the supply response to the target price, so that in fact the U.S. wheat programs supported world wheat prices to some extent rather than reducing them.

The 1979 crop year for wheat provides an instance of how the 1977 act programs work in a quite different market environment. In June 1979, at the very beginning of the U.S. crop year, it became probable that the Soviet Union would experience a possibly severe grain production shortfall. Within a few weeks in late June, U.S. cash wheat prices rose about 25 percent (in Kansas City from a $3.40–$3.60 to a $4.40–$4.60 range). This rise essentially eliminated the prospects for deficiency payments and reached the price levels requiring a cessation of storage subsidy payments in the farmer-owned reserve (FOR) program, which contained about 10 million tons of wheat at the time. These developments meant that wheat would be on essentially an open-market basis for the 1979–80 crop year (ending May 31, 1980). It has been argued that the 1977 act programs, particularly the release of FOR grain, provided a damping influence on price increases in this period. (Council of Economic Advisers, 1980, pp. 151–152.) It seems undeniable that prices would have risen even more sharply had grain stocks been as low as they were in the 1973 and 1975 episodes of excess demand. However, it is not clear that stocks were much higher than they would have been without the FOR program. Ending U.S. wheat stocks were already almost 30 million tons in 1977 without benefit of the FOR program, and were actually a little less (25 million tons) as of May 31, 1979. Nonetheless, it is true that some 3 million tons of U.S. wheat were released from the FOR program and some of it probably went into consumption and export channels that it would not have in the absence of the FOR program. Three million tons is roughly 5 percent of the U.S. wheat supply. If half this quantity went into disappearance channels, and this was caused by the program, then the program could have held prices down by 2 to 5 percent.

It seems likely, however, that a more important policy influence in 1979, as in 1978, was the price-enhancing effect of set-asides. Indeed, the absurdity of set-asides in a year of grain shortage illustrates the chief deficiency of acreage controls as a stabilizing device. For winter wheat, the decision to impose set-asides must be made up to a year before reliable information on the relevant world crop becomes available. It is too blunt an instrument, and, in contrast to stockpiling decisions, not reversible. The absence of a sharper and longer-lasting price explosion in 1979 depended more on the luck of exceptional U.S. grain yields than on the foresight of policy makers.

Corn

Although the programs for the four feed grains (corn, sorghum, barley, and oats) differ substantially, corn is most important. In 1977 it accounted for $13 billion of the $16 billion farm value of all feed grains. Although a substantially greater tonnage of corn is exported than of wheat, in percentage terms the export market is less important to U.S. corn producers. Corn prices peaked later than wheat prices in the mid-1970s, the highest prices being generated by the U.S. production shortfall in 1974 rather than the earlier export demand boom. And corn prices, while they fell by one-third between the 1975–77 peak and their 1976–77 to 1977–78 levels in real terms, generated neither the economic distress nor the political outcry that plummeting wheat prices did.

The main differences between the corn and wheat programs are: (1) the corn target price is much closer to the loan rate (market price floor), and (2) the set-aside program is more complicated but has had a smaller effect on production. The relative ineffectiveness in corn of set-asides of the type used on wheat follows from the closeness of the target price to the loan (market support) price. The 1978 target price was $82.70 per metric ton and the loan rate was $78.70. The set-aside requirement was 10 percent. Even with an allocation factor of 100 percent, the largest expected marginal revenue per ton from participation is

$$MR = (-1.1) \$78.70 + \$82.70 = \underline{\$74.83}$$

that is, the producer would expect to receive less by participating in set-asides than from not participating, since the minimum market price is the $78.70 loan rate.[5] In anticipation of this difficulty, a voluntary diversion program was put into place for corn in which an additional 10 percent of acreage could be added to the set-aside acreage, and in return the producer would receive a payment that amounted in 1978 to about $80 per metric ton not produced. At about 2.5 tons per acre, roughly the U.S. average yield, the payment is $200 per acre, far above the rental value of land. This considerable incentive resulted in participation of about 6 million acres of corn land in set-asides, at a cost to the U.S. Treasury of about $520 million in 1978 (USDA, 1979c). Nonetheless, harvested corn acreage turned out to be only about 1 million acres below the preceding year (which had no acreage restraint program), and U.S. average yield was up about 10 percent from 2.3 to 2.6 metric tons per acre.

In 1979 some adjustments were made in the corn program but the basic incentives were the same. Participation in acreage reduction was again only minimally effective and was again far outweighed by increases in yields. Nonetheless, market prices remained well above the target price because of strong export demand.

The net result for corn, and the other feed grains as well, is that the 1977 act programs, although they distributed about $1 billion per year to feed grain producers in deficiency, diversion, and disaster payments in 1978 and 1979, had only a small effect on production or market price. It is likely, however, that the CCC loan and farmer-held reserve programs did have a significant effect in that without them the very large feed grain supply (a record amount, 8.5 percent above the preceding year's supply, which was also a record) could well have driven farm prices down to the $80 per ton loan rate. At the same time, these programs have resulted in somewhat higher levels of carryover stocks of feed grains. These will help buffer sharp price rises which might otherwise have occurred in late 1979 or the years ahead. The feed grains program is thus functioning essentially as a stabilizing program with respect to market price, with occasional side payments to support producer income. This is in contrast to wheat,

[5] Eligibility for loans is also tied to participation in set-asides, and this provides additional incentive to participate. However, as long as the CCC acquires *someone's* corn to support the market price, a producer obtains roughly the same benefit even if his own corn is not eligible for the CCC loan program. It should also be noted that if a producer has a permitted alternative use for set-aside land that is almost as remunerative as corn production, it may pay him to participate in set-asides even for a small deficiency payment.

where supply control has had an effect in increasing market prices as well as producer income.

Other field crops

The other feed grain crops have similar programs, but with a few important differences. Sorghum and barley have a ratio of target price to loan rate and set-asides more nearly approaching wheat's than corn's. Oats have no target price protection or set-asides at all. Rice has the unique feature of deficiency payments tied to historical (allotment) acreage rather than current planted acreage. This feature permits the achievement of farm income support via deficiency payments to be more completely divorced from market intervention for rice than for the other crops; a producer cannot increase his payments by means of expanding output in response to the target price, so that the move from Q_o to Q_p in figure 6-1 would not occur.

Cotton is unique in the flexibility of its loan (market support) price. Subject to a floor well below market prices, the cotton loan rate is tied to a world market price. The intention is to avoid support prices which would impinge upon export demand. For similar reasons, the 1977 act empowers the secretary of agriculture to reduce the market support price of grains when the market price has declined to within 5 percent of the market support price in the preceding year. Although the 5 percent criterion was in fact met for both corn and wheat in 1977–78, the secretary chose not to exercise this option.

The market for soybeans is even less regulated than the cotton market, being protected only by a loan rate well below the market prices of recent years. However, the programs for other crops have probably had indirect effects on the production and price of soybeans. There is some reason to fear that a program that stabilizes the grain markets may destabilize the soybean market. A set-aside program for corn makes the production of soybeans more attractive at a given soybean-to-corn price ratio. To discourage such substitution, the 1977 act specifies that production of set-aside crops plus set-aside acreage plus production of other cash crops cannot exceed normal crop acreage (established by the Agricultural Stabilization and Conservation Service based on 1977 plantings) if a producer is to be eligible for program benefits. It is not clear, however, that the program provisions have countervailed cross-commodity substitution incentives created by target prices and production restraints for the grains. Unfortunately, there exist no reliable econometric estimates of such effects.

Livestock programs

Intervention in the meat markets is limited to relatively minor restrictions on imported beef. Only about 7 percent of U.S. beef consumption is imported, and the import restraints have amounted to perhaps 20 or 30 percent of the imported total. The resulting beef price increase is estimated to be in the neighborhood of 1 or 2 percent (Houck, 1974; Freebairn and Rausser, 1975). Beef import restraints are nonetheless notable in illustrating a questionable aspect of U.S. farm policy today. Limitations on beef imports have been in effect only since the late 1960s, during the period when grains policy has been becoming generally more market oriented. Until 1980, beef import restraint levels were linked to U.S. production, and the restraints were suspended altogether under presidential authorities during high-price periods. In 1980, new "countercyclical" beef import legislation was introduced, intended to expand import quotas when beef is scarce in the United States and contract quotas when beef is plentiful. The questionable aspect of this approach, which it shares with current grains policy, is a presumption that political determination of short-term price adjustments and commodity flows will yield results preferable to the results of market forces. Do we know enough to fine-tune the beef market by means of a variable protective program, and can the political will be mobilized to carry out stabilizing policies?

In any case, intervention in the livestock market through beef import controls is trivial compared to the programs for dairy products. Dairy policy involves market support prices, import quotas, marketing orders, and consumption subsidies that altogether make milk perhaps the most highly regulated of all U.S. farm commodities. And dairy farmers are the most politically active of the major commodity groups in terms of lobbying and financial support for politicians.

The Commodity Credit Corporation supports the price of milk by direct purchases of nonfat dry milk, cheese, and butter sufficient to maintain the price of milk used in producing these products at roughly 80 percent of "parity." The concept of parity was at one time a key element in discussion of U.S. farm programs, but dairy products is the only major program in which this usage remains. In ordinary language, parity means equality; in practice, it refers to tying a support price to an index of input prices. It is indexation in much the same sense that Third World countries are currently asking for indexation of international raw materials prices.

The demise of parity as a basis for price supports in grains is worth a brief digression here for the light it sheds on politics versus economics in policy formulation. Instead of parity, target prices for the major crops in the 1977 act are justified on the basis of the U.S. average cost of production for each crop. It has been argued that cost of production is superior to parity in that costs reflect productivity changes while parity does not. Therefore, cost of production should move more closely with normal market-clearing prices. However, the idea of cost of production as a basis for support prices raises serious difficulties. First, there is a substantial range of estimated costs which can be cited to justify a wide range of target prices. Second, cost is not an exogenous parameter but, under competitive pressures in the input markets, particularly the land market, average cost per unit tends to rise to equal the level of expected price. Therefore, raising support prices in itself leads to rising costs. The political point, which in practice overrides the economic rationale, is that congress or the secretary of agriculture may (and has) changed target prices independently of cost-of-production estimates. Cost estimates are therefore practically meaningless as determining factors in target prices. The choice of a parity or cost-of-production rationale merely affects the language in which political decisions are expressed.[6]

Returning to the dairy program, an important result of it is that the support prices have in the past led to unmanageably large stocks of nonfat dry milk, cheese, and butter from time to time, although these have not caused problems nearly as serious as those encountered in the European Community's dairy policy. As of 1980, the dairy support price was probably the most out of line with market realities of any major farm commodity. Governmental outlays for the program are expected to approach $1 billion.

Even when dairy product prices are at the market support levels, average prices received by farmers are well above the support price. The reason is that the price of "Class I" milk, sold predominantly for direct consumption as a beverage, is higher. Under ordinary circumstances, milk of identical quality would sell for the same price whatever its final use. However, the U.S. milk marketing system permits differential pricing of Class I and manufacturing milk (used to manufacture dairy products). The cooperatives become essentially price discriminating cartels. They can increase producers' total returns from a given quantity of milk by charging a higher price in the market with relatively inelastic demand (the Class I market). Each farmer then receives a "blend" price averaging the Class I and manufacturing

[6] For further discussion, see Johnson (1981).

revenues in his milk "pool." Unlike the classical cartel, milk marketing cooperatives are unable to control production. They are cartels with free entry. Instead of producing too little, from the social point of view, they produce too much as farmers expand output in pursuit of the higher blend price. There are no monopoly or cartel profits in the classical sense, but producers gain rents from selling more at higher prices. For a more detailed analysis, including an attempt to estimate the net social welfare losses, see Ippolito and Masson (1978).

Commodity market coordination

Despite the complexities we have been outlining, some elements of the 1977 act are making progress toward better policy coordination among the various crops than had existed in the past. On the supply side, the idea of tying target prices to cost of production is probably meaningless, as noted above, in explaining the general level of support. But the cost-of-production approach does give an indication of how target prices for different commodities can best be set relative to one another so as not to artificially encourage substitution of one crop for another. For example, there was controversy within the Carter administration as to what fraction of U.S. average cost of production to cover in the proposed 1977 farm bill, but once it was decided (with reference to wheat) that 1.5 percent of land value plus all other costs as estimated would be covered, the same formula was applied to competing grains. Coordination of this kind is important because even though there may not be much supply response if prices for soybeans, wheat, corn, cotton, and so forth, all rise 10 percent, there is likely to be a considerably greater response if the price of soybeans rises 10 percent relative to the prices of every other crop.

The tremendous regional diversity of U.S. agriculture creates special difficulties in avoiding unwanted substitution in production. In the Corn Belt, corn and soybeans are good substitutes; in the Mississippi delta, cotton and soybeans; in the Southern Plains, cotton and sorghum; in the Northern Plains, wheat and barley. In irrigated agriculture, wider production shifts are possible. Durum wheat acreage in Arizona has doubled and halved in a year. The relative prices given by U.S. average costs of production may not be appropriate for particular areas. For example, one reason oats do not have a target price is suspicion that a U.S. average cost formula would generate artificial shifts from barley and wheat to oats in the Northern Plains.

The substitution possibilities in production mean that a commodity may be substantially affected by programs for other commodities. For example, when a producer has to set aside 20 percent of sorghum acreage to qualify for deficiency payments, this can easily tip the balance to favor cotton in areas where these crops are good substitutes. The result is that a set-aside requirement for one crop tends to lead to similar requirements for other crops. And a crop like soybeans, which has no target price protection or set-asides or effective CCC loan support, may be as much affected by the grain programs as the grain markets themselves, as mentioned earlier.

On the demand side, the 1977 act was also intended to pay closer attention than previous policy to substitution between commodities. Loan (market support) prices for all the grains were set approximately equal to one another on a poundage basis. This approach was thought to be especially important for wheat relative to feed grains to ensure that when all grains were in surplus, feeding wheat to livestock was a viable use.

Unfortunately, the use of independent coordinating principles on the demand and supply sides leads to anomalies. The ratio of wheat to corn market support prices (in 1979) was 1.12, while the ratio of wheat to corn target prices was 1.55. This divergence generates a chronic tendency to violate the criterion for social efficiency that the price ratio of two commodities in consumption should be equal to the price ratio in production; that is, there is a chronic inducement to a relative oversupply of wheat.[7]

It would be useful to sum up this discussion of U.S. commodity programs with an estimate of the overall degree of protection of U.S. agriculture. This could provide a number comparable to the estimates provided by Hayami in this volume for Japan and other countries. One key difference, however, is that Hayami compares internal (domestic) prices to world prices in making his calculations. U.S. policy in the grains and cotton does not drive a wedge between U.S. and world prices; it affects the world price. This leads to the need for counterfactual analysis mentioned earlier, with the difficulties entailed. I have attempted to construct a rough overall estimate of the degree of protection of U.S. farm commodity prices, measured as the ratio of actual prices in 1978–79 compared to what prices would have been without price supports and production controls. The ratio ranged from 1.9 for sugar to 1.00 for soybeans, hogs, and poultry. Overall, it was 1.05 to 1.06; that is, programs raised the average farm price 5

[7] The oversupply does not necessarily show up, as it has in earlier programs, as chronically excessive stocks. Pricing wheat at feed value gets around this problem, in principle. The long-run problem can be summarized by saying that the United States produces wheat using resource costs of $134 per ton whose value in (feeding) use is $92 per ton.

to 6 percent. This is not a large degree of protection compared to Hayami's estimates and to estimates of 1.15 to 1.20 in the 1960s in the United States. For further discussion of the estimates, see Gardner (1981).

Noncommodity programs

The host of governmental activities in agriculture not directed at specific commodities presents too many complications to warrant detailed exposition. One set of them that should be mentioned, however, is regulatory activities aimed at improving the physical environment, protecting food consumer and farm worker health and safety, and bringing farm wages and working conditions up to urban standards. A common characteristic of these activities is that they add to production costs in U.S. agriculture. American farmers are quite concerned about these programs, most of which have become significant factors only in the past five years or so. Indeed, in many instances costly regulation is still more a threat than an actuality. An argument worth noting is that to the extent that other countries in the world do not impose them, these existing and proposed regulations reduce the competitiveness of U.S. products in world markets. Moreover, vegetable producers have argued on the import side that Mexican producers, for example, can produce tomatoes cheaper than U.S. producers because of less severe restrictions on pesticide use and lower wage and working standards, and that therefore some compensating restraint on imports of Mexican vegetables should be imposed.

Another major set of governmental actions in agriculture has had the effect of reducing costs. These include: subsidized and federally guaranteed credit programs, subsidized water for irrigation in some parts of the country, government funding of agricultural research and extension, subsidized crop insurance schemes (notably the disaster payments program mentioned above), and generous tax treatment of many agricultural enterprises. Programs of this sort have been in existence much longer, and have probably had a much greater impact, than the newer cost-increasing programs. There is evidence that some of these programs have been socially valuable in the sense of generating social benefits far in excess of program costs. Agricultural research, at least in certain areas, is the best example. Others have been more in the nature of transfers from taxpayers to farmers, and some have probably generated net social losses (for example, the Agricultural Conservation Program which the last five presidents have tried, without success, to persuade congress to end). All of these activities have tended to reduce costs and to increase supply of U.S. farm commodities. They have probably been a major factor in the rapid growth of U.S. agricultural productivity in the period since 1940. Consequently, the notion that cost-increasing regulation is a good argument for trade intervention favoring U.S. producers is a two-edged sword. Should cost-reducing programs also be compensated for on the grounds that they have given U.S. producers an unfair competitive advantage?[8]

A final set of noncommodity activities of government that should be mentioned consists of the broader economic policy steps that significantly affect agriculture. These include energy policy, social welfare programs, international currency arrangements, and most important at present, macroeconomic policy determining the rate of inflation. The acceleration of expected inflation in the past ten years has had many disruptive effects in agriculture. The most serious at present, and the one which could cause the most difficulties in the future, is the building of inflationary expectations into long-term interest rates. This creates two serious problems in agriculture: a cash flow problem and an environment of extreme uncertainty for the highly leveraged holder of real assets. Instability in the inflation rate is not a free lunch; if leveraged landholders make extraordinary gains when inflation accelerates, we should expect a corresponding opportunity for losses.

At the present time we are seeing rates of inflation exceeding earlier expectations, and consequent windfall capital gains to owners of land. Capital gains on farmland in recent years have been of the same order of magnitude as net farm operating income. Although many farmers have of course benefited from increases in land prices, there is a widespread sense among farm people that the current situation is not healthy. This feeling is expressed in the policy area as a demand for legislation that will moderate the increase in land prices. There has been discussion at the federal level, but the main action has taken place at the state level. State governments seldom if ever play a role in commodity policy, but regulation of land use and transfer is different. The main thrust recently has been attempts to prevent nonfarm investors from entering the market for farmland. A few states

---

[8] In considering agricultural exports it is necessary also to consider cost-reducing regulation that affects agricultural commodities after they leave the farm. Both inland waterway and railway transportation rates for grains are priced below the full cost of providing these services. The USDA provides valuable information and export promotion services as well as CCC export credit, even though explicit export subsidies no longer exist. And the Federal Grain Inspection Service provides export quality control, in part at the taxpayers' expense.

have enacted regulatory statutes to this end, and many more are actively considering them, particularly in restricting foreign buying of U.S. land. Nonetheless, it seems safe to predict that policies that do not change the rate of inflation, long-term interest rates, or commodity-market prospects can have no significant effect on farmland prices, except possibly for some short-term psychological effect.[9]

International issues

Policies specifically directed at international trade issues are treated by Houck in chapter 3 of this volume. This section is concerned with the international consequences of domestic farm programs. *Deficiency payments* have the same international effects as export subsidies (but very different domestic effects, the former reducing but the latter increasing domestic consumer prices). They reduce world prices and thus make foreign consumers better off and foreign producers worse off.[10] *Production restraints* reduce U.S. exports; they increase world prices and thus make foreign consumers worse off and foreign producers better off. A high market support price caused by *CCC loans and purchases* has effects similar to production restraints with the important exception that carryover stocks accumulate as a by-product of the price support effort. These stocks must necessarily be released from time to time, and when they are, they may have price-reducing effects roughly equivalent to the price-increasing effects of their acquisition. Thus, a U.S. domestic policy based on CCC loans and storage becomes an international price stabilization program. Because the stocks accumulated in the 1950s and 1960s became quite costly, it has become common to refer to the United States as "carrying the burden" of international stockpiling in these years. Of course stockpiling, if done with an eye to profitable resale, is no burden but a money-making opportunity. The "burden" is more properly called a cost of uneconomic attempts to prop up U.S. average prices above the levels consistent with long-term supply and demand conditions.

International commodity agreements

Attempts have been made to establish internationally coordinated national storage programs under a new International Wheat Agree-

---

[9] For evidence of the close relationship between U.S. farmland prices and the expected return flows from land ownership, see Melichar (1979). For further discussion of several issues taken up in this section, see Castle (1979).

[10] A clear and helpful exposition of the theoretical basis for these consequences is in Jones and Thompson (1978).

ment, but these efforts have so far been without success. The United States now has sufficient grain in storage that there is no reason for other countries to wish to undertake the financial burden of adding to them. The U.S. proposal in 1977 was for a wheat stock of 30 million metric tons, an amount which the U.S. carryover (above minimum working stocks) has subsequently approached unilaterally.

The U.S. government has also supported the International Sugar Agreement. The sugar crops have been among the most heavily protected of U.S. farm commodities. In 1978–79, policies held the U.S. market price for raw sugar at almost twice the world (off-shore) market level (Gardner, 1980). This is especially striking in that there are fewer than 15,000 U.S. sugarcane and sugar beet producers (compared to almost a million producers of corn, for example) (U.S. Department of Commerce, 1974).

The United States has also become increasingly sympathetic to international agreements for imported products, following its long-standing support of and membership in the International Coffee Agreement. Still, there appears to be growing sentiment, parallel to the increases in support for market orientation as a goal in domestic programs, that international commodity agreements should be price-stabilizing devices, not international institutions for holding long-term average prices above market-justified trend levels.

A possible exception is wheat, where the secretary of agriculture has from time to time given encouragement to producer sentiment for an organization of wheat exporting countries (OWEC). There is question about the degree of market power a wheat-exporter cartel could exercise as a practical matter; and at the policy level there is question of whether an OWEC, even if feasible, is a wise or desirable undertaking.

Embargoes, food aid, and trade negotiations

No steps undertaken for domestic political purposes have greater international implications than food aid and restrictions on exports. Food aid has been in many cases intended as an international relief activity, particularly in the aftermath of wars and natural disasters. Nonetheless, the institutionally formalized food aid established in the 1950s under the legislation known as P.L. 480 seems to have had its primary purpose as an adjunct to domestic price-support programs. The problem in the 1950s and 1960s was the disposal of the large CCC stocks. As U.S. commodity programs have moved toward the target price and deficiency payment approach, P.L. 480 has become less important domestically. And by the later 1970s, the real value of food aid under this program had fallen substantially below the value of pre-1972 shipments, in spite of high stock levels near the end of the decade. Moreover, the aims of P.L. 480 involve foreign policy issues as expressed in the Department of State influence in P.L. 480 shipment allocations and in attempts in Congress to direct food aid allocations.

Restrictions on exports are one of the few U.S. policy interventions undertaken with the intention of aiding food consumers at the expense of producers. The only actions undertaken of this sort were temporary embargoes on soybean exports in 1973 and in 1974 and 1975, on grain sales to the Soviet Union, and for a short time, Eastern Europe. It is unlikely that these restrictions had any effect on the supply–demand balance either domestically or abroad, but they did have repercussions that still have influence. First, foreign purchasers of U.S. products naturally found it prudent to increase the diversity of their sources for imports.[11] Second, the political reaction from producers was so strong as to induce both presidential candidates in 1976 to make very strong promises to avoid future export restraints.

One result of the 1973–75 events was an intensive attempt to regularize future grain trade with the Soviet Union and other trading partners. In 1975 and 1976, the United States entered into a series of bilateral agreements, of varying degrees of formality, whose intention was to make trade flows more stable and predictable. The fact that multilateral agreements, if they can be reached, are ultimately more satisfactory to this end probably explains part of the increased U.S. interest in them in the past few years.

The U.S.–Soviet bilateral agreement on grain trade functioned smoothly through the severe Soviet production shortfall of 1979, but foundered on political shoals at the beginning of 1980. The U.S. grain trade became more explicitly than ever before a tool of international politics as President Carter suspended all U.S. shipments above the minimum 8 million tons to the Soviet Union in response to their occupation of Afghanistan. Because the Soviets have apparently been able to substitute grain from other sources for U.S. grain, neither U.S. exports nor Soviet imports were reduced by as much as had at first been expected. In addition, the U.S. government entered the grain markets in an attempt to support prices at pre-embargo levels. Consequently, neither U.S. trade nor producer prices have in the short term been much different than they would have been with no embargo. Nonetheless, there could be long-term reductions in demand

---

[11] Discussion of the soybean embargo occurs in several places throughout this volume. See particularly the chapters by Houck, Talbot and Kihl, Yoshioka, and Sanderson.

for U.S. grain as a result of this reinforcement of the notion that the United States is unreliable as a source of supply.

Potential for Progress

U.S. agricultural policy is not *ad hoc*, excessively complicated, constantly changing, and in part self-contradictory simply because the policy process is perverse or because policy makers are inept. These characteristics arise because a judgment has implicitly been made that although allowing agricultural production, prices, and farm income to be determined by market forces is not satisfactory, neither is it satisfactory to have a governmentally planned and regulated agricultural sector. Thus it is the set of consumption and production decisions of individual households, farms, and marketing firms that principally determines prices in U.S. domestic markets. It is world market conditions and policy decisions in other countries that principally determine prices for U.S. exports. It is individual producer decisions that principally determine resource allocation and production choices. But the overall market prices that result from the resolution of these forces are very often found unsatisfactory by one group or another, and this dissatisfaction results, through the political process, in programs directed at the unsatisfactory outcome.

The problems of the agricultural economy that seem most important in determining the justifiable extent of U.S. governmental involvement in agriculture can be grouped in five categories: (1) a tendency to persistent low incomes in agriculture; (2) a recurrence of transitory periods of low farm incomes alternating with high prices to consumers (instability); (3) cash flow problems which, coupled with large capital investment requirements, deter entry and squeeze the living standard of heavily indebted farmers; (4) the market power of agribusiness enterprises; (5) maintaining the growth of agricultural productivity. Intervention in commodity markets can always be conducted so as to promote special interests. The question is whether and how it can promote solutions to problems in categories (1) to (5).

With respect to (1), the facts as outlined earlier suggest that, for commercial scale farmers, there is no problem. And for those rural residents for whom persistent poverty is a problem, commodity policy is ineffective because they market so little commercially.

With respect to (3), the more appropriate sources of policy improvement are in financial institutions and monetary and fiscal policy.

With respect to (4), anticompetitive practices should be treated consistently with overall commercial and antitrust policy. The decentralized, small-enterprise nature of farming provides a rationale for certain special types of governmental activity. These include, in category (4), public investment in market information and its dissemination, and in category (5), public investment in research and development.

We are left with category (2), which is in fact the main problem cited in justifying policy proposals to Congress and to the public. All the same, it seems inevitable that conflicting interests in the political process will not be content with policies in category (2), or elsewhere, directed solely at improving the general functioning of the agricultural economy in the joint interests of consumers, producers, and taxpayers. The struggle of each conflicting group, and of subgroups within the larger groups, to increase their slice of the economic pie creates seemingly inevitable obstacles to jointly optimal policy. But these circumstances also create opportunities for bargaining and compromise by which policy improvements may be accomplished. The challenge for policy makers, particularly in the executive branch of the federal government, is to administer legislation aimed at promoting special interests in such a way as to further the country's general interest.[12]

Historically, the conflicting goals of U.S. policy, and the potential for improvements, can be observed nowhere better than in the area of programs in pursuit of grain stabilization. Ad hoc CCC stock release policy was replaced by the Carter administration with a "farmer-owned reserve" policy of subsidized storage. This program involved prespecified trigger prices, originally at 140 and 175 percent of the market support price (for wheat). The idea was to leave scope for private storage within the rather broad price band between 100 and 140 percent of the loan rate. When market prices reached 140 percent of the loan rate, a situation of scarcity presumably caused by an unusual production shortfall somewhere in the world, storage inducements to keep farmer-held grain would cease. But then, in response to the political pressure represented by the American Agricultural Movement, the target price—the basis for producer incentives intended to

---

[12] It would be an oversimplification to assert that *all* agricultural policy can be understood in terms of economic interests of particular groups. For example, Secretary of Agriculture Bergland (in the Carter administration) promoted the "structure of agriculture" as a policy issue. The issue is whether farms are in some sense becoming too big, and therefore too few. This is not to date an issue that is mobilizing pressure from special interests, though many are pleased to include "to save the family farm" in the stated purpose of legislation.

represent average cost of production—was placed in 1978 at 145 percent of the support price. Thus, the "cost-of production" price ended up exceeding the stock-release price. And still further, in response to the budget costs entailed by such a high target price, production restraints were adopted that in 1978–79 resulted in the strange combination of simultaneously having artificially small production, artificially large stocks, and resulting market prices at levels originally contemplated as being indicative of extreme scarcity.

On the other hand, there is a notable tendency for U.S. farm programs not to fight for long against underlying market trends. In wheat, the subject of attempt after attempt to support market prices, the trend toward lower real prices has not been resisted in the long term (USDA, 1980). This market orientation contrasts with, for example, grains policy in the European Economic Community, whose internal support prices continued to increase relative to U.S. prices.

Domestic agricultural policy aimed at the general interest and the improved international coordination of commercial relations in agriculture are both desirable goals. Moreover, they are complementary goals in that progress in one area should make progress easier in the other. Greater predictability and stability in trade flows would make domestic price stabilization and farm income support policy easier to conduct.

One type of change that seems to hold promise in improving U.S. agricultural policy is simply better policy and program planning. Such policy planning would involve a strategic outline of the goals that policy is intended to achieve. It must include some kind of ranking of priorities among these goals, and also weights or procedures that allow rational choice when goals conflict. Otherwise, a strategic plan has nothing useful to say. We cannot usefully say in the United States that we want policies that provide consumers with high-quality food at the lowest possible cost and also make farming a more profitable activity. Of course, policies that can attain both goals simultaneously would be desirable, but the real issues do not arise here. The policies that are live issues tend to benefit one group at the expense of another. Nonetheless, it should be possible to do better than simply wait for political choices to be made. Indeed, an overall picture of an ideally organized farm sector, with value judgments underlying it laid out clearly, might help politicians to be more consistent and rational in legislative action.

Program planning involves the tactics used to achieve policy goals, the administration of policy. The problem here is that even when legislation has been enacted, for example, the Food and Agriculture

Act of 1977, the programs have been too complicated and have changed too often. Better program planning could establish with more certainty the policy instruments best suited to alternative policy goals. An irony in current U.S. policy is that while one of the best-attested reasons for governmental intervention in agriculture is the instability generated in unregulated markets, current U.S. programs appear so much in flux that instability and uncertainty, as perceived by U.S. farmers domestically and by our trading partners internationally, may actually be increased by governmental intervention.

References

Castle, Emery N. 1979. "Resource Allocation and Production Costs," in Bruce Gardner and James Richardson, eds., *Consensus and Conflict in U.S. Agriculture* (College Station, Texas, Texas A&M University Press).

Council of Economic Advisers. 1980. *Economic Report of the President* (Washington, D.C., GPO).

Freebairn, J.W., and G.C. Rausser. 1975. "Effects of Changes in the Level of U.S. Beef Imports," *American Journal of Agricultural Economics* vol. 57 (November) pp. 676–688.

Gardner, Bruce L. 1979. *Optimal Stockpiling of Grain* (Lexington, Mass., Lexington Books).

———. 1981. "Consequences of Farm Policies in the 1970s," in D. Gale Johnson, ed., *Food and Agricultural Policy for the 1980s* (Washington, D.C., American Enterprise Institute).

Grennes, T.J., P.R. Johnson, and M. Thursby. 1977. *The Economics of World Grain Trade* (New York, Praeger).

Hottel, J.B., and C.D. Evans. 1980. "Returns to Equity Capital in the U.S. Farm Production Sector," in U.S. Department of Agriculture, *Balance Sheet of the Farming Sector, 1979, Supplement* (Washington, D.C., February) pp. 51–68.

Houck, James P. 1974. "The Short Run Impact of Beef Imports on U.S. Prices," *Australian Journal of Agricultural Economics* vol. 18, pp. 60–72.

Ippolito, R.A., and R.T. Masson. 1978. "The Social Cost of Government Regulation of Milk," *Journal of Law and Economics* vol. 21, pp. 33–66.

Johnson, D. Gale. 1981. "Agricultural Policy Alternatives for the 1980s," in D. Gale Johnson, ed., *Food and Agricultural Policy for the 1980s* (Washington, D.C., American Enterprise Institute).

Jones, B.F., and R.L. Thompson. 1978. "Interrelationships of Domestic Agricultural Policies and Trade Policies," in Agricultural Extension Service, University of Minnesota, *Speaking of Trade* (Minneapolis, Minn.).

Melichar, E. 1979. "Capital Gains Versus Current Income in the Farming Sector," *American Journal of Agricultural Economics* vol. 61 (December) pp. 1085–1092.

Robinson, K.L. 1979. "Inflation and Food Prices," in Farm Foundation, *Increasing Understanding of Public Problems and Policies—1979* (Oak Brook, Ill., Farm Foundation) pp. 65–73.

Taylor, C.R., and H. Talpaz. 1979. "Approximately Optimal Carryover Levels for Wheat in the United States," *American Journal of Agricultural Economics* vol. 61 (February) pp. 32–40.

USDA. 1979a. U.S. Department of Agriculture, Economics, Statistics and Cooperatives Service. *Farm Income Statistics*, Statistical Bulletin No. 627 (October).

———. 1979b. U.S. Department of Agriculture, Economics, Statistics and Cooperatives Service. *Field Crops: Production, Disposition, Value* (Washington, D.C., April).

———. 1979c. U.S. Department of Agriculture. *Agricultural Statistics, 1979* (Washington, D.C., GPO).

———. 1979d. U.S. Department of Agriculture, Economics, Statistics and Cooperatives Service. *Balance Sheet of the Farming Sector, 1979*, Agricultural Information Bulletin No. 430 (August).

———. 1980. U.S. Department of Agriculture, Agricultural Stabilization and Conservation Service. *Wheat—1980 Program*, ASCS Commodity Fact Sheet (June).

U.S. Department of Commerce. 1974, Bureau of the Census. *Census of Agriculture, 1974, Vol. I* (Washington, D.C.).

III

The Making of Agricultural
Policy in Two Democracies

7

Agriculture and Politics in Japan

Kenzo Hemmi

Political factors seem to play a greater role in the determination and effectuation of government policy in the agricultural sector than in any other sector in Japan—a phenomenon that appears to be the case in many other developed countries of the world as well. In this respect, there hardly seems a need to single Japan out as a special case. Three reasons, however, make worthwhile the discussion of politics that is presented in this chapter. First, it is worth examining the actual manner in which farm programs in Japan are formulated through the interaction of factors in the Japanese political setting. This involves a situation in which decision making is normally based on consensus rather than majority vote and one in which a "from-the-bottom-up" process, rather than a "top-down" process is the established procedure. Second, there is some need to elaborate on the simplistic answer the Japanese are wont to give—"it's because of politics"—when queried by foreigners in international forums about the seeming irrationality inherent in their government's farm policy. Third, it is necessary

Kenzo Hemmi was dean of the faculty of agriculture at the University of Tokyo. The author heartily acknowledges the assistance of Mr. T. Iwakura of the Policy Research Board of the Liberal Democratic Party, and F. Ikeuchi and H. Wakamiya, both from the *Asahi Shimbun*. In a sense they should be coauthors. However, all views expressed are of the author alone, and not of them. They have no responsibility for the views expressed in the chapter.

to clarify the manner in which the current trend—that of visible decline in the position of the Liberal Democratic Party (LDP) against a background of advancing urbanization—is affecting the relationship between agricultural policy and politics.[1]

The chapter begins with a discussion of the relationship between the LDP and the rural farming communities; in fact it is impossible to exclude this relationship from any discussion of agricultural policy and politics in Japan, where a single-party government of the LDP and its forerunner parties has been in power much longer than in other nations that have single-party governments.[2] Next I examine the question of the extent to which the agricultural policy of the LDP, as well as the policies of the opposition parties, reflects the views of the Japanese people. Finally, I examine the actual decision-making machinery for the formulation of agricultural policy. This study will show that the LDP has within its fold a host of National Diet members who, as former top-level career officials in several government agencies, have taken direct part in the formulation and implementation of policy decisions, and that these Diet members now serve not only to enhance the policy-formulating capability of the ruling party itself but also to improve empathy between the party and the government.

Agricultural Communities and the Liberal Democratic Party

Rural communities as a political base

Why is the Japanese government forced to adopt a protectionist policy toward the nation's farming households? The question cannot be answered without considering the fact that the long-ruling Liberal Democratic Party is, after all, a political party and that its foundation

[1] The Liberal Democratic Party swept the last simultaneous elections for both houses of the Diet (June 22, 1980), winning 284 seats in the 511-seat House of Representatives and a so-called stable majority in the House of Councillors. The voters' turnabout in support for the LDP had already appeared in the 1979 general election (see figure 7-3). However, comments on this sweeping victory unanimously concluded that the trend of decline in the position of the LDP was not reversed by this. There could have been so-called sympathy votes for the late prime minister Masayoshi Ohira. It would seem also that the people have concluded that there is no safe alternative to the LDP government for the time being. Thus, the June 22nd vote was one for stability but not one of positive approval of the LDP.

[2] The Liberal Party and the Democratic Party combined to form the Liberal Democratic Party in 1955.

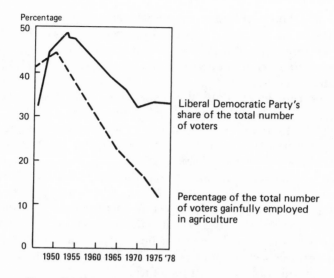

Figure 7-1. **Electoral strength of the Liberal Democratic Party in relation to farm population, 1946–78.** *Source*: Masumi Ishikawa, *Sengo Seiji Kozo-shi* (A History of the Postwar Political Structure) (Tokyo, Nikon Hyoron Sha, 1978). p 74.

rests solidly in rural agricultural communities. (On a political spectrum of liberal to conservative, the LDP is generally considered a conservative party.) Being a national party, the LDP of course has supporters elsewhere, but it is nevertheless evident from an abundance of survey data that its support in rural constituencies outstrips by far the support it enjoys in the large cities. In this regard, the party stands in striking contrast to all the opposition parties, particularly the Komeito (Clean Government Party), the Democratic Socialist Party (DSP), the Japan Communist Party (JCP), and even the New Liberal Club, a faction which broke from the LDP not long ago. The following are statistics that illustrate how much the LDP relies on rural farming communities for support.

Figure 7-1 shows a correlation between the postwar trend in the percentage of those gainfully occupied in farming and the trend in the percentage of electoral votes secured by the LDP ruling party.

The gainfully occupied portion of the population in agriculture in Japan, which had remained stable at about 14 million between the period from 1920 to 1944, increased sharply after the end of World War II to surpass 16 million by 1950. Later in the 1950s, however, it suddenly began to drop and has been on a steady downward trend ever since. The percentage of those occupied in agriculture out of the nation's total working population reached its peak of about 45 percent at the time of a 1950 survey, thereafter declining rapidly to fall below 20 percent in 1970 and subsequently down to 11.4 percent in 1975.

The percentage of electoral votes secured by the ruling LDP party also began to show an upturn shortly after the war, reaching a peak in 1952. But thereafter it also declined steadily. Since the inauguration of the LDP in 1955 (the result of a merger of conservative parties), practically every general election has seen the LDP's share of votes decline.[3] This trend resembles closely the downward curve traced by the percentage of those gainfully occupied in farming. With the beginning of the 1970s, the figures show that the decline in the LDP's share of electoral votes was finally checked, but the timing also coincides with the period when the flow of population from rural to urban areas slowed down (despite a steady decline in the number of those gainfully occupied in agriculture).

Figure 7-2 compares the relative shares of the votes secured by the LDP in four different types of constituencies—metropolitan, urban, semiurban, and nonurban types—in the general elections of 1972 and 1976. The figure illustrates that the greater the degree of urbanization of a constituency, the smaller the number of votes garnered by the LDP.

The general election of 1976, in particular, saw the LDP suffer a setback of an unprecedented scale amid an intraparty factional strife in the aftermath of the Lockheed scandal that resulted in the arrest of Prime Minister Kakuei Tanaka. The figure indicates that in the metropolitan constituencies, the LDP's standing degenerated into that of a governing party with only one-quarter of the electoral vote. Even in this election, however, the party garnered over twice the share of votes in the nonurban constituencies as it did in the metropolitan constituencies, thus managing to secure a majority of the votes in the former. Nevertheless, one can hardly overlook the fact that the LDP's serious setback was the direct result of an unprecedented margin of decline in the number of votes received by the party even in the nonurban constituencies. It may be assumed that when and if the LDP can no longer compensate for its weakness in the urban areas with its strength in the rural areas, the era of single-party government by the LDP will come to an end.

Table 7-1 shows the number of members elected from the main political parties, together with the relative percentages of these num-

[3] The exception is the last simultaneous elections.

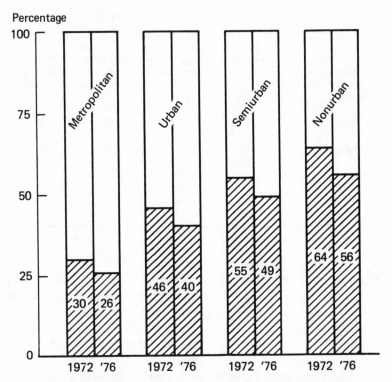

Figure 7-2. The Liberal Democratic Party's share of votes in different types of constituencies in the general elections of 1972 and 1976.

bers for each of the four constituency types in the 1976 general election. The figures again illustrate that, whereas the Komeito, the DSP, the JCP, and the New Liberal Club all depend on metropolitan and urban constituencies for support, the LDP tends to rely for support on the nonurban and semiurban electoral districts (incidentally, the pattern of support for the Japan Socialist Party (JSP), the biggest opposition party, falls somewhere between these two patterns).

An electoral constituency system that favors rural communities

The fact that the base of political support for the LDP lies solidly in the rural agricultural areas is of tremendous significance in connection with the hold the party maintains on the reins of government.

TABLE 7-1. JAPAN: NUMBER OF MEMBERS ELECTED FROM

Constituency	Liberal Democratic Party	Independent conservatives	New Liberal Club	Japan Socialist Party
Metropolitan	29	3	7	17
	(29)	(3)	(7)	(17)
Urban	64	1	7	32
	(47)	(1)	(5)	(24)
Semiurban	100	6	2	53
	(54)	(3)	(1)	(29)
Nonurban	56	8	1	21
	(62)	(9)	(1)	(23)
Total	249	18	17	123
	(49)	(4)	(3)	(24)

Note: Numbers in parentheses indicate percentage. See the note in figure 7-2.

In other words, the LDP has been able to remain in power for so long because, and only because, it has enjoyed support in rural districts rather than in the large cities with their heavy concentrations of population. The reason lies in the workings of the Japanese electoral constituency system, whose allocation of parliamentary seats is extremely favorable to rural constituencies.

Figure 7-3 compares the trend of the LDP's relative share of the votes with that of its share of the parliamentary seats won (at the time of election) in the general elections since 1955, when the party was formed. The figure shows two conspicuous trends: (1) the share of the parliamentary seats won is always greater than the share of the votes won, usually by a large margin; and (2) that compared to the steep downward trend of the share of votes, the share of seats has only a mild downward trend—and even moves upward in some places.

The relative share of the votes captured by the LDP fell below the 50 percent mark (which is to say, it became less than the combined share of the votes received by the opposition parties) as early as 1967. Nevertheless, the party was always able to hold a majority of the parliamentary seats until 1972. (As discussed later in detail, the number of elected members from the LDP shrank to less than a majority for the first time in the 1976 general election, but the party still managed to muster a parliamentary majority through the enrollment of elected members who had run as independents.)

The LDP has thus been able to control a disproportionately large number of seats in the Diet compared with its share of the electoral votes won because the system of per-district allocation of seats works

DIFFERENT PARTIES IN THE 1976 GENERAL ELECTION

Komeito	Democratic Socialist Party	Japan Communist Party	Independent progressives	Total
23	9	10	2	100
(23)	(9)	(10)	(2)	
18	10	3	1	136
(13)	(7)	(2)	(1)	
12	9	3	0	185
(6)	(5)	(2)	(0)	
2	1	1	0	90
(2)	(1)	(1)	(0)	
55	29	17	3	511
(11)	(6)	(3)	(1)	

in a manner extremely favorable to the rural areas. After the war, the numbers of seats for the electoral districts of the House of Representatives were first established in proportion to the numbers of eligible voters in the districts. However, in subsequent years, the system did not keep abreast of the large-scale migration from rural regions to the major cities despite the implementation of several revisions, so that there rapidly developed a serious imbalance between the ratio of number of voters to the number of seats on a per-district basis. In other words, despite a heavy steady depletion of population, the rural constituencies have been able to continue electing the same number of Diet members as in the past. Conversely, the metropolitan districts have not, for some time, been represented by a number of Diet members that is commensurate with the sharp population buildup.

In terms of the number of eligible voters per Diet member, therefore, the ratio between the highest and the lowest reached as much as five to one in the 1972 general election. In 1975, a statutory revision aimed at restoring balance to the allocation of seats was enacted, but it proved inadequate since it merely increased the total number of seats by twenty (the additional seats being allocated to districts with large increases in population) without reducing the numbers of seats in districts with depleted populations. As a result, the 1976 election again saw the differential in terms of the number of voters per Diet member between the highest district, Chiba Prefecture's 4th District (urban type), and the lowest district, Hyogo Prefecture's 5th District (nonurban type), exceed the three-to-one level. And this gap, moreover, is still expanding. The earlier five-to-one differential was, in

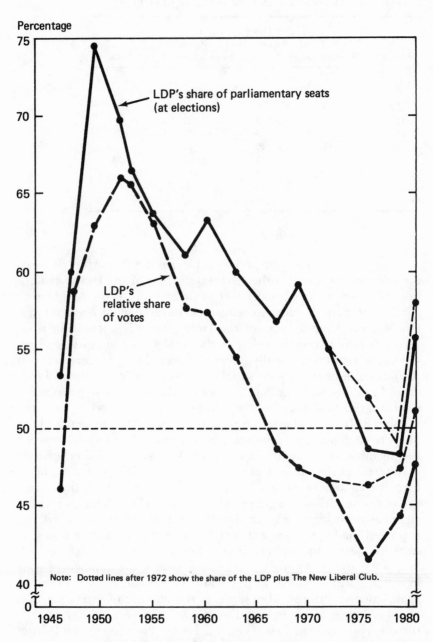

Percentage

75

LDP's share of parliamentary seats
(at elections)

70

65

LDP's
relative share
of votes

60

55

50

45

Note: Dotted lines after 1972 show the share of the LDP plus The New Liberal Club.

40

0

1945   1950   1955   1960   1965   1970   1975   1980

Figure 7-3. Trend of the Liberal Democratic Party's share of votes compared with
its share of parliamentary seats, 1945–80.

226

fact, ruled unconstitutional by the Supreme Court, but the constitutionality of the three-to-one differential is still in dispute in the same court following conflicting rulings made by two different high courts in Tokyo in the autumn of 1978.

In the House of Councillors, whose representation is said to have a more regional nature than the House of Representatives, the numbers of seats allocated to prefectural districts have not been revised since the war, and the imbalance between rural and urban representation has become even more pronounced than in the House of Representatives. For instance, the differential ratio between the Kanagawa Prefectural District, with large cities like Yokohama and Kawasaki, and the Tottori District, a seriously depopulated prefecture, is now more than five to one.

This distribution of parliamentary seats favoring the rural constituencies obviously works to the great advantage of the LDP, because the party can make maximum use of its strong rural political base to gain the election of a large number of members with a relatively small number of votes. It would not be an exaggeration, therefore, to cite this as the single, albeit sometimes obscure, factor that has enabled the LDP to maintain its singular hold on the reins of power despite the fact that its share of the electoral votes has long since slipped below the 50 percent mark.

In that sense, the party's serious setback in the 1976 general election may be blamed on the failure of this "mechanism" of parliamentary seat allocation to function as well as it had done for the LDP in the past. The failure of the mechanism was indicated by the fact that (1) the opposition parties captured most of the twenty additional members allocated to the metropolitan districts in the revision of the previous year, and that (2) the LDP's share of the votes shrank significantly even in the rural constituencies it has traditionally counted on.

Supposing, then, that the imbalance between the numbers of seats representing rural and urban constituencies is completely rectified and a more equitable representation is restored. How would the allocation of Diet seats change? Immediately after the 1976 election, the *Asahi Shimbun* made a hypothetical calculation of how the votes captured by the different parties in that election would have been reflected in the distribution of parliamentary seats if divisions and mergers of various constituencies and revision of seats had been carried out in such a way as to keep the differential in terms of the number of voters per Diet member to within the ratio of two to one at most (and without altering the total number of seats in the House of Representatives). Under this realigned distribution of seats, the newspaper's calculations revealed the number of members elected from the LDP would have totalled only 222, a number far short of a majority in the 511 seat House.

The actual number of elected LDP members in that election was 249, a number which enabled the party to secure a bare majority by admitting into its ranks 12 conservative politicians who had run as independents. Had its number of seats been as calculated for the hypothetical situation, the addition of a dozen independents would still not have made up a majority, so that a continuation of government by a single party would have been a much more difficult proposition.

As for the opposition parties: they would all have captured more seats in the hypothetical situation, with the Komeito counting 67 elected members instead of the actual 55, the JCP 36 members instead of 17, the DSP 31 members instead of 29, and the New Liberal Club 20 members instead of 17. The only exception would have been the JSP, another party with some traditional dependence on rural constituencies, which would have had 116 elected members instead of the actual 123, for a loss of 7 seats.

Given this background, then, the LDP is perhaps understandably not very enthusiastic about revision of the present seat allocation. The JSP, the largest of the opposition parties, will be in the same position. It is also evident that if the LDP is to stay in power, it will be imperative that it continue to strengthen its support in the rural constituencies that have been its traditional stronghold.

In the context of the relationship between the existing constituency system and Japan's agriculture, it is also worth mentioning that the Japanese House of Representatives is based on the so-called medium constituency system, allocating from three to five seats to a district, rather than on a small constituency system. What this means is that there are practically no electoral districts that do not include some farming areas, with the exception, of course, of a few metropolitan constituencies.

The electorate for the House of Representatives resides in a total of 130 districts, of which the only constituencies consisting entirely of strictly urban areas are the contiguous 21 districts located in the cities of Tokyo, Yokohama, Osaka, Nagoya, Kyoto, and Kobe. The total number of seats for these districts is 83, which amounts to only 16 percent of the 511 seats of the house. Even in Saitama Prefecture, where an influx of new residents who commute to neighboring Tokyo has resulted in a significant population increase, the four constituencies are all districts containing urban, suburban, and rural areas. Similarly, none of the cities that has over a million population, such as

Sapporo, Kitakyushu, and Fukuoka, possesses a single constituency that consists of one purely urban municipality. There is likewise not a single constituency in the country consisting entirely of a regional consumer city or industrial city. Simply put, then, practically all constituencies contain farming areas, to a greater or lesser extent.

If the electorate for the House of Representatives were to be reorganized into a small-constituency system by dividing each existing district into from three to five small districts, there would emerge new urban constituencies (leaving aside the question of their precise degree of urbanization) in all parts of the country—not only in the metropolitan areas—and these constituencies would logically give rise to a host of new urban-oriented members of the Diet. Under the present constituency system, however, even a member whose base of political support lies in a regional consumer city cannot afford to ignore the demands of voters in the peripheral farming areas of his constituency. Worse still, given the greater voice and organizational strength of the agricultural producers compared to those of the consumers (along with the comparative reliability of the former's practical support during election campaigns), it is not surprising that some legislators "willingly" choose to abandon their obligations as representatives of their urban constituents.

Interdependence between farmers and Diet members—the situation in a constituency in Tohoku Region

So far the discussion has been focused on the high degree of dependence of the LDP's government on rural farming communities for electoral support. Just how, then, do the members of the National Diet maintain their ties with the farming communities? The nature of the interdependence between the farmers and Diet members who represent them should be examined at this point.

As might be expected in farming regions, there are producers' organizations, such as the agricultural cooperatives, which have virtually inseparable ties with the local town- and village-size communities. It is, in fact, no exaggeration to state that such organizations coincide exactly with the hierarchy of political power within local society. This structure might be better explained by describing the situation in a typical constituency in the Tohoku Region, one of Japan's representative rural, predominately agricultural areas.

Take the hypothetical case of a young man aspiring to reach a position of influence in the regional community. The logical start for him would be to become an activist for the youth section of his local agricultural cooperative society, or *nokyo*. (Frequently, *nokyo* youth sections recruit politically aware and active young men from regional communities around them.) If he distinguishes himself in his work and wins a measure of confidence from the upper echelons, he will, at the age of about thirty, be assigned to the position of "head of a production team" or "head of a primary agricultural society." The person in this position is responsible for a local *nokyo* unit, consisting of from 50 to 100 farming households. His new duties might include allocation of irrigation water and organizing of collective rice seedling production projects.

The heads of these societies must have not only the technological expertise to help secure above-average crop yields, but also the ability to skillfully coordinate the interests of the different farmers. If our hypothetical farmer shows he can perform these functions to everyone's satisfaction, he will become a respected local figure well on his way to eventual promotion to such positions as member of the local agricultural committee, and the local *nokyo* board. Using such posts as stepping stones, he will eventually have a chance to run for president of the local *nokyo* chapter, or even for member of the local municipal assembly to represent perhaps seven or eight local villages or hamlets. Later still, he may go on to become mayor of a town or a city. Of course, many rural communities still retain vestiges of feudalistic power structures dominated by a few influential families. Still, it may safely be assumed that such practical experience in the management of local affairs as that sketched above is an essential attribute for anyone who seeks to play a leading role in rural agricultural communities.

Meanwhile, members of prefectural assemblies and the National Diet are in a position to utilize these power structures for their own canvassing activities. In the case of Mr. "A," an LDP member of parliament from the fictitious constituency of our case study, electoral support on the grass-roots level is typically organized into local village or hamlet units, with men in such posts as heads of production teams or primary agricultural societies, or agricultural committee members given the responsibility for actually canvassing for votes in each local community. Using the organizational skills and abilities that they have built up, these men work hard to line up votes behind their candidate.

It is thus only natural that the appointment of agricultural committee members and *nokyo* officers in each locality, village, and town is a matter of serious concern for prefectural assembly members as well as for National Diet members. In other words, they would like to see men from their own political machinery fill these positions, and it is therefore not at all unusual for these politicians to bring their influence to bear for this purpose. The relationship established is thus one of reciprocity, with each side supporting the position of the other. In cities, towns, and villages, meanwhile, Mr. A's *koenkai* (support organization) has local chapters that are headed by local and regional municipal assemblymen who have maintained this type of relationship with him throughout their political careers. Little wonder, then, that members of the National Diet take an active interest in municipal assembly elections in their constituencies. Against this background, campaigns for House of Representatives' elections always tend to become overheated, since general election results will eventually affect the outcome of regional and local elections at every level, and local canvassers realize that their own positions are also at stake.

There are other agricultural organizations, such as the crop insurance associations, which, among other things, handle compensation for losses caused by natural disasters and crop failures. The association's employees in Mr. A's constituency are also mobilized into frenzied activity during his election campaigns. In this way, the politician will reap considerable benefit from his own earlier efforts to improve the working conditions of the association employees. In addition to those interests, locally organized social groups and study groups for youths, typically bearing names such as the Society for Studying Agriculture, will provide Mr. A with frontline campaigners and canvassers. As part of his day-to-day routine at home, the politician will have made it a point to appear in person as often as possible before these groups, or to arrange for interesting speakers to address their meetings.

The position of National Diet members in rural constituencies is not, of course, secured merely by taking an active interest in the local elections in their constituencies. The decisive factor is what they can accomplish to meet the farmers' demands in the area of their own prime concerns—the needs of their daily lives and needs concerning agricultural production—and whether they can effectively exhibit their actions and achievements in this regard. This is an absolute prerequisite for every member of the Diet whose political base is in a rural area. Specifically, the farmers' demands usually include guaranteed prices for rice and other crops and produce, as well as adequate subsidies for land improvement, farm land consolidation, and river improvement projects.

Leaving the question of the price of rice for later discussion, a politician can best prove his mettle to the voters by procuring government subsidies. In the case of Mr. A, a young member of the Diet who is beginning to consolidate his position as a legislator specializing in agriculture and forestry, his activities at the government level can be outlined as follows.

When a village-size community is, let us say, applying for subsidy for a land improvement project, the normal administrative channel would be to apply via the local municipality to the prefectural government, which would, after a decision to approve the application, advance the matter to the Tohoku Office of the Ministry of Agriculture, Forestry and Fisheries, which would finally refer the application to the ministry in Tokyo. The farmers have an important vested interest in getting their request approved, because projects of this kind are subsidized to a large extent by the national and prefectural governments with minimal financial burden on the farmers themselves. But with so many other communities competing for limited budgetary allowances, the farmers in question have little hope of securing the necessary funds through normal administrative channels. So they send representatives to lobby Mr. A., their representative in the Diet: they would like him to wield his influence on their behalf.

Mr. A, in turn, will either dispatch his secretaries or go himself to the Ministry of Agriculture, Forestry and Fisheries or the prefectural administration to present his case. His effort will have been a success if the government or prefectural offices respond by saying, in effect, "If we give in to every one of these lobbies, we would be bankrupt— but if it is Mr. A's wish, we cannot refuse," and he will thus be assured of victory in the next election.

For those in the Ministry of Agriculture, Forestry and Fisheries and the prefectural government, the factor that determines their response is how much Mr. A has been helping them in his position as a legislator specializing in agriculture and forestry matters. For example, Mr. A may make frequent visits to the Ministry of Finance during the formulation phase of the annual budget to secure allocations for the Ministry of Agriculture, Forestry and Fisheries. There is thus also a standing relationship of give and take between the Ministry of Agriculture, Forestry and Fisheries and this Diet member.

Apart from members of parliament from the opposition parties, there is in Mr. A's constituency another Diet member from the LDP, Mr. B, with whom Mr. A is constantly vying for greater influence. Leaving his connections with other government offices aside, Mr. B is not as influential as Mr. A as far as the Ministry of Agriculture, Forestry and Fisheries is concerned. If the latter wants to eat into Mr. B's base of electoral support, therefore, he can utilize his connections with the ministry to maximum advantage. For example, he may gain access to information that a certain district in Mr. B's territory has applied for a subsidy but is having difficulty getting it approved. Mr. A will then casually approach influential figures in that district and offer his "cooperation." Needless to say, he may, in return for his favor, ask for help in the election: for instance, perhaps 30 percent of the votes in that district.

There is a more subtle method as well. When petitioners from the said district go to the Ministry of Agriculture, Forestry and Fisheries to lobby their cause, Mr. A can solicit the support of ministry officials by having them tell the petitioners, in effect, that "you might get somewhere if you approach us again through Mr. A." This way, there is little doubt that the district's representatives will come to Mr. A of their own accord. At this point, there should already be a basic agreement between Mr. A and the ministry officials on approval of the subsidy, but on the record the matter of the application will be treated as just having gotten off the ground. Eventually, Mr. A will be able to claim a lion's share of the credit by widely publicizing his "success" in securing the budget allocation.

There are also many cases in which local representatives will, from the start, solicit the support of a number of politicians in an attempt to secure an allocation for a given project. Here, the critical factor is who will be the first to break the good news of "allocation secured" to the voters. The one to break the news will be considered the most influential legislator vis-à-vis the government office concerned.

In this way, the relationship of interdependence between farmers and politicians is, in a sense, a game of influence peddling with "subsidies" (in other sectors as well as agriculture and forestry), with "votes" as the stakes. "The age of decentralization" is one phrase that has been gaining popularity in Japan in recent years as a reaction to this situation. An increasing number of citizens are supporting the argument that it is none other than "government by subsidies," as controlled by the central administration, that spoils the spirit of autonomous rule in the regions. But as for actual reform of government by subsidies, there is very little likelihood of any specific action being taken, although all would agree in principle to the necessity for reform. The main reason for this, apart from strong opposition from the central administration, is that no member of the Diet from a rural constituency could—in his right mind—support such a reform. For without the subsidy system, there can be no influence-peddling games of promising subsidies in return for assurance of votes. The dynamics of interdependence between farmers and politicians via the medium of subsidies and votes applies to a greater or lesser extent to practically all rural farming constituencies. It is the ability to gain maximum leverage from this dynamics of influence, as the party in power, that gives the LDP its political strength and it is, as such, an integral factor behind the party's long stay in power.

The power relationship between farmers and politicians, however, does not necessarily remain static. The question of whether a lobby effort will remain at the level of a mere "request" or will escalate into a "pressure" depends, of course, on the amount of influence wielded by the asking side. The more universal the goal of a request is within a constituency, the more likely it is to assume the tenor of pressure. A typical case in point would be the perennial demands for a higher price for rice. Demands of this nature, which transcend the domain of local constituency-level politics and represent the universal wish of farmers across the land, are thrust upon Diet members of all political parties in every constituency. As a result, the politicians are placed in the tough position of being rated by their electorate solely on the basis of their enthusiasm and concrete actions toward the fulfillment of the demand, in the absence of a power relationship that normally enables them to play the influence-peddling game. Should a politician stand apart in ignoring such a demand, he is bound to suffer the consequences in the next election.

But for individual constituencies, there are frequently issues that are more serious than the price of rice. In such a case, the very fact that a given demand is not nationwide often tends to enhance the sense of crisis within the constituency involved to make the pressures brought to bear on its legislators much more intense. A good example here would be the controversies surrounding the importation of such commodities as oranges, beef, and, on a more local level, cherries. Moreover, even demands like these, which are of an intrinsically regional nature, become public issues with nationwide implications virtually whenever an *nokyo* decides to take them up on an organization-wide basis. For instance, Yamagata Prefecture, which faces a problem over importation of cherries, is not strictly speaking concerned with oranges or beef. But as long as the *nokyo* consider them issues warranting joint action, the farmers of Yamagata Prefecture cannot remain aloof to these questions. There is, of course, merit for them in this arrangement as well, in that their cherry issue will not be shunted aside as merely a local problem.

It would also be fair to assume that it is none other than the rice price that ensures for an *nokyo* the unity of action it needs. And such unity also functions as a force that tends to restrict the activities of the legislators, a situation that undeniably stands in the way of compromises at times and leads to a lack of flexibility on both sides.

It should also be noted that, although working for the realization of the farmers' demands, on the one hand, the legislators are also responsible on the other hand for having to inform their constituents about the limitations of governmental policy—a role which adds to the complexity of their interrelationship.

Politics and government support of the rice price

In Japan, rice is not just a commodity but a sacred commodity. Food and livelihood had meant just rice until recently. The price of rice may be thought of as representing politics itself in Japan.

The existing system of staple food control is, strictly speaking, based on the Staple Food Control Act of 1942, although government controls on staple foods originated with the Rice Act of 1921, enacted after the Rice Riots of 1918. The Rice Act of 1921 and its amendments were systems of indirect control.

When faced with the food shortage situation in World War II, however, the government was no longer able to keep down the price of rice through indirect control, and the government was compelled to resort to direct controls. (See also the historical background of Japanese agricultural policy in chapter 5 by Egaitsu in this volume.) The Staple Food Control Act of 1942 is a system of direct control. As the demand–supply situation gradually improved over the ensuing years to finally reach the point of surplus production, the system evolved into a blessing for the farmers because it assured them of a stable volume of purchases at prices just to the producers. Overproduction of rice became a conspicuous trend sometime after 1965, a period during which the government also began to get deeply involved in the procedure for setting the annual price of rice.

By 1970 the amount of old rice in storage reached 7.2 million tons. The government cut back on rice acreage by an equivalent of 1.4 million tons through what it called a "temporary adjustment." In 1971, the production adjustment programs went into full operation as a temporary measure with a five-year time limit. The government purchase price of rice, the producers' price of rice, also had to remain fixed for two years in a row in 1969 and 1970. It was during the price-setting procedures in 1971 that "politics" for the first time took precedence over the demand–supply balance.

Activities surrounding the setting of the producers' price of rice for the 1971 crop reached a peak of intensity in late April of that year. Although then Prime Minister Eisaku Sato had spoken for some time of "freezing the price of rice for three years," the mood of dissent within the ruling Liberal Democratic Party seemed stronger than ever before. In the end the prime minister had to give in to demands from his own party. Even though the rate of price increase was a slim 3 percent, the mere fact of an increase at a time of overabundance of supply was evidence enough of the considerations of politics. Soon the general public itself was beginning to accept the idea that "politics sets the price of rice."

Why, then, was the prime minister compelled to give in to party demands that year? To be sure, the influence of the Sato regime was on the decline after its relatively long stay in power. But more important, the Japan Communist Party had made many gains while the LDP showings had been less than impressive in the nationwide local elections that had just been held and, moreover, the House of Councillors election was coming up shortly, in late June. In fact, LDP members of the upper house moved to adopt the 6.3 percent price increase plan proposed by the Comprehensive Farm Policy Research Committee (Sogo Nosei Chosa Kai), one of the LDP party organs, as the "consensus of the House of Councillors." The situation was so tense that some upper house members were heard to exclaim "I can't run if this proposal doesn't go through!" in sessions of the LDP Executive Council (Somu Kai), the party's highest decision-making organ. And the sense of crisis was mounting among LDP members of the House of Representatives as well as among the upper house members. One veteran lower house member from Hokkaido was reported to have gone straight to the prime minister at his official residence to say: "You are the only one opposed to raising the price of rice. You know, the party can even expel its president!" It is assumed that without the solid backing of farm votes this legislator could not have confronted so boldly the prime minister, who still wielded tremendous influence in his own right.

There was no question about the political clout of the farmers, their collective vote, and of the national *nokyo*, the Federation of Agricultural Cooperative Associations. One prefectural federation of *nokyo* chairmen from the Tohoku region went so far as to declare in a newspaper interview that "our 'enemies' are the Prime Minister and the Minister of Agriculture and Forestry. Many of us in [the] Nokyo feel that we should enter our own rival candidates in the Upper House election, to teach the LDP a lesson." Indeed, one legislator from Tohoku, who played a leading role among a group of LDP Diet members active in rice matters (the so-called rice legislators), had had the unnerving experience of witnessing LDP incumbents in the prefectural assembly suffer heavy losses to candidates backed by *noseiren,* a branch of the *nokyo* which concentrates its activity on lobbying, in the recent nationwide local elections. The experience led him to express concern about what would happen if the farmers simply abandoned the LDP. The concern was all the more serious among National Diet members who had been returned to their seats only a few times and who, as a result, were not confident they commanded a solid base of political support. For instance, one relatively young upper house member who had spent his career in the Budget Bureau of the Ministry of Finance went around soliciting support by saying, "I will lose the election if the price of rice is not raised"—only to be ridiculed by his former subordinates at the ministry, who told him: "Weren't you the one who used to reject the farmers' demands by saying 'we have to do something about the deficit in the staple food control budget'?" The excitement of an election can apparently make some politicians lose their heads. Still more examples of politicians ready to cast aside their principles and beliefs in the face of election pressures will be cited later on.

In the ninth House of Councillors election, held on June 27, 1971, the LDP did not do as well as had been expected by most analysts. In this first National Diet election of the 1970s, the party could win only sixty-three seats—one short of sixty-four, the number needed if the LDP wanted to maintain the same number of seats in the upper house as before. The main reason for the poor showing was an unexpectedly large number of setbacks suffered in the so-called one-seat districts of a constituency system that favored the LDP more than any other political party. While the party had only lost three of the total twenty-six single-seat districts in the previous upper house election in 1968, this time it lost eight. Single-seat districts are, in fact, constituencies in which farming communities make up the largest bloc of voters. At the time of this election these districts should have had a rural population percentage of 40 percent or thereabouts. Therefore, the LDP defeat there could only be attributed to the unpopularity of the government's policy of holding down the price of rice and adjusting production instead.

Still smarting from the sharp slap the farmers delivered to it in the 1971 House of Councillors election, the ruling LDP resorted to the strategy of having rice price deliberations in 1974 moved to after that year's upper house election. The move proved a success. Although the ballot held on July 7, 1974, appeared to have resulted in a "crushing LDP defeat," with the party winning not even half the number of the seats being contested and their margin over the total number of seats held by opposition parties shrinking to a single-digit figure, the LDP managed to win in all of the single-seat districts except Oki-

nawa. There were constituencies in which the party had lost eight
seats in the previous election. Had the LDP not recovered in these
rural constituencies, the balance of power between the LDP and opposition political forces would have been completely reversed and an
end marked to the single-party rule by the LDP.

Before the campaigns for the 1974 elections began, many observers
thought that the LDP might be rejected by the farm vote. These
observers had their reasons, for many constituents in rice-producing
areas of Tohoku and other regions were demanding that rice prices
be set before the upper house election, and their campaigns for winning higher prices were gathering momentum with unusual speed.
From one prefecture to the next, youth sections and women's sections
of prefectural *nokyo* federations began issuing such statements of intention as "No support for the LDP," "No cooperation with the LDP,"
and "Cast a blank vote"—a development which slowed the activities
of the traditionally LDP-oriented *nokyo* top echelon officials. The developments surrounding the rice price issue were generally interpreted by observers of the pre-election climate as working in favor of
the Japan Socialist Party (JSP) and other opposition parties. As matters
evolved, however, the farmers' expression of anti-LDP sentiments did
not materialize as votes against the party. The farmers, in the end,
had apparently no choice but to turn to their old standby, the LDP.

In turn, of course, the LDP administration had no choice but to
extend an appropriate "compensation" to the farmers who had helped
prevent an overwhelming victory by the opposition parties in such a
critical situation. On July 22, two weeks after the LDP's "defeat" in
the House of Councillors election, the government set its basic purchase price of rice at ¥13,615 per 60 kilograms—actually a 32.2 percent increase over the previous year's price. Adding to this the benefits
of various subsidy and assistance programs, the increase in actual
receipts per ton of producers came to 37.4 percent, the largest increase
since the chaotic period of the immediate postwar years. The government and the LDP had believed that, judging from past experience, a hike of 30 percent at the maximum would be enough for
coming to terms with the farmers. The tentative margin of 25.5 percent that the government first proposed to the Rice Price Deliberation
Council had allowed for an additional 5 percent margin for "political
considerations." The producers, meanwhile, feeling the painful effect
of an inflated economy that was especially difficult for the agriculture
and forestry sector, demanded a sizable price increase of 64.7 percent.
And the opposition parties, emboldened by their recent success in the
upper house election, began lining up support behind this demand

in order to bring considerable pressure on the government, with such groups as the Rice Price Joint Struggle of All Opposition Parties (Zen Yato Beika Kyoto) and the Japan Federation of Farmers' Unions (Nihon Nomin Kumiai Rengokai), backed by the JSP and the Japan Communist Party (JCP)) spearheading the drive. The combined strength of those forces evidently compelled the government and the LDP to give in to a considerable extent.

The electoral defeat in the House of Councillors set off something of a panic among the LDP's "rice legislators," and the late night session of the LDP Executive Council held on July 20, for instance, was dominated by voices demanding that the party leadership renegotiate the price of rice with the government. Their sentiments were typically that "we can't expect the farmers to settle for so little." Their arguments were strong enough to silence counterarguments from city-based Diet members who said that urban white collar workers will abandon the LDP if it keeps working together with just the farmers. A group of LDP "rice legislators" calling themselves the Rice Price Council (a group nicknamed the Viet Cong by the media, for reasons to be explained later) found its ranks swelling to as much as 80 percent of all LDP Diet members. The group demanded a very substantial increase of about 50 percent. It is reported that they went as far as to threaten the party leadership that they would "rally the Rice Price Council members to take group action if the party tried to hold the price of rice down to an unreasonable level."

No discussion of the "rice legislators" in the LDP would be complete without discussing the group dubbed the Viet Cong by the media. The word Viet Cong, of course, was used in Japan as in the United States to refer to the National Liberation Front during the Vietnam War. It probably became the nickname of the rice legislators because of the similarity in pronunciation to the word *beikon,* the Japanese abbreviation for the Rice Price Meeting of Diet Members (Beika Taisaku Giin Kondankai). Every year, when the time for rice price deliberations rolls around, groups of LDP Diet members—sometimes numbering over 300—materialize, seemingly out of nowhere, to hold meetings on the price of rice. Once they win their price increase demand, the groups then disappear, again as if by magic. In number of participants, these gatherings have consistently been the largest of all the meetings held by LDP legislators for at least the past ten years.

When the price-setting deliberations begin each year, usually in July, the Viet Cong legislators are found "making the rounds" in Tokyo rather than in their own constituencies, despite the fact that the National Diet is normally in recess then. They accompany and entertain petitioners from rural communities coming to Tokyo to lobby their causes, sometimes even taking care of their accommodations and meals in a frantic effort to curry their favor. It is important that these Diet members also attend the national meetings of rice price petitioners held in Tokyo and pay their respects to farmers from their home constituencies. Within the party, these legislators will present the views of their rural constituents through the Rice Price Council (or any other name adopted by the group for the particular year). The message is always simple—"Raise the price of rice." The Executive Council often provides the Viet Cong legislators with an ideal forum for their "show of force" activities. Besides the Viet Cong legislators who sit on the Executive Council, others who do not will also come to the council conference room to present their "nonmember's reports" and apply more pressure on the party leadership.

For many years, the Viet Cong legislators comprised the mainstream of the LDP. More precisely, there had never been another force strong enough to counter them in the party. But a strong rival group eventually emerged: the so-called comprehensive farm policy faction (Sogo Noseiha)—politicians who gained influence through their work with the Comprehensive Farm Policy Research Committee. During the days of the Sato administration, Kakuei Tanaka (the expremier) at one time served as chairman of this committee after being forced out of the key post of the party, the secretary-generalship. Originally a pressure group intended for securing a higher price for rice, the Comprehensive Farm Policy Research Committee gradually became a stronghold for the young and middle echelon members of the LDP's right-wing elements around the late 1960s when rice production was beginning to show a surplus. The comprehensive farm policy program of the Ministry of Agriculture, Forestry and Fisheries, launched in 1968, gave rise to the acreage reduction program of 1969 and the introduction of a semirationed rice distribution system. It was around this period that the "comprehensive farm policy faction" emerged. Although the acreage reduction program did not officially go into effect until 1971, it is obvious that the faction was central to introduction of the program.

Within the LDP, 1976 was also an important year. In response to the proposed increase of 5.2 percent, a margin which the producers' organizations had already tried to reject as being far too small, some members of the faction boldly asserted that "2.5 percent would be quite enough." A few years back such a statement would have triggered a flood of strong protest from the farmers. And since a general election was scheduled, the statement was seen as one that completely ignored the farm vote.

Behind this seemingly bold move was the growing ineffectiveness of the rice issue as a tool for lining up votes behind selected candidates. More specifically, the regional *nokyo* machinery that had once been so useful to the LDP Diet members for gathering votes was no longer under their influence. Labor unions were formed in one *nokyo* office after another by employees willing to work for candidates supported by the opposition parties. Consequently, LDP legislators began to feel a need for creating their own organizations of supporters. In the meantime, the LDP was sinking to the position of a "party backed only by one-third" or "party backed only by one-quarter" of the voters in urban constituencies. Diet members representing these districts naturally began to assert that "the setting of a high rice price in concert with farmers' organizations will only alienate the urban consumers." This argument gradually gained support. The perennial "rice price struggle" rapidly declined in force through 1977 and 1978. Attendance at the farmers' rice price rallies by members of parliament was becoming a purely perfunctory affair, and the farmers, for their part, were abstaining from pressing unreasonable demands. In 1979, when the season for rice price deliberation rolled around, the producers appeared unable to arouse any enthusiasm at all. More remarkable still, the national conference of *nokyo* representatives, which met on June 18, did not even adopt the usual slogan of "let's win the rice price we demand." By now, LDP Diet members were deserting the cause as quickly as they could manage. The Viet Cong regulars remained on the scene, but they plainly showed a lack of enthusiasm, as evidenced, for instance, by the renaming of their organization from the previous "LDP National Diet Members' Council on Producers' Price of Rice" (or the Rice Price Council) to "National Diet Members' Council on Promotion of Agriculture and Forestry."

In response to this show of weakness on the producers' side, agriculture, forestry and fisheries minister Watanabe unveiled a new policy line tougher than anything previously seen in the sector. He proposed to introduce a graduated price scale system for the government purchase of rice according to which the produce would be divided into five different quality grades. That appeared to be a reasonable measure, consistent with the comprehensive farm policy faction's earlier assertions that "it is ridiculous that tasty rice and not so tasty rice should bear the same price." There was, however, a political pitfall. When examples of the "not so tasty rice" were given, members of parliament from the areas where the crop received the lowest rating became quite angry. On July 13, the Rice Price Deliberation Council submitted a report essentially constructed around a deferment of price increases and the introduction of a graduated pricing system.

The following day both a joint meeting of the LDP's Comprehensive Farm Policy Research Committee and the Agriculture and Forestry Subcommittee and a meeting of the party Executive Council became extremely stormy. In the final settlement, which materialized in the early hours of July 15, the party made a compromise by promising "to supply the amount equivalent to five-sixths of the price reduction that would accompany the introduction of graduated prices as a cushioning measure against the sharp price fluctuation."

The June 1980 simultaneous elections for both houses of the Diet seemed to the producers' organizations an extremely good occasion for attaining an increase in the producers' price of rice since the elections were not expected earlier at all, and all candidates were not confident of being returned. The producers' organization asked all parties and all candidates to make clear (a) their basic ideas concerning food and agricultural policies, (b) their attitudes toward the 1980 rice price, (c) their thinking about the government rice production adjustment program, and (d) their thinking about the staple food control system. In responding to these questions, almost all candidates clearly showed that they were favorable to the national *nokyo's* demands. After the elections, the producers' organizations asked each of the LDP legislators to act on what he said during the campaign. The result of these actions was a 2.3 percent increase in the producers' price, half of which was offset by reduction of subsidies to rice growers. The existence of a huge rice surplus did not permit any large percentage increase.

National Sentiments

The climate surrounding politics in Japan

As pointed out in countless discussions on Japan and its people, there is little reason to doubt that the accepted mode of decision making in Japan, whether at the level of the national government or at the level of individual private enterprises, has placed the greatest emphasis on the maintenance of internal *wa*, or harmony, with the forging of a consensus among constituent members of a given organization—even at the expense of some loss in time—always the primary consideration. In Japan, even those in the highest executive positions, for example, government cabinet ministers or directors of private enterprises, tend to be reluctant to exercise unilaterally their responsibility as decision makers, preferring instead to wait for the formation of an internal consensus that amply reflects the views of the lower echelons before making the final decision. Even in a situation like the election of the members of the National Diet, there is little individual activity in the Western sense of the term, because collective action within and by various groups is the norm.[4]

It is hardly surprising that this aspect of Japanese tradition survives best in the rural communities. In the metropolitan areas, especially the new residential belts in the suburbs, hardly any new community based groups have developed, so that local traditions as such have been lost (with the exception of internal traditions within business enterprises and enterprise-based labor unions). Several factors could account for the survival of traditional customs and practices in rural parts of the country. In irrigation farming, the most widely used method of farming, it is necessary for all farm households in a given watershed to work together for the fair distribution and control of the water resources. In paddy rice farming, therefore, there can be no dissenters. Moreover, people who harbor dissatisfaction with this indigenous, rural tradition have by now to a large extent migrated to the cities in the long history of population shift since the days of the Meiji Restoration, leaving only those who essentially feel no conflict with the traditional values in the rural parts. Also, the redistribution of rural assets in the land reform implemented just after World War II gave rise to a widespread middle class mentality in farming communities across the country. (As one result, for instance, the Japan Farmers' Union, backed by the JSP, rapidly lost influence after the land reform.)

Against this background, the basic unit of any action, be it political or economic, cannot in most practical situations be an individual or an individual household, but must be a group of people within a community unit. These community-size groups collectively serve as a substructure for village- and town-level municipalities and cooperative associations functioning respectively as the local administrative and economic units.

It is thus hardly surprising that the implementation of national farm policy in the form of commodity programs, like rice price control and the granting of subsidies, emphasizes the role of these groups from the basic levels upward. Moreover, it even appears at times as if the national government is trying to strengthen its influence over the regional municipalities (governments) by using the grants at its dis-

[4] Although prone to exaggeration in places, Ezra F. Vogel's work (1977) is useful for understanding this aspect of Japanese tradition.

posal as leverage. In a sector as heavily dependent on government expenditure as agriculture and forestry, the relationship of mutual understanding with the long-ruling LDP is of crucial importance for rural communities, so that the electorate naturally tends to choose conservative leaders. In contrast, urban voters, who do not necessarily subscribe to traditional Japanese values and who do not have an organized means of having their views reflected in government policies (as the rural constituencies have with their cooperatives), often tend to assume an anti-LDP stance. In the past, many a regional election has been fought as a choice between "the conservatives linked directly to the central government," and "the progressives representing the wishes of regional citizens."

As will be explained later in detail, neither urban dwellers' representatives nor the opposition political parties are actually opposed to the policy of protecting agricultural interests. This is because, in the first place, urban constituents are not presently finding it difficult to bear the burden of protecting the agricultural sector, either as consumers of farm products or as taxpayers. There are other reasons as well:

1. Opposition political parties based in urban areas have in the past opposed the importation of American farm products, perceiving it as part of the U.S. "economic invasion of Japan." They argued that this invasion by U.S. agricultural products resulted in the destruction of agriculture as Japan's traditional industry, thereby making the nation less self-sufficient in food supplies in a development amounting to the loss of independence for the Japanese economy. The opposition parties asserted that this argument was underscored by past cases of importation of U.S. grains under the U.S.–Japan Mutual Security Agreement.

2. The population of metropolitan areas also includes a large number of people born in rural regions. As of 1970, the total population of Tokyo, Yokohama, Osaka, Kobe, Nagoya, and their peripheral regions (together referred to as greater metropolitan areas) numbered 47,340,000—a figure representing an increase of 14,820,000 since 1955. According to another set of statistics, the total population influx from non-greater metropolitan areas to the greater metropolitan areas between 1954 and 1972 reached 20.1 million, while the population flow in the opposite direction amounted to 11.4 million.[5] These people who have migrated to

[5] The figures in 2. are calculated from tables in a work by the Government Population Council (Jinko Mondai Shingikai, 1979, pp. 190, 196).

the cities relatively recently still tend to retain a strong senti-
mental attachment to the rural communities they came from,
choosing to follow, for example, the custom of returning for a
visit during the summer and New Year vacations every year.

3. Because of the relatively slow formation of social overhead capital during the rapid growth of the Japanese economy, the quality
of the living environment in the large cities has deteriorated to
such an extent that urban dwellers have come to assume a negative attitude toward the heavy and chemical industries. This,
in turn, has led to arguments calling for the strengthening of
the agriculture and forestry sector to counterbalance the weight
of these industries.

On food and agriculture

For the people of Japan, a country of limited land area with moun-
tainous terrain accounting for much of the space, pre-modern national history amounts to a series of struggles against starvation. In
particular, the period from about 1700 to the Meiji Restoration in
1867 saw many famines sweep the country. The new Meiji government
made agricultural development one of its priority items in its national
economic development plans and invited agricultural experts from
the Western nations to teach advanced farming. Even so, the rate of
increase in food production in the years up to World War II was not
enough to compensate for the high rate of increase in population
during the same period. When the Japanese economy entered a phase
of brisk activity with the outbreak of World War I, the general standard of living improved and consumption of rice began to increase
rapidly. As a result, the price of rice immediately skyrocketed. By
1918 the overall food supply situation had become so tight that rice
riots broke out. It was after these riots that the government began
serious efforts to improve the general level of food consumption through
such steps as increased production of rice in Korea and Taiwan, increased production of soybeans in Manchuria, increased production
of sugar in Taiwan, and promotion of development in the fishing
industry.

The noteworthy point in this connection is that many of the efforts
undertaken after 1918 to increase food supplies were implemented
in lands outside the present Japanese national boundaries. This, then,
was the real reason the food situation became so critical in Japan
following its defeat in World War II. After the war, the government
implemented a series of ambitious programs to increase food pro-

duction, and the nation was finally able to achieve self-sufficiency, at least in terms of rice, by around 1955.

The diet of the Japanese people, of course, improved tremendously in the ensuing years because of the rapid growth of the economy, but it should also be noted that much of this improvement was achieved through the importation of feed grains, barley, wheat, and other agricultural products. The importation of such vast quantities was made possible by the relatively stable situation in world food markets, combined with the rapid increase in Japan's exports. The percentage of foods and agricultural raw materials in the nation's total imports has since declined from 46.5 percent in 1955–1959, to 21.2 in 1970–1974.[6]

The history of the food supply situation in Japan outlined above tells us, first of all, that the only time that food has been abundant enough to allow the Japanese to consume as much as they wanted to was the rather short period since 1955, and that throughout their long history up to the time of World War I, they have had to farm every inch of arable land merely to ward off starvation. Second, the Japanese also experienced a serious food shortage after World War II, and this memory is still fresh in the minds of the older population. And third, the Japanese people have come to harbor an attitude of serious concern toward the issue of securing adequate food supplies, in the wake of such developments as the crises in world grain trade and oil in from 1973 to 1974. They also came to feel that an economic life devoid of efforts to "farm every inch of arable land" was somehow unnatural. As might be expected, the feeling of concern about food supply has been further intensified by such developments as the U.S. restriction on soybean exports, the adoption of new 200 mile fishing zones by several countries, and the publication of a Japanese translation of the work by the Club of Rome (D. H. Meadows and coauthors, 1972).

In Japan, there is no concept quite like agricultural fundamentalism in the sense in which the term is applied in Western societies.[7] In fact, a tendency to look upon rural communities as a semifeudalistic society persisted until relatively recently, in part as a result of the designation of rural communities as "undemocratic societies" in the land reform directive issued by the occupation authorities just after World War II. Of course, since Japan had primarily an agricultural economy until

[6] The figures are calculated from various issues of the White Paper on Commerce (The Ministry of Trade and Industry, various years).

[7] A concept stressing the importance of family farms as the backbone of democracy is in (Griswald, 1947).

fifty years ago, there have always been advocates of the idea that agriculture should in fact form the basis of both the national economy and society. As mentioned earlier, recent years have seen the emergence of another school of thought that stresses the importance of the agricultural and forestry sector in light of the deterioration of the urban living environment caused by the relatively slow formation of social overhead capital during the years of rapid economic growth. But to put it very simply, agriculture is considered important in Japan today as a source of food supply, and not as something to be valued because of the quality of life in farming communities. Agriculture will be considered important as long as people are feeling insecure about their food supply situation. Apart from the postwar generation, the Japanese generally believe that the period of twenty-odd years since 1955 has been a really exceptional era in the course of Japanese history and that their food supply situation could in fact quickly deteriorate if they do not remain vigilant.

In May 1975, a National Food Conference brought together sixty-nine representatives of the academic world, the agriculture and forestry sector, the world of business and finance, labor organizations, consumers' groups, and the media (about one-third of those attending were from the agriculture and forestry sector), with Prime Minister Takeo Miki, Deputy Prime Minister Takeo Fukuda, Minister of Agriculture and Forestry Shintaro Abe, Finance Minister Masayoshi Ohira (their titles at the time), with other members of the cabinet also attending. After three sessions, the conference submitted the following proposal to the government. It represents a view shared by the leaders of Japan at the time (Norindaijin Kambo Kikakushitsu, 1975, pp. 287–288).

> Considering the future of the world food situation and the state of our land resources, the assurance of a stable food supply in the future for the nation's 100 million people and of the future adequate life for those in the farming and fishery industries, are fundamental tasks for the national administration. From this standpoint, it is to be hoped that the government will give special consideration to the items listed below in its formation of policy measures in the future.
>
> 1. The basic objective of food policies is to consolidate the structure of agricultural production with the capacity for self-sufficiency. In particular, the most pressing tasks at the present time are considered to be: the securing of the land and water resources necessary for farming, and their systematic development and improvement; education and training of those farmers who will play a key role in future agricultural production; establishment and development of livestock farming through such measures as development of a fod-

der production base; and formation of an appropriate farm price policy.

2. Recognizing the reality that Japan will continue to have to rely on overseas suppliers for a considerable part of the food requirements of the population in the years to come, it is necessary to take an active part in international cooperation efforts to resolve the world's food problems while developing, at the same time, a system for the stabilization and storage of farm produce imports.

*   *   *   *

3. Out of consideration for the health of the Japanese people of to-morrow, a standard menu based on the distinctive features of the country's natural conditions and civilization should be defined. In particular, ways of improving school lunch programs should be studied.

4. Considering the social changes that have taken place in Japan in recent years, educational and informational programs should be actively promoted henceforth, for deepening public understanding of farming and fishery activities that are conducted within the natural ecological system; efforts should also be made to improve the living environments of agricultural and fishing communities.

Although the world grain market was stabilized and the rice surplus has become a serious domestic problem, the House of Representatives unanimously passed the following resolution on April 8, 1980, which was approved almost without change by the House of Councillors two weeks later:

Resolution on the Improvement of the Capacity
for Self-Sufficiency in Food

The agricultural and fishery industries in Japan are currently experiencing severe difficulties. As a result of diversification of diet patterns, a serious imbalance has arisen in food supply and demand. To combat this problem, the Japanese Government has implemented measures for adjustment of rice production, although the resulting effects have imposed severe difficulties on producers. Meanwhile the rate of self-sufficiency in food has steadily declined and food imports have increased every year, further aggravating the instability of food supply.

The Japanese fishery industry also faces serious problems of production and supply, mainly brought about by the imposition of 200-mile-limit regulations.

World food supply/demand trends in the 1980's will grow increasingly unstable, reflecting rapid population growth, improvement in living standards and the use of food as a tool of diplomacy. The repercussions of these trends will profoundly affect the food situation in Japan. Under these critical conditions, it is imperative that Japan secure a stable food supply by improving its self-sufficiency in food, the level of which is far behind that of other developed countries. Be it resolved that, in the interest of national security, the Japanese Government must institute proper measures to improve the capacity for self-sufficiency in food and to increase productivity in the agriculture and fishery industries.

Results of opinion polls

For the purpose of corroborating statistically some of the assumptions discussed so far, we can examine the results of two opinion polls conducted by the Public Relations Section of the Prime Minister's Secretariat. The first poll was conducted in August 1975. The second was conducted in August 1978.[8] A comparison of the two opinion polls shows the effect of the passage of time following the world grain crisis.

First, the degree of pessimism in the Japanese people's outlook on the future of the food situation may be seen in tables 7-2 and 7-3. In 1975, 58 percent of the respondents believed that the food situation in Japan would be worse after ten years, while only one in every four respondents thought it would be better or remain unchanged. Three years later, those believing that the situation would get better or remain unchanged recorded a sharp increase, but 46 percent of the respondents in 1978 still believed it would get worse. Understandably, the number of those responding "it will get much worse" diminished by about one-half in the same period.

Another interesting finding is that whereas the ratio of the respondents who were pessimistic about the food situation ten years hence to those optimistic was about the same for metropolitan areas, other cities, and towns and villages (rural communities) in the 1975 poll, the 1978 poll shows that the more urban the living environment of the respondents, the more pessimistic their responses. A similar trend is seen in the distribution by occupation in the 1978 poll.

Table 7-4 shows responses to the question of whether Japan's food should be imported or whether domestic production should be increased. A majority of the Japanese, as indicated here, believe that the production of foods that can be supplied domestically should be expanded for domestic consumption. As might be expected, the percentage of such advocates of self-reliance diminishes somewhat from

---

[8] In both polls, samples were selected on the basis of sex, age, occupation, and density of population (size of population of each municipal district). After sending each sample a letter explaining the import of the poll, a reporter interviewed the sample. Therefore, there might be cases where the sample was not at his or her residence when the reporter visited his or her place. Each poll was intended for a sample of 5,000. In the 1975 polls (with 789 people either out of contact or, in a few cases, refusing to respond), answers from 4,211 respondents were collected and analyzed. In the 1978 polls, 925 individuals were either out of contact or unwilling to respond, so that responses from 4,075 people were processed and analysed (Naikaku Soridaijin Kanbo Kohoshitsu, 1975 and 1978).

TABLE 7-2. OPINIONS IN 1975 ABOUT WHAT JAPAN'S
(percentage)

Category of respondent	Will worsen	Will worsen much	Will worsen little
Overall	58	16	42
By region			
Ten large cities	58	17	41
Other cities	58	16	42
Towns & villages	57	15	42

1975 to 1978, and is obviously the highest for those working in the agriculture and forestry sector.

Table 7-5 shows that the percentage of the proponents of self-reliance is rather high even in the large cities (with the exception of the Tokyo metropolitan area, where it is somewhat lower). Also, the percentages of the proponents of self-reliance in such job categories as commercial, industrial, and service sectors and self-employed, managerial, and skilled jobs, and students—people who usually tend to assume a position critical of the nation's agricultural sector—are the same as the percentages for all respondents. It is also noteworthy that the percentage of the proponents of importation—those who feel that foreign produce, if cheaper, should be imported for domestic consumption—is as high as 30 percent for those in managerial and skilled jobs.

The greatest task facing the Japanese government in agricultural administration today, it is well known, is the solution of the rice surplus problem. In addition to the accumulation of a large amount of surplus rice, the government's staple food control budget is showing a huge deficit, which imposes a serious burden on the total government budget. In addition, the producers' price of rice in Japan is much higher than that in the world market. This situation notwithstanding, only 10 percent of the respondents in the 1978 poll attribute the cause of the rice surplus to the domestic price being too high. Most people attribute it to factors such as increased consumption of bread and noodles (49 percent), increased consumption of supplementary food items (10 percent) and the serving of bread with school lunches (10 percent).

FOOD SITUATION WILL BE LIKE IN ABOUT TEN YEARS

Will not differ from now	Will improve	Will improve much	Will improve little	Don't know
19	5	5	0	18
20	5	5	0	17
20	4	4	0	18
19	5	5	1	18

Those attributing it to the government's mismanaged agricultural policy amounted to a very small 8 percent.

As another reflection of such attitudes toward the rice surplus, 51 percent of the respondents in table 7-6 say that the current deficit in the staple food control budget is "inevitable, given the present situation." While the high percentages of those who think this way in the rural communities (and those occupied in the agriculture and forestry sector) are to be expected, the percentages are also markedly high among metropolitan residents and those in occupations which tend to be critical of agriculture and rural communities. As a result, those who maintain that this deficit should be eliminated consistently amount to 40 percent or less, except among those in managerial and skilled jobs where the proportion reaches 46 percent.

There are, to be sure, reasons behind the consumers' seemingly generous attitude toward the high price of rice. Although the consumer price of rice rose 2.6 times between 1965 and 1978, the amount spent on rice per wage-earner's household during the same period increased only 1.7 times. Because the total amount of consumption expenditure per wage-earner's household increased 4.2 times during the same period as well, the proportion of the amount spent on rice to the total expenditure of a single consumer shrank from 6.6 percent to 2.6 percent during that period. In other words, it was the consumption of less rice and the increase in their total food bills that led the consumers to assume a more magnanimous attitude toward the rising price of rice. It should, incidentally, be mentioned that the consumption of foods other than staple foods grew during the same

TABLE 7-3. OPINIONS IN 1978 ABOUT WHAT JAPAN'S FOOD SITUATION WILL BE LIKE IN TEN YEARS (percentage)

Category of respondent	No. of respondents	Will improve	Will improve much	Will improve little	Will not differ from now	Will worsen	Will worsen much	Will worsen little	Don't know	Total
Overall	4,075	10	1	9	27	46	38	8	17	100
By region:										
Tokyo wards	268	7	1	6	26	50	40	10	17	100
Nine large cities	500	6	1	5	26	53	43	10	15	100
Cities of 100,000 or more	1,429	10	1	9	25	48	39	9	17	100
Cities under 100,000	822	11	1	10	28	44	37	7	17	100
Towns and villages	1,056	13	1	12	29	42	35	7	16	100
By sex:										
Male	1,753	11	1	10	27	48	39	9	14	100
Female	2,322	9	1	8	27	45	37	8	19	100
By occupation:										
Self-employed:										
Agri, forestry & fishing	297	16	1	15	31	32	27	5	21	100
Commerce, service, free-lance	410	9	1	8	26	48	40	8	17	100
Other employed:										
Managerial, professional, & technical	180	12	2	10	34	45	34	11	9	100
Clerical	532	9	1	8	27	54	43	11	10	100
Laborers	785	9	1	8	24	51	42	9	16	100
Unemployed wives	1,211	9	1	8	27	47	40	7	17	100

TABLE 7-4. OPINIONS IN 1975 ABOUT WHETHER JAPAN'S FOOD SHOULD
BE IMPORTED OR DOMESTIC PRODUCTION INCREASED
(percentage)

Category of respondent	In principle, domestic production should be increased whenever possible	It is better to import less expensive foodstuffs rather than increase domestic production	Don't know
Total replies	71	17	12
Those employed in agriculture, forestry & fishing	76	11	13

TABLE 7-5. OPINIONS IN 1978 ABOUT JAPAN'S FOOD CONSUMPTION
PRACTICES

Category of respondent	No. of respondents	Better to consume domestic products	Better to consume imported products if they are less expensive	Don't know
		(————————(percentage)————————)		
Overall	4,075	67	20	13
By region:				
Tokyo wards	268	60	20	20
Nine large cities	500	65	21	14
Cities of 100,000 or more	1,429	66	21	13
Cities under 100,000	822	68	22	10
Towns and villages	1,056	70	17	13
By occupation:				
Self-employed:				
Agri, forestry & fishing	297	80	10	10
Commerce, service, free-lance	410	71	21	8
Other employed:				
Managerial, professional, & technical	180	67	30	3
Clerical	532	70	24	6
Family employed:				
Agri, forestry & fishing	153	77	9	14
Commerce, service, free-lance	146	68	21	11
Unemployed:				
Unemployed wives	1,211	63	21	16
Students	40	65	20	15
Other unemployed	321	64	14	22

253

TABLE 7-6. JAPAN: SHOULD THE STAPLE FOOD CONTROL BUDGET
DEFICIT BE ELIMINATED?

Category of respondent	No. of respondents	Deficit should be eliminated	Inevitable given the present situation	Don't know
		(———————(percentage)———————)		
Overall	2,668	36	51	13
By region:				
Tokyo ward	149	40	46	14
Nine large cities	325	40	44	16
Cities of 100,000 or more	938	40	48	12
Cities under 100,000	569	30	57	13
Towns and villages	687	31	57	12
By occupation:				
Self-employed:				
Agri, forestry & fishing	238	25	66	9
Commerce, service, free-lance	317	40	54	6
Other employed:				
Managerial, professional, & technical	153	46	49	5
Clerical	399	39	53	8
Laborers	484	36	51	13
Unemployed wives	681	36	45	19

interval, with consumer spending on nonstaple foods increasing 3.8 times. Nevertheless, the share of the same in consumers' total expenditures declined from 27.8 to 24.8 percent.

There are no statistics for gauging exactly how public sentiment stands on the food situation and food prices at this particular point in time. Nevertheless, recent years have seen mounting criticisms of the existing protectionism in agricultural policy. Such business and industry groups as the Federation of Economic Organizations (Keizai Dantai Rengokai), the Japanese Federation of Employers Associations (Nihon Keieisha Remmei), and the Japan Committee for Economic Development (Keizai Doyu Kai), along with the Japanese Federation of Labor (Nihon Rodo Sodomei), one of the major federations of labor unions, have begun advocating a policy shift from this protectionism. A sharp appreciation of the Japanese yen, which reached a peak in 1978, placed the nation's export industries in severe financial difficulty, with the employees of the affected enterprises bearing much of the brunt in the form of curtailed or frozen wages. Inevitably, the focus of public attention turned toward the relatively high food prices. Moreover, public concern about the inflationary effects of the rising price of oil led to demands for lower food prices. At the same time, given the increasingly stringent state of public finances, the deficit in the government's staple food control budget has become a target of mounting criticism.[9]

Agricultural policies of political parties

The agricultural policies of the political parties are all protectionist toward the farming sector. The JCP and the JSP both stress the importance of self-reliance in food, while the Komeito and the DSP tend to lean toward the interests of the consumers. The DSP policy, in particular, reflects the views of the Japanese Federation of Labor, the labor group with which that party has close ties. One of the measures the DSP calls for, "the establishment of long-term demand and supply targets in staple foods," includes the idea of selecting the types of foods for which Japan should rely on imports from overseas. This party takes the position of advocating a balance between the argument that insistence on complete self-reliance would be pointless given the size of Japan's land mass, and the one that calls for efforts toward 100 percent self-reliance. The LDP takes a position halfway between those of the JSP and the JCP on the one hand, and those of the DSP and Komeito on the other. It is also seen that while the JSP and JCP advocate increased production through expansion of the total area of farmland and acreage under cultivation, the DSP and Komeito call for maintenance of the existing level of food production, increased production through the improvement of available arable land and improvement of farming techniques, or both. The LDP takes a middle position in this regard as well. (See appendix 7-A for a short description of each party's program.)

Although all of the parties support the strengthening of the pricing policy, their actual positions on this subject vary significantly. The JSP and the JCP are pushing the concept of strengthening the existing staple food control system to the point, eventually, of covering other farm produce. Consequently, they argue for an increase in fiscal outlay for price support measures. The LDP, whose position faithfully

---

[9] See, for example, the February 4 and 5, 1979, editions of *Nihon Keizai Shimbun* and the March 3, 1979, edition of *Asahi Shimbun*. The latest influential report is one on the staple food control system by the Japan Economic Research Institute (Nihon Keizai Chosa Kyogikai, 1980).

reflects the farm policy of the government, intends to cut down the deficit in the present staple food control budget and also takes into account the position of the nations that export farm produce. While not specifying their positions on pricing policy, the Komeito and the DSP nevertheless assert that the guarantee of a fair income for the farming population should be achieved through improvement of productivity rather than through higher prices.

Machinery for Making National Policy Decisions

Interparty relations—the treatment of separate pieces of legislation

It goes without saying that policies in general can be divided into those that require the enactment of new statutes or amendment of existing ones, and those that require neither. The policies over which opposition parties usually take issue with the ruling party are those that require enactment or amendment of statutes, although opposition members may also address other policy-related issues in connection with budget and other deliberations. In other words, administrative actions based on existing statutes usually only require some form of agreement between the government and the party in power. Of course, in order to secure in advance a measure of favorable response from the opposition parties on new pieces of legislation, the government is required to show some understanding of issues and questions raised by the opposition over administrative actions that are not subject to parliamentary debate.

In preparation for the enactment of specific statutes, the LDP and the government will make whatever adjustments that may be necessary to reach a basic agreement before introducing these bills in the Diet. The role of the LDP in the Diet may thus be described, without exaggeration, as consisting entirely of efforts to seek smooth passage of government-sponsored bills. The position of the opposition parties is rather different because they do not take part in preliminary adjustments within the government. In a sense, it is in the committee deliberations on policy measures that the opposition parties have their initial official contact with government representatives. For this reason, most of the deliberation time in the Diet is taken up in questioning by members of the opposition parties. When LDP members raise questions themselves, they frequently tend to be for the purpose of confirming items agreed to with the government in advance, or for helping the deliberations to proceed more smoothly.

In contrast, the questions from opposition members usually cover numerous, detailed aspects of the issues involved. Because the LDP members still make up the majority, however, these questions are rarely aimed at securing substantive revision of proposed legislation and are often utilized for external public relations purposes. Therefore, a large number of their questions are aimed at securing purely *pro forma* revisions or at bringing about resolutions of a rather moralistic nature. In fact, the opposition party legislators often use copies of minutes of parliamentary committee meetings and other sessions for public relations material in their constituencies. Thus it is not uncommon for different opposition parties to pose questions repeatedly on essentially the same points in sessions with government officials—a practice which obviously causes tremendous delay in debate. In other words, the Diet is often used as a forum by the opposition parties for public relations activities aimed at various constituencies.

In addition to taking part in these sessions, the LDP as the majority party may sometimes arrange the order in which bills are to be deliberated on to its best advantage. To achieve the passage of the maximum number of all LDP-sponsored bills, it is important to arrange them in such an order that the opposition members will not be able to use delaying tactics to advantage to hold up the passage of bills they oppose.

With these aims in mind, the political parties make numerous deals with each other through the apparatus of the parliamentary committee of each party. Agricultural and related bills per se would pass relatively more easily than those concerning education, national defense, labor, and other areas, because the differences of views between the majority and opposition parties tend to be smaller on agricultural issues. Nevertheless, agricultural bills sometimes fail to pass, because the parties are often more interested in the fate of important bills in other areas, and because the majority and opposition parties often take opposing positions over such pieces of legislation.[10] The Kokkai Taisaku Iinkai (Committee for Steering the Deliberations in the Diet) of each party is responsible for the above strategies.

[10] During the period from the 63rd Session (1970) to the 80th Session of the Diet (1977), the Ministry of Agriculture, Forestry and Fisheries introduced eighty-seven bills into the Diet, of which seventy-eight passed, eight bills were subject to continued deliberation in the following sessions, and only one bill failed. It is said that the Agriculture, Forestry and Fisheries Committee in both the upper and lower houses is a "nakayoshi club" (a bosom friend club) (Matsuura, T., 1977).

The government, the Liberal Democratic Party, and the national Diet

Ties between the national government and the political parties may be examined in terms of two kinds of relationships. The *first* relationship stems from the practice of appointing members of the Diet belonging to the majority party as heads of the different administrative branches. In the case of a cabinet minister who is appointed from the private sector, however, the relationship between the administrative branch involved, that is, the cabinet, and the majority party would be channeled through the minister without the involvement of other Diet members. In this connection, it should be noted that no minister of agriculture and forestry has been appointed from the private sector since World War II.

The first relationship obviously exists solely between the government and the majority party, the LDP. Within the context of this relationship, the party may choose to exercise its influence in personnel appointments in certain administrative branches. In this connection, it is worth noting that whether or not the party's involvement in personnel appointments in an administrative branch like the cabinet will have a positive effect on the relationship between the government and the ruling party depends, to a large extent, on how well a person thus appointed to a ministerial post can get along with the apparatuses concerned within the LDP. (For instance, the counterpart apparatuses for the minister of agriculture, forestry and fisheries would be the party's Sogo Nosei Chosa Kai [Comprehensive Farm Policy Research Committee] and Norin Suisan Iinkai [Agricultural and Forestry Subcommittee].) In this regard, the relationship between the minister of agriculture, forestry and fisheries and concerned apparatuses within the LDP has been working smoothly in recent years, since the post has usually been filled by men who had previously served as officers for the party's Comprehensive Farm Policy Research Committee. (In the history of Japanese politics, the appointment of cabinet ministers has always been strongly influenced by factional interests so that "having the right man for the right job" is not always the primary consideration.)

When the administrative branches are about to set down new policy measures, their ties with the concerned organs within the LDP obviously assume a great deal of importance. For example, the successful conclusion of the 1979 farm product trade negotiations between Japan and the United States was due, to a considerable extent, to the mutual good faith between Minister of Agriculture, Forestry and Fisheries

Ichiro Nakagawa and the Agriculture and Forestry Subcommittee of the LDP.

The second relationship is that between the administrative branches of the government, the Diet, and the political parties to which individual Diet members belong. The second relationship, of course, also consists of relations between the government and opposition parties in addition to those between the government and the LDP.

In the context of relations between the government and the LDP, the main activities that occur involve deliberations on various bills and drafts of budget bills to be submitted, but consultations about matters concerning negotiations with the opposition parties, pressure groups, the governments of exporting countries, and the like, are also an important part of their work. As far as the relations between the government and the LDP Agriculture and Forestry Subcommittee and Comprehensive Farm Policy Research Committee in particular are concerned, their work includes consultations about the setting of government support prices for certain farm products, in addition to deliberation of the aforementioned bills. Above all, the setting of the price of rice is an extremely serious matter that concerns the fundamentals of the nation's farm policy. Because such matters must be worked out with the LDP at the basic level, the government is required to devote considerable effort to make the necessary adjustments with the party. Needless to say, when the LDP is seeking passage of legislation through its house members, the party's internal apparatuses must make an intensive effort to arrive at necessary adjustments with the government before the pieces of legislation are actually submitted to the House of Representatives. Without such preparatory work, there may be problems in implementing the legislation (such as the establishment of needed ordinances and regulations). In fact, bills formulated for passage by house members often span the jurisdiction of many different government agencies so that the work of making all the necessary adjustments frequently becomes quite cumbersome.

Of course, when the government consults the Agriculture and Forestry Subcommittee and other apparatuses within the LDP on administrative matters—particularly those that have a major bearing on individual private interests (such as the allotment of rice cultivation acreages to be converted to acreage for other crops among the different prefectures)—whatever adjustments that are made tend to be aimed at securing a general consensus on matters of principle, so that discussion of specific issues and arguments for or against specific positions are frequently avoided.

The relationships between the government and the different opposition parties often develop in the form of approaches made by the
government after the latter have already made adjustments with the
LDP. This relationship, of course, does not extend to bills submitted
by the LDP itself to a vote by house members (nor to bills submitted
by opposition parties, which usually do not pass), since in such cases
the task of laying the groundwork with regard to opposition parties
for their passage must be handled entirely by LDP members of the
Diet within the framework of parliamentary activities. At times, the
government may be subjected to questioning by the opposition parties
on the issues involved.

As for direct approaches to the opposition parties by the government, these consist in the main of various efforts to ensure that whatever revisions that may be made in the course of Diet deliberations
will remain within a scope defined by the existing consensus between
the government and the LDP. During the implementation of such
efforts, consultations between the government and the LDP naturally
become more frequent.

These, then, are some of the relationships that exist between the
government and the political parties. Generally speaking, the absolute
number of acts of legislation submitted for vote to members of the
House is relatively small compared to other countries. This is explained by the fact that given the limited capacity of individual parties
for policy planning and drafting of proposals, approaches from the
government to different political parties comprise the most important
element of the legislative formulation process.[11]

In addition to these relationships, there are activities which may not
necessarily be widespread practice but which nevertheless take place
usually on a behind-the-scenes level—namely, approaches by agencies
of the government to one of the political parties, made through Diet
members who previously served in the government bureaucracy. The
party most often involved, not surprisingly, is the LDP. Some former
bureaucrats in the Diet may ignore completely the intentions of the
agencies they used to serve, whereupon these agencies are no longer
able to exert influence on the party—and obviously the rating of such
legislators within the concerned agencies will suffer as a result. In the
case of legislators whose former agencies have some other influence

[11] In the book by the farm policy journalists (1977) one of them confessed that while
he had worked as a farm policy journalist for long, to his regret, he could not define
what the farm policy of each of the opposition parties was. The other confessed in the
book that although there were spaces for farm policy issues in the *Akahata* (Red Flag,
the daily newspaper of the JCP), the articles there consisted solely of explanatory
remarks about government policies (Nosei Journalists no Kai, 1977, pp. 142, 147).

on the party, on the other hand, these agencies may, conversely, be influenced by the party through these members of parliament. This interrelationship is by and large regarded as favorable by both the government bureaucracy and the majority party.

Pressure groups and other organizations

The number of organizations that can be defined as pressure groups is countless. For present purposes, the discussion can be limited to those organizations that have an interest in the government's farm policy, although the scope can be expanded to include the mass media. All in all, a list of these groups would include *nokyos* and other farmers' organizations, consumer groups, the labor unions, business and industry organizations, and the mass media, among others.

Starting with the *nokyos*, there was a period when the national federation of *nokyos* felt compelled to mount intensive campaigns to press their price demands whenever the government was setting or revising prices of various farm products. Most notably, the national federation organized rice price rallies all over the nation in a massive concerted campaign whenever the government was setting a new producers' price for rice. In the course of these campaigns, officers of the national *nokyo* and affiliated organizations could count on the support of local officers and members of local cooperatives all over the country. The situation, however, changed drastically when overproduction of rice and other farm produce became a reality. If the national federation had simply continued to press for higher and higher prices despite overproduction, it would have merely resulted in stretching the gap between the feasible price and the demanded price, with eventual loss of faith in the upper echelon officers of the federation on the part of the rank-and-file cooperative members.

While the overriding interest of the farmers may still be focused on the present prices of their produce, there also seems to be a shift of emphasis today toward prospects for the future. The *nokyos'* support for the existing food control system at the fundamental level can be considered a manifestation of this attitude; another is seen in the fact that price demands by farmers' organizations in recent years have been accompanied by references to such issues as rationalization of agricultural production, needs to raise the consumption levels of certain farm products, and demands for regulation of farm produce imports. In addition, one should not overlook the effect of the efforts of three entities—the Ministry of Agriculture, Forestry and Fisheries; farmers' organizations; and the LDP Comprehensive Farm Policy Re-

search Committee—which have been holding frequent informal consultations. These meetings are to help iron out various problems while
strengthening mutual faith through forging of a common basis for
their positions. The informal tripartite meetings started at the time
the government began the rice production adjustment at the initiative
of the late Tetsuo Minato, then the chairman of the LDP Comprehensive Farm Policy Research Committee, and are still being held
today. What this means in overall terms, therefore, is that the farmers'
organizations are now able to discuss matters at the level of central
government from a position of common perceptions, although it would
appear that there still remains something of a credibility gap vis-à-vis
representative organizations on the prefectural level.

As for consumer groups, they rarely have access to the kind of
direct influence enjoyed by the farmers' organizations although they
do, like the farmers' organizations, send representatives to government-sponsored deliberative meetings such as the Rice Price Deliberation Council (Beika Shingi Kai). Politically speaking, these groups
have been more effective in recent times in terms of their ombudsman-
like role in representing the voices of the general public. They have
also been helped by the mass media. In this connection, one may recall
that only recently, during the U.S.–Japanese negotiations over trade
in farm products, the media in amplifying the voices of demands from
the consumers-at-large helped to make their views a kind of pressure
in the government's formulation of its farm policy: the U.S. side
sought to press its demands concerning such commodities as beef by,
among other things, trying to correlate them with those demands
expressed in the media by Japanese consumers. This is one example
in which the mass media, by merely playing their intended role, themselves functioned as a pressure group of sorts. The media played a
similar part several years ago when there was mounting concern over
the possibility of a food crisis.

More important, however, is the growing influence of the consumer
vote in elections at all levels. This arises from the fact that there is
increased nonfarm population in areas which in the past had sent
farm-oriented legislators to the Diet. Within these constituencies, there
are areas where communities have been replaced by new towns and
apartment complexes. Those candidates running for Diet seats in
these districts formerly relied on farm votes alone for election. Now
they are finding it difficult to get elected without the additional votes
from a good number of nonfarm districts within their constituencies.
The influence of farmers' organizations, incidentally, is, again, no
longer strong enough to win seats for individual candidates although

farmers certainly still exercise enough influence to ensure the defeat of a particular politician.[12] As a tendency, their capacity for the latter is growing because of increasing support for the opposition parties on the part of the rank and file of these organizations, the generally pro-LDP position of their executive officers notwithstanding. This development is, of course, of critical significance to an LDP which has intrinsically depended on the farming communities for fundamental support.

The labor unions and various business and finance groups, on their part, have of course been promoting their views on farm policy against the economic backdrops of periods in the past. During the era of rapid economic growth, business and industrial interests advocated rationalization of the farming sector and importation of farm products—given their reliance on labor forces from rural communities for their increasing manpower needs. In the years following the oil crisis, however, the economy entered an era of slow growth under which it became unrealistic to expect wage increases comparable to those of the days of rapid growth. Having no choice but to give top priority to efforts to hold down the cost of living, both the labor unions and business and industrial interests were soon persistently calling for importation of farm products as well as levelling repeated criticisms at the government's farm policy. But at the same time, it also appears that the talk of a possible food crisis several years ago served to dampen simplistic arguments calling for greater dependence on foodstuffs imported from overseas. At any rate, neither the labor unions nor business and industrial organizations are functioning effectively today as agricultural pressure groups in the strict sense of the term. Nevertheless, should the nation's fiscal situation deteriorate to the point of making heavier taxation an inevitable issue, one may expect to hear stronger criticisms of the government's protectionist policy measures for the agricultural sector—including the staple food control policy.

As for the mass media, mentioned earlier in connection with consumer groups, they rarely function as pressure groups on their own because of their intrinsic nature, but may still work in a manner similar to pressure groups by serving to amplify specific views.

---

[12] Of course, the national federation of farmers' cooperatives can win seats for the organizations in the national constituency in every election of the House of Councillors. Even the influence of such national organizations as the National Association for Land Reclamation (Zenkoku Tochi Kairyo Kyokai), the National Federation of Tobacco Leaf Producers (Tabako-Kosaku Kumiai Zenkoku Rengokai) and others is still strong enough to win a seat or seats for each organization in each election campaign in the national constituency of the House of Councillors.

The Liberal Democratic Party

Within the LDP, policy measures are discussed by various subdivisions of its Political Affairs Research Committee (Seimu Chosa Kai). These are essentially subcommittees whose areas of responsibility more or less correspond to those of the permanent committees in the National Diet. In addition, there are various research groups for discussing basic policy measures in the different policy areas. In the area of agriculture and forestry, the party has a Comprehensive Farm Policy Research Committee and a Forestry Policy Research Committee (Rinsei Chosa Kai). In addition, the party also has various special committees for considering specific issues of particular importance, including the Special Committee on Development Measures for Mountain Communities (Sanson Shinko Taisaku Tokubetsu Iinkai), and special committees for the development of various regions such as that for Kinki Region Development (Kinki-ken Kaihatsu Tokubetsu Iinkai), and that for Hokkaido Development (Hokkaido Kaihatsu Tokubetsu Iinkai). Policy measures worked out by these internal party organizations are all submitted to the parent Political Affairs Research Committee, which examines them in terms of overall coordination and balance.

But before these measures can be submitted to the National Diet as LDP-sponsored proposals, they must be considered by the LDP Executive Council for adoption as official party policy. After the Executive Council, which must evaluate these proposals on a political basis, adopts them as official policy, they can be submitted to the Diet.

In brief, that is how the decision-making process for policy measures works in the LDP. The process is next examined more closely in the setting of a basic farm policy measure that is currently under study.

In the aftermath of the oil crisis, the Japanese economy entered a new era of slow growth. In the ensuing years, this slowdown has brought about a curtailment of growth in demand for farm produce as well as a reduction of opportunities for farming households seeking new side businesses. This situation called for an overall review of the entire spectrum of national farm policy, including a revision of long-term projections of supply and demand for selected farm products (targeted for 1985) adopted by the government in 1975. As a result, the government is currently undertaking a review of its farm policy measures, with the LDP's Comprehensive Farm Policy Research Committee also conducting related studies in reference to reports sent to it by the government from time to time.

In the course of the studies and discussions of policy measures that the government conducts through the Farm Policy Deliberation Council (Nosei Shingi Kai), the LDP's Comprehensive Farm Policy Research Committee is briefed on the government's progress from time to time, and the latter's views, in turn, are fed back to the government. The committee's views, formed originally at the level of key Diet members in agriculture- and forestry-related areas, are passed on to a conference of chairmen and vice-chairmen of the Comprehensive Farm Policy Research Committee and the Agriculture and Forestry Subcommittee before being finally fed back to the government as official views of the research committee (or of the joint conference of the committee and the subcommittee). The determination of policy measures in overall terms, however, is implemented by the aforementioned process through the government's Farm Policy Deliberation Council.

Given this general decision-making process, the important question, obviously, is what sort of decisions are made at what levels? The views of a political party must, of necessity, reflect closely the wishes of the elements of its base of support. With its foundation resting solidly in the rural communities, the LDP (and traditionally, the conservative force in general) has always advanced views that strongly reflect the wishes of the farming sector. To individual Diet members and regional assemblymen, grass-roots views may be aired in the form of "wishes" of prominent members of supporting organizations in the constituencies, or in the form of views of various pressure groups, as mentioned earlier. These views are of course aired directly to the party through the pressure groups as well.

With regard to the basic farm policy measures mentioned so far, the frequently held informal tripartite meetings (between top officials and officers of farmers' organizations, the government, and the LDP's Comprehensive Farm Policy Research Committee) have, among other things, helped to minimize the credibility gap that exists with the farmers' organization level. For the party's agriculture- and forestry-related organs, this means fewer instances of pressures brought to bear directly by various organizations as well as less pressure from supporting organizations of Diet members at the constituency level—so that the decision-making process becomes relatively easier overall for key Diet members specializing in agriculture and forestry. It also means that views of the latter are more likely to be adopted by the various related organs at their respective levels of authority.

In the case of issues involving large regional interests (such as the recent introduction of the new graduated price scale system for government rice purchases), however, the decision-making process at the level of these key Diet members is no easy matter.[13] Ordinarily, such

[13] See page 242.

issues are carefully considered in the conferences of the chairmen and vice chairmen of the LDP's aforementioned agricultural committees and subcommittees, with the participation of representatives from regional groups that hold large vested interests. (Generally speaking, such groups are the rule rather than the exception in these cases.) On these issues, too, the key Diet members in agriculture and forestry will also hold meetings to pave the way for a smoother decision-making process in the expanded conference of chairmen and vice chairmen. Once decisions are made in the expanded conference, the officers of the Comprehensive Farm Policy Research Committee or the agriculture and forestry subcommittees (or a joint conference of them) do their utmost to ensure the adoption of those decisions by these organizations. Their efforts to back these decisions will persist into the subsequent meetings of the Political Affairs Research Committee, and later, into the meetings of the party's Executive Council. In terms of a more specific method of operation, the officers may lay the groundwork by informally approaching, in advance, the heads of the organizations taking part in these meetings, or may arrange for statements to be made from observers' seats during the meetings in the form of "outside" views. Should they encounter a great deal of difficulty in their efforts, they may even make behind-the-scenes approaches to the party president or heads of factions to which members opposed to their cause belong.

As mentioned earlier, the Executive Council, whose function is to evaluate and rule on proposed measures on a political basis, is responsible for determining the party's platform. Thus, it is in the deliberations of this highest decision-making organ of the party that the opponents of proposed measures will make a final stand, using all the influence they can muster. It is therefore not rare for the Executive Council to leave the final decisions in the hands of the top officials of the party (the secretary general of the party, the chairman of the Executive Council, and the chairman of the Political Affairs Research Council) when the council's deliberations have ended in a deadlock. Entrusted with the substantial responsibility of having to make these final decisions, the top party officials must, in advance, make the necessary adjustments with the most influential figures involved, within a suitably defined framework, before entering into negotiations with each other. At the same time, executive officers of the Comprehensive Farm Policy Research Committee must similarly establish a measure of agreement with the government within the same fixed framework and work toward the necessary adjustments of views vis-à-vis the top party officials. Needless to say, the success or failure of this effort will depend on the cumulative effect of all the efforts undertaken at the preceding levels of decision making.

If concrete results then emerge from the final negotiations among top party officials, they will again be referred to the Executive Council for approval, and this will constitute the final step of the long decision-making process inside the party. That, in short, is how policy measures are adopted within the machinery of the LDP.

For the political parties of Japan, there are no privately financed research organizations available for consultation on policy matters such as, say, the Brookings Institution in the United States. Consequently, most legislative acts result from the adoption of government proposals, the exception being occasional bills proposed by individual Diet members. Even the various subdivisions of the Political Affairs Research Committee, on their part, can only evaluate and rule on materials prepared by the administrative branches on the basis of fragmentary information and data—and make, at best, a few modifications. To be sure, the issues are becoming increasingly more complex, so that few problems can be resolved within the jurisdictions of individual administrative agencies—a situation creating greater need for consolidation of views by political means. Faced with this situation, the secretariat of the agriculture and forestry section of the LDP's Political Affairs Research Committee must play its own part by, for instance, setting up private research organizations with government representatives included in the staff. Such organizations could formulate general ideas for incorporation into bills drafted by the government agencies, or by organizing their own version of the aforementioned tripartite meetings, they could strengthen basic mutual understanding. It should be noted that such activities are not a common practice in other sectors, but they need to be taken into account when examining the whole decision-making process in the area of farm policy.

Concluding Remarks

The sections above show that the politics of agriculture is still firmly based on protectionism, although there are several signs of change. Moreover, the politics of agriculture is at the core of the Japanese political scene. Without change in the whole scene of Japanese politics, the politics of agriculture may not significantly change. It is said that many Japanese are tired of the single-party domination by the LDP, which has lasted since 1955. It is also said that many Japanese are not quite convinced of the ability of the opposition parties to hold administrative power. In this concluding section, several facts about the politics of agriculture are restated with additional comments.

1. All political parties are protectionist, and Japanese consumers are still tolerant of the high prices of several foods and of the large deficit in the staple food control budget. Therefore, in any agricultural trade negotiation, either bilateral or multilateral, the Japanese government has to deal with issues within a very narrow range of options. The government may try to widen the range by educating its people in the course of the negotiation, but the government's effort may be disrupted or disturbed by actions of legislators in either the LDP or in other parties. Moreover, journalists may often encourage the actions of legislators.

2. The political influence of the farmers' organizations has been less and less powerful in recent years. Moreover, the existence of huge rice surpluses (and surpluses of other produce such as milk) has further weakened the farm organizations. There is a growing opinion that the staple food control system should be changed drastically.[14]

3. With the last simultaneous election for both houses of the Diet in June 1980, the sweeping victory of the LDP may encourage the LDP to redirect the government farm policy. Dominant opinion now is that there will not be any election for the House of Representatives for at least two years from the last elections. Without a change in public opinion about the future world food situation, there will not be any drastic change in government farm policy, which is now highly protective, because present government farm policy probably reflects accurately national sentiments on food and agriculture.

[14] The report on the staple food control system by the Japan Economic Research Institute has attracted wide attention (Nihon Keizai Chosa Kiyogikai, 1980).

Agricultural Programs of the Major Political Parties as of 1979

The Liberal Democratic Party (LDP)

Until now the importance of the role of agriculture has been emphasized primarily in terms of supplying food for the population and securing necessary income for farm households. Agriculture is, however, also playing an important role in terms of maintaining the stability of Japanese society, and can, as such, be considered an "industrial sector essential for the security of the nation." Therefore, agricultural policy in the days ahead should call for increased production that is consistent with trends in demand and thus maintain and improve the nation's capacity for self-reliance in food supply. Also, improvement in the structure of farming assumes vital importance under conditions of stable economic growth. A pricing policy that ignores the supply-and-demand situation is bound to fail. For this reason, it is necessary to undertake a policy of thoroughgoing improvements in the structure of agriculture. In order, then, to recruit persons having superior ability and dedicated interest in agriculture for positions of responsibility, and to promote the formulation of prosperous regional communities with a base in agriculture, it is necessary to create a more pleasant living environment in farming communities, and at the same time foster a sense of solidarity among the members of these communities. It is also necessary to work for a more efficient farm produce distribution system, and for the establishment of policies for promoting prosperity in the food industry itself, for the purpose of ensuring the consumption of domestic farm produce amid the diversifying of dietary demands of the consumers.

Mainly from the September 28, 1979, edition of the *Zenkoku Nogyo Shimbun*.

The Japan Socialist Party (JSP)

Agriculture is considered a key sector, bearing such important social responsibilities as provision of staple foods for the population through intensive and renewable farming of all available land, stabilization of employment, development of regional economies, and conservation of the natural environment. The party is strongly opposed to the LDP policies of reliance on food supplies from overseas and giving priority to big business while curtailing the agricultural sector. Under its "Regional Agricultural Promotion Plan for Rebuilding the Agricultural Sector and Furthering Self-Reliance in Food," the party would raise the rate of self-sufficiency in grains to 60 percent within five years and to 69 percent in ten years in an effort concentrated in the area of the nation's basic foods such as rice, wheat, soybean, meat, milk, and feed grains. Toward this end, the party would actively promote development of both farmland and substructure consolidation activities and will make such adjustments to the conditions of production as intensified use of arable land, communal use of farming machinery, organization of production cooperatives, and improvement of various agricultural facilities. Also, it would introduce a system of regionally specialized multicrop farms under which the basic products of rice, livestock, and fruits would be produced collectively and cooperatively in combination with other crops in such a way as to ensure year-round farming. In order to stabilize this farming system, the party would strengthen the price support system and introduce a low-interest financing system, as well as eliminate the gap in the quality of housing, transportation, education, cultural amenities, and medical care between urban and rural communities.

The Komeito (The Clean Government Party)

Based on the premise that agriculture is a "fundamental sector for the survival of the Japanese," the party intends to incorporate a new concept into the Agricultural Basic Law, which at present is completely oriented toward economic rationalism. According to this concept, which would be called the "new agriculturalism," due recognition will be given to the fact that farming and rural communities fulfill such important functions as producing food, stabilizing local economies and society, helping to create culture, and conserving the natural environment. In addition, the party maintains that concrete stipulations and regulations regarding formation of a national consensus on rural reconstruction should be included in the said law. Their goal should be to strengthen such agriculture-related policy measures as a national food policy and accompanying measures concerning rural environment and welfare and consumer oriented measures. Also, stipulations in the law concerning modernization of agriculture should be reexamined with a view to the ethics of training of managerial personnel and an added emphasis on the ecosystem.

Also, the party maintains that while self-sufficiency in feed grains would be difficult, efforts should be made toward the reconstruction of agriculture and greater self-reliance in food production by establishment of a "food importation coordinating council" comprising producers, consumers, scholars, and others. This council would lay down independent guidelines concerning imports that the government would take into account, thereby introducing a shift away from the complacent importation policy presently controlled primarily by the government and industrial and financial circles. It would seek to raise the rate of self-sufficiency in terms of primary caloric intake to 80 percent, as well as to improve the pricing policy that is now in the process of weakening—all in all promoting integrally the implementation of these comprehensive measures. In ordinary times, however, an appropriate amount of importation should be maintained to support the existing level of dietary life.

The Democratic Socialist Party (DSP)

From the perspective of maintaining the nation's economic security and conserving land, it is a vital national task to treat agriculture as a basic sector of the national economy and to foster its growth into a key sector of the regional economies.

Toward this end, our party would implement the following measures: (1) To promote reorganization of the production structure to conform to demands of consumers and to reflect the consumers' views, the party will make an effort to establish medium- and long-term targets for self-reliance and a regional specialization of production based on allotment of different crops to respective producing areas of suitable conditions. It will also encourage the voluntary adoption of crop rotation by such means as a comprehensive price guarantee system and improvement of the basic production structure for farmland amenable to crop rotation. (2) To develop the agricultural sector into a highly productive industry capable of meeting international competition, the party would take drastic steps in terms of investments for such purposes as the training of specialists, accumulation of large-scale farms, improvement and strengthening of land improvement projects, construction of food-processing complexes, and introduction of a substantial financing system for farm modernization efforts. (3) To shatter the traditions of bureaucratic administration of the agricultural sector and to develop self-reliant regional agriculture centered around capable specialists throughout the nation, the party would move toward launching a council for development of regional agriculture, adoption of an un-itemized regional subsidy system, and other measures. The party is opposed to the raising of the consumers' price of rice.

The Japan Communist Party (JCP)

The present policy of "transforming Japanese industrial structure" advocated by the LDP is designed to expand the importation of foods and to curtail and reorganize the agricultural sector in response to demands from the United States and financial and industrial circles. An important element of this policy is abandonment of government guarantees on prices, as seen in its structural policy aimed at eliminating part-time farm households through the revision of the Agricultural Land Law, and in its efforts to render the food control system toothless.

The Japan Communist Party would implement radical *reconversion* of the ruinous existing agricultural policy of dependence on the United States and subordination to big business interests, and, holding agriculture to be the most important and basic producing sector, undertake the reconstruction of the sector, overcoming the critical situation through the stabilization of the livelihood of small- and medium-size farms by means of a reinforced pricing policy, among other measures. In addition, increased production of wheat, soybeans, and feed grains should be undertaken. The party would expedite the reinforcement of conditions amenable to the voluntary adaptation of crop rotation by the farmers. And by cutting imports in accordance with the increase in domestic production, and by combining the advanced techniques of the farmers with modern science and industrial capabilities, the party would work toward a multifaceted development of the agricultural sector and a drastic improvement in the rate of self-sufficiency in food. The party would protect rural communities from "development" for the sake of big business interests and undertake the development of the agricultural and forestry sector and local industries utilizing favorable natural conditions and such resources as farmland and forests. It would also consolidate the social and economic substructure in order to create prosperous and comfortable agricultural communities.

The New Liberal Club

Agriculture is not merely an industry for the production of food, but an extremely vital economic sector having such functions as maintenance of national security, development of the national lands, conservation of the natural environment, and fostering of culture. There is a tendency to belittle the importance of the nation's agriculture against a background of economic rationality and the argument for international division of different economic activities, but this way of thinking is ill conceived.

Given the worldwide shortage of food and unstable international relations, Japan should seek to raise its rate of self-sufficiency in food rather than increase its dependence on food from overseas. Toward this end, it is necessary to implement a comprehensive program consisting of four main targets: namely, greater use of available farmland, strengthening of the basic productive structure, research and development in farming technology, and a proper pricing policy. Since the alternative forms of full-time and part-time farm households will develop naturally in the process of implementing these objectives, there is no need to devote a special effort to the training and development of full-time farmers.

There is a tendency to denigrate farming in rural communities as well as cities. Such an attitude should be corrected, and indeed, a government policy which places farming in a status that would correct this is desirable. It should also be recognized that the future of the nation as well as its identity will be determined to a large extent by how well the agricultural sector fares.

References

Asahi Shimbun (Tokyo). 1979. March 5.

Griswald, A. W. 1947. *Farming and Democracy* (New York, Harcourt Brace).

Ishikawa, Masumi. 1978. *Sengo Seiji Kozo-shi* (A History of the Postwar Political Structure) (Tokyo, Okurasho Insatsu Kyoku).

Jinko Mondai Shingikai. 1979 (Government Population Council). *Nihon Jinko no-Doko* (Dynamics of the Japanese Population) (Tokyo, Okurasho Insatsu Kyoku).

Matsuura, T. 1977. "Hokaku Ainori wa Dokomade Tsuzuku" (The Future of the Presently Friendly Relationship Between the LDP and the Opposition Parties) in Nosei Journalist no Kai (Farm Policy Journalists Association), *Tato-ka Jidai no Nosei* (Tokyo, Norin Tokei Kyokai).

Meadows, Donella H., Dennis L. Meadows, Jørgen Randers, and Willian W. Behrens III. 1972. *The Limits to Growth* (New York, Universal Books).

Naikaku Soridaijin Kanbo Kohoshitsu. 1975 (Public Information Section, Prime Minister's Secretariat). *Shoku Seikatus oyobi Shokuryo ni Kansuru Seron Chosa* (Japanese Opinion About Future Food Consumption and Supply) (Tokyo, Naikaku Kanbo).

————. 1978 (Public Information Section, Prime Minister's Secretariat). *Shokuryo ni Kansuru Seron Chosa* (Japanese Opinion About Future Food Supply) (Tokyo, Naikaku Kanbo).

Nihon Keizai Chosa Kyogikai. 1980 (Japan Economic Research Institute). *Shokkan Seido no Bapponteki Kaisei* (A Proposal for Drastic Reformation of the Staple Food Control System) (Tokyo, Nihon Keizai Chosa Kyogikai).

Nihon Kieizai Shimbun (Tokyo) 1979a. February 4.

————. (Tokyo) 1979b. February 5.

Norindaijin Kambo Kikakushitsu. 1975 (Planning Section, Agriculture and Forestry Minister's Secretariat). *Nihon no Shokuryo Seisaku o Kangaeru* (Review of Japanese Food Policies) (Tokyo, Norinsho).

Nosei Journalist no Kai. 1977 (Farm Policy Journalists Association). *Tato-ka Jidai no Nosei* (Farm Policy Under the Losing Dominance of the LDP) (Tokyo, Norin Tokei Kyokai).

Vogel, Ezra F. 1977. *Japan As Number One* (Cambridge, Mass., Harvard University Press).

Zenkoku Nogyo Shimbun (Tokyo). 1979. September 28.

8

The Politics of Domestic and Foreign Policy Linkages in U.S.–Japanese Agricultural Policy Making

Ross B. Talbot and Young W. Kihl

As political democracies with representative forms of government, Japan and the United States pursue economic policies that reflect their respective national interests and ideologies. Major policy conflicts sometimes occur. One area of conflict has been—and continues to be—in agricultural trade relations. Before explaining why this is true and what can be done about it, we offer a set of propositions.

1. In economic terms, the agricultural trade relations between Japan and the United States are complementary. The natural limitations imposed on the Japanese agricultural sector have resulted in a food deficit situation, which has grown incrementally because of dynamic increases in national wealth and very moderate increases in national population. At present, approximately half of Japan's food requirements come from imports. In contrast, the natural advantages of the U.S. agricultural industry have often resulted in food surpluses followed by declining market prices for agricultural products. American agriculture has become quite dependent on the existence of foreign (dollar) markets for its products; over time, Japan has become the number one export market for U.S. agriculture. Thus, there has de-

Ross B. Talbot and Young W. Kihl are professors of political science at Iowa State University.

veloped a harmony of interests between U.S. and Japanese agriculture, at least as viewed in terms of the economic theory of comparative advantage.

2. In political terms, the agricultural trade policies of both Japan and the United States tend to be dominated by agricultural political interests owing to the strong rural base of the Liberal Democratic Party in Japan and the highly decentralized nature of the American political party system. To some extent this is a reflection of the difference in the structure and orientation of the two political systems. The United States has a federal system, with a national government characterized by separated powers; Japan is a unitary state, with a parliamentary-cabinet form of government. Although farmers are a minority group in both countries, and especially so in the United States (approximately 12 percent in Japan and 3 percent in United States), the farm vote continues to have political credibility, for somewhat different reasons. Thus, food and agricultural policies in both are strongly influenced by domestic political considerations and competing sectional and commodity interests, although the latter are of relatively greater significance in U.S. food politics.

3. In the two countries, rather diametrically opposed ideologies are proclaimed by their respective agricultural political interests; these ideologies are, at least in part, camouflages for the respective economic interests. U.S. farm groups (general and commodity), the U.S. Department of Agriculture (notably the Foreign Agricultural Service), and powerful Congressional agriculture committees advocate the superiority of the economic theories of free trade and comparative advantage. In contrast, the Japanese agricultural power structure (the farmer cooperatives, the Ministry of Agriculture, Forestry and Fisheries, and the agriculture committees in the Diet) advocate with equal vigor the vital necessity of implementing the principles of self-sufficiency and protectionism.

4. The agricultural political establishments of both the United States and Japan then attempt, not without moderate success, to isolate themselves from the subordinate although significant role that each would occupy if the national interests of both countries were the primary concern of the respective governments. More specifically, U.S.–Japanese national and international economic policies are primarily concerned with issues of mutual security, world peace, and domestic prosperity, and yet their respective agricultural interests tend to pursue policies that isolate their particular economic interests from these primary goals. Moreover, in both nations, other domestic industrial and welfare interests also have major and coordinate concerns which

need to be, and to some extent are, accommodated in both the domestic political processes and in the foreign policies within and between the two nations.

5. In consequence, ways and means need to be devised that will
accord both Japanese and U.S. agricultural interests a significant, but
still secondary, role in the overall relations between the two nations.
Institutions and strategies need to be developed which will build flexibility, diversity, and mutual understanding in the decision-making
process between the two governments. Peace, freedom, security, and
prosperity are their mutual goals, and rational agricultural trade relations are definitely valuable to both nations in the pursuit of those
goals.

To explain and analyze these basic propositions, we contend that
in the post–World War II period both the U.S. and Japanese political
systems have endeavored to institutionalize and make operational,
although in somewhat different manner, form, and degree, four concepts of political democracy: polyarchy, pluralism, populism, and participatory democracy (Fowler and Orenstein, 1977, especially chapter
3). In the process of doing so, conflicts of interests and policies in the
field of bilateral agricultural trade relations have necessarily occurred.
These conflicts of interest and ideology have proved to be an exac-
erbating and disruptive factor in the political and economic relationships between the two nations. Their causes and effects need to be
explained, and from this explanation one can envisage ways and means
to bring about their accommodation.

The first section of this chapter is a review of our conceptual framework and its application to the historical and, in particular, contemporary developments of U.S. agricultural and food policies. In
essence, we ask three principal questions: Who commands? under
what conditions? and to whose benefit? Then we examine these questions by applying our conceptual framework to the American political
scene relative to changing developments in agricultural and food
policies.

In the succeeding section we apply these same concepts and in-
quiries to postwar agricultural and food policy developments within
the Japanese political system. The third section is a general overview
of the changes in power relationships and politico-economic perceptions in this policy area that have occurred during the last thirty-five
years. In the final section, we briefly critique the conceptual framework in terms of its utility as an explanatory and predictive tool and
explain why it needs to be modified somewhat in its application to

the Japanese political system (the framework was devised primarily with the American political system as the working model).

An underlying major premise of our conceptual approach is that agricultural trade relations between the nations constitute a subsector process, a partial reflection of their respective political and economic realities and ideologies. Therefore, our analysis is predominantly an interpretation of the political power structure of food within each nation rather than a descriptive review of the politics of their agricultural trade relations. The latter, we contend, can be best understood through an explication of the former.

U.S. Food and Agricultural Politics and Policies: A Conceptual Framework and Analysis

Modern political science seeks to provide more depth and scope, both normatively and empirically, to the classical political concept (notably of Aristotle) that governments are controlled by the one, the few, the many, or some combination thereof and that public policies are the consequent outcome. To some extent, the new classification—polyarchy, pluralism, populism, and participatory democracy—is the pouring of new wine into old bottles. Following the lead, however, of Stanley Hoffman, among others, that classification has been given a better empirical foundation through asking and elucidating three particular questions: Who commands? Under what conditions? For whose benefit? (Hoffman, 1978, pp. 181–201).

We will use those concepts of democracy and that framework of inquiry to examine decision making in the U.S. and Japanese political systems relative to agricultural and food policy developments within and between those two nations, with principal reference to the postwar period (1945–1980).

Who commands? The making and implementing of U.S. food policy

The American democracy is approaching its 200th anniversary; its national constitution stands much as it was constructed in 1787, then amended in 1791 (the Bill of Rights) and in the post–Civil War period. Throughout the nation's history, farmers have played a powerful role in its political institutions at all levels of government—national, state, and local. American elections, political parties, interest groups, legislative decision making, the rise of bureaucracies, and judicial interpretations have all been influenced by the needs, desires, demands, and aspirations of its farmers. This was particularly true in the nineteenth century, significantly so throughout the first half of the twentieth century, and surprisingly so even in the decade of the 1970s, by which time the U.S. farm population had dwindled to less than 3 percent of the nation's.

The history of nineteenth century American politics was often an unfolding of events centering on agricultural issues. Taxes, tariffs, disposal of public lands, slave labor, foreign trade, and subsidies were among the issues often, and sometimes bitterly, debated. With the coming of the twentieth century new kinds of issues and controversies were encountered, the impact of science and technology, the concept of parity as a surrogate for justice, the purity and nutritive qualities of food, the multiple demands of the second environmental movement, ways of legitimizing the regulation of farm production, public credit strategies, experiments in crop insurance, programs of food aid to the poor at home and to the new nations, among numerous others.

Our major generalization arising from this is that as the number of farms and farmers diminished, the relevant concept of democracy has been revised, at least in practice if not in rhetoric, sometimes more by indirection and happenstance than by plan and foresight. The somewhat unsteady historical sequence has been from participatory democracy to populism to pluralism to polyarchy. Throughout this process the old concepts have not been discarded. Indeed, they are periodically revived in new form and through different strategies, but the trend is as we have observed, in the main. We will try to give substance and interpretation to that generalization in our discussion of U.S. agricultural and food policy developments in the postwar period and will conclude with some speculative comments relative to likely directions in the near future.

Grass-roots democracy: participatory democracy

The direct and active participation of the citizen in the political decision-making process is a fundamental ideal in American democracy, and this certainly includes rural America. The Jeffersonian concept of grass-roots democracy and the belief that the backbone of this democratic republic is the family farmer are operative ideals which have withered but, for reasons that seem more mystical than rational, still seem to retain some efficacy in the American political culture—and, quixotically, even within metropolitan America. The rise of the farm cooperatives in the early 1900s, culminating in the Capper-Volstead Cooperative Marketing Act of 1922, and eventuating in the development of fairly powerful producer and marketing cooperatives today, were landmark events in U.S. food and agricultural policies. The programs of the Farm Credit Administration have a definite, though declining, grass-roots underpinning. The development of price support programs in the early New Deal years, through the two agricultural adjustment acts, brought closely in their wake the creation of farmer-elected county committees and local committeemen. In addition, referenda were held (and still are for tobacco and peanuts) in order to determine whether voluntary (usually) or compulsory acreage or quota controls could legitimately be imposed on participating farmers, or even on those who chose not to participate. With the passage of the Soil Conservation and Domestic Allotment Act in 1936, there followed the creation of local soil conservation districts and their farmer-elected county boards. The creation of the rural electric cooperatives and the now-defunct Farm Security Administration in the 1930s is further evidence of the participatory model in action.

Today, however, this operative ideal seems to have less potency in rural America. The environmentalists, nutritionists, land ecologists, United Farm Workers, and counterculturists, among others, have co-opted the ideal of direct democracy, and to some considerable extent their policies and programs have been viewed by rural America as a threat to farmers' economic interests and their increasingly business-oriented way of life. The participatory democrats of the 1970s and early 1980s stress the use of "organic" techniques of crop rotation, soil fertilization, and pest control. There is a studied emphasis on the quality of food products rather than on their efficient production, and all of this—according to its advocates—should take place through a renewed emphasis on the use of "intermediate" types of farm technology.

We are not attempting to downplay the participatory-type movements of today. If they should prevail even in modest proportions, relative to achieving their means and ends, there would occur at least a modest decline in farm production, in terms of quantity. This would have some effect on the U.S. food export situation and could have some effect on U.S.–Japanese agricultural relations. We do not believe, however, that the effect will prove to be of more than marginal consequence.

Nineteenth and twentieth century varieties of agrarian protest: populism

Populism has always been an important concept in the American heritage, and particularly so in rural America. Its essence is born out of the spirit of democratic theory: the people are sovereign; government should be responsible to the majority, not vested (such as railroad, land, and financial interests)—groups often wrathfully referred to as the plutocracy, Wall Street, robber barons. Populism breeds panaceas, the panaceas become clichés, the clichés become the promises of political parties, the promises become rallying cries and campaign slogans. One could argue that the populists' heyday was in the 1870s with the rise of the Grange Movement (the "corrupt" land policies and shipping rates of the railroads were the principal targets) followed in the late 1880s and early 1890s by the Populist movement, which soon became the People's Party. But the major political parties (Democratic and Republican since the Civil War) have always overcome these movements by absorbing the main planks of their platforms into their own, and thereby diminishing the passions of fear and hatred which had given them birth. Historically, low farm prices breed rural populism; good farm prices dissipate the discontent, whereupon the people's movement would fail, or mature and be transformed into an interest group. Such seems to have been the almost relentless cycle of agrarian populist movements.

Now the rise of the American Agriculture Movement (AAM) in the late 1970s has proved, once again, that a resurgence of bitter deep-seated farmer discontent will manifest itself in the form of another, this time quite unusual, populist movement. The use of expensive farm tractors to block the Fourteenth Street Bridge leading to the huge South Building, which houses a major portion of the U.S. Department of Agriculture's (USDA's) bureaucracy, and to nearly cordon off access to the U.S. Capitol and the House and Senate office buildings, constituted a remarkable scene in the nation's capital. But these actions—along with camping on The Mall, piling corn on Independence Avenue where it fronts on to the agriculture department's administration building, and invading the secretary's office of that department—proved that the spirit of populism is still alive in rural America. Moreover, these moderately radical tactics were not in vain. A bewildered Department of Agriculture and a beleaguered Congress responded. Populist-based tactics were also clearly influential in the passage of the Emergency Agricultural Act of 1978 (L. Mayer, 1978).

It is a reasonable, though debatable, thesis that the farmer interest groups of today are offspring of the populist movements of yesteryear. Today's National Grange is a modest shadow of the radical Grange movement of the 1870s. The present National Farmers Union (NFU) is not the firebrand it was in the first half of this century. Major sections of the cooperative movement have been organized into a business-minded, establishment-oriented confederation, the National Council of Farmer Cooperatives. The National Farmers Organization (NFO) burst into prominence in the late 1950s. Caused by low farm prices and motivated by the desire to establish countervailing power, it was willing to use radical tactics to try to make effective its holding-action strategy. In recent years, however, the NFO has become more moderate in its demands and business oriented in its procedures. Now the AAM seems to be in the process of transforming itself from a radical to a liberal interest group, in terms of its demands and strategies.

In numerous respects, this modernized agrarian populism is an anachronism. The principal ideological characteristics of populist theory were: (1) an ". . . overweaning commitment to the principle of popular rule . . ." and (2) ". . . its combination of democratic and conspiratorial qualities and its susceptibility to Bonapartism, to demagogic leadership claiming legitimacy from the consent of the Mass . . ." (Minar, 1964, p. 349). American farmers today hardly seem to have the political strength that would enable them to mold those ideological beliefs into a functional strategy. Even so, the political observer has to be impressed by at least the short-run effect of the American Agricultural Movement.

American populism is not without significance to the Japanese. To the extent that the AAM, for example, is successful in imposing its will upon the U.S. Congress, there would ensue a substantial increase in farm commodity loan rates and target prices, higher costs to the U.S. Treasury, probably less farm production, and higher food costs at home and for commodities exported. What this would mean in terms of Japan's interests would be rather speculative; quite possibly it would mean higher consumer food costs, a modest lowering in the public costs of domestic food programs, and a minor diminution in the demands of Japan's farmer interest groups to reorganize their production practices and the structural conditions of their industry.

Interest group politics: a diversity of triangles: pluralism

Much of the political ideology and the political realities of American farm politics can be encompassed in the concept of pluralism, from James Madison's argument in Federalist Paper No. 10 concerning the naturalness and the value of interest groups in a democratic republic, to David Truman's superb study in the 1950s in which he developed a general theory of interest groups to both explain and justify policy making in the United States as a clash of interest groups, either active or potential (Truman, 1951).

There were farmer-interest groups of a type in the nineteenth century, but the modern farm organization began with the formation of the American Farm Bureau Federation (AFBF) in the 1920s, followed by the modernization of the National Farmers Union (NFU) in the 1930s. In time, farm policy became more and more the product of cooperation between the corners of what we will refer to as the "food triangle." The first corner is the powerful congressional agricultural committees that, owing to the relative weakness of American political parties, have historically dominated legislative decision making in the nation's capital. The second corner is the rise and proliferation of farmer interest groups, both general and commodity, during the New Deal years and thereafter. Farm prices came to be made in Washington, D.C., or so many believed, and this meant that farmers needed to have their own representatives making particular demands, backed by subtle or outspoken threats of retribution at the ballot box. The third corner came about because of the rise of the U.S. Department of Agriculture—notably during and since the 1930s—as a powerful, dynamic, expanding bureaucracy serving primarily the research, informational, and analytical needs of its two principal constituents—the relevant congressional committees (including, definitely, the House and Senate agricultural appropriations subcommittees) and the aforementioned farmer-interest groups and their members. This food triangle, in motion, has been referred to as a "whirlpool of power."

One should quickly note, however, that the pluralist type has never been a pure specimen; conflicts of ideology, the geography of sectionalism, the increasing specialization and the consequent rise of special commodity groups, and bureaucratization within the farm organizations are evident features of contemporary farm politics. Food triangle is a generic term; there are many types thereof.

Consequently, the main difficulty with the pluralist food triangle concept is that it does not enable one to see the diversity of ideologies and interests that exists within American agriculture. Even a breakdown into variant types will miss some of the richness of differences found in farm politics and farm policy. However, we believe that three types should be quickly reviewed; then a fourth one (the food export triangle) will be presented in more detail.

There are some definite and occasionally deep-seated ideological conflicts in farm politics, and they have existed since the early 1930s and particularly so since the end of World War II. The first variant we shall call the liberal food triangle. Its corners are a Democratic U.S. Department of Agriculture (the administrations of Charles Brannon and Orville Freeman, in particular), the National Farmers Union (and later the National Farmers Organization), the National Farm Coalition, and the southern and midwest Democrats on the afore-mentioned congressional committees (Youngberg, 1979). The ideology is Jeffersonian in tone; there is much rhetoric about the family farm; its strategy tends to favor an upward push on price supports, loan rates, and target prices.

A second type, the conservative food triangle, is made up of a different set of actors, although it should be stressed that there are often political crossovers and renegades. However, this variation takes on a much more Republican, social Darwinist, successful farmer kind of composition. The USDA administrations of Ezra Taft Benson (1953–60) and Earl Butz (1968–72) are primary case studies of this type. They were ably supported by the American Farm Bureau Federation, and the ideological emphasis was decidedly toward a free market focus. Their successes were limited because only during the first two years of the Eisenhower administration did the Republicans control Congress, and the Democratic-controlled agriculture committees looked forward to rough and tumble bouts in committee with both Benson and Butz.

Our definite impression is that the established farm organizations, which means essentially all of them except for the new, shakily organized American Agriculture Movement, have become less ideological over the last decade. To be sure, the Farm Bureau has never been in the National Farm Coalition, while the National Farmers Union was but withdrew during the legislative struggle over the 1973 farm bill (Barton, 1974). Our contention is that American farm organizations, including by and large the commodity organizations, often reconstitute themselves into a third type that might be viewed as a consensus food triangle. Admittedly we exaggerate somewhat, but recent hearings in the House regarding the National Agricultural Bargaining Act of 1979 is a case study in consensus. The official American Farm Bureau Federation weekly newspaper headlined the story: "Farm Groups unite on farm marketing bill." (AFBF, 1979). The Agricultural Trade Act of 1978 is another example of the moderate trend toward interorganizational consensus. There are three principal reasons for this trend. One is that the modern commercial farmer is gradually becoming "a farmer in a business suit." A modern farm is a complex, expensive, hazardous investment, which is not the kind of an environment in which agrarian populism can flourish for long. Second, the general farm organizations are heavily involved in service functions to the farmer: insurance in several varieties, sales of many types of inputs (fertilizer, seed, pesticides), marketing cooperatives, and the like. Third, to use Don Paarlberg's phrase: there is a new agenda (1980). The old agenda, the agricultural establishment, is under severe challenge by the new agenda composed of nutritionists, ecologists, civil rights advocates, rural labor unions, and conservationists, among others. (At a later point we will return to this agenda concept.)

The food export triangle is an important variant of the pluralist food triangle, a group consisting of the Foreign Agricultural Service (FAS) and the "cooperators" (food commodity groups) who have organized themselves into an Agricultural Cooperators Council (along with the pertinent Congressional committees and subcommittees). This is a special variation (a subset) of the food triangle of power. Its uniqueness is in its origin, objectives, and mode of operation.

The Foreign Agricultural Service was established by the Department of Agriculture in 1930 ". . . to provide systematic representation in U.S. embassies to promote sales of U.S. farm produce" (Hardin, 1967). In 1939, the service was transferred to the Department of State; in 1954, it was moved back into the agriculture department. To some degree, presumably, this was a squabble over turf, but much more significantly, these transfers were concerned with a basic policy question: who should direct the promotion of U.S. farm exports abroad? The controversy over whether to upgrade the position of agricultural attaché to the rank of counselor, which was a subissue in the Agricultural Trade Act of 1978, was just one more manifestation of this brooding controversy. All U.S. foreign economic activities abroad should be channeled through the ambassador's office, according to the State Department; the populistic instincts, deeply embedded in the food triangle, have never trusted the "striped pants, cookie-pushing, Eastern elite" (to characterize the populist's stereotype) to be aggressively dedicated to the sale of U.S. farm exports abroad. In any respect, the Foreign Agricultural Service has developed into one of the major bureaucracies within the agriculture department, with (as of Sept. 30, 1978) 772 employees (37 are not fulltime), with 445 of them in Washington, D.C. and 292 located in seventy embassies abroad; and with a budget in fiscal 1979 of almost $54 million. Its functions are to: (1) maintain a worldwide agricultural intelligence and reporting service, (2) analyze agricultural information essential to the assessment of foreign supply and demand conditions, (3) develop foreign markets for U.S. farm products through market promotion activities, and (4) direct and coordinate the USDA's participation in the formulation of trade programs and agreements (U.S. Congress, 1979a, p. 108).

The cooperator program of the Foreign Agricultural Service was a direct offshoot of Public Law 480 (McKenna, 1978). A minor portion of the foreign currencies accumulated through Title I sales were authorized for use by the service to induce the joining (cooperation) of public and private agricultural interests in the construction and implementation of diverse trade promotional strategies abroad. And by early 1979 some forty-five "cooperators" (U.S. food and fiber commodity organizations) were under contract with the service (U.S. Congress, 1979a). These cooperators have established themselves as an interest group, the Agricultural Cooperators Council (a third corner of the food export triangle) and its member organizations are listed in table 8-1. Furthermore, these cooperators are subsidized by the U.S. government, almost wholly with dollars rather than foreign currencies. In fiscal 1977 this subsidy amounted to $11,719,000 (U.S. Congress, 1979a).

This FAS–cooperator arrangement is actually a special variation of the typical triangular relationship. (USDA, 1975, pp. 10–11, 20–21). Participating therein are the forty-one state departments of agriculture and their five regional associations (for example, the Mid-Atlantic International Agri-Trade Council [MIATCO], which includes the twelve Midwest state departments of agriculture). Also included in this arrangement are the foreign cooperators. "These are governments, private firms or trade associations of foreign countries that also have something to gain from U.S. market development programs. . . ." For example, Japanese cotton spinners and garment manufacturers undertake cooperative consumer advertising with the U.S. Cotton Council International promoting the sale of 100 percent cotton garments in Japan (McKenna, 1978, p. 11). These foreign cooperators have now come to be the major contributors to this U.S. cooperator program so that by fiscal 1977 the figures were: the Foreign Agricultural Service, $12,517,000; U.S. cooperators, $12,575,000 (with $1,951,000 of that in contributions of food and services); foreign cooperators, $16,845,000—for a grand total of $41,937,000 (U.S. Congress, 1979a).

We must not downplay the congressional side of this triangle. Charles Hardin documents the intense interest that Congressman Jamie Whitten (Democrat from Mississippi), the longtime chairman of the agricultural appropriations subcommittee, and since 1979, of the full committee, has had in this program since its inception (Hardin, 1967). Congressional involvement depicts a global concern in some instances; in many others it is decidedly constituency oriented. For example, Congressman De La Garza's (Democrat from Texas) comment at a hearing in 1978 on U.S. trade with Japan: "I very simply would like to sell more beef and citrus products to Japan" (U.S. Congress, 1979b,

TABLE 8-1. MEMBER ORGANIZATIONS OF THE
            AGRICULTURAL COOPERATORS COUNCIL

American Angus Association	Holstein-Freisian Association of America
American Brahman Breeders	International Brangus Breeders'
Association	Association, Inc.
American Hereford Association	Leaf Tobacco Exporters
American Polled Hereford Association	Mohair Council of America
American Quarter Horse Association	National Association of Animal Breeders
American Seed Trade Association	National Peanut Council
American Soybean Association	National Renderers Association
Burley and Dark Leaf Tobacco Export	of America
Association, Inc.	Poultry and Egg Institute of America
California Almond Growers Exchange	Protein Grain Products International
California Cling Peach Advisory Board	Rice Council for Market Development
California Raisin Advisory Board	Santa Gertrudis Breeders International
Cotton Council International	Sunkist Growers, Inc.
Diary Society International	Tanners' Council of America, Inc.
D-N-E Sales, Inc.	Tobacco Associates, Inc.
EMBA Mink Breeders Association	U.S. Feed Grains Council
Florida Department of Citrus	U.S. Meat Export Federation
Great Plains Wheat, Inc.	Western Wheat Associates, U.S.A., Inc.

Source: *Hearings and Markup: Agricultural Exports and U.S. Foreign Economic Policy,*
House Committee on International Relations, 95 Cong., 2 sess. (1978) p. 282.

p. 8). The triangles of food power whirl in many directions, and not
least—according to the pluralists—toward a U.S. senator's state and
a U.S. representative's district. As stated recently and colloquially by
an FAS official: "We have this constituency down on the farms. We
scratch their backs and they scratch ours" (M. Mayer, 1980, p. 148).

As indicated earlier, this program is a direct offshoot of Public Law
480 and was principally designed for the avowed purpose of increasing the dollar sales of U.S. food products in foreign markets. Over
some twenty-five years, the Foreign Agricultural Service and the private cooperators (U.S. and foreign) have developed an imaginative
and diverse set of strategies and tactics (trade fairs, food exhibits, food
sales teams, media programs) in pursuit of the goals of the program.
As expressed in the subtitle of a recent article in *Fortune* magazine:
"The Foreign Agricultural Service hired some farm boys with PhDs,
and they have helped push U.S. agricultural exports from $7 billion
to $35 billion in just one decade" (M. Mayer, 1980, p. 146). The
service's professional-business orientation was nicely summarized in
the same article, by a high-ranking FAS administrator: "We are basically economists—economists and salesmen."

TABLE 8-2. U.S. FOREIGN AGRICULTURAL SERVICE EXPENDITURES,
WITH ESTIMATED U.S. AND THIRD PARTY COOPERATOR
CONTRIBUTIONS

(dollars)

Expenditures	Fiscal 1977	Fiscal 1978	Fiscal 1979
FAS	11,719,000	14,805,000	19,430,000
U.S. cooperator contributions:			
Cash	10,529,000	11,370,000	14,124,000
Goods & services	1,951,000	2,070,000	2,397,000
Total U.S. cooperator			
contribution	12,480,000	13,440,000	16,521,000
Foreign cooperators	16,845,000	17,406,000	19,398,000
Total cooperator projects	41,044,000	48,651,000	55,349,000

Source: U.S. Congress, Agriculture, Rural Development, and Related Agencies Appropriations for 1980, part 5, Hearings before the House Subcommittee of the Committee on Appropriations, 96 Cong., 1 sess. (Washington, D.C., GPO) pp. 92–103.

Albeit, a minor but persisting political controversy continues to be heard (GAO, 1975). The question at issue is: Has the cooperator program evolved into a type of pork-barrel[1] operation in which the commodity organizations (the cooperators) continue to receive public funds for promoting their products after a successful prosperous market has been developed? As table 8-2 indicates, the cooperator program does incur a fair-sized and increasing cost to the U.S. government.

The position of the House of Representative's Committee on Government Operations has been that once a market has been successfully developed, then ". . . further U.S. government support should not be required. The cooperator organizations' economic self-interest should be sufficient to maintain the market" (GAO, 1975, pp. 55–56). The General Accounting Office's principal recommendation, in its 1975 report, was in the same vein: the secretary of agriculture should " . . . establish criteria for determining when products supported under the cooperator program are well established in a market and no longer warrant FAS assistance" (GAO, 1975, p. 66).

The U.S. Department of Agriculture's response to this criticism was sharply negative: reducing the U.S. government's investment in this program would result in large cutbacks in the export promotion program; markets lost are difficult to regain; U.S. competitors (Australia, Canada, France, and others) are actively involved in their own promotion programs; this cooperator program has been eminently suc-

[1] A government project or appropriation yielding rich patronage benefits.

cessful; it should be (and is) carefully scrutinized, monitored, and audited, but no basic changes should be made in it (GAO 1975, pp. 82–87). The comments from the Department of State were ambiguous but, at least by indirection, that department seemed to agree with the Government Accounting Office's recommendations concerning the cooperator program (GAO, 1975, pp. 92–93). Obviously the cooperator program imposes direct costs on the U.S. Treasury, and it could well be that both U.S. and foreign cooperators should incur a greater share of the costs or possibly the total cost. In President Carter's proposed budget for fiscal 1981, there was a recommendation to the effect that market development funding should only be made available to cooperators that provided at least 50 percent of the funding for that program. Perhaps so; however, by fiscal 1979 the FAS' share of the costs for the cooperator program had declined to 31 percent (U.S. Congress, 1980, pp. 391–392). If the proposed 50 percent rule is implemented, then this would prevent the Foreign Agricultural Service from using public funds to initiate new and heavily subsidized cooperator programs, which it has often done with the avowed intent (generally adhered to) of decreasing incrementally that subsidy when a particular program proved successful. This tactic seems to be fair and prudent, at least as viewed in terms of the national interest of the United States.

We have included table 8-3 for the purpose of relating the cooperators' program more specifically to U.S. agricultural trade relations with Japan. Eight U.S. cooperators have permanent offices in Tokyo: American Soybean Association, California Cling Peach Advisory Board, National Renderers Association, Poultry and Egg Institute of America, USA Dry Pea and Lentil Council, U.S. Feed Grains Council, U.S. Meat Export Federation, and Wheat Associates, U.S.A. Other cooperators have programs that are pursued on a more special, *ad hoc* type of arrangement. No U.S. agricultural trade office has been set up in Japan (six had been established throughout the world, by 1980, under the provisions of the Agricultural Trade Act of 1978). However, it seems quite clear that the Foreign Agricultural Service would have done so if the cost had been less prohibitive. That is, FAS' initial estimate for setting up a trade office in Tokyo was $1.2 million, which would have exceeded the total cost for establishing all of the six trade offices (U.S. Congress, 1980, p. 375). Note, too, that the table indicates that the cooperators, U.S. and foreign, contributed that year almost 75 percent of the funds for administering the program.

In summary, our general impression is—although we have not probed into the cooperator program in depth—that the program, in general,

TABLE 8-3. U.S. COOPERATOR PROGRAM IN JAPAN: FAS EXPENDITURES AND ESTIMATED U.S. AND THIRD PARTY CONTRIBUTIONS, FY 1978

(dollars)

U.S. cooperator	FAS expenditures	U.S. cooperator contributions[a]	Foreign cooperator contributions	Total
American Soybean Association	486,096	406,000	1,791,764	2,683,860
Western Wheat Association	453,388	216,000	1,563,665	2,038,653
Cotton Council International	410,039	87,000	541,451	1,038,490
U.S. Feed Grains Council	335,415	147,000	732,554	1,214,969
International Institute for Cotton	310,000	0	1,129,670	1,439,670
Calif. Avocado Commission	204,995	211,000	0	415,898
Poultry & Egg Institute of America	201,945	140,000	284,881	626,835
National Renderers Association	178,635	111,000	56,835	346,470
Calif. Cling Peach Advisory Board	127,251	219,000	468,700	814,951
Calif. Raisin Advisory Board	110,925	131,000	509,622	751,547
U.S. Meat Export Federation	96,414	146,000	73,697	316,111
USA Dry Pea & Lentil Council	30,376	22,000	3,097	55,473
National Peanut Council	19,050	24,000	3,710	46,760
National Potato Promotion Board	12,009	24,000	0	36,009
EMBA Mink Breeder Association	8,653	24,000	0	32,653
Calif. Apricot Board	1,364	0	0	1,364
Export Incentive Program	632,782	2,483,613	93,446	3,219,787
FAS Projects	225,241	45,476	0	270,717
Total	3,854,533	4,437,089	7,253,092	15,544,714

Source: U.S. Department of Agriculture, Foreign Agricultural Service, to the authors, August 31, 1979.

[a] Prorated based on FAS expenditures.

has been a pronounced success. Even after discounting for the political hyperbole, there seems to be a fair amount of merit in Vice President Mondale's adulation of the Foreign Agricultural Service: " . . . the contribution you make to this Nation's strength is truly incredible" (USDA, 1979a, p. 7). Perhaps not "incredible," but according to one recent study, ". . . the White House has been looking rather wistfully at the FAS as a possible model for a new industrial program" (M. Mayer, 1980, p. 154).

Nevertheless we do insert a word of caution about the strategy and tactics of the Foreign Agricultural Service. Put more bluntly, there are those who view FAS' tactics as too aggressive and demanding, too insensitive to Japan's peculiar food predicament. After all, the critics argue—and with some credibility—Japan is the number one market in the world for U.S. agricultural commodities; why doesn't the U.S. food export triangle of power (to use our terminology) recognize that economic reality, modulate its demands, and become more gentlemanly in its choice of selling tactics? Again, our firsthand observations of the FAS bureaucracy in action are much too limited for us to attempt to arbitrate this controversy. Our general observation is: The FAS bureaucracy acts essentially as one would expect, under the given political and economic conditions. To employ a current aphorism, how one stands on an issue depends on where one sits. Perhaps it would be useful, to both the FAS and Japan's Ministry of Agriculture, Foresty and Fisheries, if there could be a mutual understanding, if not appreciation, of the validity of that suggestion.

Two food networks: polyarchy

The polyarchal model is essentially elitist. "It specifically leaves policy choices to the elite rulers, while reserving to the public periodic selection among these elites. People do not govern under polyarchy; they merely choose their governors. It gives leaders considerable leeway and legitimacy as long as they regularly ask for approval at stated intervals" (Fowler and Orenstein, 1977, p. 32).

In the American agricultural scene, and undergirding the structure of the food networks, is the development of a scientific, heavily technological, highly productive agriculture (Heclo, 1978). The U.S. system of land grant universities, which was established by the Morrill Act of 1862, may have begun as the "people's colleges," but over a century of time these land-grant universities have assumed a leading role in educating a new elite—not by intent, but in result. Agribusiness in all of its ramifications—the farmer-businessmen, the development of new animal breeds and crop varieties, the ever-increasing com-

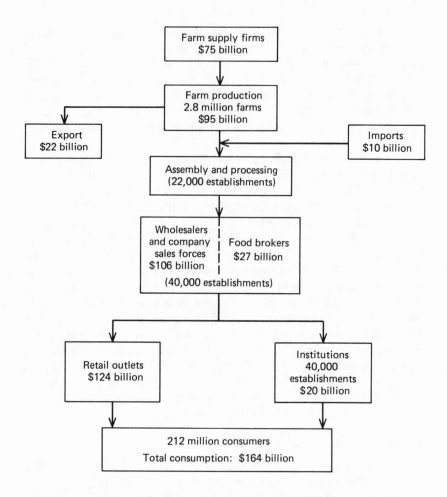

Figure 8-1. Functional organization of U.S. food agribusinesses, 1974. *Source*: Ray A. Goldberg, unpublished paper, as reprinted in Gail L. Cramer and Clarence W. Jensen, *Agricultural Economics and Agribusiness* (New York, Wiley, 1979) p. 34. Reprinted with permission of John Wiley & Sons and Ray A. Goldberg.

plexity and immensity of farm technology, the chemical revolution in terms of both its growth-inducing and growth-preventing effects, the burgeoning of a scientific-technological and regulatory bureaucracy (the Department of Agriculture)—has been a principal factor in the proliferation of the food industry into nearly every phase of American economic life. Moreover, the American food industry has also become deeply involved in international politics—in market economics (Japan), socialist economies (the Soviet Union and China), and the Third World economies (Egypt and Pakistan).

Polyarchal theory leads one to deduce from the evidence that there are two food networks in the United States—the agribusiness network and the Washington food network. We have included figure 8-1 to depict in brief form what is taking place in the development of an agribusiness network. It constitutes a vast and complex input–output model. The result is the most productive farm-food industry in the world, but one which has become heavily dependent on food and fiber exports if it is to be profitable to at least the major elements in the agribusiness industry.

Viewed from the perspective of the polyarchal model, the agribusiness industry has both a positive and negative face. According to the main agribusiness actors—fertilizer, grain trading, farm machinery, chemicals, transportation, supermarket chains, as examples—the food industry, like every other major American industry, is in the process of adjusting to the demands of a highly technological urban society and an interdependent world. As viewed by its advocates, agribusinesses pursue a positive sum strategy; at home and abroad American farm products are produced in quality and abundance; they are then sold at attractive prices; therefore, all of us are winners, from producers to consumers.

According to those who advocate and pursue the populist and participatory democracy models, agribusinesses personify a persistent evil of elitism—the few are exploiting the many (that is, the food consumer) in terms of excess profits through the production and sale, ofttimes, of health-hazardous and only marginally nutritious foods, and through the undermining of the family farm. The pluralists' view is more ambivalent—agribusiness should be both loved and feared; the first when the end result is more profit for the producer; the latter when the result is a loss of individual freedom in decision making. But after one filters away the rhetoric it is difficult not to come to the socioeconomic conclusion that agribusinesses have become the dominant force in the American food industry.

In polyarchal theory, and especially that of the liberal variety, a bureaucratic (executive and congressional) food network had to be, and has been constructed, as a countervailing force to the agribusiness network. We have termed this "the Washington food network." U.S. national and international interests in matters of food policy would be more effectively pursued by creating new executive bureaucracies which would have the responsibility and authority to direct food policy decisions more in the public interest, at least this was the liberals' claim. Typically, this construction and allocation was hastily conceived and inadequately thought out, more a matter of muddling through than of any systematic planning. We do note that this condition was apparently changed for the better in the late 1970s (Hopkins and Puchala, 1980, chapter 4). We have included figure 8-2 to portray graphically the complexity and diversity of this particular food network, although the chart is certainly not complete. According to the General Accounting Office, "over 26 agencies and 30 full Congressional Committees have some responsibility in food programs and policies" (GAO, 1979, p. 5).

The result has been the creation of confusing and conflicting jurisdictional lines; political infighting over boundary questions constantly occurs. But food has become too important to be left to the agribusiness network or the special interest-oriented food triangle, or so the argument runs. Moreover, the dividing line between foreign and domestic policy decisions has become more indistinct; food has become just one more sectoral area among many, which means that the advice and counsel of the Office of Management and Budget (OMB), the U.S. Treasury, the Council of Economic Advisors (CEA), and the Environmental Protection Agency (EPA), among others, should become more prominent and influential. And the internationalization of U.S. food has increased the level of concern and involvement in food policy issues of the National Security Council, the Agency for International Development (AID), and (of particular importance to agricultural trade relations) the Office of the Special Trade Representative (STR).

In Congress, jurisdictional proliferation is just as evident. According to the same GAO study, "seven standing committees are responsible for most major food policy matters" (U.S. Congress, 1976, p. 26). Of even more relevance has been the rather dramatic professionalization of congressional staffs and support organizations such as the Congressional Research Service, Congressional Budget Office, Office of Technology Assessment, General Accounting Office, House and Senate budget offices, and the much expanded staffs of the food-related standing committees. To some extent this development has occurred to provide the members of Congress and congressional committees with their own sources of "intelligence" (expertise), thereby lessening the often overwhelming superiority of the executive bureaucracies in terms of information and analysis. One could contend, of course, that

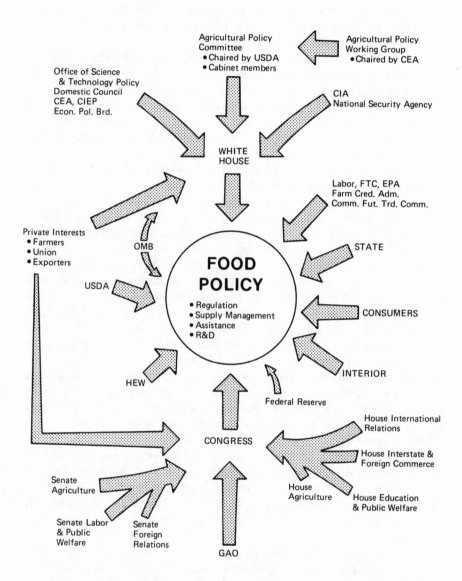

Figure 8-2. Major influences on food policy. *Source*: U.S. General Accounting Office, *Food, Agriculture, and Nutrition Issues for Planning*, CED 79–36 (Washington, D.C., January 29, 1979) p. 6.

this professionalization has been a principal cause of executive–congressional confrontations. Perhaps so, but it is our position that these congressional staffs have generally tended to convey, in their advice and counsel, a perspective, an outlook on life, which is more national, and often international, in its vision than is generally found, for example, in the food triangles of power.

On the other hand, the staffs of the individual members of Congress may be considerably more influential in molding and unifying behavior than are the congressional staff organizations. One of the dominant calculations in the political lives of members of Congress is their steadfast concern about reelection. And the members of their respective staffs also have a very considerable interest in acting in ways that will enhance the attainment of that same objective.

Historically (during and since the New Deal years) the U.S. Department of Agriculture has been the bureaucratic linchpin between these two networks, refereeing the disputes and sanctions, sometimes even calling the signals, but the political trend has been one of decline in USDA power and influence. Liberal forces would claim that the USDA is biased in favor of agribusiness; the conservatives would counter that it has been too easily misled by organized labor and "cheap-food" urban Democrats. In either case, the department suffered losses in authority and prestige during the late 1960s and early 1970s. However, during the Carter-Bergland years (1977–80) that department was able to establish fairly well (some wins, some losses) its desired role as the dominant coordinating and equilibrating bureaucracy relative to policy conflicts between and within the two polyarchies. Nevertheless, in really critical situations affecting U.S. food policies, national and international, power will continue to move to the White House.

In summary, we believe that the conceptual framework presented herein is a useful tool for providing perceptive insights into the political question of who commands? in the area of U.S. food policy. But we are confronted with a major and fairly obvious difficulty. In the matter of U.S. food and agricultural policies, there are elements of participatory democracy, populism, pluralism, and polyarchy at work, although we claim that fairly definite trend lines can be denoted. To some extent, moreover, decision making is a dependent variable; those who command are actually manipulated by major economic, political, and sociopsychological forces over which they have little control. In the concluding section of the chapter we will try to relate that general observation to the specific matter of U.S.–Japanese agricultural trade relations.

Under what conditions?

The question of "who commands" must be answered, in part, by posing a contingent question—under what conditions? Those who have power, and the means to influence the instruments of power, employ particular strategies in an attempt to achieve certain ends, but they do so within a changing social environment.

Historically, the major conditions that have influenced U.S. agriculture have been: its rich natural endowments; the effect of Jeffersonian agricultural fundamentalism; the development of a scientific agriculture in the latter part of the nineteenth century; the origins and growth of nationally controlled, farmer-administered credit and regulatory (production) programs in the 1920s, and especially in the 1930s; and the maturing of agricultural economics as a science during the first half of this century. Such conditions have influenced the changing structure of political power, relative to U.S. agricultural and food policies. It is, however, the post–World War II period that is particularly relevant to the subject of this book.

Our review of the evidence has led us to conclude that the following eight conditions have been of major significance in the remolding of the four concepts of democracy since 1945. Although we endeavored to list those conditions in historical sequence, this effort proved only partially successful. Conditions arise and are revised in multiples. They overlap and interact, then are redefined and reanalyzed; whereupon new strategies and structures are devised to meet different estimates of changing situations. Nevertheless, we will proceed as if there has been an historically linear progression of changing conditions.

The declining political power of the farmer

The logic of democratic theory is based on the proposition that political power moves when people move; that is, the principle of majority rule must be institutionalized. Farm population in the United States (and the definition of a farmer has been liberally devised) has shrunk from 23 million in 1950 to an estimated 6.3 million in 1979; that is, less than 3 percent of the U.S. population (Penn, 1981). Many, including numerous political scientists, predicted accordingly that there would be a severe decline in the political influence of American farmers. Surely their political importance has declined, but in no way proportionate to the massive decline in farm population. Why not? Certain particular, if not peculiar, features of the American political system have their cushioning effects: the weakness of American po-

litical parties; the single-member district elections to the House of
Representatives (rural nonfarm population has risen from 31.5 million in 1950 to an estimated 47.2 million in 1977); the equality of
representation in the U.S. Senate (Iowa has two senators, so does
California); the election of the president through the electoral college
system; the continuing efficacy of the family farm ideology in urban
as well as rural America; the dominance of the rural states in the
congressional committees on agriculture, and on the appropriations
subcommittees; and—very important—the enduring insight in Wood-
row Wilson's dictum that, "congressional government is committee
government." The food triangles of power, general and commodity,
liberal and conservative—admittedly less politically potent than they
used to be—have still succeeded in winning more legislative battles
than has usually been predicted.

The continuing political efficacy of the family farm ideology

Myth and reality have been in conflict in this regard. In reality, the
farmer has become a key component in an agribusiness network, an
important link in an industrial chain. Still, the myth of the family
farm refuses to die, and indeed most farms are operated as family
businesses, corporate or otherwise. But the U.S. Department of Agriculture estimates that by the year 2000 one percent of the farms will
produce 50 percent of the agricultural output and this trend has been
well underway for some thirty years (USDA, 1980, p. 12).

Politically, the myth provides the populists with one slight hope of
success, gives more legitimacy to the farmer committee system than
is deserved, exaggerates the importance of the food triangles of power,
functions as a political barb that constantly pricks the agribusiness
establishment, sustains the agriculture department as it clings to nos-
talgia for political supports, but thwarts that bureaucracy as it en-
deavors to propose realistic policies.

Overproduction and price–income instability in farm commodities

As agricultural economists have observed for some years, the aggregate demand for and the supply of farm commodities are severely
inelastic (W. Cochrane, 1979, p. 409 and passim). In the vernacular,
this means that the more the farmer produces, the less he profits.

Since 1929, the food triangles of power have called upon the federal
government to redress the balance—that is, through incentives (but
rarely by compulsion) to require them to do as a group (by commodity)
what they would not do as individual entrepreneurs. In consequence,

from March 31, 1938, to September 30, 1978, there was a net restoration of capital by the U.S. Treasury to the Commodity Credit Corporation of almost $59.5 billion. This means that price support programs, alone, had an average annual cost of nearly $1.5 billion a year for each of the last forty years.

This public expense has been difficult for the food triangles of power to sustain politically. Indeed, the passage of the Food and Agriculture Act of 1965 required a more market-oriented approach for nearly all commodity programs. But such changes in the rules of the game only changed the political tactics of the farmer interest groups. Legislative and administrative battles now came to be over the amount and conditions of set-aside payments, loan rates, target prices, and release requirements for farm-based reserves. And in those contests, the food triangles have been modestly successful.

In any respect, the moderate-to-heavy costs of federal farm programs have occasioned changes in the structure of political power. Farmer interest groups have had to form coalitions with urban, organized labor, and welfare groups—often with considerable reluctance—in order to build sufficient political support for their own price and income programs. Tradeoffs came to be a political necessity; expensive food stamp, school lunch, and welfare-nutrition programs were the result.

Food surpluses as an instrument of U.S. farm and foreign policy

Food has been used as an instrument of U.S. foreign policy ever since World War II. Public Law 480, passed in 1954, has been of particular importance to American farmers although mutual security acts have also been of significance. In the beginning Public Law 480 was dominantly a surplus disposal program, a dumping program as some have viewed it, although it has gradually evolved into an effective instrument of foreign policy (Hopkins and Puchala, 1980, chapter 3). From July 1954, through Sept. 30, 1978, the cost of these programs has been over $31.6 billion; over 262 million metric tons of commodities were shipped under the various titles of P.L. 480.

Politically, these oft-named Food for Peace programs have caused new alliances of power. Religious organizations and secular welfare groups have become involved in making decisions about how much, to whom, and for what. The Agency for International Development (AID) has become an influential actor; so has the Department of State, especially during and since the Kissinger regime; the foreign relations committees in Congress have acquired some jurisdictional powers and responsibilities. At the same time, the Washington food network has, in general, been ambivalent toward these food aid programs. More specifically, as U.S. food surpluses declined, so did the political desire to use them; shipping relatively scarce food to the Third World raised consumer food prices at home. The traditional food triangles have supported international food aid programs with reluctance when farm prices have been on the rise; when surpluses built up, word went out to U.S. embassies abroad: negotiate more shipments under P.L. 480, although current budget legislation has practically closed that surplus valve.

During the 1970s, P.L. 480 became of decreasing importance to farm groups, although it continued to be of considerable value to U.S. church and welfare organizations with international health and development programs, and of marginal importance to the Department of State and AID as an instrument of U.S. foreign policy. In 1960, some 26 percent of U.S. agricultural exports were shipped under P.L. 480 provisions; by 1970, this percentage had declined to less than 14 percent, and by 1979, that figure had become 3 percent. It seems fair to generalize that P.L. 480 is now more symbolic than substantive, and relative to its effect on the U.S. political economy, probably of more value as a political than an economic issue and instrument.

The rise of the environmental movement

From the mid-1960s through the early 1970s, Congress enacted more important, far-ranging, regulatory-environmental legislation than would ever have been believed possible as early as the Kennedy administration. Indeed, the sweep of this legislation extended beyond the protection and purification of natural resources; hunger, poverty, occupational safety, and unorganized labor also came to be highly placed items on the political agenda. Within the social sciences, agenda-building came to be widely discussed and theorized about: whoever controls the public agenda controls policy output, so to speak. Within the academic and bureaucratic food establishment, Don Paarlberg came to be the principal innovator of the concept of an "old agenda" and a "new agenda" in matters concerning food and agricultural policies (D. Paarlberg, 1980, especially chapters 3 to 5 for his latest version). To use his metaphor: "Making public policy is like playing a football game: you can't win if your side doesn't have the ball" (that is, control of the public agenda). The traditional food triangles of power (to use our terminology) have too often lost the ball; even more seriously they often do not seem to realize that they are now the defense, or if they do, their defensive strategies are ill conceived in concept and ineptly pursued in action.

We concede that Paarlberg's propositions have merit and insight. The agribusiness network (including the colleges of agriculture in the land grant universities) has become the defender of the old agenda; new and reinvigorated structures of political power have come into play in the form of the Environmental Protection Agency, the Council on Environmental Quality, a host of liberal–radical environmental interest groups, and reorganized and recharged congressional committees. However, it is our general observation that a counterrevolution is underway; whether this is good or bad, viewed nationally and internationally, is not our immediate concern. The agribusiness network and the food triangles of power are regrouping and are beginning to win in the game of administrative regulations, research studies, and judicial decisions. In any respect, the new environmental movement is a significant and present condition of power; populism and participatory democracy have been given a modernized dose of political adrenalin; the traditional triangles of food power are engaged in a new type of confrontational politics; the agribusiness network has become more clearly identified and perhaps better understood.

The ascent of the United States into the role of the dominant world food power

This changing condition is obviously of major importance in a discussion of the politics of U.S.–Japanese agricultural trade relations. But, in terms of its major political and economic aspects, the domestic and foreign policy implications of this condition are so vast and complex that we have had great difficulty in fitting together a set of general observations that would be useful in its elucidation. To begin, however, the United States has moved from the position of a residual supplier of agricultural products to that of the dominant world food power. Among several causes was congressional enactment of the Food and Agriculture Act of 1965, with its emphasis on farm price supports being set at or near the world market price.

In 1975, Lester Brown brought this issue onto the political and intellectual agenda with his discussion of "the North American breadbasket," which includes Canada, of course. According to Brown, "North America's unchallenged dominance as a global food supplier began in the forties. The scale of exports expanded gradually during the fifties and sixties. During the seventies, North American grain exports have doubled in response to the explosive growth in import demand from around the world" (Brown, 1975, p. 10). Our table 8-4 is from Brown's latest book; the dependency has become so dramatic that "today over a hundred countries rely on North American grain" (1981, p. 93).

TABLE 8-4. THE CHANGING PATTERN OF WORLD GRAIN TRADE
(million metric tons)

Region	1934–38	1948–52	1960	1970	1980
North America	+5	+23	+39	+56	+131
Latin America	+9	+1	0	+4	-10
Western Europe	-24	-22	-25	-30	-16
E. Europe and USSR	+5	0	0	0	-46
Africa	+1	0	-2	-5	-15
Asia	+2	-6	-17	-37	-63
Australia and N. Z.	+3	+3	+6	+12	+19

Note: Plus sign indicates net exports; minus sign, net imports.
Source: Lester R. Brown, Building a Sustainable Society (New York, W. W. Norton, 1981) p. 92.

This changing condition was certainly dramatic, if not revolutionary, because of its immediate impact and long-run potential. According to the Department of Agriculture, in 1970 U.S. agricultural
exports were about $5 billion; in 1980, the total had climbed dra-
matically to more than $41 billion. In terms of volume (million metric
tons), the change was less exciting, perhaps: from more than 106
million in fiscal 1973 to almost 164 million for fiscal 1980. Some
viewed this transformation in terms of its creation of wealth; others
were concerned more about political and economic power. But the
use of food as an instrument of power, in the pursuit of either foreign
or domestic policy goals, was not auspiciously successful during the
early 1970s. The Russian grain sales in 1972 were a near fiasco; as
President Nixon commented later to Andrei Gromyko, the United
States was "snookered." The short-lived soybean embargo in 1973,
and particularly its application to Japan, proved to be a major economic
mistake, coupled with adverse political repercussions. Subsequently,
the Ford-Butz administration negotiated a grain-sales agreement with
the Soviet Union, and in November 1975 an important U.S.–Japanese
"understanding" was arrived at through an exchange of letters between
U.S. Secretary of Agriculture Butz and the Japanese minister of
agriculture, Shintoro Abe.
   A prelude to this agreement was the United States–USSR food
export imbroglio that took place throughout most of 1975. Heavy
U.S. grain sales to the Soviet Union coincided with a stretch of bad
weather in the Midwest, leading to a tightening of available grain for
export, which culminated in a "temporary suspension" of sales to the
Soviet Union, followed by the refusal of the longshoremen's union to
load ships of grain destined for that nation. After some complicated
negotiations between the two superpowers, a U.S.–USSR Grain

Agreement covering the period of October 1, 1976, to September 30, 1981, was ratified.

In political terms, the agribusiness network, the Washington food network, and the food export triangle prefer to follow a market economy-type strategy of all-out sales. An increase in profits and some mitigation of the balance of payments problem are the principal motives. Major difficulties arise, however, when U.S. food supplies move toward short supply. At some point on the food prices-inflation scale, the Washington food network, probably under the personal direction of the president, must move to a managed economy, regulating food shipments abroad and perhaps even food prices at home.

The Soviet invasion of Afghanistan in late 1979, followed soon by the U.S. embargo on grain shipments (above 8 million tons) to the USSR, is further proof that foreign policy considerations may override the economic interests of all the food structures of power (R. Paarlberg, forthcoming). Our surplus–scarcity continuum is no longer the principal indicator that guides decision making. It seems fairly predictable that the Afghanistan situation is not an isolated incident, and the likelihood of future embargoes of this type is one principal reason for the Japanese concern over their extensive dependency on U.S. food exports.

The weather-climate equation

Mention must be at least made of the vagaries of weather and climate as constraints on the planning and implementation of policy. The 1972–74 world food crisis was, in part, caused by extremely adverse weather conditions in several important grain-growing areas. Future crises of this type could possibly be prevented if an extensive international grains agreement were to be negotiated and ratified by at least the major food-producing and food-consuming countries, but this likelihood seems to recede with each passing year since the World Food Conference in 1974.

Are we entering an age of food scarcity?

In recent years there has been an undercurrent of speculation that the world may be moving into a condition of food scarcity, although there is certainly no consensus on this matter. A recent USDA publication views the future, although not without qualification, in this vein: "The long period of overproduction, burdensome surpluses and depressed farm prices now seems to be behind us, although there may still be occasional years of excess production . . . We face an increasingly tight and significantly more volatile world food balance ahead" (USDA, 1981, pp. i, 26).

This statement, together with chapter 2 in this volume, provides an overall perspective of what is likely to be the world food situation throughout this decade. Viewed on a surplus–abundance–scarcity continuum, it is fairly obvious that food demand–food supply behavior patterns have important implications for both U.S. and Japanese food policy strategies. It is even probable that the matter will occasionally, perhaps often, become involved in high-level politics. If the trend moves toward scarcity, political intensity will increase somewhat commensurately, and fundamental considerations relating to Japanese–U.S. defense and trade policy matters may have to be reviewed and recalculated.

It could be argued that all of these conditions, some more than others, point to what Willard Cochrane has recently designated as the central policy issue in American agriculture: *"How are consumers and farmers in the United States to achieve a tolerable degree of price and income stability where the food and agricultural sector of the United States is integrated into the world market through the important export crops—wheat, coarse grains, cotton and soybeans?"* (italics Cochrane's) (1979, p. 163). To a lesser degree, he could have said the same for the consumers and farmers of Japan.

Thus uncertainty, instability, and variability are built into the American food industry. An elaborate, extensive, and expensive national grain reserve system would probably enable the United States to smooth out nearly all of those humps, but such a reserve scheme is not politically feasible nor perhaps would it be economically wise. This means that the politics of instability and uncertainty will lead to continuing political struggles over answers to the questions of who benefits? and who should benefit?

Who benefits?

Every phase of the U.S. food and fiber system has its political costs and political benefits. The system is an intricate and complex infrastructure which is intertwined in nearly every sector of the political economy of the nation, and increasingly so of the world. Viewed politically, one important question is: Who benefits from the agricultural and food legislation enacted by Congress and then implemented (primarily) by the U.S. Department of Agriculture? Viewed in terms of political philosophy that question leads to a serious normative problem: Should the winners have won? We will only allude to possible and alternative answers to that question. Viewed empirically, the question is still difficult to grapple with. How do we define what is meant by winners and losers? How can we say that one concept of democracy became stronger and another weaker? Again, our treatments of those questions are deductive and rather problematical.

As discussed earlier, one of the most significant changes in the world food scene has been the incremental but dramatic movement of the United States from the role of a residual supplier of world food exports to that of the dominant world food export power. The importance of that changing situation to the fiscal health of the nation and the special welfare of the U.S. food industry and foreign consumers has obviously been of very considerable significance.

Successful policies are viewed as such, by and large, because they have evolved from a positive-sum strategy—that is, all major groups involved are winners in that they receive more positive advantages than negative disadvantages from the policy—the U.S. farmer-held reserve system, for example, at least as it is now functioning. But the incremental industrialization of American agriculture has brought many new players into the game of food; new technologies breed new politics. At each stage of the input–output function of U.S. agribusiness (see figure 8-1) political decisions have to be made.

In 1977, U.S. consumers spent $180 billion for food; of that amount $124 billion covered the costs of transporting, processing, and distributing the food that originated on U.S. farms; the farmers' gross return was $56 billion. The cost of labor—which, in political terms, means labor unions—constitutes the major part of the total food marketing bill. Labor used by assemblers, manufacturers, wholesalers, retailers, and eating places cost $58 billion in 1979, which should be compared with the $56 billion (gross return) received by the producing farmers (USDA, 1978, p. 35).

The agribusiness network has been a fairly clear winner in this transformation of American agriculture from a special way of life to a conglomerate of modestly capitalized (usually) businesses located in rural America. The applied (including managerial) scientific and technological underpinning of U.S. agriculture has brought into being a complicated and intricate U.S. food system. Added to this is the fact that agribusiness interests have often formed mutually productive alliances with the food triangles of power.

Another beneficiary has been the innovator farmer-businessman, who is indeed one of the main spokes in the production–processing–marketing wheel which we have termed "agribusiness." Table 8-5 depicts what is taking place within American agriculture. Some 6.6

TABLE 8-5. U.S. FARM PROFILES BASED ON 1974 NATIONAL CENSUS DATA[a]: STRUCTURAL CHARACTERISTICS BY SIZE CLASSIFICATION

| | Size Classification | | | | |
| | Declining sector | | | Expanding sector | |
General structural characteristics	"Part-time and subsistence" farms (sales of less than $10,000)	"Small" farms (sales of $10,000–39,999)	"Medium" farms (sales of $40,000–99,999)	"Large" farms (sales of $100,000–199,999)	"Largest" farms (sales of $200,000+)
No. of farms[b]	1,203,004	631,782	324,310	101,153	51,446
Percent of farms[b]	52.2	27.3	14.0	4.5	2.1
Avg. farm size in acres	203	416	761	1,299	2,826
Percent of land	23.3	25.7	24.1	12.8	14.1
Percent of farm sales	4.7	16.9	24.7	17.0	36.8
Average Market value of agricultural products sold ($)	5,321.00	21,696.00	61,890.00	136,012.00	581,996.00

Source: General Accounting Office, Changing Character and Structure of American Agriculture: An Overview, CED-78-178 (Washington, D.C., U.S. General Accounting Office, Sept. 26, 1978) p. 77, table 19 (modified).
[a] Published December 1977.
[b] These figures represent all farms, not just commercial farms with sales of $2,500 and over.

percent of the farms accounted for almost 54 percent of farm sales in 1974. Even more significant, perhaps, is the degree of concentration taking place within all of the sectors depicted in figure 8-1, although this oligopoly–competition controversy is subject to various interpretations that cannot be examined in this chapter. In two noteworthy speeches in 1979, Secretary of Agriculture Bergland analyzed these trends, pondered over their meaning, and proposed a national dialogue on the subject. It might be possible politically to slow down or redirect this trend toward the industrialization of the American food industry. If the major food triangles of power could be synchronized under USDA guidance and direction, then a national food policy, with an emphasis on the stabilization of the power of the family farmer, might be constructed and enacted. But we are very skeptical.

Colleges of agriculture and the USDA's Agricultural Research Service (ARS) have also benefited; in fact some would argue that they have been a principal factor in the building up of surpluses. Establishing the logic that the cure for farm surpluses is more science and technology has not impressed the Washington food network in recent years, and the members of the House Agriculture Committee, in particular, have begun to be disbelievers. In the latter's case, how to win the next election is the dominant motivation, or so is the current orthodoxy in political science (Mayhew, 1974; Fiorina, 1977). And fewer farmers mean fewer constituents, which means redistricting, and that could bring about the incumbent's demise.

Another strong winner (beneficiary) is the U.S. Department of Agriculture. Farm prices may, or may not, be made in Washington, but farm legislation—in draft form—usually emanates from within the offices of the department. To be sure, the USDA is usually not "one big happy family" when it comes to proposing new or revised farm and food legislation, or in its implementation. For example, the Agricultural Stabilization and Conservation Service (ASCS) has one set of interests, the Agricultural Research Service may have quite a different set, and the Economics, Statistics and Cooperatives Service (ESCS)[2] may disagree with both; but the differences will be ironed out, probably not to the full satisfaction of any of the involved bureaucracies. What the secretary of agriculture decides to ask for, or how he decides to act, is not necessarily (as we have explained earlier) what the Executive Office of the President will concur with, but the secretary continues to be the principal actor in the Washington food network.

[2] On July 1, 1981, the Economics, Statistics and Cooperatives Service was split into three separate services: the Economic Research Service, the Statistics Research Service, and the Agricultural Cooperatives Service.

Farmer interest groups have also benefited from the national farm programs of the last forty years, and they have certainly proliferated. Specialization follows from industrialization, and this has led to a proliferation of commodity-based interest groups, of almost inordinate variety. James Madison would surely be astounded, if not painfully appalled, at their bounteous proliferation. We can be assured that the interest groups as bureaucracies, have benefited from the politicization of farm policy (Yekes and Akey, 1979). Whether this has been to the benefit of their constituents is another matter. The political rhetoric of nearly all general farmer interest groups (with the American Farm Bureau Federation as a principal exception) is often heavily populistic, ardently espousing participatory practices, but their political strategies are seldom harmful to the interests of the "largest" farms (as defined in table 8-5).

The participatory democracy movement of the mid and late 1960s had several spin-offs, one of which was a hard, close look at hunger in America. The idea of food stamps for low-income persons was hardly a new idea, but the farmer interest groups (the National Farmers Union excepted) have tended to treat domestic food schemes primarily as useful surplus disposal rather than nutrition-building programs. However, one result of the new food agenda was a substantial increase in funds allocated for several varieties of domestic food programs. In the appropriations for fiscal 1980, over half of the USDA's appropriations, more than $8.5 billion out of a total of nearly $16.7, was for such programs, with a large portion of that allocated to food stamps.

On the other hand, participatory democracy advocates in neither the "first" nor the "second" conservation movements (Fleming, 1972) have been able to elevate the natural resource issue to a top ranking on the nation's political agenda. Modern agricultural practices continue to "mine" one of the nation's most precious natural resources, notably its farmlands (Crosson and Frederick, 1977, especially chapter 7). Although we cannot review the evidence in this study, we are definitely of the opinion that U.S. agricultural practices over the last fifty years have caused very serious agronomic and economic damage to the nation's soil.

Since the passage of soil conservation legislation in 1936, the USDA has, in a half-hearted and off-handed manner, used the "carrot" approach—namely, the use of agricultural conservation payments, on a cooperative basis, to institute (ostensibly) soil conservation practices. Since the passage of the 1972 and 1977 amendments to the Federal Water Pollution Control Act of 1956 it would be possible for the U.S.

Environmental Protection Agency to use the "stick" approach—namely, the enforcement of regulations pertaining to non-point source pollution. But politically the legislation is essentially unenforceable. Somehow the landowner and the land renter will have to be subsidized to protect farmland which is both his and the nation's. Along with this subsidy will have to come public regulations that are both enforceable and efficacious. This is a matter of seminal importance to all citizens of the United States; indeed, to food consumers worldwide. All of us, present and future, are the "losers" thus far.

The principal beneficiary of U.S. food programs has been placed last, even though this is the most important category—namely, food consumers, both domestic and foreign. The USDA has devoted a great deal of resources, with heavy emphasis on the printed word, to prove that food is a bargain, both at home and abroad, in terms of quality, quantity, and price. Although the statistics revolving around the food-is-a-bargain issue come in many varieties, the following statement will suffice: "In general, 1 hour's work in a factory buys more food today than 10 or 20 years ago" (USDA, 1978, p. 36).

The impact of U.S. food exports on foreign consumers, and particularly the Japanese consumer, is of special significance in this study. As noted earlier, the most important changing condition in U.S. food policy has been the tremendous growth in food exports. We must limit ourselves, however, to two observations. First, the shipment of food under P.L. 480 and other food aid programs has been of substantial proportions, at least until 1972. But although food aid has several pluses—millions of starving people have been fed, food costs for the urban poor in developing nations have been moderated—at the same time it has a minus in the sense that economic incentives of the peasant farmers have sometimes been blunted. On balance, and it is a speculative but heartfelt calculation, we believe that food aid under P.L. 480 has been a positive good. The second observation is that U.S. food exports to Japan have also grown immensely. Oft quoted is the statistic, which must be crudely calculated, that more U.S. acres (14 million) than Japanese acres are utilized to produce food for the Japanese consumer. The variety and nutritive quality of the Japanese diet has surely been enhanced over time because of these exports. It must be kept in mind, of course, that herein lies a mutual harmony of interests extended across a vast ocean!

In summary, and in view of past and present U.S.–Japanese trade relations, both Americans and Japanese need to be acutely aware of the question of who commands? in the making and implementation of U.S. food policy. If the models of populism and participatory democracy had become effectively institutionalized, there would now be more stress on equality rather than liberty, fewer inputs of chemicals, more emphasis on mandatory soil practices, higher import restrictions, an increase in subsidies to the family farmer, compulsory acreage and probably production restrictions, among other features. Whether such policies would have benefited rural and urban America, and over what period of time, is not at issue here. What does seem clear, however, is that less food would have been produced and at a higher cost to both the American and Japanese consumer.

What did take place in the politics of American agriculture, and notably so over the last forty years, was the short-run, perhaps benighted success of farmer interest groups and food triangle politics, and the gradual development of two elites (a dual polyarchy) in both the public and private sectors of American agriculture. The high, rigid price-support advocates lost to the flexible price-support, market economy advocates. Efficiency criteria became effectively imbedded in U.S. food legislation, more stress was placed on liberty (of the producer), less credence was given to the concept of parity, and—of particular importance to Japan—more food was produced at a lower cost, as compared with the populist-participatory democracy alternatives. The long-run implications of these policy changes are really not perceivable, but there appears to be a definite tendency toward the continuing development of the agribusiness and Washington food networks, with farm interest groups allying themselves with one network or the other, in practice if not in political rhetoric, and with their choice based on political party and ideological preferences. Agricultural trade relations are simply one subsector, albeit a prominent one, in which the food political economies of the two nations are interacting, both domestically and diplomatically.

Japanese Food and Agricultural Politics and Policies: A Conceptual Framework and Analysis

A similar, parallel question of who commands the Japanese agricultural policy system is important to ask if we are to obtain an accurate and balanced picture of U.S.–Japanese agricultural trade relations. Food and agricultural policies of contemporary Japan, like other important governmental programs, are expressed in the form of major legislative bills to be enacted by the National Diet. The political system of Japan, unlike the United States, is a parliamentary democracy characterized by more centralized decision making. As a parliamentary democracy, Japan has adopted a cabinet form of government whereby the prime minister is leader of the majority party in the National Diet. All public policies and programs, including the ones in agriculture, are thus adopted and implemented by the government, which operates under the stewardship of the prime minister as the principal political leader.

The process of agricultural and food policy making in Japan at the initial stage typically involves a series of consultations (called *nemawashi*) between the two principal agricultural policy actors; namely, the Ministry of Agriculture, Forestry and Fisheries (MAFF) and the ruling political party, which since 1955 has been the Liberal Democratic Party (LDP) (as detailed by Hemmi in chapter 7). This is followed by an official approval by the cabinet presided over by the prime minister before the measure is sent to the lower house of the Diet and its appropriate committees for deliberation and voting. The Japanese prime minister, as head of the ruling party in parliament, stays in office as long as he is able to move major bills through the legislature and to command a majority seat in the lower house of the Diet. During his tenure of office the prime minister normally adopts and executes national agricultural policies which more or less reflect consensus decisions arrived at by the participation of various interest groups and individuals in the food and agricultural system of Japan. In the subsequent discussion we shall examine the question of who commands the agricultural and food policy system of Japan, followed by a brief examination of the changing conditions for policy making, and then the question of who benefits.

Who commands? The making and implementation of Japanese food policy

The literature of political studies on contemporary Japan gives us some clue as to who commands the national agricultural and food policy system in Japan. Although competing explanations of Japan's policy making are possible, the single most popular and influential model of decision making in Japan is probably the elitist model, or polyarchy (Fukui, 1977, pp. 22–35). This theory is based on the concept of a tripartite power elite composed of the ruling Liberal Democratic Party, senior bureaucrats of the government ministries, and "big businessmen." According to those subscribing to this view of elitist theory, these three major groups form a regular and effective alliance and control decision making on major policy issues. Since the making of Japanese food and agricultural policies is no exception to the rule, a variation of the ruling triumvirate model should apply to the issue area of agricultural and food politics in contemporary Japan.

Japan's agricultural establishment: polyarchy

Who, then, are the members of Japan's agricultural establishments? It appears that Japan's agricultural political structure, resembling the food-triangle model of the U.S. decision system, consists of three institutional actors: the ruling party, the farmer's cooperatives, and the agricultural bureaucracy. Those who occupy these institutional positions, respectively, are (1) the politicians in the National Diet who belong to the conservative Liberal Democratic Party, and are generally elected from rural districts; (2) the spokesmen of the powerful agricultural interest groups, including the National Federation of Agricultural Cooperative Associations, known as *nokyo;* and (3) the senior bureaucrats in the Ministry of Agriculture, Forestry and Fisheries of the central government. Although the National Diet is formally responsible under the system of parliamentary democracy, the adoption of Japan's food and agricultural policies results from the interplay of influences as well as the convergence of interests among the three policy actors. We shall discuss each of these occupants of Japan's agricultural establishment in turn.

The Liberal Democratic Party has as a political base the rural communities of Japan, as pointed out vividly by Hemmi in chapter 7. While the conservative LDP depends on the continuous electoral support of rural voters to stay in power, the rural communities are benefited by the agricultural and food policies of the government under the LDP rule. The latter may include generous government subsidy programs, such as, (until recently) maintaining high price supports for rice production and providing incentive payments to farmers who participate in the riceland diversion program. A close tie exists therefore between the rural electoral support of the LDP and the pro-farmer policies and programs of the LDP government.

The mutually beneficial arrangement between the two political forces, the conservative party and the rural electoral support, is an important variable in the equation of Japan's domestic politics. The significance of such a rural coalition in Japan's electoral politics becomes self-evident when we account for two important developments in postwar Japan. First, as also discussed by Hemmi in chapter 7, is the progressive decline of the electoral support of the conservative Liberal Democratic Party in the national parliamentary elections. Since 1967, the LDP has failed to capture a majority of the votes in the national election and since 1976, a majority of the seats in the lower house of the Diet. Although the LDP had an electoral comeback in the 1980 general election, capturing 284 of the 511 seats in the lower house and thereby increasing by 26 more seats, it stays in power basically as a result of the opposition parties' failure to unite and merge into a cohesive group. Typically, it receives the support of some independents and members of the New Liberal Club, a dissident group of the ruling party in the lower house. The latter increased its seats in the lower house from 4 to 12 in the 1980 election. Although the party has thus far successfully avoided forming a coalition cabinet, it may not be that lucky next time. The second important development is the relative decline of the size of the rural voting bloc to which the LDP is heavily indebted because of the migration of population from villages into urban areas in the past years. According to Hemmi, the manipulation of the electoral constituency system to favor rural communities is one reason the LDP stays in power.

It is interesting that many members of the Diet who represent rural districts, whether of the ruling or opposition parties, are anxious to receive the endorsement of their candidacy from the prefectural and local-level organizations of the farm cooperatives. Sometimes the farm cooperative association puts forward its own candidate to run for the lower house of the Diet. Not surprisingly, the elected representatives are expected to speak for rural interests, while the LDP by gerrymandering electoral district systems enjoys the strength of a disproportionately larger rural bloc in the Diet.

In the process of agricultural policy making, the LDP plays an important leadership role. The party coordinates its farm and agricultural policies and programs with the National Diet, government ministries, various pressure groups, and other organizations, as detailed by Hemmi in chapter 7 of this volume. The agricultural committee of the National Diet deliberates on and adopts the legislative measures that have already been approved by the policy-making bodies of the LDP, which include the Policy Affairs Deliberation Commission (Seichokai) and the executive council (Somukai). Prior to this stage, the party attempts to arrive at policy consensus on the proposed legislative bills. For this purpose, the Research Commission on Agricultural Policy (Sogo Nosei Choshikai) and the Agricultural Committee (Norinbukai) of the LDP, which have some 200 members, conduct a series of consultative meetings to formally discuss the proposals with the key policy actors in Japan's agriculture. The latter entails, of course, the representatives of agricultural interest groups and the officials of the Ministry of Agriculture, Forestry and Fisheries. The policy adopted is, therefore, based on a policy consensus of the party, the cooperatives, and the bureaucracy.[3]

Farmers' cooperatives, known as *nokyo*, constitute the "big business," or a kind of monopolistic Zaibatsu, in agriculture. The national *nokyo* is a conglomerate of political and economic interests in Japan's agricultural world, and constitutes "an incredibly complex, loosely knit, and unwieldly organization" (Donnelly, 1977, p. 143). At the national level the farmers' cooperatives in Japan consist of three separate bodies: the National Federation of Agricultural Cooperative Associations called Zenno, a central cooperative bank of agriculture, called Norinchuoginko or Noringinko, and a Central Union of Agricultural Cooperatives called Zenchu. Through the mobilization of their large membership and financial resources, the farmers' cooperatives in Japan exert strong pressure on the government to protect the cooperatives' interests. In this endeavor they have been very effective.

In 1977 the National Federation of Agricultural Cooperative Associations (Zenno) claimed to have a membership of 7.7 million, organized into fifty-seven prefectural unions, and then into some 7,000 local cooperatives that are basically of two types: multipurpose and specialized cooperatives. Multipurpose cooperatives are engaged in several lines of business that include marketing, purchasing, and processing of agricultural products; financial credit; mutual insurance; warehousing; and farm guidance. Specialized cooperatives generally engage in a single line of business in agricultural products such as fruits, horticulture, or livestock. It should be noted, however, that the number of farm households in Japan was estimated to be only 4.9 million in 1975, and in each subsequent year that number has been declining. This means that practically all farm households in Japan are members of the cooperatives and so are a sizable number of those who are nonfarmers but are engaged in agriculture-related activities in the rural towns and nearby cities. To differentiate farmers from nonfarmers, the cooperatives maintain two types of membership: full members and associated members, which were listed in 1977 as 5.8 million and 1.9 million, respectively (Suda, 1978, p. 22). Many leaders of farmers' cooperatives have subsequently become politicians by running for public office themselves or by endorsing the candidates of their choice who belong mostly to the Liberal Democratic Party.

Farmers' cooperatives in Japan help administer government programs through the purchase and sale of rice, and by collecting, packing, storing, and selling grain on behalf of the government. They also purchase and distribute fertilizer, farm chemicals, feedstuffs, farm

[3] Tomozo Iwakura, LDP head office staff, to Young Kihl, July 4, 1979.

machinery, and other materials needed for agricultural production, as well as such nonagricultural items as textile goods, electric appliances, furniture, and automobiles. The National Federation of Agricultural Cooperative Associations coordinates the handling of these commodities on behalf of the local cooperatives and prefectural federations. Established on March 30, 1972, after the consolidation of Zenkoren (the National Purchasing Federation of Agricultural Cooperative Associations) and Zenhanren (the National Marketing Federation of Agricultural Cooperative Associations), which had originally been established in 1948, the National Federation of Agricultural Cooperative Associations had paid-in capital of 10,128 million Japanese yen in 1976, with a total business volume of nearly 4.5 trillion yen (some $14.6 billion) in fiscal year 1975–76 (Zenno, n.d., p. 6; Suda, 1978). Zenno actively promotes the import of agricultural goods and raw materials for fertilizer, farm chemicals, and feedstuffs by maintaining direct business contacts with overseas producers and has offices located in New York, Los Angeles, Hong Kong, Sao Paulo, Sydney, and Bangkok. It is one of the major trading companies in Japan, the sixth in rank among all general trading organizations (generally referred to as GTOs) (Suda, 1978, p. 9).

The central cooperative bank of agriculture (Noringinko) is the most important economic organization for Japanese farmers. It is said to be the second most important bank in Japan in terms of the size of customer savings. It not only extends credit to farmers but also acts, among others, as the agent of the government for financial dealings with the activities and operations of the agricultural cooperatives. Most of the money deposited by farmers tends to flow out of the other sectors that have a stronger demand for funds, even though this violates the purpose for which the central cooperative bank was established, that is, to supply funds for agricultural investment. Nonetheless, the central cooperative bank is blessed by abundant funds available for agricultural investment which are supplied and replenished by government subsidies through the Agriculture, Forestry and Fishery Finance Corporation (Noringyogyo Kinyukoko).

The Central Union of Agricultural Cooperatives (Zenchu) coordinates the activities of farmers' cooperatives through its leadership role in the affairs of the National Federation of Agricultural Cooperative Associations. The chairman of Zenchu acts as the national spokesman for the farmers' cooperative movement in Japan and maintains, through the elective executive council and professional staff, close ties with members of the Diet and senior bureaucrats of the government ministries responsible for agricultural policies. Japan's farmers' cooperatives even have a political organization called the National Farmers' General Federation (Zenkoku Nomin Sorenmei) which, although claiming independence, is generally regarded as a political arm of the Central Union of Agricultural Cooperatives; its support goes almost exclusively to LDP candidates.

The third policy actor, the Ministry of Agriculture, Forestry and Fisheries, is an important link in the tripolar agricultural power structure of Japan. A few dozen senior bureaucrats in the ministry, who are typically graduates of well-known universities, such as Tokyo University Law School, exercise an inordinate amount of influence in developing Japan's food and agricultural policies. They wield almost absolute power in the formulation and implementation of agricultural policies. They not only collect information on agriculture but are selective about what they publish. The MAFF bureaucrats are, therefore, almost autonomous in policy matters and are not checked by the Japanese Diet to the same extent that the U.S. Congress controls the federal bureaucracy.

The Ministry of Agriculture, Forestry and Fisheries initiates the process of food and agricultural policy making through its formulation of agricultural plans and programs. It also supervises and monitors the implementation of these programs by the local level governments in Japan. In this task the ministry is aided not only by the National Federation of Agricultural Cooperative Associations but also by the National Agricultural Committee System (Zenkoku Nogyo Kaigisho). The latter is an officially sanctioned, pyramidal structure of the National Chamber of Agriculture, prefectural chambers of agriculture, and local agricultural committees in cities, towns, and villages throughout Japan.

From the preceding discussion it is obvious that Japan's agricultural political structure is characterized by an interlocking system and a pattern of influence that are interwoven through the ruling political party, farmers' cooperatives, and the government bureaucracy. What happened in the national election of 1977 is one of the many examples illustrating the existence of a symbiotic relationship between the dominant institutions in Japan's agricultural establishment. In the upper house election that year the farmers' cooperatives were credited with electing at least eight councillors to the House of Councillors. Seven of those eight elected were new members; five of them were LDP members with cooperative association ties, and three were former bureaucrats of MAFF. In that election, the ruling LDP barely received a simple majority of the seats in the upper house. Without the successful campaign by farmers' cooperatives, therefore, the ruling party would have suffered a major electoral defeat, which would have put an end to the LDP's domination in parliamentary party politics in the postwar era.[4]

The Japanese agricultural power structure, thus described, generally advocates protectionism in foreign agricultural trade. To them the goal of achieving food self-sufficiency, although impossible in reality to attain, is of the most importance and value. Thus there is considerable political merit in keeping this goal of food self-sufficiency as a high-ranking item on the domestic policy agenda. This is why they continue to advocate a policy of agricultural modernization and government subsidy to equalize productivity and income between agriculture and other sectors of the economy. They believe that as a rich country Japan can afford to support agricultural subsidy programs, no matter how expensive they are, because of the successful development of the Japanese economy and the national policy of export-led industrialization.

Balancing competing interests: pluralism

A second credible model of policy making in contemporary Japan can be called pluralism. In many ways it resembles polyarchy. Unlike polyarchy, however, in pluralism more emphasis is given to the role of various interest groups in decision making and the balancing of competing interests represented by different groups. Japan's food and agricultural policies are then the outcome of the give-and-take politicking among the contending groups—not only among the agricultural interest groups, but between the latter and the nonagricultural groups and organizations as well. According to those subscribing to pluralism, the spokesmen for various interest groups in Japan exert differential amounts of pressure on power holders and convey the wishes of their respective memberships into the corridors of political power. As different groups vie for influence and their interests clash, the pluralists believe that the public interest is somehow protected in the balancing process.

Without denying the pivotal role of the ruling LDP in formulating Japan's food and agricultural policies, the pluralists would assert that other opposition parties in parliament, such as the Japan Socialist Party (JSP), bring important counterweights and pressures to bear on the ruling party, thereby protecting the public interest. In fact, the JSP has been equally supportive of rural interests in legislative politics by endorsing, for instance, higher rice price supports than the LDP is willing to accept. (See appendix 7-A in this volume for the agri-

[4] Susumu Yamaji, *Nihon Keizai Shimbun* editorial writer, to Young Kihl, July 5, 1979.

cultural programs of the major Japanese parties.) Also, it is important to realize that other government ministries and agencies, besides the MAFF, are involved in the process of developing and implementing Japan's food and agricultural policies. The Ministry of Finance (MOF) and Ministry of International Trade and Industry (MITI) are the cases in point. The finance ministry is involved in the determination of the government rice price policy in its financial aspects, while the MITI is involved in the foreign currency holding and current accounts of foreign agricultural trade (Johnson, 1977, pp. 227–279; Fukui, 1978, pp. 75–170).

It is also important to identify various nonagricultural interest groups that influence the evolution of Japan's food and agricultural policies. These groups include the business organizations, trade companies, labor unions, mass media, consumer interest groups, among others. The interests of "big businessmen" in Japan are represented by such powerful economic organizations as the Japan Federation of Economic Organizations (Keidanren) and the Japan Committee for Economic Development (Doyukai). By virtue of their close proximity to and association with the leaders of the ruling Liberal Democratic Party, and through contributions to the party and individual political figures, the voice of the Keidanren is likely to be reflected in the party programs on economic issues, including food and agriculture. On matters of liberalizing agricultural trade, which would allow more imported agricultural goods to Japan, many trading companies are likely to endorse and benefit from any change in the existing government policies of protectionism and restrictive agricultural trade.

The role of the trade union movement in agriculture is limited in contemporary Japan because it is overshadowed by the success of farmers' cooperative movement. Nonetheless, two trade unions in agriculture are closely aligned with political parties in Japan: the All-Japan Federation of Farmers' Unions (Zennihon Nomin Kumiai Rengokai) with the Japan Socialist Party and the National Farmers' Alliance (Zenkoku Nomin Domei) with the more moderate Democratic Socialist Party. Both farm unions view farmers as workers rather than as entrepreneurs or small businessmen entitled to rent and profits (Donnelly, 1977, p. 158). The latter view, of course, is the ideology of the farmers' cooperative movement in Japan. The All-Japan Reclamation Federation (Zennihon Kaitakusha Renmei) is a national organization for farmers who have settled on land reclaimed for agricultural purposes. This group, together with the National Farmers' Alliance and the National Farmers' General Federation (already mentioned as the political arm of the Central Union of Agricultural Cooperatives), is in support of the position of the National Federation of Agricultural Cooperative Associations on the key policy issue of high price supports for rice. These groups, for instance, jointly sponsor the annual rallies for rice price supports that are held in the second week of July and for which the National Federation of Agricultural Cooperative Associations provides leadership.

The press in Japan plays a positive role in articulating the issue of agricultural and food policies in contemporary Japan. For instance, the *Mainichi Shimbun* carried an article on September 5, 1978, on "Why Oranges in Japan Cost a Dollar Each" in which it criticized the practices of trade companies making an unfair profit at the expense of the consumer (U.S. Congress, 1979d, pp. 77–78). From time to time the *Japan Economic Journal* urges liberalization of beef imports and the lowering of the price of rice so as to protect the consumer's interest (*Nihon Keizai Shimbun*, February 28, 1979). In so doing, the press helps educate the Japanese consumer and the public on the complex issue of agricultural and food policies. It generally tends to speak for the interests of consumers and housewives, who are surely the silent majority in Japan. The role of academicians and experts is also important in articulating issues and educating the public on the relative merits of existing and proposed agricultural policies (WEISS, 1978).

On the policy issue of foreign trade in agriculture, the economic organizations and trade companies are generally supportive of the policy line of liberalization of agricultural trade, as exemplified by the lifting of artificial barriers to imports such as quotas and tariffs. According to these advocates, the beneficiary of liberalized agricultural trade will be the consumer because he can enjoy cheaper prices for food products, whether domestically produced or imported from abroad. Thus, in the long run, they argue, the public and consumers would benefit from such a major change in the existing policy of protectionism. This line of liberalization is, of course, vehemently opposed by the spokesmen of the agricultural establishment in Japan at the present time.

Agricultural bureaucracy: factionalism and patronage

The political culture of Japan is unique and different in many ways from that of the Anglo-American democracies. Students of Japanese culture (for example, Nakane, 1970) often point out the more hierarchical and group-oriented nature of Japanese politics and society, as contrasted with the egalitarian and individualist pattern of Anglo-American political culture. One manifestation of these characteristics in agricultural and food policy making in Japan is the preeminent role exercised by the government bureaucracy and the pervasive influence of factionalism within and patronage without the agricultural ministry of the central government. If we are to grasp the dynamics of agricultural policy making in Japanese democracy we need to examine, therefore, the cultural phenomenon of Japan's agricultural bureaucracy although in so doing we are diverging slightly from the analytical model of who commands?

The bureaucracy of the Ministry of Agriculture, Forestry and Fisheries, and the factions within it, are ultimately the source of decision-making power for food and agricultural policies in contemporary Japan.[5] The ministry enjoys almost absolute power in implementing agricultural policies and programs, although it is responsive to its constituencies in the farm sector, which include, among others, the Diet members representing farmers and farmers' cooperatives. On policy matters, the agricultural bureaucracy is almost autonomous and capable of controlling dissent by mobilizing its network of patronage outside the ministry. The latter consists of various deliberative councils on agricultural policies whose members are appointed rather than elected. This network also includes several public and private corporations in agriculture that are directly and indirectly subsidized by the ministry and are staffed by the ex-bureaucrats of the ministry upon their retirement from government service.

The agricultural bureaucracy is generally conservative in attitude and orientation. Two agricultural ministers in recent years, Michio Watanabe and Ichiro Nakagawa, were leaders of a right-wing LDP Diet group called Seirankai which, among others, opposed a peace treaty with China in 1978. The agricultural bureaucracy generally resists any change in the status quo, including revision of the Basic Agricultural Law. Many MAFF officials take the view that, although prices are high, it is in the national interest for Japanese consumers to pay rice prices which are three or four times higher than those of the world market. To agricultural bureaucrats, beef and oranges are not really significant in the consumers' diet. They console themselves by saying that "Japanese can eat pork and mikans (mandarin oranges) instead." They also point out that the Japanese do not complain much about higher rice prices, even though they know they are way above world market prices, because incomes are up and rice purchases represent a decreasing share of disposable income. The net social cost of

[5] In chapter 7, Hemmi attributes less influence to the Ministry of Agriculture, Forestry and Fisheries in the making of Japanese agricultural policy than we do in this section. We have given this matter further consideration and concluded that our interpretation is basically accurate. Obviously there is a difference of opinion, and we would suggest that this is an important issue needing further research.

Japan's restrictive practices on agricultural trade for eight major food items is estimated by two USDA agricultural economists to be as high as 2 percent of Japan's GNP, nearly $8 billion by fiscal 1985–86 (Bale and Greenshields, 1977, p. 19).

The fact that the agricultural ministry is so powerful and autonomous can be both an asset and a liability. The lack of effective countervailing forces tends to drive the ministry to pursue producer-oriented goals without much consideration of overall domestic policy or the international implications of its action. The ministry suffers from the failure of coordination of its policy with other ministries—such as the Ministry of Finance (MOF), the Ministry of International Trade and Industry (MITI), and the Economic Planning Agency (EPA)—or even between bureaus of the ministry, which may themselves be pursuing conflicting goals. Thus, within the MAFF, the practice of sectionalism, known as *tatewari* or *monobetsu* administration, sometimes causes inefficiency in policy making. Agricultural policy tends to be determined individually in each division of the ministry, without sufficient coordination with other divisions, and each division has a subordinate organization to execute its own policy. Moreover, agricultural policy is often devised commodity by commodity so that conflicts arise among the policies, and policies generally lack totality or consistency of purpose.[6]

The agricultural bureaucracy perpetuates its own system of patronage within and outside MAFF. A network of patron-client relations based on factional ties is important to reckon with in examining the rise and fall of certain bureaucrats or ex-bureaucrats. Thus, Tokyo University graduates tend to climb to positions of influence within the ministry, ultimately emerging as either director generals or vice ministers. If promotion at the right time is not attained, the officials in question must retire from the ministry so as to give way to the next eligible candidates in the line of succession. The retired officials, listed in the MAFF directory as "Old Boys," are rewarded with executive positions in associations or private firms, which are as a rule subsidized by MAFF. These positions—known as *amakudari*, or golden descent from heaven—are reserved for a government retiree and given to him as reward for life-long service and patronage (Johnson, 1974, pp. 953–965). In 1979, the MAFF directory listed twenty-six such Old Boys who had served in the high echelons of the ministry before retirement. This network of Old Boys provides a direct link between the MAFF's bureaucracy and the agricultural industry, serving as the

---

[6] Masayoshi Honma, agricultural economist, to Young Kihl, September 20, 1979.

primary channel for disseminating information and administrative guidance.[7]

Some retired officials then pursue a political career by running for national office as LDP candidates. These bureaucrats-turned-politicians are typically those who served the ministry with distinction at the top level before retirement, such as administrative vice ministers and directors-general of major bureaus like the Food Agency. In 1979, there were five former officials of MAFF who subsequently became members of parliament in the lower and upper houses of the Diet. These people provided the leadership in the deliberations on legislative bills on agriculture in the Diet because they had sufficient knowledge to challenge the agricultural policies and programs developed by the ministry. Other Diet members who come from rural constituencies are not so well informed on complex issues and are usually dependent on the agricultural bureaucracy for information on issues and even for advice about how to vote. It may be no exaggeration to say that it is MAFF which leads the Diet rather than the other way around.

The Ministry of Agriculture, Forestry and Fisheries appoints members of certain deliberative councils on agricultural policy and also of various public corporations in the agricultural industry. Two examples are the Rice Price Deliberation Council and the Livestock Industry Promotion Council. Although the council members enjoy a degree of autonomy in their deliberations, the agricultural bureaucracy exercises a strong influence on them and their recommendations. The Rice Price Deliberation Council, consisting of fifty members representing all walks of life in Japan, makes recommendations that are nearly mandatory on the government purchase and sales prices of rice, wheat, and barley (Donnelly, 1977). In arriving at the price of rice, the council takes into account the wage rate increases in other sectors of the economy, which are normally determined about two months before the meeting of the council. The rice price decision has become an annual ritual for which many agricultural interest groups, particularly the *nokyo*, have been actively involved. The Livestock Industry Promotion Council also determines the upper and lower limits of the prices for meats and dairy products. The council decisions are to a certain extent manipulated by MAFF through a process called *nemawashi*, a prearranged decision whereby the agricultural bureaucracy tells the experts in the council what the latter's recommendations should be.

[7] Susumu Yamaji, *Nihon Keizai Shimbun* editorial writer, to Young Kihl, July 5, 1979.

Since the price decisions by the rice or livestock councils affect the jurisdiction of the Ministry of Finance, the agricultural bureaucracy often manipulates and mobilizes its own constituency to put its position through. The latter may consist of Dietmen, cooperatives, and even the council itself in the attempt to exert pressures that favor the position of the ministry over that of the Ministry of Finance. The Livestock Council, through the Livestock Industry Promotion Corporation, actually approves quotas for beef imports and then sets the sale price for this beef at a much higher level (Longworth, 1976; 1978b). In all cases the agricultural industry ends up reaping a huge profit from the transaction. Although these profits are primarily used for purposes of upgrading the livestock industry—which is the official policy—some of the funds are likely to be diverted and used as business expenses for the purposes of perpetuating and reinforcing the privileged position of MAFF's patronage system in the livestock industry.

Agrarian populism and mass participation

No strong agrarian populist tradition exists in contemporary Japan as it does in the United States, although in pre–World War II Japan, agrarian discontent and radicalism were exploited by the militarists for their overseas expansionist policies (Havens, 1974, pp. 308–310). Nonetheless, the participatory democracy movement by farmers is still active and vocal in contemporary Japan. The farmers often join in mass demonstrations to make their demands known to the public.

During an early week of July each year, timed to coincide with the convening of the Rice Price Deliberation Council to determine the government policy on rice price support, representatives of various farm groups, led by *nokyos,* typically create mass demonstrations in Tokyo to display the solidarity of the rice farmers. And in making their demands for higher rice price support, farmers at the local level organize letter-writing campaigns, demonstrations, and petitions. They even launch fund-raising campaigns to help finance the travel costs of demonstrations to Tokyo (Donnelly, 1977, p. 164). The purpose of the annual ritual demonstrations is to impress the members of the Rice Price Deliberation Council that the farmers' interests need to be protected. They also make their pleas directly to the politicians in the LDP and the National Diet by visiting them in their offices.

There is heightened concern over the potential danger of the use of pesticides and food additives to the health of humans. The environmental movement in Japan has been demanding more rigorous and forceful government control of the use of chemicals in agriculture and food processing, and it is gaining momentum and increasing support from the attentive public (Enloe, 1975, p. 231). In this endeavor the press and mass media make valuable contributions through educating the public on the importance of environmental policy and the role of agriculture in it. The voice of environmentalists in agricultural policies relative to regulating the excessive use of chemicals, preventing industrial pollution from harming agriculture, and maintaining ecological balance through agriculture, is still relatively weak and ineffective in Japan. It is certainly less pronounced than in the United States.

Under what conditions?

Major decisions about Japan's food and agricultural policies reflect changing conditions in the political and socioeconomic environment. As noted by Kuroda in chapter 4, Japan's defeat in World War II, rapid economic growth since 1955, changes in food and dietary habits, and perceptions of food shortages and food security are some specific examples of the context within which Japan's major agricultural policies and programs are articulated and implemented.

The gist of the long-term agricultural and food policies of Japan at the end of the 1970s can be summarized in a set of policy goals. They are: (1) self-sufficiency in food production to the maximum extent possible, (2) food security through imports of essential commodities, (3) modernization and rationalization of agricultural production, (4) raising farm income to levels comparable to incomes in other sectors, and (5) preservation of a viable rural sector so as to control migration of the rural population to urban centers. Given the large population and limited space and cultivable areas in Japan, the first goal of food self-sufficiency has proved almost impossible to attain. A more viable alternative for Japan seems to be the second goal of assuring a stable and reliable supply of food commodities from abroad. This is why Japan needs to maintain good relations with the United States, the principal supplier of its food imports, and at the same time to diversify its sources of supply to lessen its food dependency on a single country.

The attainment of the three remaining policy goals has also been affected by changing circumstances within and outside Japan. Although modernization of rice production has been achieved from a technical standpoint, the large government subsidy and rice price support policy does not lend itself to rationalization of agricultural production from an economic point of view. Moreover, from the perspective of international trade, the protective agricultural policy regarding rice cultivation is grossly inefficient and is in violation of the principles of free trade and comparative advantage—principles that are among the factors which enabled Japan to prosper economically in the first place.

As emphasized throughout this volume, the farm sector benefited from the dynamic growth of the economy generally. The export-led growth of the economy increased the size of the economic pie, and the level of farm income was also raised as a result of the "trickle-down" effect. Moreover, dispersion of manufacturing industries to the nonmetropolitan regions led to the creation of new jobs and non-farm employment for many rural residents. There was also a steady increase in investments in rural infrastructure, which has thereby enhanced the quality of rural life. Thus, the implementation of the fourth and fifth objectives of Japan's agricultural and food policies—raising farm income and preservation of a viable rural sector—has been greatly facilitated by Japan's rapid economic growth since 1955.

Who benefits?

Food self-sufficiency for Japan, although impossible to achieve, has become an important national purpose and political symbol which rallies the support of many Japanese voters. A kind of national sentiment and consensus therefore exists on the desirability of achieving a certain amount of food self-sufficiency to the extent that it is possible to do so (see chapter 7 by Hemmi in this volume). But food self-sufficiency for Japan is not only an economic but a political and social issue as well, and the Japanese are well aware of the necessity for balancing the two competing values.

By providing political leadership, through the conservative rule of the LDP government since 1955, Japan has successfully managed the task of economic growth and has allocated the resultant wealth in ways that have benefited most of its citizens. In their efforts to redesign social and political values, Japanese leaders have effectively used the slogan of food self-sufficiency and have manipulated the symbol to assist the farm sector which was lagging behind the urban and industrial sectors of the economy. By exploiting popular sentiment and support for achieving this national goal of food self-sufficiency, the LDP government adopted agricultural policies and programs which would bring about, in effect, a modest shift in distribution and redistribution of wealth in society.

Japan's commitment to the goal of food self-sufficiency also implies a continued policy of government support and subsidization of agricultural production, which must be financed through taxation, and results in high food prices for the consumers. The share of the MAFF budget in a given year, for instance, has been approximately 8 to 11 percent of the total national budget (see table 4-A-27). Of this, some 30 to 40 percent of MAFF's budget has been spent for purposes of food subsidies of various types. The transfer payments from the general account budget to the special account for food control increased to as high as 40.6 percent of the MAFF budget for fiscal year 1968, although the trend since then has been on the decline (Donnelly, 1977, p. 187). The deficit in the food control account for fiscal year 1978 was estimated at ¥75 billion, resulting from the fact that the government subsidized the wholesale price of rice by reselling it to authorized dealers at prices below the purchase price. Although the purchase price of rice by MAFF's food agency remained virtually unchanged at about ¥286,000 per metric ton of brown rice in 1977 (approximately three to five times the world price level), the government-controlled consumer price of rice and the resale price was considerably lower—¥3,235 per 10 kilograms for standard rice as of February 1, 1980 (U.S.–Japan Trade Council Report, p. 3). (For more about the rice support program, see Houck in chapter 3 and Egaitsu in chapter 5.)

The Japanese government recently adopted a series of measures to help convert rice paddy fields to farmland suitable for upland crops, such as wheat, soybeans, and feed grains. These programs are intended to help achieve the goal of food self-sufficiency for crops other than rice by curbing the import of grains from abroad. Rice consumption in Japan, estimated at 11.7 million tons annually, is falling behind a potential production capacity of 13.4 million tons. Because rice is a heavily supported crop, however, the Japanese government must pay farmers subsidies to encourage them to make a changeover from rice cultivation to other crops. The government incentive payments in 1978, already amounting to ¥260 billion, and accounting for 10 percent of the general account budget relating to agriculture, resulted in the conversion of 430,516 hectares of rice paddies in 1978 (U.S.–Japan Trade Council Report, p. 2). If the current ten year program, called the Measure for the Reorganization of the Use of Paddy Fields, is successfully implemented, the agricultural ministry expects—rather optimistically—that by the year 1990 the self-sufficiency rate for wheat and soybeans will increase from 4 percent and 3 percent respectively in 1977 to the 1960 levels of 39 percent for wheat and 28 percent for soybeans (Agricultural Policy Outlook for the 1980's, 1980, p. 4). Since the program is immensely costly, it will result in a further reshifting and reallocation of the nation's fiscal resources.

This protective agricultural policy of Japan, which benefits the farmers as producers, should be regarded as a social and political, as well as an economic program. Agriculture in industrialized Japan is like a "public good" whose costs are paid in the same way that costs for other public goods, such as education and national defense, are paid for.

The Japanese government has made many adjustments in some commodity areas of agricultural trade. There is no restriction on the importation of feed grain, for instance, so as to encourage development of the livestock industry. Through cheap, imported feed grains, the general livestock industry including the beef, dairy, hog, and poultry industries have become well established in Japan. The wheat import policy has also been liberalized in Japan, although imports of other food items such as beef and citrus products are still controlled by the government through quotas and tariffs. The government's restrictive trade policy on food imports is defended on the grounds of protecting domestic industry, particularly the meat and *mikan* (mandarin orange) industries from possible damage from foreign competition. But recent concessions by the Japanese government relative to its increase of import quotas for oranges, beef, and cherries from the United States, which had been agreed upon in the Strauss-Ushiba memorandum of January 1978, will provide a small measure of benefit to the food consumer in Japan. (See chapter 3 by Houck in this volume.)

Even if Japan continues to pursue agricultural adjustment farm policies, benefits of the distributive type (that is, to the farmer) are likely to increase. During the 1979 Japanese fiscal year, for instance, the MAFF budgeted some ¥159 billion for livestock and feed programs to finance new and old projects. Among them were ¥4.1 billion for integrating calving and feeding production units and ¥1.4 billion to modernize the meat distribution systems (U.S. Embassy Agricultural Attaché, Tokyo, 1979, p. 26). The suppliers of industrial sector inputs to agriculture are also beneficiaries of the agricultural subsidy system. The mechanized agricultural implements like farm tractors reflect the small size of Japanese farming operations. Rather minuscule in size and simple in operation, they can safely be used by the elderly and the children in the farm household. Furthermore, most Japanese farm families strongly prefer farm implements which are individually owned rather than collectively shared. The agribusiness industries of Japan, some of which are owned and operated by the agricultural cooperatives, are also the beneficiaries of the existing land and farm subsidy programs.

The goal of food security for Japan is likely to remain a national objective for some time to come. It is understandable that the Japanese are deeply concerned about the danger of possible food shortages. The 1973–74 world food crisis also added further anxiety to the already very sensitive food security nerve. The maintenance of reliable supplies of food from abroad, buttressed possibly by the establishment of an international grain reserve system, is therefore an important policy consideration for Japan. (See chapter 10 by Hayami in this volume.)

Convergence and Divergence of U.S. and Japanese Food Aid and Trade Policies

Since World War II, U.S.–Japanese agricultural trade relations have gone through five overlapping phases. *Phase one* was characterized by food surpluses in United States and severe deficits in Japan. This covered the period in Japan from the beginning of the occupation in 1945 until the enactment of the Agricultural Basic Law in 1961. In this period there was a strong convergence of food policy interests.

The general direction of U.S. policy was approximately that which was stated by John Emmerson in 1946: "We [United States] shall assure ourselves of a 'favored position' in Japan if we succeed in effecting lasting reforms, in giving impetus to a genuine liberal movement, and in starting the process of democratization in Japanese education" (1978, pp. 284–285). This policy was, of course, far more fundamental and far reaching in its potential scope and significance than U.S.–Japanese food trade policies. But food has been an important means in the pursuit of that objective.

In 1947, Robert Cochrane—who had been the head of the Tokyo Bureau of the *Baltimore Sun* from 1945 to 1946—reviewed the two years of what he termed the "MacArthur era" in Japan. Among his many observations were these: "Only the 900,000 metric tons of food contributed by the United States in 1946 staved off widespread urban starvation, and this year [1947] at least twice as much will be needed. . . . Starvation and confusion walk the streets of Tokyo and Osaka and Nagoya. . . . Japan today is the sick man of Asia" (pp. 283–284).

By 1954, this "sick man" was moving down the road to recovery. The USDA's Foreign Agricultural Service (FAS) was, however, only mildly impressed with the trend in U.S.–Japanese agricultural relations. "Since World War II," noted an FAS report, "the U.S. has become Japan's main agricultural supplier, although her imports have not reached 1935 levels" (USDA, 1955, p. 16). In the United States, it was the agricultural sector which was "sick," with surpluses. That same year (1954) Congress passed the Trade Development and Assistance Act (Public Law 480), and extensive efforts were made by the Department of Agriculture to move U.S. farm products into the world market through not only P.L. 480-type sales, but also through Export-Import Bank loans and Commodity Credit Corporation (CCC) subsidized sales. Japan's use of P.L. 480 occurred primarily in fiscal years 1956 and 1957. Title I sales (for Japanese yen) totalled a little over $213 million dollars in the 1955–66 period, and by 1966 they had ceased altogether; barter transactions, also under P.L. 480 provisions, were almost equal in value during that same time period (over $207 million).

During the *second phase,* the Japanese "miracle" period (1961 to 1972), the Japanese economy rebounded in a well-nigh miraculous fashion, as did the increase of U.S. food exports to that nation. On the U.S. food side, the Foreign Agricultural Service-cooperator strategy, which we have discussed earlier, was initiated and implemented.

Significant, too, in increasing U.S. agricultural trade have been the aforementioned loans and credit sales. According to statistics generally available at the U.S. Department of Agriculture, over the 1955–73 period, Export-Import Bank loans totalled slightly more than $1.3 billion, while Commodity Credit Corporation credit sales in that period amounted to more than $424 million. United States rice exports to Japan have also had a mercurial history. There were nearly $14.5 million worth under P.L. 480 in 1956, thereafter dwindling quickly to zero by 1960. In the 1963–64 period, there was an increase to more than 150,000 metric tons (from 1,406 the previous year), then 221,261 metric tons in 1964–65, to more than 218,223 metric tons in 1965–66, to almost 101,700 in 1966–67, whereupon the rice shipments shrank dramatically and have now declined to almost zero.

Dollar sales of U.S. agricultural exports to Japan increased dramatically from more than $485 million in 1960 to $750 million in 1965, to more than one billion dollars in 1970. For the next two years, the volume of trade remained rather constant, but the 1973 sales (almost $2.3 billion) nearly doubled those of the previous year: a splendid example of a positive sum strategy.

The *third phase*, the embargo period or the soybean shock syndrome, took place between 1973 and 1975. As background, the United States experienced differing types of food crisis politics in the early 1970s, specifically the food price controls episode in 1972, and the temporary and partial food export embargoes (understandings) of 1973, 1974, and 1975 (Destler, 1978; Nau, 1978). Hathaway's perceptive analysis of the first episode has, by and large, become recognized as the authentic version (1974). Relative to the 1973 embargo, U.S. Secretary of Commerce Dent decided in late June, for a variety of political and economic reasons, that it was necessary to declare a "complete, temporary embargo" on U.S. exports of soybeans and the products thereof (Destler, 1978, pp. 51–56). Although the embargo was partially lifted on the following August 1, and completely so during the next month, the political and economic damage had been done. In Japan, the soybean shock of 1973 was devastating, and it has continued to affect U.S.–Japanese agricultural trade relations in a serious way. A rather extensive case study has been made of this affair, and Graziano (1975) has concluded:

> The soybean export control decision was essentially a domestic political decision which involved domestic economic consideration. Foreign economic policy considerations were given short shrift by the key actors who had neither the time nor the inclination to involve themselves in international consultations or negotiations (p. 33).

In consequence, a number of acts of food diplomacy had to be undertaken. In 1974 the USDA found it necessary to work out an "understanding" with Japan's Food Agency concerning limited purchases of corn, pending final determination based on that fall's corn harvest. This was followed in August 1975 by a somewhat more formal "letter of understanding," which was agreed to by Secretary Butz and Minister of Agriculture Abe, but the economic and political damage had been done.

All of which leads to a few general observations. First, the Butz-Abe letter of understanding seemed to resolve this controversy in a satisfactory manner, from the U.S. viewpoint. But, second, it was a principal indicator to the Japanese that they must search diligently, through trade and foreign investment, for other reliable sources of supply. Finally, the soybean scare syndrome became a meaningful symbol in the minds of Japanese policy makers. There is a tendency in the Washington food policy network, and especially within the USDA, to view this scare as a political sham ("after all, U.S. soybean exports actually increased in 1973—the Japanese agricultural interests are using the 'scare' as a justification for their policy of protectionism"). There is probably considerable truth in that contention; nevertheless, U.S. policy makers cannot overlook the significance of symbolic politics. In terms of perceptions, the Japanese did—and still do—see this episode as a serious divergence of values and interests in its relations with the United States.

The *fourth phase*—when the Tokyo Round negotiations ended in 1979, the implementation process began. The initial offers of the Japanese were minimal. Even as late as April 1978, Alan Wolff, U.S. deputy special representative for trade negotiations, was testifying before a subcommittee of the Senate Committee on Foreign Relations to the effect that: "In agriculture, the Japanese offers are entirely unsatisfactory, and we expect that it will be a difficult negotiation," but he then became more hopeful: "We think there will be improvements" (U.S. Congress, 1978b, p. 6). That same month, the late Congressman Leo Ryan (a Democrat from California) noted the "bitterness" among businessmen from northern California toward the avowed obduracy of the Japanese toward entering into serious negotiations: ". . . there is rapidly growing resentment toward Japan in the American business community on the West Coast, and specifically in California. This simply is not sufficiently well understood by the Japanese Government" (U.S. Congress, 1978b, pp. 18–19).

The U.S. media seemed to accord considerable coverage to this ongoing controversy. There was admittedly a touch of levity in their treatment of the U.S.–Japanese version of "the chicken war" (Talbot, 1978), although this time it was beef, oranges, cherries, and grapefruit juice. This accord was designed ostensibly to ease several U.S.–Japanese trade tensions, including those involving the agricultural commodities noted above. Then in the following December a second incremental increase in quotas for those products was negotiated. The Tokyo Round negotiations are now over; the U.S. Senate has consented almost unanimously to the implementing legislation (the "dairy" senators were the principal opponents), and the proof of the deed now rests in its implementation by GATT and the major participant nations (see chapter 3 by Houck). At a press conference in January announcing the Strauss-Ushiba "understanding," Ushiba had "warned" Japanese reporters that "it will be necessary for Japan to open more of its domestic market to foreign goods." Even so, as a diplomat noted, "there is a big difference between being able to promise something and being able to fulfill that promise" (*The New York Times*, 1978, pp. 1, 4).

The *fifth and final phase* is a crystal-ball look at the 1980s. We have only minimal confidence in our predictions, but see this phase, dimly, as one of "learning to live politically with the status quo" for the next ten years. Other things being equal, it seems doubtful that U.S. agricultural exports to Japan will increase or decrease appreciably, at least in real (constant) value. Since 1974, Japan's share of total U.S. agricultural exports, in dollars, has remained quite constant: 1974, 15.8 percent; 1975, 14.1 percent; 1976, 15.5 percent; 1977, 16.3 percent; 1978, 15.1 percent (Kaplan, 1979, p. 27). In fact, the United States incurred a market share loss in total Japanese food imports of 4.3 percent from 1968–79 to 1976–77 (U.S. Congress, 1978a, pp. 4–5). Moreover, our interviews with several U.S. cooperators, both in Washington, D.C., and Tokyo, provided us with some empirical support for our forecast. By and large these cooperators believed that the most viable strategy will be to "work hard to keep the share we have"; however, many U.S. fruit and vegetable interests are much more demanding.

This could, of course, prove to be a contentious period for U.S.–Japanese agricultural trade relations. Again, the surplus–scarcity continuum is very important on the American side. If U.S. grain stocks (including soybeans) move to either extreme, there could be trouble. If it is a matter of surpluses, the U.S. food export triangle will push too hard for increased sales; if shortages occur, then the Washington food network will have serious problems of allocating scarce commodities, and the domestic economy will almost surely be favored. On the Japanese side, the main point of controversy will likely center around the self-sufficiency debate. If heavy production subsidies cause a major change in the prevailing structure of trade relations, this would then result in another round of charges and countercharges. Finding an equilibrium position, politically, and then maintaining it, will not be a simple strategy to accomplish.

Two Policy-Making Processes in Competition: A Review of the Conceptual Model

The fourfold conceptual model of democracy, as applied to agricultural and food policy making within and between the United States and Japan, has proven to be useful and valid. The two nations are political democracies, with generally compatible national aspirations, goals, and interests; both have developed political and economic institutions that are capable of negotiating the requisite, mutually advantageous compromises necessary in all major policy areas. Both democracies, moreover, have been beset by a series of complex policy problems and issues pertinent to the difficult adjustments in agricultural and food policies. These have been caused by rapid changes in the industrialization of their rural and farm economies, with attendant socioeconomic effects on their respective political systems. In short, the likenesses of the two political systems are more prominent than their differences.

We found, however, that our fourfold conceptual model cannot be transposed literally to the case of Japan without certain modifications. Polyarchy and pluralism are valuable as conceptual tools in explaining the process of food and agricultural policy making in Japan, as well as in the United States. In Japan, however, we view the factionalism-patronage system as a modified form of political polyarchy, a combination of the polyarchy and pluralism models. This modified model reflects the special characteristics of the Japanese political culture and is an essential tool for explaining agricultural and food policy making in that nation.

On the other hand, participatory democracy and populism, although relevant to Japanese democracy, are not strong and they do not seem to have been of particular value in explaining the Japanese agrarian and rural political scene since the end of World War II. Therefore, if we are to rank the four analytical models in terms of their relative explanatory value, we would list the bureaucratic factionalism and patronage form of polyarchy as first, followed at a modest distance by pluralism, leaving populism and participatory democracy at the end.

On the American side, we have stressed the major importance of the dual polyarchies of agribusinesses and Washington food networks, followed quite closely by pluralism (the food triangles of power), with populism and participatory democracy trailing in that order. One last word of caution, however. More urbanized forms of populism and participatory democracy—the environmental and consumer movements, broadly defined and (ironically) elitist in leadership—could become increasingly influential in the food and agricultural policy-making area of both nations, for reasons already elaborated on. Much depends on the economic intelligence, the political wisdom and skill, the perceptive sensitivity to "new agenda" issues, and the good fortune (favorable weather—no major war) of the food polyarchies and the food triangles of power in Japan and the United States.

References

AFBF. See American Farm Bureau Federation.

American Farm Bureau Federation (AFBF), *Farm Bureau News*, July 16, 1979. "Agricultural Policy Outlook for the 1980's." 1980. *Japan Report* vol. 26, no. 2 (February 1) (Issued by the Japan Information Service, Consulate General of Japan, New York).

Bale, Malcolm D., and Bruce L. Greenshields. 1977. *Japan: Production and Imports of Food—An Analysis of the Welfare Cost of Protection*, Foreign Agricultural Economic Report No. 141 (Washington, D.C., USDA, November).

Barton, Weldon, V., 1974. "Coalition-Building in the U.S. House of Representatives: Agricultural Legislation in 1973," in James E. Anderson, ed., *Cases in Public Policy-Making* (New York, Praeger).

Brown, Lester R. 1975. *The Politics and Responsibility of the North American Breadbasket*, Worldwatch Paper 2 (Washington, D.C., Worldwatch Institute).

———. 1981. *Building a Sustainable Society* (New York, W. W. Norton).

Cochrane, Robert D. 1947. "MacArthur Era: Year Two," *Harper's Magazine* (September) pp. 283–284.

Cochrane, Willard W. 1979. *The Development of American Agriculture* (Minneapolis, Minn., University of Minnesota Press).

Crosson, Pierre R., and Kenneth D. Frederick. 1977. *The World Food Situation: Resource and Environmental Issues in the Developing Countries and the United States* (Washington, D.C., Resources for the Future).

Destler, I. M. 1978. "United States Food Policy, 1972–76; Reconciling Domestic and International Objectives," in Raymond F. Hopkins and Donald J. Puchala, eds., *The Global Political Economy of Food* (Madison, Wisc., University of Wisconsin Press).

Donnelly, Michael. 1977. "Setting the Price of Rice: A Study in Political Decision-Making," in T. J. Pempel, ed., *Policymaking in Contemporary Japan* (Ithaca, N.Y., Cornell University Press).

Emmerson, John K. 1978. *The Japanese Thread: A Life in the U.S. Foreign Service* (New York, Holt, Rinehart and Winston).

Enloe, Cynthia H. 1975. *The Politics of Pollution in a Comparative Perspective* (New York, David McKay).

Fiorina, Morris P. 1977. *Congress: Keystone of the Washington Establishment* (New Haven, Conn., Yale University Press).

Fleming, Donald. 1972. *The Second Conservation Movement*, Volume VI, *Perspectives in American History* (Cambridge, Mass., Harvard University, Charles Warren Center for Studies in American History).

Fowler, Robert, and Jeffrey Orenstein. 1977. *Contemporary Issues in Political Theory* (New York, Wiley).

Fukui, Haruhiro. 1977. "Studies in Policy Making: A Review of the Literature," in T. J. Pempel, ed., *Policymaking in Contemporary Japan* (Ithaca, N.Y., Cornell University Press).

———. 1978. "The GATT Tokyo Round: The Bureaucratic Politics of Multilateral Diplomacy," in Michael Blaker, ed., *The Politics of Trade: U.S. and Japanese Policymaking for the GATT Negotiations, Occasional Papers of the East Asian Institute* (New York, Columbia University) pp. 75–170.

GAO. 1975. General Accounting Office. *The Agricultural Attaché Role Overseas: What He Does and How He Can Be More Effective*, ID-75-40 (Washington, D.C., General Accounting Office, April).

Graziano, Edward F. 1975. "Commodity Export Controls: The Soybean Case, 1973," in Commission on the Organization of the Government for the Conduct of Foreign Policy, *Appendices*, vol. 3 (Washington, D.C., GPO).

Hardin, Charles M. 1967. *Food and Fiber in the Nation's Politics*, Volume III (Washington, D.C., GPO for the National Advisory Commission on Food and Fiber, August).

Hathaway, Dale E. 1974. "Food Prices and Inflation," in Arthur M. Okun and George L. Perry, eds., *Brookings Papers on Economic Activity*, Volume I (Washington, D.C., The Brookings Institution).

Havens, Thomas. 1974. *Farm and Nation in Modern Japan: Agrarian Nationalism 1870–1940* (Princeton, N.J., Princeton University Press).

Hayami, Yujiro. 1979. "Trade Benefits to All: A Design of the Beef Import Liberalization in Japan," *American Journal of Agricultural Economics* vol. 61, no. 2 (May) pp. 342–347.

Heclo, Hugh. 1978. "Issue Networks and the Executive Establishment," in Anthony King, ed., *The New American Political System* (Washington, D.C., American Enterprise Institute for Public Policy Research).

Hjort, Howard W. 1978. "The Relationship between Domestic and International Food Policy," in *International Food Policy Issues, A Proceedings*, Foreign Agricultural Economic Report No. 1943 (Washington, D.C., U.S. Department of Agriculture).

Hoffman, Stanley. 1978. "Domestic Politics and Interdependence," in Lincoln Gordon, ed., *From Marshall Plan to Global Interdependence* (Paris, Organization for Economic Cooperation and Development).

Hopkins, Raymond F., and Donald J. Puchala. 1980. *Global Food Interdependence: Challenge to American Foreign Policy* (New York, Columbia University Press).

Johnson, Chalmers. 1974. "The Reemployment of Retired Government Bureaucrats in Japanese Big Business," *Asian Survey* vol. 14, no. 11, pp. 953–965.

———. 1977. "MITI and Japanese International Economic Policy," in Robert Scalapino, ed., *The Foreign Policy of Modern Japan* (Berkeley, Calif., The University of California Press) pp. 227–279.

Kaplan, Eugene J. 1979. *Japan's Tariff and Nontariff Barriers: The Perception Gap* (Washington, D.C., United States-Japan Trade Council).

Longworth, John W. 1978a. "Feeder-Calf Price-Support Policies in Japan," *Review of Marketing and Agricultural Economics* (Australia) vol. 46, no. 2 (August) pp. 103–127.

———. 1978b. "The Japanese Beef Market: Recent Development and Future Policy Options," *Review of Marketing and Agricultural Economics* (Australia) vol. 46, no. 3 (December) pp. 167–195.

———. 1976. "Institutions and Policies Influencing Japanese Beef Imports," *Review of Marketing and Agricultural Economics* (Australia) vol. 44, nos. 1–2, pp. 19–43.

Mayer, Leo V. 1978. "The Farm Strike," *Policy Research Notes* (Washington, D.C., North Central Regional Public Policy Research Committee, U.S. Department of Agriculture, Economics, Statistics and Cooperatives Service).

Mayer, Milton. 1980. "Our Butter-and-Egg Men Are Winning Big Abroad," *Fortune* (May 19) pp. 146–154.

Mayhew, David R. 1974. *Congress: The Electoral Connection* (New Haven, Conn., Yale University Press).

McKenna, David A. 1978. *U.S. Government-Sponsored Agricultural Export Market Development Programs*, A. E. Ext. 78-29 (Ithaca, N.Y., Cornell University, Dept. of Agricultural Economics, September).

Minar, David W. 1964. *Ideas and Politics: The American Experience* (Homewood, Ill., The Dorsey Press).

Nakane, Chie. 1970. *Japanese Society* (Berkeley, University of California Press).

Nau, Henry R. 1978. "The Diplomacy of World Food: Capabilities, Issues and Arenas," in Raymond F. Hopkins and Donald J. Puchala, eds., *The Global Political Economy of Food* (Madison, Wisc., University of Wisconsin Press).

Ogura, Takekazu. 1967. *Agrarian Problems and Agricultural Policy in Japan.* (Tokyo, The Institute of Asian Economic Affairs).

Organization for Economic Cooperation and Development. 1974. *Agricultural Policy in Japan* (Paris, OECD).

Paarlberg, Don. 1980. *Farm and Food Policy: Issue of the 1980's* (Lincoln, Neb., University of Nebraska Press).

Paarlberg, Robert L. Forthcoming. "Food as an Instrument of U.S. Foreign Policy," in Don F. Hadwiger and Ross B. Talbot, eds., "Food Policy and Farm Programs" (New York, The Academy of Political Science).

Pempel, T. J. 1977. "Japanese Foreign Economic Policy: the Domestic Bases for International Behavior," *International Organization* vol. 31, no. 4, pp. 223–774.

Penn, J. B. 1981. "The Changing Farm Sector and Future Public Policy: An Economic Perspective," in *Agricultural Food Policy Review: Perspectives for the 1980's*, AFPR-4 (Washington, D.C., U.S. Department of Agriculture) table 4, p. 37.

Sanderson, Fred H. 1978. *Japan's Food Prospects and Policies* (Washington, D.C., The Brookings Institution).

Schertz, L. P., and coauthors. 1979. *Another Revolution in U.S. Farming?* (Washington, D.C., U.S. Department of Agriculture).

Suda, Yugi. 1978. *Nokyo*, Jiji Mondai Kaisetsu No. 37 (Tokyo, Kyoyukusha).

Talbot, Ross B. 1978. *The Chicken War: An International Trade Conflict Between the United States and the European Economic Community, 1961–64* (Ames, Iowa, Iowa State University Press).

Truman, David. 1951. *The Governmental Process* (New York, Alfred Knopf).

U.S. Congress. 1975 and 1976. Technology Assessment Board. *Hearings: Food Information Systems*, 94 Cong., 1 and 2 sess. (Washington, D.C., GPO).

————. 1978. House Committee on Ways and Means, Subcommittee on Trade. *Background Articles on United States–Japan Trading Issues*, 95 Cong., 2 sess. (Washington, D.C., GPO).

————. 1978b. Senate Committee on Foreign Relations Subcommittee on East Asian and Pacific Affairs. *Hearing: U.S./Japanese Relations*, 95 Cong., 2 sess. (Washington, D.C., GPO).

————. 1979a. House Subcommittee of the Committee on Appropriations. *Hearings: Agriculture, Rural Development, and Related Agencies Appropriations for 1980*, Part 5, 96 Cong., 1 sess. (Washington, D.C., GPO).

————. 1979b. House Committee on International Relations, Subcommittee of, *Hearings: United States Trade with Japan*, 95 Cong., 2 sess. (Washington, D.C., GPO).

————. 1979c. House Committee on Agriculture. *Hearings: State of Agriculture*, 96 Cong., 1 sess. (Washington, D.C., GPO).

————. 1979d. House Committee on Ways and Means, Subcommittee on Trade. *Task Force Report on United States–Japan Trade*, 95 Cong., 2 sess. (Washington, D.C., GPO).

————. 1980. House Subcommittee of the Committee on Appropriations. *Hearings: Agriculture, Rural Development, and Related Agencies Appropriations for 1981*, Part 2, 96 Cong., 2 sess. (Washington, D.C., GPO).

USDA. 1955. U.S. Department of Agriculture, Foreign Agricultural Service. *Trading in Competitive Markets* (Washington, D.C., GPO).

————. 1975. U.S. Department of Agriculture, Foreign Agricultural Service. *Foreign Agriculture*, Special Issue on Market Development (May 26).

————. 1978. U.S. Department of Agriculture. *Fact Book of U.S. Agriculture*, Misc. Publ. 1063, revised (Washington, D.C., GPO).

————. 1979a. U.S. Department of Agriculture. *Foreign Agriculture* (August) p. 7.

————. 1979b. U.S. Department of Agriculture. *Press Release* (31279), February 6, p. 1.

————. 1979c. U.S. Department of Agriculture (Foreign Agricultural Service). "Vice President Mondale Lauds American Agriculture on FAS 25th Anniversary," *Foreign Agriculture* (May).

————. 1980. U.S. Department of Agriculture. *U.S. Farm Numbers, Sizes, and Related Structural Dimensions: Projections to Year 2000*. Technical Bulletin no. 1625 (July).

————. 1981. U.S. Department of Agriculture. *Agricultural Food Policy Review: Perspectives for the 1980's*, AFPR-4 (April).

U.S. Embassy. 1979. *Agricultural Situation* (Tokyo, U.S. Embassy Agricultural Attaché, January 24).

U.S.–Japan Trade Council Report. 1980. *Greater Food Self-Sufficiency in Japan: Some of the Costs*, no. 18 (Washington, D.C., May 9).

WEISS (World Economic Information Services), ed. 1978. *Shokuryomondaino Kokusai Kozoto Nihonno Sentaku* (International Structure of Food Problems and Japan's Option) a symposium (Tokyo, WEISS).

Yakes, Nancy, and Denise Akey, eds. 1979. *Encyclopedia of Associations: National Organizations of the United States*, Vol. 1, 13th edition (Detroit, Mich., Gale Research Co.) Section 1 for Trade, Business and Commercial Organizations, and Section 2 for Agricultural Organizations.

Youngberg, I. Garth. 1979. "The National Farm Coalition and the Politics of Food: New Interest Group in a Changing Environment," paper presented at the Hendricks Public Policy Symposium, Lincoln, Nebr., April 5–6.

Zenno, n.d. *The National Federation of Agricultural Cooperative Associations* (pamphlet in English) (Tokyo).

IV

Agricultural Interdependence

9

The Personal View of a Japanese Negotiator

Yutaka Yoshioka

Significance of Japan's Agricultural Reform and Food Aid from the United States

The agricultural and food supply situation in Japan continues to show strong influences from the years immediately following World War II. It was during the years of occupation by the Allied Forces that the United States brought to Japan its agricultural expertise along with large amounts of food aid. The agricultural sector was shaken loose from its prewar feudalistic characteristics by a democratic "revolution." In such a setting it was later possible to introduce and extend new technology that greatly increased productivity in agriculture. The seeds of a major change in Japanese eating habits were also planted at this time when shipments of American wheat and milk were sent to feed the Japanese, including school children, many of whom were near the point of starvation because of wartime destruction of the agricultural and fishery industries. Recently, it has become possible in Japan to replace in part the traditional diet of rice and fish by a Western meal. The long-term effects that these years have had on postwar U.S.–Japanese agricultural relations have been considerable.

For two to three years after the end of the war, U.S. government officials "advised" the Japanese government on how it should democratize its agricultural sector. In this connection, the major components of the reform enforced by the Japanese government included

Yutaka Yoshioka is executive director of the Agricultural Policy Research Committee (Nohsei Chohsa Iinkai).

many new programs to achieve a comprehensive land reform, plus the establishment of a cooperative system, an agricultural extension service, and an agricultural research system. The land reform itself forced the major landowners (who owned 40 to 45 percent of the country's farmland) to release 80 percent of their holdings to their former tenants. Although later modified,[1] the basic features of these programs were never changed, functioning as the base of the postwar agricultural system.

Before the war, the Japanese Ministry of Agriculture and Forestry had attempted to pass several land reform bills to protect the interests of tenant farmers but these efforts were always blocked by the Diet which was dominated by landowners and others with strong vested interests in the status quo.[2] Ultimately, it took the support of the postwar occupation forces to carry out the ministry's goal. At that time, the general headquarters of the allied powers had a group dispatched from the U.S. Department of Agriculture, and it was with their idealism and good will that the general headquarters, together with the reformist faction of Japan's agriculture ministry and farm groups, studied Japanese agriculture and promoted democratization of rural areas. This at least is the way Japanese agricultural leaders have interpreted the total situation, even though they recognize that there were different views and opinions about Japan's agricultural reform between the general headquarters and the Japanese agriculture ministry.

The former tenant farmers who in most cases were allowed to own their land were then organized into agricultural cooperatives. By this means an element of stability and prosperity was introduced into the rural areas of Japan, which, in turn, set off a favorable chain of events that spread prosperity to the rest of the national economy and laid the foundation for the period of rapid economic growth that followed. The newly independent farmers aggressively began to adopt new agricultural technologies[3] that greatly stabilized and increased the

[1] For instance, under the revised Agricultural Land Law, an agricultural cooperative can possess farmland in some cases, while only operator-farmers could possess farmland under the original law. Consolidation and separation of agricultural research stations were instituted to meet new situations.

[2] In 1927, the cabinet refused to send to the Diet a bill for farm tenants, which had been drafted by the minister of agriculture and forestry. In 1931, the same bill, with various modifications, was proposed by the cabinet to the Diet, but the Diet did not pass it. In 1938, the ministry succeeded only to the extent that the Diet passed the Bill of Agricultural Land Adjustment, which was insufficient to protect the interests of tenant farmers in their relations with landowners.

[3] More fertilizer and chemicals and a new method of nursing seedlings were started using new varieties of rice. At a later stage, a complete system of mechanized paddy rice production with smaller machines was adopted by most rice-growing farmers.

production of rice, the principal staple food of the nation. The resulting higher level of self-sufficiency in food allowed precious foreign exchange reserves to be used to import the raw materials needed for industry. In turn, the increasingly prosperous farming communities served as necessary consumer markets for the manufactured goods.[4] The memory of the significant American role in establishing the postwar agricultural system still remains today among Japanese agricultural leaders and facilitates the resolution of frictions that arise in relations between the two countries.

The second great contribution that the United States made to Japan during the immediate postwar period was its food aid.[5] For several years, the American government supplied various food products— food without which many people would have starved in Japan. Wheat and dry milk were also supplied through school lunch programs that were started in 1946. Regardless of whether or not this was merely a convenient way to dispose of surplus American agricultural production, the end result was that the Japanese, along with their gratitude for the food, gradually became accustomed to Western foods, thus making possible the rapid Westernization of the Japanese diet that took place ten years later during the period of rapid economic growth. The change in diet also created a large demand for agricultural imports from the United States and other food-exporting countries.

Liberalization of Imports

As the reconstruction period drew to an end, Japan became a member of the General Agreement on Tariffs and Trade (GATT) in September 1955 and reentered international society (see Houck in chapter 3 of this volume). As a new member of GATT, Japan entered into tariff negotiations with about twenty countries. At that time, the most important negotiations were with the United States. Over the years since then many negotiations involving tariff reductions and other matters of trade liberalization have continued to be held. As a result of these negotiations and also of unilateral initiatives taken by the

[4] However, the land reform also had the adverse effect of preventing the exploitation of economies of scale because the transfer in ownership of farmland was strictly regulated to protect newly independent farmers and land was not always in the hands of the most productive users.

[5] Between 1945 and 1951, using American aid funds, Japan imported more than 9 million metric tons of foods (wheat, wheat flour, corn, peas and beans, canned foods, barley, rye, milo, soybean flour, sago palm starch, chestnuts, tapioca, sorghum starch, nonfat milk powder, sugar, and the like (Obara, 1952).

Japanese government, many important measures for developing agricultural trade were adopted and implemented. For example, the First Trade Liberalization Plan was implemented from 1960 to around 1965; the Kennedy Round of GATT negotiations concluded in 1967; and the Tokyo Round held from 1973 through 1978. Accordingly, in addition to a considerable reduction in tariffs, the number of items under residual import restrictions has decreased from seventy-six agricultural (including forestry and fishery) and seventy-nine manufacturing items in 1963 to twenty-two agricultural (including three fishery) and five nonagricultural items in 1980. Several agricultural items are under state trade approved by the GATT. It is a common feeling among Japanese agricultural leaders that the present protection level of Japan's agriculture is not far behind the European Community's (EC's), even though farm size is considerably smaller (see tables 9-1, 9-2, 9-3, and 9-4).

When Japan became a member of GATT, Japanese agricultural policy makers had to start preparing for rapid import liberalization and simultaneously consider the pressing and often contradictory need to modernize the agricultural sector in conjunction with Japan's industrial development. Fortunately for Japanese policy makers and for American and other foreign exporters, the rapid growth of the Japanese economy and the Westernization of the diet increased the demand for many agricultural products. This increase in demand, together with mechanization of farming operations accelerated by the labor shortage in rural areas, stimulated agricultural productivity. However, the concomitant rapid increase in wages and income in the industrial sector necessitated raising agricultural price supports to a level that would enable farmers to have incomes comparable to those in the industrial sector. Nor have increases in farm size and farming operations satisfied Japanese policy makers. At the same time, this rise in demand, together with a corresponding liberalization of import restrictions, has led to a phenomenal increase in food and feed imports over the last twenty years, making Japan one of the largest importing countries in the world. In 1979, Japan imported agricultural products worth $16,540 million, in which the U.S. share was $6,104 million, or 36.9 percent. Traditionally, the United States is the largest agricultural supplier to Japan, and Japan is the largest agricultural customer for the United States (Japan Trade Center, 1980, p. 70).

The accomplishment in liberalization referred to earlier was by no means easy to achieve, as explained later. Domestically, the Japanese government had to deal with mutually contradictory demands from various sectors to promote agricultural adjustment.

TABLE 9-1. AVERAGE SIZE OF FARMLAND MANAGED PER FARMER, IN
MAJOR COUNTRIES 1975

Country	Hectares per farm
Japan	1.1
Italy	7.7
Germany	13.8
France	24.5
U.K.	68.5
U.S.	157.6

Sources: The Commission of the European Communities, The Agricultural Situation in the Community (Brussels, 1976); data from the U.S. Department of Agriculture; Norinsuisansho (Ministry of Agriculture, Forestry and Fisheries), Stable Supply of Foods and the Role of Agriculture (Tokyo, 1979) p. 61.

The philosophy behind import liberalization of agricultural products

As the Japanese came to understand it, the U.S. trade philosophy throughout the Kennedy and Tokyo rounds and other negotiations held off and on during the Johnson and Nixon administrations was one of free trade based on comparative advantage, even in agriculture. This philosophy, which did not discriminate between agriculture and industry, was interpreted by the Japanese agricultural sector as advocating an international division of labor in which Japan, concentrating on industrial production, would rely on imported agricultural products. Many feared this would undermine small-scale Japanese farmers who would have to compete with low-cost, large-scale American agriculture. The Japanese agricultural sector, in turn, did not hesitate to publicize the above views for political purposes. The American arguments were the same as those used by the Japanese industrial sector: that agricultural imports should be increased in return for manufactured exports from Japan to the United States. To protect its position from attacks from both within and without the country, the Japanese farm sector had to oppose the position taken by the United States on agriculture, although eventually ministry officials and other agricultural leaders came to believe that to protect the agricultural sector from domestic as well as international pressures as described above, it was necessary to make minimum concessions. At the time, there did not exist a united consensus in Japan on liberalization of agricultural imports.[6]

[6] Imports of feed grains had been liberalized at an earlier stage in the postwar period.

TABLE 9-2. JAPAN: TWENTY-TWO AGRICULTURAL PRODUCTS SUBJECT TO RESIDUAL IMPORT RESTRICTIONS, 1980

Classification	Number of items	Heading no. of customs tariff schedule	Description
Key farm products:			
Dairy products	3	04.01	Sterilized or frozen milk and cream and other cream with fatty content of 13% or more, fresh, not concentrated or sweetened
		04.02	Milk and cream, preserved, concentrated, or sweetened
		04.04	Processed cheese; other cheese and curd (excl. natural cheese)
Meat and processed meat products	2	02.01	Meat and offals of bovine animals, fresh, chilled, or frozen, excl. tongue and internal organs
		16.02	Other prepared or preserved meat and offals of bovine animals or pigs; other preparations chiefly meat and offals of bovine animals or pigs (excl. ham and bacon, sterilized and packed in airtight containers)
Rice and wheat processed products	2	11.01	Wheat flour; rice flour; barley flour (incl. beardless barley flour)
		11.02	Groats and meal of wheat and rice, excluding germs thereof; other worked wheat and rice (for example, rolled)
Fruits, vegetables, and processed products	6	08.02	Oranges, fresh; tangerines, fresh
		08.11	Oranges, temporarily preserved by sulphur dioxide or other gases; tangerines, temporarily preserved by sulphur dioxide or other gases
		20.05	Fruit purée and fruit pastes

		Description
Regional specialties and related items as corumn	5	
	20.06	Pineapples with added sugar or spirits; fruit pulps with added sugar or spirits, excl. apricots and nuts; other pineapples, prepared or preserved; other fruit pulps, excl. apricots and nuts
	20.07	Fruit juices with added sugar, excl. lemon juice; other fruit juices, excl. sloe bases, lemon, and lime; tomato juices, with a dry weight content of less than 7%
	21.04	Tomato ketchup and tomato sauce
	07.05	Small red beans; broad beans and peas, excl. seeds for growing vegetables; other dried leguminous vegetables, excl. seeds for growing vegetables
	12.01	Groundnuts, excluding those to be used as materials for groundnut oil under customs supervision
	11.08	Starches and insulin
	17.02	Grape sugar, without added flavoring or coloring; milk sugar (without added flavoring or coloring matter), less than 90% pure milk sugar content; other sugar, without added flavoring or coloring; sugar syrup, excl. maple syrup; caramel; artificial honey; other sugars and syrups, without added flavoring or coloring (excluding sorbose)
	12.08	Edible seaweeds in rectangular papery sheets not more than 430 sq cm per piece; seaweeds of genus Porphyra and other seaweeds mixed with *Porphyra* and other edible seaweeds, edible, excl. those in heading no. 12.08–3–(1) of the customs tariff schedule; other edible seaweeds (*Entromorpha, Monostroma, Kjellman-iella,* and *Laminaria*); tubers of *konnyaku* (*Amorphophallus*), whether or not cut, dried, or powdered
Fish, shellfish, and seaweeds as corumn[a]	3	
	03.01	Herring: cod (incl. Alaska pollack) and its roes, yellowtail, mackerel, sardines, horse-mackerel, and sauries, fresh (live or dead), chilled, or frozen

(Continued)

347

TABLE 9-2. *(Continued)*

Classification	Number of items	Heading no. of customs tariff schedule	Description
		03.02	Hard roes of cod (incl. Alaska pollack), salted, in brine, dried, or smoked; cod (incl. Alaska pollack), herring, yellowtail, mackerel, sardines, horse-mackerel, and sauries, salted, in brine or dried, *niboshi* (small boiled and dried fish for seasoning use)
		03.03	Scallops, cuttlefish, and squid (excl. *mongo ika* [*Sepia subaculeata*]), live; scallops, predators of shellfish, cuttlefish, and squid (excl. *mongo ika*), fresh, chilled, or frozen; scallops, predators of shellfish, cuttlefish and squid (excl. *mongo ika*), other than live, fresh, chilled and frozen
Other	1	21.07	Food preparations with added sugar, excl. rations, peanut butter, sweet corn, and Korean ginseng tea; ice cream powder, prepared milk powder for infants, and other preparations mainly consisting of milk; food preparations of seaweeds (*Porphyra, Enteromorpha, Monostroma, Kjellmaniella,* and *Laminaria*); *mochi* (rice-cake), cooked rice, roasted rice flours, vitamin-enriched rice, and other similar food preparations of rice, wheat, and barley (incl. beardless barley)

Source: Norinsuisansho (Ministry of Agriculture, Forestry and Fisheries) *Staple Supply of Foods and the Role of Agriculture* (Tokyo, 1979) p. 65; Import Notice as of July 1980.

[a]Seaweed is included in heading 12.08 under regional specialties and related items.

TABLE 9-3. JAPAN: STATE TRADE[a] ITEMS

Item	Applicable regulatory laws
Agricultural products:	
Condensed milk, dried milk, butter, milk powder, whey powder	Law concerning price stabilization of livestock products
Wheat, meslin (mixture of wheat & rye)	Food grains control law
Barley	
Rice	
Raw silk	Raw silk price stabilization law
Items controlled by Finance Ministry:	
Tobacco	Tobacco monopoly law
Salt	Salt monopoly law
Alcohol	Alcohol monopoly law
Items controlled by Health and Welfare Ministry:	
Opium	Opium regulation law

Source: Norinsuisansho (Ministry of Agriculture, Forestry & Fisheries).
[a] State trade (in contrast to private trade) is authorized under GATT provisions.

The major source of theoretical support for the "lonely" Japanese agricultural sector was the existence of the similar Common Agricultural Policy of the European Community. The purpose of this policy, as interpreted by Japanese farm interests, was to protect the smaller European farmers from the larger scale farmers of agricultural exporting countries. The reasoning was that if this policy could be exempted from the American comparative advantage arguments, the Japanese, with even smaller scale farming and greater dependence on food imports, were justified in expecting even more sympathy from the Americans. Supporting this line of thinking was the belief that the recent large increases in agricultural imports and progress in trade liberalization in Japan made Japan's position much more open to imports than Europe's. Frustration within the Japanese agricultural sector grew all the more vehement when Australia and New Zealand began to demand that Japan open up its market for their livestock products as a result of Britain's subscribing to the European Community's Common Agricultural Policy.

Even in view of the agreement on the agricultural sector reached by the United States and the European Community in the negotiations of the Tokyo Round, it was acknowledged that it was very difficult to translate the philosophy of comparative advantage into acceptable domestic policies. Japan came to have some doubts about the motives

TABLE 9-4. RESIDUAL IMPORT RESTRICTIONS APPLYING TO FARM PRODUCTS IN MAJOR COUNTRIES, 1979

Country	Number of items	Major items	Remarks
U.S.	1	Beet sugar, cane sugar	U.S. import restrictions under GATT include waivers on 13 items BTN (1–24 group) wheat, flour, processed wheat products, peanuts, milk and cream, butter, dairy products (such as ice cream); in addition, the importation of beef is regulated under a special law.
Canada	4	Milk and cream, butter, cheese, curd	
W. Germany	3	Potatoes, potato starch, prepared vegetables	Protection provided by EC nations mainly in the form of levy under the Common Agricultural Policy (described below). Import quotas are supplementary.
U.K.	1	Bananas	
Italy	3	Bananas, grapes, citrus fruit juice	
France	19	Horse, sheep, mutton, natural honey, cut flowers, vegetables, bananas, pineapples, grapes, prunes, melons, prepared fish products, etc.	
Benelux	4	Cut flowers, vegetables, grapes, etc.	

Notes: Levy system applies to European Community (EC) farm product imports. Surcharges are levied on the following items to maintain common support prices for major products within the region: (1) surcharge (basic type)—grains, dairy products (prices supported within the region); (2) surcharge (processed products)—pork, eggs, poultry meat (prices not supported); (3) surcharge plus tariffs—beef (prices supported); (4) surcharge plus deficiency payment—durum, olive oil (prices supported); (5) tariffs plus adjustment levies—vegetables, wine, etc. (prices supported).

Source: Compiled from Norinsuisansho (Ministry of Agriculture, Forestry and Fisheries). *Stable Supply of Foods and the Role of Agriculture* (Tokyo, 1979) p. 61, and other ministry sources.

behind the United States' basic stance on comparative advantage. In the Japanese–U.S. negotiations, the U.S. side was not forced into the position of having to defend its protected sectors (dairy products, beef, sugar, and the like) because Japan, of course, did not have any meaningful agricultural products to export to the United States. In U.S.–European Community negotiations, however, Japan observed that there were many difficult arguments about dairy products that compromised the philosophy of comparative advantage and came to suspect that much of the rhetoric was just an opportunistic cover for American self-interest.

Also, as the U.S. side made an issue of U.S.–Japanese agricultural relations whenever it suffered a large balance-of-payments problem, Japan came to have doubts about how much the United States cared about cultivating a stable, long-term trade relationship in agricultural products. In Japan it is generally believed that bilateral trade in food and agricultural products is an integral part of overall, long-term friendly U.S.–Japanese relations, from which a stable supply of food is secured. It is also believed that agricultural trade issues, therefore, should not be dealt with only in conjunction with temporary balance-of-payments problems between the two nations. More attention is paid in Japan to the overall development of U.S.–Japanese agricultural trade than to the increases or decreases in trade of each specific commodity. In other words, while the United States considers U.S.–Japanese agricultural trade in terms of commercial gain and loss, Japan puts more emphasis on securing a stable supply of food in total.

Of course, behind the historic Japanese reaction against the American comparative advantage argument lie, to some degree, vested interests in maintaining the status quo. Although the U.S. argument could be useful in promoting rationalization of agriculture, in actuality, it tended to result in an extremely defensive attitude within the Japanese agricultural sector because the gap in the scale of farming between the United States and Japan is formidable.

To develop U.S.–Japanese agricultural trade without harmful conflict, it is necessary to recognize not only the comparative advantage of small-scale farming in Japan but also the wider problem of Japan's need for social stability, and its concerns about community problems, industrial adjustment, environmental protection, and self-sufficiency in food.

Domestic opinion about import liberalization of agricultural products and how that opinion has changed over time

As mentioned previously, American demands that Japan liberalize its import restrictions (including those on agricultural products) were made strongly whenever Japan built up a considerable surplus in the two nations' bilateral trade. By way of a response to the intense American pressures, the various Japanese ministries usually hastily drew up a government import liberalization plan and, then, after consultation with the Liberal Democratic Party (LDP), the government would issue and implement new liberalization measures, including those for agricultural products. In the process of arriving at these liberalization policies, it was necessary to harmonize and overcome the great rivalries that existed among the various government ministries, industries, and political interest groups, with each group doing its best to protect its particular products from competition from the outside.

As can be inferred from the above process, Japan's trade liberalization has developed as a passive response to outside pressures without any overall long-term trade liberalization scheme, except for a vague notion of "liberalizing as fast as possible." Moreover, the products or industries that lost their trade barriers because of outside pressure were generally understood to be making sacrifices for the sake of smoothing Japan's relations with the outside world. Consequently, there was a consensus among the affected industries, the government agencies, and the business community as a whole that compensation for the industries was justified by the losses they suffered from trade liberalization.

Naturally, however, the chief proponents of the liberalization trend were those manufacturers in the export sector, especially those that became internationally very competitive, that stood to benefit greatly from trade liberalization. The heavy and chemical industries were the foundation for Japan's rapid economic growth, and the profits that grew as liberalization proceeded were regarded as the profits of the nation. As Japan became a member of GATT and adopted trade liberalization as a national policy, it became very difficult for anyone to voice opposition to this trend. In most cases the number of manufactured and agricultural items that had to be liberalized was determined on the initiative of the Ministry of Foreign Affairs and the Ministry of International Trade and Industry (MITI). The Ministry of Agriculture, Forestry and Fisheries usually determined the specific items under its authority and drew up a detailed plan designed to forestall vigorous opposition by farm groups and politicians.

In the case of agricultural commodities, those products that are less important for Japan's agriculture in the future, less vulnerable to liberalization, and whose production does not require extensive manpower were selected for liberalization, because these industries either would not suffer seriously from liberalization or could be diversified into other agricultural production.

Thus, the process was dominated by the producers, leaving little concern for consumers' interests. When the liberalization targets were determined, post-liberalization aid to target industries was simultaneously planned. And the effectiveness of these assistance measures usually had a great influence on the identification of target industries. While the Finance Ministry was most concerned that the industry chosen would put the least possible burden on the national budget after liberalization, the major concern of the Ministry of International Trade and Industry (MITI) and the Ministry of Foreign Affairs was with liberalization of those items that trading partners, including the United States, desired to export aggressively. Agricultural cooperatives and other interest groups always strongly resisted liberalization, insisting that it would seriously damage Japan's agricultural sector and also that an international division of labor would greatly impair Japan's self-sufficiency in food. All over the country, agricultural organizations put great pressure on the Diet representatives of their election districts and government officials regardless of political party affiliation.

In contrast, there was no sign of the consumer group activity that might have been expected to appear. The only defense of consumer rights, little as it was, came from the mass media. These different demands from various interest groups were, in the end, reconciled at the Agricultural Committee meetings of the ruling Liberal Democratic Party, with participation of officials of the Agriculture Ministry, and then approved at the top levels of the LDP. In the party discussions, officials of the Agriculture Ministry always had to play a role as proponents of liberalization, a role that was most unpopular with the politicians.

The rapid pace at which liberalization took place, despite the obstacles described above, can largely be attributed to the rapid growth of the Japanese economy and to the stable reign of the LDP government. However, there were adverse political and economic side effects that came from the hasty and often *ad hoc* liberalization of agricultural products. These were, among others, an imbalance between the levels of protection provided for agricultural products and processed products, a substitution of liberalized commodities for protected products, an emotional rivalry between the various agricultural areas of Japan, and political disagreements.

Compared to the past, however, the industrial sector has greatly lessened its direct pressure on the agricultural sector in Japan for several reasons: the importing climate for agricultural commodities in Japan, which has become better developed because of import liberalization; the lack of food surpluses in many nations; the energy crisis; and the establishment of the 200-nautical-mile fishing zone regime. Besides, as the LDP has lost some strength, partly as a result of urbanization in Japan, it has become clear that support from the remaining rural agricultural areas is very important to the stability of conservative rule. Furthermore, it has become obvious that in many countries—whether they are advanced, socialist, or developing—a healthy agricultural sector is considered essential for economic and political stability, and this has helped Japan's agricultural sector to define its proper position vis-à-vis the entire economy.

Today, the agricultural protectionist policies in Japan are criticized more because they are a drain on the nation's financial resources than because they are improper trade policies. And several labor unions, which insisted on liberalization during the later stages of the Tokyo Rounds on the ground that it could decrease food prices, have ceased to press their demands now that energy prices have been raised dramatically, inflation has become severe, and the international environment has become less stable.

The one-sidedness of U.S.–Japanese agricultural trade

The one-sided nature of postwar U.S.–Japanese agricultural trade, with the commodities flowing only from the United States to Japan, has been an impediment to smooth trade relations between the two nations. Before World War II, raw silk was a major export item bringing international orientation to the Japanese agricultural sector. However, during the postwar period, the increase in wages and land prices in the agricultural sector (which led to increasing domestic production costs), the growing domestic market for agricultural products, the increasing number of farmers who branched out into off-farm jobs, and the improvement in the balance-of-payments situation owing to the successful exporting of Japanese manufactured goods were all factors which lessened the need for, and ability of, the agricultural sector to export. Thus the manufacturing sector became overzealous in its export efforts while the agricultural sector became overly dependent on the domestic market. The agricultural sector did its utmost to preserve the domestic market for itself and to restrict imports. In international negotiations, Japan has gone to the extreme of refraining from demanding concessions from negotiating partners for exportation of several agricultural products lest it should be subject to requests for more concessions in relation to liberalization of Japanese markets.

Furthermore, whenever there appeared a danger of an oversupply in the Japanese market, the agricultural organizations would immediately coordinate a nationwide cutback of production in order to stabilize market prices (which was possible since agricultural cooperatives are legally exempt from the antitrust law) and farmers' incomes, or in the case of the latter, demand that the government enact measures to the same effect. Even in the United States, if domestic production is reduced under the law, the right to take measures restricting imports is officially authorized. A provision to the same effect is included in the GATT. Under similar conditions in Japan, however, it is not by law per se that domestic production is reduced, but by an understanding or consensus reached among the agricultural groups or under government administrative guidance. It is therefore difficult to invoke the GATT provision to justify Japan's import adjustment measures in such cases, but in practice such measures are frequently called for under excess supply conditions.

Among the advanced countries in the world, Japan is the only one with such insignificant agricultural exports. (In 1979, Japan imported over $16 billion worth of agricultural products, while it exported only $750 million worth of agricultural and food products.) Today, there is a common recognition that the domestic market for many agricultural products has been expanded to its maximum limit.[7] Against this background, it would be of great significance for the internationalization of the Japanese agricultural sector as well as for the cultivation of more markets for excess products, if a two-way flow of agricultural commodities could be initiated by Japan's exporting farm products such as seeds, fruits, and certain vegetables that are internationally competitive. (The fact is that a realistic interest in promoting exports of agricultural products is *not* increasing. Overpowering it are complaints about the difficulties that would be involved.)

[7] (1) Besides a quite stagnant food market situation, per capita total calorie intake was decreased by 1.1 percent per year from 1973 to 1975 and increased only by 0.5 percent per year from 1975 to 1978. No significant increase is projected (see tables 3-2, 4-A-5, 4-A-6 in this volume). (2) The present pattern of Japan's per capita caloric intake—12.8 percent from protein, 22.7 percent from fats and oils, and 64.5 percent from carbohydrates—is quite similar to the USDA guidelines (USDA-USDHEW, 1980).

Japanese systems for protecting agricultural sectors

Beginning in 1979, Japan's export of rice became a source of trade friction between Japan and the United States, but the issue was resolved in 1980 through discussions between the two governments. In general, Japanese rice is not competitive on the international market because of its rather peculiar characteristics and its relatively high domestic price. Thus Japan has never exported rice on a large-scale commercial basis and has traditionally been an importer. However, as Japan had experienced starvation conditions following the end of World War II, there was a strong desire to attain self-sufficiency in rice, and a policy aimed at increasing production was pursued throughout the postwar period. (See the Houck, Kuroda, and Egaitsu chapters in this volume for discussion of the rice support policy and self-sufficiency in general.) And by the 1960s, with annual production levels having reached 13 to 14 million metric tons, Japan was able to achieve the nationally desired goal of total self-sufficiency, thus giving the Japanese people a tremendous sense of psychological security.

Ironically, with the increased consumption of meat and wheat products, Japanese annual per capita rice consumption began to decline from its peak of 118.3 kilograms in 1962. By 1979 per capita annual consumption had decreased by 33 percent to 79.8 kilograms, a trend that is expected to continue. In principle, the Japanese government buys the rice from the producers and then resells it to distributors. Because of this system, the concomitant increase in production and decrease in consumption resulted in excess government rice reserves of 7.2 million metric tons (roughly equivalent to six months' consumption) in 1969. Again in 1979, because of a larger than expected harvest and a further decrease in consumption, government reserves again reached 6.5 million metric tons despite efforts to promote the cultivation of alternative crops and to dispose of excess reserves (Norinsuisansho, 1980, p. 79).

The disposal of reserves had primarily taken the form of discounted sales for industrial use and for use as fodder; however, the government also began exporting rice as assistance to needy countries. (Japan has agreed with the United States that from 1981 to 1983 such exports will not exceed 400,000 tons annually.) Thus Japan has adopted the policy that exporting rice is a temporary phenomenon for the purpose of dealing with excess reserves, and that exports will be carried out after consultation with the FAO Subcommittee on Food Reserves and within the limits set forth by the agreement between Japan and the United States. With the domestic price of rice several times the international price, production for export as aid or for industrial use requires huge subsidization and puts a great financial burden on the government. As an economic policy it is extremely inefficient and is infeasible. It is unlikely that the government desired such a policy, or that it desires to continue such a policy.

Over the past ten years, the American and Japanese systems for protecting their agricultural sectors (farm incomes) have developed greatly. This has given rise to many of today's bilateral trade problems and will in all probability continue to do so even in the near future.

For many years in the United States, price support (loan-rate) programs have covered the main agricultural products under the operations of the Commodity Credit Corporation (CCC) in order to guarantee incomes, with the products covered ranging widely from dairy products and cotton to wheat and feed grains. Complementing these domestic price support programs were the necessary import adjustment measures. At the beginning of the 1970s, however, the United States adopted a new approach in addition to the price support system. This was a target price system, under which most of the direct government payments that the grain farmers received came to be introduced. At the same time, the level for the price support has come to depend on the price level prevailing in the world market.

In contrast, the programs protecting farm income in Japan consist mainly of price support systems. There are several basic reasons why this approach dominates in Japan,[8] but in any case, the support price levels that are set to protect the small farmers' incomes are by necessity considerably higher than those on the world market. The method used at the border to regulate imports is mainly the quota system and state trade. The import quota system, which is also employed by the United States in the case of dairy and other products, is by no means as well accepted by the international community as, for example, the import levy system. The import levy system is widely used by the European Community as a common agricultural policy tool to regulate

[8] The several basic reasons are as follows: (1) Price supports are the most effective assurance for farmers' incomes. (2) The Ministry of Finance has always been against a deficiency payment system, because as a matter of government policy, the burden on the consumer should be easier in terms of prices than in terms of taxes. (3) A deficiency payment system is not adaptable and workable because: the number of farmers is so great, the production cost varies extensively among the producers, the quality of the products is not well standardized, and the marketing channels are so complicated and numerous. (4) Producers have strongly opposed the deficiency payment policy because the government's soybean policy, which was to protect domestic production after the import liberalization, failed completely, and soybean production decreased substantially. The target price was so unsatisfactory to the farmers and soybean marketing channels were so numerous and complicated that the cases of deficiency payments were quite limited, resulting in a drastic decrease in soybean production.

imports. Because the system does not directly control the exact quantity that can be imported, it looks at first glance to be not far from free trade, but in real terms it is often a more effective way to restrict imports than quantitative restrictions. The quantitative restriction system can be flexibly adjusted according to domestic demand conditions and, therefore, can be adjusted to allow more imports if these are promised at international negotiations.

To meet the new demands for food brought on by the rapid economic growth that began in the mid-1960s and by the rapid Westernization of the Japanese diet, some farmers who traditionally grew rice had to begin to diversify their production into livestock, vegetables, and fruit. This called for a change from small-scale, general to highly efficient, specialized farming. At that time, with the rapid flow of farm labor to other industries, agricultural policy sought to encourage large-scale, high-efficiency farming, thereby hoping to lower domestic production costs in the near future to the world market price levels. The plan therefore was to gradually lower the price levels of the price support systems, but the unexpectedly rapid economic growth completely upset this. What actually happened was that to keep farmers' income levels equal to wage earners', the prices of agricultural products under the above program increased as fast as, if not faster in some cases, than general wages. The gap between Japanese and world price levels of most agricultural products, therefore, did not close at all, except for a few items such as pork, broilers, and eggs (which could be produced with abundant feed grains imported mostly from the United States, with less land, and with the higher efficiency of new technologies).

Nevertheless, because employment opportunities were even more attractive in the manufacturing than in the agricultural sector, a large part of the rural labor force moved to the factories and cities. Thus a decrease of labor in the agricultural sector, imports attributable to the expanded domestic market, and import liberalization necessitated large-scale restructuring of Japan's agricultural sector. For example, domestic production of wheat, barley, and soybeans almost completely ceased and was replaced by imports from the United States and other exporting countries. Livestock industries such as hogs, broilers, and eggs developed rapidly in various areas. Sixty-five percent of the 4.6 million Japanese farm households have come to be part-time farmers, depending on nonfarming jobs for most of their income. In other words, the majority of Japanese farmers are, in actuality, laborers who happen to own a small amount of farmland. Such a major restructuring, taking place within a short ten-year period, is probably unprecedented in history. (See the Kuroda and Egaitsu chapters in this volume.) One result of this process was the development and growth of American production of soft wheat, semihard wheat, feed grains (especially grain sorghum), soybeans, lemons, grapefruit, and other fruits with the Japanese market in mind. Japan has become not only the best all-round customer for American agricultural exports, but also the number one customer for many individual export items. It was this major restructuring of Japan's agricultural sector that made possible the massive exports from the United States, Australia, Canada, and other developed and developing countries.

From the point of view of the American agricultural sector, this is probably the greatest success story in its history. From the viewpoint of the Japanese agricultural camp, however, it cannot be called a success story. The reason is that most of the exports from the United States are temperate-zone products and therefore *could* have been produced in Japan, if cost were ignored. The Japanese agricultural camp feels that liberalization has allowed cheaper foreign products to rob it of the market that was originally its right to serve. (Nobody denies that domestic raising of hogs and poultry and to some extent, beef-cattle, was also made possible and developed remarkably by inexpensive imports of feed grains, but since this does not involve farming of the land within Japan and the number of producers is relatively small, it had little effect on the sentiments of Japanese farmers as a whole and their representatives.) Thus it can be said that the above restructuring of the Japanese agricultural sector was the result of reactions to events rather than the intended consequence of well-planned policies. Against this background, Japanese farmers and agricultural interest groups have tended to attribute the failure to resist foreign pressures to liberalize trade, which resulted in the restructuring or collapsing of the agricultural sector against their will, to the weakness of the Agriculture Ministry and some Diet members of the ruling party representing the agricultural sector's interests.

Thus, although the American agricultural sector can regard as a success story the growth of its exports to Japan and its "complementarity" with the Japanese agricultural sector, the Japanese agricultural bureaus and farm leaders find it as difficult to call it a success story as the American car and television industries would find it difficult to praise their "complementarity" with their corresponding sectors in Japan. (A difference between the United States and Japan may lie in the fact that strong consumer groups exist in the United States that do not care whether goods are produced abroad or domestically as long as they provide good value for consumers.) Nevertheless, looking back over the past twenty years, whether the Japanese agricultural sector likes it or not, the transformation that took place in the farming villages was clearly a restructuring of the agricultural sector that resulted in mutual complementarity with the American counterpart. And it is important for the U.S. side to recognize that this restructuring took place with unprecedented speed and scale among the advanced industrialized countries.

Nor can the transformation of the Japanese agricultural sector be said to have taken place in a balanced fashion. In fact, the transformation had greatly different effects on different types of agricultural products. For example, domestic producer prices have come to differ greatly from the international market price in the case of those "land-based" products, such as grains, beef, and dairy products, whose production costs are greatly affected by scale of operation. With "facility-based" products, such as hogs, broilers, eggs, and greenhouse vegetables, this is less true.

Problems of Food Security

Differences in U.S. and Japanese public opinion about self-sufficiency in food

For Americans, probably the most incomprehensible aspect of postwar U.S.–Japanese agricultural relations, particularly after the world food crisis in 1973, is the Japanese obsession with being self-sufficient in food. This desire is held not only by Japanese farmers themselves, but by the nation as a whole. The United States is the world's largest producer and exporter of agricultural products. It may at times suffer from problems of surpluses, but it has never experienced a food shortage as a nation. In terms of food supply, the general American public has not suffered greater hardships than an occasional fluctuation in consumer prices. It may be relevant to compare the two countries' wartime experiences. One American who grew up as a boy in the Midwest during World War II when questioned said, "What I remember about food during the war is that hamburgers got a little thinner." It cannot be compared with the obsession for finding food that many Japanese, on the verge of starvation, developed—an obsession that led them to eat wild grass and sweet potato leaves. Accordingly, since the war, one of the foremost concerns of the government, regardless of who was in power, has been that of ensuring a dependable supply of food, and especially of the principal grains, through promotion of domestic production. Whatever the actual results have been, there has never been an administration in power that has not promised greater national self-sufficiency in food as one of its slogans. Furthermore, the opposition parties have never ceased to attack the party in power for being lax in its efforts to increase self-sufficiency. On this general point, therefore, the parties in and out of power have been constantly in accord.

The best institutional expression of the notion that the government is responsible for promoting food self-sufficiency and a stable supply of primary food can be found in the government control system for rice and wheat. Under this system, a special division of the Ministry of Agriculture, Forestry and Fisheries, the Food Agency, is allocated a special account. Using agents located throughout the country, the agency does everything from buying up the rice and wheat from the farmers (and importers) to storing and distributing it for sale. It even regulates and guarantees the prices and amounts of grains that will be bought and sold. The producers' prices and those for resale are set once a year by the government and are effective for the length of that fiscal year. As a result, the domestic prices of these items did not waver even during the year of the world food crisis (1973), in stark contrast to the violent price changes and shortages of nonregulated items such as soybeans and even toilet paper.

During the three years between 1973 and 1976 when the world prices of many grains rose sharply, the Food Agency sold its wheat and barley at predetermined domestic price levels that were much lower than the prices at which it was bought. As a result, 419 billion yen in losses were accumulated and had to be absorbed in the national budget. If the Japanese government had directly and immediately passed on the increase in costs for wheat to the consumers, the prices of bread and noodles would have risen sharply in contrast to the stable price of rice under the surplus condition and there would have been a definite short- and long-term adverse effect on the consumption of wheat. Of course, when world prices drop or the yen strengthens, the special account for rice and wheat sometimes shows a profit, a situation which often leads to the United States making an issue of the government's wheat management program. But if it is made clear that the goal of this government operation is to stabilize the amount and prices of primary food supply (rice and wheat) and that balance between plus and minus in relation to wheat will break even in the long run, the significant role played by this system in stabilizing the consumption and import of wheat could be better understood.

Judging from the great concern that the Japanese have shown about the self-sufficiency issue in food, it might be assumed that they are pursuing an irrational goal of eventually growing *all* their food domestically. Such a conclusion would be mistaken. The government goal is a very realistic one of striving, at least, not to drop below the present level of self-sufficiency. There are no concrete policies pointedly related to raising the self-sufficiency level to a certain percentage for certain products. Rather, the intent is to present a general projection for production based on forecasts of future demand. However, all Japanese agricultural interests have demanded that the government establish a self-sufficiency target in order to show the farmers guidelines for production and the consumers a projection of domestic supply. The state of future U.S.–Japanese agricultural relations will depend greatly on how well Americans can comprehend the importance to the Japanese of maintaining a certain level of self-sufficiency in food.

Japanese reactions to world events

Two events that occurred in 1973, the world food crisis (including the American government's embargo of soybean exports), and the oil crisis, further increased the Japanese people's traditional concern with self-sufficiency in food production—a concern which had lessened up until 1973 because of the worldwide grain surplus—and greatly influenced Japanese agricultural policy after that time. These reactions indicate the importance of assuring Japan of a secure food supply as a basis for future negotiation on the subject of food trade between the two countries.

In 1973, the United States did not, in effect, reduce soybean exports to Japan. The Americans therefore criticize the Japanese for exaggerating the effect of the so-called soybean shock. After the export embargo was imposed, the U.S. Department of Agriculture did, in fact, work to ensure that Japanese needs were met at least at previous years' levels, and import levels were effectively maintained. Japanese interests are fully aware of the American government's intention to cooperate in this situation. That the Japanese government still continues to cite the soybean shock stems from the larger implications of this crisis.

First, the sudden shortage of soybeans, the raw material for two traditional Japanese foods, *natto* (fermented soybean) and *tofu* (soybean curd), followed by an abrupt rise in the price of soybeans, sent small producer-retailers of the soybean products throughout the country into a panic. They were soon joined by housewives and the mass media. As the panic spread among the mass of the people, the problem became a political issue, and the government, totally unprepared for such an emergency, came under attack for its negligence. In Japan, the sphere of government responsibility is far more extensive than it is in the United States. The Japanese public was anxious lest the shortage of soybeans be followed by shortages of staple foods such as rice and wheat. However, it soon became clear that government controls applying to wheat and rice guaranteed that there would be no need to worry about additional shortages, and, as a result, people felt renewed confidence in the concept of government control. The government took the opportunity afforded by this wave of public support to stockpile rice and wheat and to encourage and subsidize private stockpiling of soybeans for human consumption. Although the public's fears were finally calmed once a supply of soybeans was secured from the American source, the crisis did make people acutely conscious of Japan's dependence on other countries located far beyond the ocean for its food supply—a fact which will not soon be forgotten.

Japanese policy makers have been most concerned about the following points:

1. As long as poor crops continue to occur in Soviet Russia at a considerable rate of one every few years, sharp fluctuations in world supply and demand conditions could also occur frequently in the future. It is then imperative that Japan have a long-term policy for securing a stable supply of food—especially when such fluctuations take place at a time when stockpiles are depleted. When that happens, the price rise of agricultural products in the world market reduces the difference between Japanese producer prices and international prices, and thus with a situation favorable to domestic Japanese producers, it becomes easier to appeal to the public for an increase in domestic production.

2. There is concern about the fact that the American government's decisions are made for the benefit of domestic agriculture, and to encourage stable domestic food prices for the consumers. To the Japanese, this proves that the American government—and for that matter, maybe all governments—gives priority to the immediate benefit of a domestic majority in making final decisions. Nonetheless, realizing that it is difficult for any government to avoid emphasizing domestic politics, Japanese government planners believe it essential

that Japan formulate a basic and firm policy governing (a) food imports from overseas and (b) increased production in domestic agriculture.

3. Japanese government and business leaders had taken the overly optimistic and unsubstantiated view that since Japan was a traditional customer for American agriculture, the American government would provide special treatment for Japan. It soon became evident, however, that once American exports become subordinate to diplomatic decisions, the American government will not be able to treat Japan or any one country more favorably than it treats its other allies.

Thus, in 1973 the question of securing a supply of food became a national political issue. At that time, representatives of producers, consumers, the mass media, and the trading companies attended a national conference on the issue of food supply presided over by Prime Minister Miki. The conference agreed on a long-term statement of basic principles that would ensure a stable supply of food. This policy has remained essentially unchanged to the present. It consists of:

- Improving the international flow of information regarding the supply and demand conditions of food (improvement of the FAO Information System).
- Improving the exchange of information between Japan and the United States and obtaining guarantees of a stable grain supply (the Abe-Butz agreement, 1975–77).
- Building domestic reserve stocks of important grains (rice, wheat, corn, soybeans) to meet short-term fluctuations in supply and demand.
- Strengthening agricultural development assistance to developing countries to lessen the strain on the world food supply.
- Implementation of a policy to increase domestic production of wheat and soybeans, which are necessary for traditional foods.

The above principles obviously do not include the types of drastic policies designed to stimulate domestic production that are viewed with disfavor by the United States and other exporting countries. Instead, it can be seen that these are extremely commonsensical political decisions, especially in view of the fact that they were taken at a time of grave public concern in Japan.

The greatest effect of the world food crisis of 1973 on Japan was on the consumer movement. Although the Japanese movement is not as strong as that of the United States, groups of housewives led by a relatively small number of leaders, combined in cooperative movements and have been steadily increasing since the end of World War II. Right up to the day before the American embargo on soybean exports, their leaders complained that Japanese food prices were unreasonably high and advocated liberalization of imports, saying that the government only protected the farmers and forced Japanese consumers to consume overpriced food products by restricting imports. But immediately following the soybean embargo, these same leaders retracted their demands for import liberalization and instead adopted a new stance of supporting increased domestic agricultural production for the purpose of increasing self-sufficiency in food. To achieve this they were now willing to cooperate with the farmers, even at the cost of more expensive food. Moreover, because environmental problems were becoming more serious at that time, the consumer groups directed their aims away from lowering food prices toward upgrading the safety of food products; the consumer movement thus developed into a movement to restrict and prohibit the use of preservatives and additives in foods. This change in the nature of the consumer movement lies behind the diplomatic conflicts that developed in 1976–77 concerning the use of preservatives on American citrus fruits.

During the Tokyo Round negotiations, when beef and oranges became a serious point of contention, some members of the U.S. Congress became irritated by the Japanese consumers' dull response to high prices for these items, and it was jokingly suggested that Ralph Nader should be sent to Japan to arouse the slumbering Japanese consumer. To a certain extent, such jokes reveal a lack of understanding by the Americans of the Japanese consumer movement. Historically, the movement has been highly conscious of its "solidarity with the weak," and this consciousness, in turn, forms the basis for the movement's claim of "solidarity with the farmers." And, in fact, the movement's opponents are mostly the strong: the government, manufacturers, distributors, trading companies, and other industries. When this inherent tendency to side with the "weak" farmers is combined with the aforementioned Japanese anxiety about obtaining a secure supply of food, it is easy to understand why Japanese consumers are more concerned with attaining self-sufficiency through domestic production than with the problem of cheaper food prices and why the Japanese consumers tended to express little support for the American position during the Tokyo Round negotiations. It is important to recognize the difference in consumer behavior in the two countries.

The Beginning of Agricultural Reorganization in Japan and Implications for the Two Countries' Relations

Once the immediate post–World War II period was over, U.S.–Japanese agricultural relations centered primarily around the problems of liberalization of trade (of agricultural products other than grains) on the American side and obtaining a secure supply of food and feed (essentially grains) on the Japanese side. Up to now in both countries these matters have been dealt with almost entirely as problems of trade relations, and even though the agricultural systems of both countries have been discussed in the context of trade negotiations, the scope of the discussion has not been sufficiently broad or deep. Yet agricultural relations between Japan and the United States will become increasingly complex in the 1980s; unless each country seeks a deeper understanding of its partner's agricultural system and policy objectives, it will be extremely difficult to maintain harmonious agricultural relations between the two nations.

World grain supply and demand conditions are also beginning to reflect the destabilizing effect of external factors such as energy and currency problems. It also seems to us that American agriculture has decreased the production flexibility it once had. With the increase in wages, land prices, investment costs, and environmental problems, it will become more necessary to protect American family farms, especially those in the marginal producing areas.

In Japan, instability and a slowdown in economic growth are restricting the domestic food market. It is already apparent that there is a surplus of many agricultural products, including livestock products. Nutrition experts point out that the Japanese have already attained the average level of nutrition necessary for a balanced diet. Under these market conditions, it will be very difficult for the government to raise the price support level as easily as in the past. New policy measures, such as a combination of price supports and deficiency payments, should be considered, aiming at more productivity in basic agricultural products so that those products can compete at least with the European Community's products. Yet despite the conditions of the domestic market, Japan, now a major economic power, will continue to be pressured by foreign countries to increase imports of agricultural products. In this harsh environment of the 1980s, the Japanese agricultural sector will have to substantially decrease production of rice, its major product, in order to match a forecast decrease in its demand, and Japanese farmers will have to face the difficult task of switching over to the production of other crops. In other words, within ten years one-fourth of the fields now reserved for rice will have to be planted with other crops in accordance with the government guideline. It would be socially and politically infeasible for Japan, a country which has limited space for agricultural production and which already must import great amounts of agricultural products, to allow these fertile rice fields to lie semipermanently fallow. The new crops planted in this rice land will probably compete to some extent with imported agricultural products. And it is likely that the competing products will be grains such as wheat, soybeans, and feed grains, which up to this time have not been a serious issue in U.S.–Japanese agricultural trade negotiations.

References

Norinsuisansho. 1979. (Ministry of Agriculture, Forestry and Fisheries) *Stable Supply of Foods and the Role of Agriculture* (Tokyo).
————. 1980. *Annual Report on the State of Agriculture in Fiscal Year 1980* (Tokyo).
Obara, Yoshio. 1952. *Imported Foods and Foreign Foods* (Tokyo, Grain Importers Association).
Ohwada, Keiki. 1980. "Agricultural Land Reform in Japan," in Japan Trade Center, *Trade in Agricultural, Forestry and Fishery Products* (Tokyo).
USDA-USDHEW. See U.S. Department of Agriculture-U.S. Department of Health, Education and Welfare.
U.S. Department of Agriculture-U.S. Department of Health, Education and Welfare. 1980. *Nutrition and Health: Dietary Guidelines for Americans* (Washington, D.C.).

10

Adjustment Policies for Japanese Agriculture in a Changing World

Yujiro Hayami

Development of Trade in Agricultural Products

Whenever there is friction between Japan and its trading partners, mention is invariably made of the closed nature of Japanese agriculture. The United States, Europe, and the Oceanic countries have repeatedly demanded that Japan liberalize its imports of agricultural products. Moreover, the high price of food has also occasioned criticism in Japan itself of the country's closed agricultural policies.

It is clear from table 10-1 that the food prices charged Japanese consumers are high by international standards. Although these figures collected by agricultural attachés to the U.S. Embassy tend to overstate Japanese prices, other data substantiate the conclusion that Japanese food prices are generally higher than those in the West.[1] It is obvious that such prices result from a protectionist agricultural policy. Of the twenty-seven items subject to import quota restrictions

Yujiro Hayami is professor of economics at the Tokyo Metropolitan University. The text of this chapter draws heavily on a study by the author for Prime Minister Ohira's Study Group on External Economic Relations (Hayami, 1980).

[1] This conclusion remains basically unchanged even in consideration of the data in MAFF (1979).

at present, twenty-two are agricultural products. Thus, it is no wonder that agriculture is a lightning rod for trade liberalization pressure.

Yet, this is not to imply that Japan's level of protection is substantially higher than that of other countries. Trade in agricultural products was rapidly liberalized in the process of Japan's rapid economic growth. As seen in table 10-2, the number of agricultural and marine products subject to import quota was reduced from seventy-three to twenty-two (see also table 10-3). Although Japan still continues to rank alongside France among the industrialized countries having the largest numbers of agricultural products subject to import quotas, these figures do not accurately reflect the extent of agricultural protection. The United States, for example, supplements its quota restrictions with General Agreement on Tariff and Trade (GATT) waivers on thirteen items, such as dairy products, and there are also legal provisions for invoking import controls when imports of meat exceed certain levels. The European countries' trade protection centers around variable import levies that are designed to eliminate the price difference between imports and domestic products; the levies thus collected are used to finance the European Community's (EC's) common agricultural policy. By comparison, Japan does not appear that protective of its agriculture relative to other industrialized countries.

In fact, Japanese agricultural and marine product imports increased sharply during the period of rapid economic growth, as shown in table 10-4. From 1965 to 1979, imports of agricultural, forestry, and marine products rose approximately fivefold, and imports of agricultural products alone 3.5-fold. Because there was only a marginal increase in agricultural, forestry, and marine product exports during this same period, a net foreign currency disbursement for agricultural, forestry, and marine products increased nearly sixfold, and there was likewise a 3.6-fold increase in the agricultural trade deficit. With the extremely rapid increase in the imports of industrial materials, agricultural products did come to account for a smaller percentage of the total import bill; yet Japan's doors may be said overall to have been very rapidly opened to agricultural imports.

The result has been a decline in Japan's self-sufficiency in foods (see table 10-5). There has been a precipitous drop in self-sufficiency in crops such as wheat, feed grains, and soybeans that are heavily land intensive and with which Japanese production is at a comparative disadvantage. Although complete self-sufficiency or even surplus production is maintained for rice with price supports, the self-sufficiency for all cereals is less than 40 percent, the lowest of any major industrialized country.

TABLE 10-1. INTERNATIONAL COMPARISON OF

	Food prices as percentage of Tokyo prices		
Cities	Boneless sirloin steak	Pork chops	Broiler chickens
Washington	24	56	43
Canberra	27	63	77
London	40	56	71
Paris	30	67	125
Bonn	36	77	77
Rome	34	67	83

Note: Ratios were calculated using the exchange rates current at the time of the survey.

Source: U.S. Department of Agriculture, *Foreign Agriculture* (October 1979).

The Logic of Agricultural Protection

Despite such rapid expansion in agricultural imports and the steep decline in food self-sufficiency, world opinion continues to press Japan for liberalization of its trade in agricultural products. Why is this? The long-term cause is the decisive comparative advantage which Japan has achieved in manufacturing production, and the short-term cause stems from Japan's export drives and major trade surpluses, which have occurred cyclically during the periods of economic recessions (such as the final stage of the Tokyo Round negotiations). In this sense, it is understandable that agricultural producers seek protection and should resist being sacrificed to preserve the advantages of other sectors.

It is almost an empirical law that agricultural protection increases when a country attains the more advanced stages of industrialization. Japan has been no exception. Table 10-6 gives a comparison of Japanese and West European protection or support for agriculture as measured by the ratios between agricultural output values in domestic prices and in international prices. As Japan's economy jumped to West European levels in the decade since beginning its rapid growth in the mid-1950s, so did Japanese agricultural supports also rise to West European levels.

RETAIL FOOD PRICES AS OF SEPTEMBER 4, 1979

Food prices as percentage of Tokyo prices

Eggs	Butter	Milk	Tomatoes	Rice
83	71	67	63	67
100	38	53	67	67
143	56	59	77	83
167	83	59	56	111
125	83	63	48	91
125	77	59	77	91

TABLE 10-2. INTERNATIONAL COMPARISON OF IMPORT QUOTA RESTRICTIONS

Country	Year	Number of commodities subject to import quotas		Total
		Agricultural and marine products	Mining and manufacturing products	
Japan	1969	73	45	118
	1970	58	32	90
	1971	28	12	40
	1972	24	9	33
	1973	23	8	31
	1974	22	7	29
	1975	22	5	27
	1978[a]	22	5	27
France	1978[a]	21	24	45
W. Germany	1978[a]	8	3	11
Italy	1978[a]	4	7	11
U.K.	1978[a]	6	6	12
U.S.	1978[a]	1	3	4

Source: Data provided by the Ministry of Agriculture, Forestry and Fisheries, Tokyo.
[a] January 1978 only.

TABLE 10-3. JAPAN: COMMODITIES SUBJECT TO IMPORT QUOTAS
UNDER THE JURISDICTION OF THE MINISTRY OF
AGRICULTURE, FORESTRY AND FISHERIES

Category and number of products	Commodities
Dairy products (3)	Milk and cream (fresh) Evaporated milk, etc. Processed cheese, etc.
Meats and processed meat products (2)	Beef Mixed meats and other processed products
Processed grain products (2)	Flour Flour meal and cracked barley
Fresh and processed fruit and vegetables (6)	Oranges, etc. (fresh) Oranges, etc. (temporary storage) Fruit juices and tomato juice Fruit purees and fruit pastes Processed pineapple products, etc. Tomato ketchup and tomato paste
Starches and sugars (2)	Dextrose, lactose, etc. Starch
Local agricultural products and seaweed (3)	Beans Peanuts (except for crushing for oil) *Konnyaku* roots and edible seaweed
Fish and shellfish (3)	Herring, cod, yellowtail, and some other fish as well as cod eggs (fresh, refrigerated, or frozen) Same as above (salted or dried) Scallops, scallop eyes, and cuttlefish (excepting *Monko* cuttlefish)
Others (1)	Other processed foods

Source: Data provided by the Ministry of Agriculture, Forestry and Fisheries, Tokyo.

In this connection, it should be noted that the public cost of supporting agriculture is more than the simple differential between the international price and the domestic consumer price. As taxpayers, the people also bear the burden of the government's price support disbursements (food control program budget deficits, and the like). According to D. Gale Johnson (1973, chapter 3), the total cost of

TABLE 10-4. JAPAN'S EXPORTS AND IMPORTS OF AGRICULTURAL PRODUCTS, SELECTED YEARS, 1965–79
(absolute numbers in billion yen)

Item	1965	1970	1979	1979 ÷ 1975
Exports				
Aggregate export value	3,042.6	6,954.4	22,531.5	7.4
Value of agric. & marine prod. exports	216.8	315.8	396.6	1.8
Value of agricultural product exports	64.0	139.7	165.0	2.6
Value of agric. & marine prod. exports as % of aggregate export value	7	5	1.8	—
Value of agric. prod. exports as % of aggregate export value	2	2	0.7	—
Imports				
Aggregate import value	2,940.8	6,797.2	24,245.4	8.2
Value of agric. & marine prod. imports	1,242.5	2,249.5	6,318.7	5.1
Value of agric. prod. imports	1,018.1	1,511.3	3,604.9	3.5
Value of agric. & marine prod. imports as % of aggregate import value	42	33	26	—
Value of agric. prod. imports as % of aggregate import value	35	22	15	—
Trade balance				
Aggregate export value – aggregate import value	101.8	157.2	−1,713.9	—
Value of agric. & marine prod. exports – value of agric. & marine prod. imports	−1,025.7	−1,933.7	−5,922.1	5.8
Value of agric. prod. exports – value of agric. prod. imports	−954.1	−1,371.6	−3,439.9	3.6

Note: Dashes = not applicable.
Source: Ministry of Finance, *Customs Statistics* (Tokyo, various issues).

TABLE 10-5. INTERNATIONAL COMPARISON OF FOOD SELF-SUFFICIENCY
(percentage)

Foods	Japan				France	W. Germany	Italy	Netherlands	U.K.	U.S.
	1960	1970	1975	1978[a]	1975	1975	1975	1975	1975	1975
All grains	83	48	43	37	152	80	74	23	64	174
Food grains	90	79	76	75	177	89	96	48	52	307
Rice	102	106	110	111	n.a.	n.a.	n.a.	n.a.	n.a.	n.a.
Wheat	39	9	4	6	n.a.	n.a.	n.a.	n.a.	n.a.	n.a.
Feed grains	66	6	2	2	138	74	54	15	71	151
Beans	44	13	9	9	70	30	96	11	28	120
Vegetables	100	99	99	97	94	35	115	201	76	102
Fruit	100	84	84	78	67	40	129	37	30	99
Dairy products	89	89	82	89	111	107	75	268	55	98
Eggs	101	97	97	97	105	80	95	168	99	101
Meats	93	89	77	79	98	84	73	183	73	97
All food products	91	79	76	75	—	—	—	—	—	—

Note: n.a. = not available. Dashes = not applicable.
Sources: Norinsuisansho (Ministry of Agriculture, Forestry and Fisheries), Shokuryo-Jikyu-Hyo (Food Balance Sheets) (Tokyo, various years); Organization for Economic Cooperation and Development, Food Consumption Statistics, 1970–75 (Paris, 1978).
[a] 1978 data are provisional.

TABLE 10-6. COMPARISON OF AGRICULTURAL SUPPORT RATIOS IN
JAPANESE AND WEST EUROPEAN COUNTRIES
(percentage)

Country	1955	1965
Belgium	34.4	28.9
France	21.6	29.2
W. Germany	27.4	36.8
Italy	35.3	37.9
Netherlands	12.9	18.3
U.K.	33.7	18.3
Japan	8.9	38.6

Note: Agricultural support ratios are calculated by subtracting the value of agricultural production
in international prices from the value of agricultural production in domestic prices and dividing
the remainder by the value of agricultural production in domestic prices.

Sources: Data prepared by the Japan Economic Planning Agency in Kenzo Hemmi, Nogyo (Agriculture) (Tokyo, Chikuma Shobo, 1970) pp. 90–91.

agricultural protection, including both the cost of higher consumer
prices and the burden of government disbursements, was equivalent
to 55 percent of agriculture's gross domestic product in the countries
of the European Community and 38 percent in the United States in
the late 1960s. Kenzo Hemmi (1978) has calculated the figure for
Japan in the same period at 51 percent.

This high degree of agricultural protection among the industrialized countries basically derives from the need to maintain social
stability within the growth process. Agricultural production may generally be characterized as inseparable from family life, and the farm
is both a place of production as well as family life. As the result, the
transfer of resources between the agricultural and the nonagricultural
sectors, especially the movement of labor, requires a period of adjustment measured in generations. On the other hand, since the demand for agricultural goods is inelastic, it is feared that relying purely
upon market mechanisms to restructure a shrinking agricultural sector in the face of rapid industrialization may well result in a sharp
reduction in the rate of return to agricultural labor and an income
differential between farm and city so great as to imperil social stability.
Failure to implement agricultural protection policies would likely have
made it difficult to maintain political stability or the underlying stability of rural life, which in turn would have threatened the political
basis on which Japan's rapid economic growth has been built.

Aside from the need for political stability, there are other reasons
why the protection of agricultural production is appealing. Basic is
the recognition that agriculture has a value far beyond a narrow

economic accounting. Ensuring stable food supplies is a case in point. Food is a primary need, and anyone who lived through the war will remember the nightmare of food shortages. Another reason for valuing agriculture beyond its narrow economic worth is that farms and rural villages play an important role as havens where the natural environment survives. Both security and nature are the public goods for which demand increases when per capita income rises. The fact that agriculture is more protected in highly industrialized economies derives from this increased preference for such nonmonetary values as social stability, food security, and environmental protection.

Problems of Structural Adjustment

Having achieved rapid economic growth and having clearly established the comparative advantage for its industry, Japan is inexorably faced with pressures for liberalization of agricultural imports. However, if this liberalization of agricultural imports is to mean a destruction of domestic agriculture, it will be resisted not only by the farmers but by all people who value the contribution which agriculture makes to society above and beyond its purely economic aspects. Herein lies the conflict between international harmony and agricultural protection.

The only long-term answer is to achieve structural adjustments in agriculture in order to foster domestic agriculture efficient enough to compete internationally. In fact, ever since the 1961 Agricultural Basic Law was enacted with the goal of making agricultural income levels equal to those in other industries, the Japanese Ministry of Agriculture, Forestry and Fisheries (MAFF) has worked untiringly to achieve this target through improving the agricultural structure (see chapter 5 by Egaitsu in this volume).[2] As indicated by the "selective expansion" slogan, this has meant policies designed to raise agricultural production efficiency and farm income by transferring resources from the production of farm products of low-income elasticities to those of high-income elasticities and by expanding the scale of operations. Yet despite these policy efforts, it proved impossible to achieve income equalization through agricultural restructuring alone and protective policies had to be resorted to, primarily because the rapid

[2] For more detail about the process of agricultural adjustments, see Hayami and coauthors (1975, chapter 3).

TABLE 10-7. INTERNATIONAL COMPARISON OF SCALES OF
AGRICULTURAL OPERATION
(hectares)

Country	Land per agricultural worker		Land per farm household	
	Agricultural land	Arable land	Agricultural land	Arable land
France	16	9	28	15
W. Germany	8	5	15	9
Italy	6	3	9	4
U.K.	28	10	70	26
U.S.	103	45	158	69
Japan	1.1	0.9	1.1	1.0

Notes: Arable land includes both cultivated land and land under perennial plants. Agricultural land includes arable land and permanent pastures. Land areas are from 1977 and populations from 1978 except for Japan where all data are from 1978.

Sources: U.N. Food and Agriculture Organization, Production Yearbook, 1978 (Rome, 1979); European Community, Yearbook of Agricultural Statistics, 1978 (Brussels, 1979); U.S. Department of Agriculture, Agricultural Statistics, 1978 (Washington, D.C., 1979); Prime Minister's Office, Bureau of Statistics, Rodoryoku Chosa, 1978 (Labor Survey) (Tokyo, 1979); Norinsuisansho (Ministry of Agriculture, Forestry and Fisheries), Nogyo Chosa, 1978 (Agriculture Survey) (Tokyo, 1979).

economic growth induced such rapid increases in nonagricultural income that agricultural restructuring and the improvements in labor productivity in agriculture could not keep pace.

The basic factor limiting Japanese agricultural productivity is the small size of farms. Looking at the scale of operation, Japan's average farm of 1.1 hectares of agricultural land, or 0.9 hectare of arable land, is well below the farm sizes of the other industrialized countries, as shown in table 10-7. Under the circumstances, it is difficult for Japanese agriculture to make efficient use of modern labor-saving technologies that would make them internationally competitive.

The average farm size showed virtually no increase during the period of rapid economic growth. As seen in table 10-8, the number of persons employed in agriculture declined by approximately half between 1960 and 1978 to bring agriculture's share of the total labor force down from 27 to 11 percent. Yet there was only a 20 percent decline in the number of farm households, and this, together with the conversion of some agricultural land to nonagricultural uses, held the average farm size to a 15 percent increase over the period (0.8 percent per annum)—a rate of increase which would require some ninety years for a mere doubling.

Obviously, the reason there was so little decline in the number of farm households despite the decline in the agricultural population is

TABLE 10-8. JAPAN: AGRICULTURAL LABOR, FARM HOUSEHOLDS, AND AREA UNDER CULTIVATION, SELECTED YEARS 1960–78

Item	1960	1965	1970	1975	1978	1978 ÷ 1960
Total labor population (000)	44,650	47,540	51,100	52,400	54,270	1.22
Agricultural labor population (000)	11,960	9,810	8,110	5,890	5,710	0.48
Agricultural labor population as percent of total labor population	26.8	20.6	15.9	11.2	10.6	—
Farm households (000)						
Full-time	2,080	1,220	850	620	620	0.30
Class A part-time	2,040	2,080	1,810	1,260	880	0.43
Class B part-time	1,940	2,370	2,740	3,080	3,280	1.69
Total	6,060	5,670	5,400	4,950	4,790	0.79
Area under cultivation (000 ha)						
Wet paddies	3,380	3,390	3,420	3,170	3,110	0.93
Fields	2,690	2,610	2,380	2,400	2,390	0.89
Total	6,070	6,000	5,800	5,570	5,490	0.91
Cultivated area per farm household (ha)	1.00	1.06	1.07	1.12	1.15	1.15

Note: Dash = not applicable.
Sources: Prime Minister's Office, Bureau of Statistics, *Rodoryku Chosa* (Labor Survey) and *Kokusei Chosa* (National Census) (Tokyo, various issues); Norinsuisansho, *Nogyo Census* (Agricultural Census) and *Sakumotsu Tokei* (Crop Statistics) (Tokyo, various issues).

the increase in the number of part-time farm households. Whereas approximately one in three farm households was engaged in farming full-time in 1960, the number has now declined to one in eight. During the same period, the number of class B part-time farm households (those whose nonagricultural income exceeds their agricultural income) has jumped from 30 percent to 70 percent of the total. It thus became common for farmers with secure nonagricultural employment to hold on to their land and to continue farming in their spare time by drawing upon supplemental labor from available family members. (For a more detailed discussion of part-time farming, see chapters 4 and 5 in this volume.)

As a result, full-time farmers have found it difficult to expand their operational scale. As of 1977, the per-farm area under cultivation for full-time farm households was a mere 2.3 hectares, and the average for "self-supporting" farm households (those whose income from agriculture is at least equivalent to the income of workers in other industries), a mere 3.7 hectares. Given this small scale of operation, it is impossible to develop internationally competitive agriculture in Japan.

Consequently, full-time or self-supporting farmers wishing to expand their scale of operations have had to turn to livestock, greenhouse crops, or other modes which do not require much additional land. As seen in table 10-9, full-time farmers and class A part-time farmers (those earning the majority of their income from farming) account for large percentages of the total livestock and greenhouse agricultural production while class B part-time farmers account for much of the rice production. Although only 8.9 percent of all farm households, self-supporting farms produce nearly 67 percent of the livestock and 64 percent of the greenhouse vegetables. However, these same self-supporting farms produce only 20 percent of Japan's rice crop.

Part-time farm households tend to concentrate on rice farming because it is a very stable crop offering a high return on only intermittent labor. Because rice marketing is carried out exclusively by the government, rice farmers are guaranteed a high price and can easily sell their harvest through agricultural cooperatives, the sole agents of government rice marketing. In addition, agricultural research and extension services have traditionally concentrated on the rice crop to the extent that rice cultivation has become highly standardized and there is little difference in productivity between part-time and full-time farmers. The fact that the production of Japan's staple crop has been geared to part-time farming in this way is thus a major factor

TABLE 10-9. JAPAN: COMPOSITION OF AGRICULTURAL PRODUCTION BY FARM CATEGORY, 1978
(percentage)

Farm category	Farm households	Area under cultivation	Agricultural production value			
			Total	Rice	Livestock	Greenhouse vegetables
Full-time farmers	12.5	24.3 (2.27)	28.1	15.3	42.6	44.4
Class A part-time farmers	17.8	31.6 (2.08)	39.8	36.3	44.6	46.5
Class B part-time farmers	69.7	44.1 (0.74)	32.1	48.4	12.8	19.1
Total	100.0	100.0 (1.15)	100.0	100.0	100.0	100.0
Self-supporting farmers	8.9	28.7 (3.72)	38.8	20.3	66.5	63.5
Others	91.1	71.3 (0.90)	61.2	79.7	33.5	36.5
Total	100.0	100.0 (1.15)	100.0	100.0	100.0	100.0

Note: Numbers in parentheses are average farm sizes in hectares.
Sources: Norinsuiansho (Ministry of Agriculture, Forestry and Fisheries), Nogyo Chosa, 1979 (Agricultural Survey) and Nokakeizai Chosa, 1978 (Farm Household Economy Survey) (Tokyo).

encouraging part-time farming and impeding any decline in the number of farm households.

The farmer's attachment to his land is another fundamental factor that has promoted part-time farming. This love of the land has been buttressed by a number of factors, among them an ancestral identification with the land, a desire to maintain the farm as a productive postretirement vocation, and the expectation of higher land prices in the future. More basically, the land tenure policies pursued since the postwar agrarian land reform have rejected any separation of ownership and cultivation rights.[3] Tenancy rights have been very strongly protected, and it has been almost impossible for landlords to evict tenants in any circumstances. Land rent has been controlled at an extremely low level, thus giving part-time farmers no incentive to lease out their holdings. Although a number of ways have been found to get around this in keeping with the recent drive to expand operational scale, including consigning the land or its management to the agricultural cooperative or establishing usage rights under a consolidation program, the fear still prevails that once let, land is lost forever. Under the circumstances, it is only natural that most farm sons, even those who secure stable employment in nonagricultural industries, tend to hold on to their land through part-time farming even if their operation is very inefficient.

The spread of part-time farming has in turn impeded attempts by full-time and self-supporting farmers to expand operational scale and improve productivity. It should be pointed out, however, that the increase in off-farm earnings has made it possible to achieve the goal of income equalization between farm and nonfarm families. As seen in table 10-10, in the 1960s average farm household income was well behind urban wage earners' income, by 11 percent on a per-household basis and 32 percent on a per capita basis. Yet this disparity was narrowed during the process of rapid economic growth until per capita farm household income exceeded per capita urban wage-earner income in 1975. The main force behind this rapid increase in farm household income has been the off-farm earnings. The nonagricultural income rose from approximately 50 percent of all farm household income in 1960 to over 75 percent in 1978. The importance of this nonagricultural income is also evident from the ironic fact that class B part-time farmers whose average farm is the smallest have the highest incomes, and full-time farmers whose farm size is the largest, the lowest.

[3] For postwar institutional reforms including land reforms, see Hayami and coauthors (1975, chapter 3).

TABLE 10-10. JAPAN: INCOME OF FARM AND URBAN WAGE EARNER HOUSEHOLDS, SELECTED YEARS 1960–78
(absolute numbers in thousand yen)

| | Farm households | | | | Urban households | | Income ratio | |
| | Per household | | | | | | | |
Item	Agricultural income	Nonagri-cultural income[a]	Total (1)	Per capita (2)	Per household (3)	Per capita (4)	Per household (1) ÷ (3)	Per capita (2) ÷ (4)
1960	225	224	449	78	502	115	0.89	0.68
1965	365	470	835	157	797	194	1.05	0.81
1970	508	1,084	1,592	326	1,390	358	1.15	0.91
1975	1,146	2,815	3,961	867	2,897	760	1.37	1.14
1978	1,197	3,823	5,020	1,113	3,702	969	1.36	1.15
Full-time	2,770	1,491	4,261	1,012	3,702	969	1.15	1.04
Class A part-time	3,042	2,254	5,296	1,074	3,702	969	1.43	1.11
Class B part-time	553	4,628	5,181	1,149	3,702	969	1.40	1.19

Sources: Norinsuisansho (Ministry of Agriculture, Forestry and Fisheries), Nokakeizai Chosa (Farm Household Economy Survey) (Tokyo, various issues); Prime Minister's Office, Bureau of Statistics, Toshi Kakei Chosa (Urban Household Economy Survey) (Tokyo, various issues).
[a] Nonagricultural income for farm households includes money earned by family members as seasonal laborers.

Policy Issues

Japanese agriculture in prospect

In seeking economic development that is based on international cooperation, it is necessary to liberalize agricultural trade. When applied to Japan, this further implies the need to foster agriculture of comparable scale and productivity with the industrialized countries of the West. So far, the expansion in part-time farming has been seen as a factor inhibiting expanded operational scale for full-time farmers. However, this same turn to part-time farming has also helped to equalize agricultural and nonagricultural income levels and has contributed importantly to social stability by preventing rural depopulation and urban overcrowding.

Such being the case, the dual demands for creating an internationally competitive agriculture and preserving social stability can best be met by enabling part-time farmers to stay in the rural villages and to reduce their own operations by consigning production to full-time farmers. Because the farmer's strong attachment to the land and the expectation that such land will become increasingly valuable make it impossible to expand the scale of agricultural operations through transfering land ownership, the only way left to expand operational scale is through activation of the land rental market.

Japanese agriculture should thus aim at creating the following features looking ahead to the twenty-first century. First, while guaranteeing highly stable employment opportunities in nonagricultural sectors, it should promote greater fluidity of cultivation rights so that some 90 percent of Japan's 5 million farm families can remain in rural villages keeping areas for home gardens while they work in nonagricultural occupations and consign the cultivation rights of the rest of their land to full-time farmers. If this is done, the approximately 10 percent full-time farmers will be able to expand the scale of their operations to an average of 8 to 10 hectares. This is comparable to the West German scale and, given Japan's good land productivity, would make it possible for Japanese agriculture to compete internationally.

Structural policies

Greater fluidity in land use rights is essential to the shift to such an agricultural structure, and this in turn requires assurances that rented land will be returned to landowners upon their request. Although schemes such as those for subcontracting cultivation under the auspices of agricultural cooperatives or village administrations should be encouraged, Japan should also effect drastic reforms in agricultural land laws.

Even if an expanded scale of operation is promoted, this will not in itself mean the achievement of internationally competitive agriculture, given the current production structure. Even if Japan achieves an operational scale on par with European Community levels, it will be difficult to compete internationally in wheat or feed grains with countries in new continents such as the United States or Australia. A major reorientation of agricultural production will be required for the shift to an open trade system. The Netherlands in table 10-5 is illustrative. The Netherlands has the lowest self-sufficiency in grains of any European country, even lower than Japan's, but at the same time is a major exporter of garden and livestock products because it has succeeded both in using its scarce land very efficiently and in maintaining an essentially pastoral environment. When cheap grains began to pour into Europe from the New World in the nineteenth century, France, Germany, and other European powers erected tariff barriers to protect domestic agriculture, whereas the Netherlands transformed its agriculture by making positive use of these cheap grains and specializing in production of the commodities that had a comparative advantage.

I believe the Netherlands is indicative of a direction Japanese agriculture should take. Of course, we must be fully aware of the differences between the economic environment in which Japanese agriculture operates today and that which existed for the Netherlands in the nineteenth century. Japan's industrialization has been very rapid in comparison to Europe's in that century, and thus our transition period must necessarily be shorter. At the same time, it will not be easy for Japanese farmers accustomed to agriculture centering on the traditional rice and cereal crops to switch to livestock-centered farming and to bring their productivity up to international standards. Therefore, greater governmental investment in technology and land infrastructure will be needed if the desired agricultural adjustments are to be achieved.

Rice prices and rice policies

The main obstacle to such a restructuring of Japanese agriculture is the high level of rice price supports. The price of rice paid to Japanese farmers was virtually at an international level until the mid-

1950s. It was raised sharply during the era of rapid economic growth until it is now five times or more international levels. During the period when the producers' price for rice soared, investments in technological development, extension services, and land improvement were concentrated on rice production to make rice Japan's most stable and most standardized crop. The result, as explained before, is that part-time farmers have come to rely upon rice. Meanwhile, there has been little expansion in the scale of operation of full-time farmers. The shift of agricultural resources from rice to other crops of high income elasticities has been blocked. Deficits in the rice-dominated Food Control Account have, together with the costs involved in the control of areas planted in rice, come to account for 30 to 40 percent of all MAFF budget items (see table 10-11). The fact that the Food Control Account eats up a large portion of the government's expenditure for agriculture makes it difficult to increase investments for agricultural restructuring.

Therefore, the price of rice must be held down before adjustments can be made that would lead to an open trade system. Although lower rice prices may not be welcomed by farmers, they will ultimately benefit even those self-supporting farmers who specialize in rice cultivation by promoting fluidity in cultivated land and, thereby, enabling them to expand their scale of operation. Holding down the price of rice is also needed to encourage the shift away from rice, where demand has been declining 2 to 3 percent per annum, to other crops where demand is increasing.

This shift away from rice cultivation must be promoted with a continuing concern for a desirable agricultural structure under free trade arrangements. The shift to barley or soybeans is now encouraged by the government. However, such a shift represents a most inefficient expediency in terms of comparative advantage. Rather, the main shift must be to roughage as the basis for livestock production, which is expected to continue a very rapid demand growth. As seen in table 10-12, Japanese intake of animal protein is still low by international standards. Because it is difficult to hope for any major increase in fish production, demand for meats, milk, and dairy products will likely continue to grow rapidly. There has been an especially sharp increase in consumption of beef and other meats over the past few years. Although milk and dairy products are currently in surplus, this glut is caused by a temporary stagnation in demand coupled with a sudden increase in production stimulated by excessive price supports. Demand for milk and dairy products can be expected to continue its long-term growth with appropriate pricing.

TABLE 10-11. JAPAN: THE FOOD CONTROL ACCOUNT IN THE TOTAL GOVERNMENT BUDGET AND THE MINISTRY OF AGRICULTURE, FORESTRY AND FISHERIES BUDGET
(absolute numbers in billion yen)

Year	Total government budget (1)	MAFF budget (2)	Food Control Account			Percentage of total budget (5)/(1)	Percentage of MAFF budget (5)/(2)
			Transfers to Food Control Special Account (3)	Costs of shift away from rice production (4)	Total (3) + (4) (5)		
1960	1,765.2	166.9	29.0	—	29.0	1.6	17.4
1965	3,744.7	404.9	120.5	—	120.5	3.2	29.8
1970	8,213.1	992.1	374.6	81.8	456.4	5.6	46.0
1975	20,837.2	2,289.2	811.4	106.1	917.5	4.4	40.1
1976	24,650.2	2,491.9	822.9	78.7	901.6	3.7	36.2
1977	29,346.6	2,770.7	730.5	95.6	826.1	2.8	29.8
1978	34,440.0	3,225.9	631.2	304.5	935.7	2.7	29.0
1979	39,667.6	3,621.8	753.8	228.1	981.9	2.5	27.1
1980	43,681.4	3,776.5	652.1	303.4	955.6	2.2	25.3

Note: Dashes = not applicable.
Source: Food Agency, Beika ni Kansuru Shiryo (Rice Statistics) (Tokyo, July 1981) pp. 156–157.

TABLE 10-12. INTERNATIONAL COMPARISON OF ANIMAL PROTEIN
            CONSUMPTION
(grams per person per day)

Year and country	Meats		Eggs and dairy products	Fish and shellfish	Total
	Beef	Total			
1975					
Australia	27.1	47.8	26.6	3.0	77.4
France	12.4	35.6	28.3	5.6	69.5
W. Germany	9.5	30.0	25.1	3.4	58.5
Italy	9.5	23.5	21.6	4.4	49.5
U.K.	10.3	25.7	27.5	2.2	55.4
U.S.	23.0	40.3	29.6	2.4	72.6
Japan	1.3	9.1	9.1	17.5	35.7
1978					
Japan	1.7	10.9	9.9	17.8	38.6

Sources: Norinsuisansho (Ministry of Agriculture, Forestry and Fisheries), Shokuryo-Jikyu-Hyo (Food
Balance Sheets) (Tokyo, 1978); Organization for Economic Cooperation and Development, Food
Consumption Statistics, 1970–1975 (Paris, 1976).

Although it may be difficult to shift profitably from rice toward
roughage production, given the current state of the art in Japan, it
should surely be possible to develop highly efficient mixed farming
if operational scale can be expanded and appropriate research and
extension activities promoted.

Price and trade policies

Concerted efforts for such structural adjustments seem to be the
only way to adapt Japanese agriculture to an open trade system. At
the same time, the international pressures on Japan make it impossible
to delay the liberalization of agricultural imports until structural adjustments are completed. It is thus necessary to formulate price and
trade policies consistent with the maintenance and development of
domestic agriculture.

As already noted, Japanese agricultural protection and trade restrictions are not especially severe in comparison with those of the
other industrialized countries. Rather, the problem is that Japanese
protection is concentrated in a small number of items such as beef
and oranges which, because their domestic price levels are so far out
of line with international prices, have become symbols of Japanese
protectionism. This is a highly undesirable situation, detrimental to
both our international relations and domestic consumer interests.

For a product such as beef, where the domestic industry is still in an infant stage and where demand is elastic enough that liberalization is expected to generate substantial increases in demand, there is every possibility that a combination of import liberalization and deficiency payments could meet the dual aims of promoting international cooperation and sustaining the maintenance and development of the domestic industry.[4]

In the case of oranges, rather than holding out for the negative policy of simply resisting import liberalization, it would be better to initiate a positive policy of seeking the *quid pro quo* of expanded U.S. imports of Japanese mandarin oranges (now restricted for plant quarantine reasons) and trying to expand both domestic and international demand by mixing imported orange or grapefruit juice with Japanese mandarin orange juice for a better quality, higher value product.[5]

There are also many possibilities besides juice where the liberalization of agricultural imports can be turned to an increase in exports of processed goods. In fact, there are a number of products such as spaghetti and *arare* (rice cookies) in which imports have increased so rapidly as to imperil the processing industry because the liberalization of product imports has not been accompanied by a similar liberalization in raw material imports. Moreover, this affliction is spreading to *miso* (bean paste), *shoyu* (soy sauce), *sake* (rice wine), and other industries as well. Such developments can only make matters worse for an already slumping rice demand. Here too, there is a need for reorienting agricultural policies hitherto based upon import restrictions.

The formulation of policies aimed at both international cooperation and domestic agricultural development requires a full and accurate understanding of supply, demand, production, and other aspects. While the Ministry of Agriculture, Forestry and Fisheries' statistical compilations are among the best in the world in the areas of production and the rural economy, the use of these data for market analysis and policy evaluation is not quite so well developed. The

[4] Such a plan for beef import liberalization was proposed by the Forum for Policy Innovation, a voluntary association of social scientists in Japan (Forum for Policy Innovation, April and June 1978). For an English summary, see Hayami (1979).

[5] At present, Japanese mandarin orange exports to the United States are restricted to Washington, Oregon, Idaho, Montana, Hawaii, and Alaska because of the fear of citrus canker. Moreover, except for Alaska, the other states have plant quarantine procedures that are much too rigorous, and it would not be unreasonable for Japan, in keeping with the principle of trade reciprocity, to demand a broader export market and a streamlining of quarantine procedures in return for allowing expanded U.S. orange exports to Japan.

ministry should try to expand analytical capability in those areas in cooperation with academic circles.

Food security

Until now, concern for food security has been used primarily to ward off liberalization and to promote food self-sufficiency. Yet the logical basis for developing such an argument is fragile indeed.

In discussing Japan's food security, it is first necessary to define the possible crises which may occur. These may be broadly classified into (1) diminished supplies and higher prices for foods as a result of poor harvests worldwide, such as happened in 1972–74; (2) a halt to imports because of war or some other catastrophe; and (3) a Malthusian crisis which might emerge if population grew relative to food supplies.

For the first case, it would not be very effective to increase the food self-sufficiency rate ignoring considerations of comparative advantages. The U.S. embargo on soybean exports is a frequently cited example of such a crisis, yet raising Japan's self-sufficiency in soybeans or wheat from between 3 and 4 percent at present to a future 10 percent would do very little to alleviate the panic caused by such a crisis. Moreover, any attempt to raise Japan's self-sufficiency to a meaningful extent would necessarily entail socially unacceptable costs. Effective policies to cope with such a crisis would be to diversify import sources and to cooperate with international stockpiling programs.

Nor would the maintenance of domestic self-sufficiency be at all effective in a crisis of the second type, a war-induced or other halt to imports. Because Japanese agriculture is heavily mechanized, and because any situation that would cut off food imports would also cut off oil supplies, peacetime self-sufficiency levels would be irrelevant to coping with such a crisis. The first means for preparing for such a crisis would be to enlarge domestic stockpiles. Expanded livestock farming would also be a very effective contingency step in that livestock can be slaughtered for meat in times of shortage and stockpiles of feed grains can themselves be used for food. Yet it is essential that the policies designed to survive such a crisis be implemented before the crisis is upon us. The seeds, materials, and manpower mobilization plans must be ready so that food rationing can be instituted, and pastures, golf courses, and other areas organized for cultivation as soon as the crisis strikes.

Dealing with the third possible crisis, a Malthusian food shortage, does require that Japan's agricultural production capability be maintained and enhanced. However, the need is for potential productive capacity, and not for continued production of products with which Japan is at a comparative disadvantage. So long as irrigation facilities and other land improvements are kept up, the land can be used for roughage production now and can be easily converted to grain production later should the situation demand. Agricultural research and experimentation must also be enhanced from the long-term point of view. Although domestic production of barley, soybeans, and other crops may be inefficient at present, this situation could change if the global supply–demand balance deteriorated sharply in the future. Our long-term security needs thus mandate that research be steadily pursued in preparation for such a contingency. Above all, the best policy for coping with such a Malthusian crisis is to cooperate with agricultural development in the developing countries thereby forestalling the crisis. Agricultural research and development is the most effective means for such cooperation.

Ensuring food security is one of the state's most important responsibilities, and food policies must be forcefully promoted to this end. However, to tie food security to a short-term improvement in domestic self-sufficiency not only impedes preparations for an open trade system but carries the very considerable risk of detracting attention from the programs that need to be undertaken for true security.

Conclusion

It is a general tendency that agricultural protection and supports increase when a country achieves a high level of industrialization. In this, Japan has been no exception. Yet this does not mean that Japan must ape the industrialized West in preserving its inefficient domestic agricultural sectors. Japan's part-time farmers have enabled it to solve the very difficult problems of equalizing agricultural and nonagricultural income levels while maintaining social stability in rural villages. It will be a truly unprecedented achievement if we can build upon this success to create a dual structure of (1) a small number of internationally competitive full-time farmers and (2) the rural majority continuing to hold titles to their land even as they earn the bulk of their income from nonfarm occupations while they continue to live in the villages earning the same income level as the efficient full-time farmers. In terms of this goal there is no tradeoff between trade liberalization and rural well-being. Such a goal cannot be achieved by agricultural policies alone. It must be based upon concerted efforts for industrial decentralization, improved transport systems, and other measures to ensure stable nonagricultural employment opportunities for people residing in rural villages. It must be planned and promoted as an integral part of a comprehensive national economic plan.

References

European Community (EC). 1979. *Yearbook of Agricultural Statistics 1978* (Brussels).

FAO. 1979. U.N. Food and Agriculture Organization. *Production Yearbook 1978* (Rome).

Forum for Policy Innovation. 1978a. "Gyuniku Yunyu Jiyuka-An" (A Plan for Beef Import Liberalization) mimeo (Tokyo, April).

————.1978b. "Gyuniku Yunyu Jiyuka-An no Hihan ni Kotaeru" (Reply to Criticisms on the Plan for Beef Import Liberalization) mimeo (Tokyo, June).

Hayami, Yujiro. 1979. "Trade Benefits to All: A Design for Beef Import Liberalization in Japan," *American Journal of Agricultural Economics* vol. 61, pp. 342–347.

————.1980. "Taigai Chosei to Ngoyo Mondai" (Agricultural Problems in External Coordination), in International Economic Policy Study Group, *Taigai Seisaku no Kihon* (Guidelines on International Economic Policy) (Tokyo, The Bureau of Finance Printing Office) pp. 181–214.

————, Masakatsu Akino, Masahiko Shintani, and Saburo Yamada. 1975. *A Century of Agricultural Growth in Japan* (Tokyo, University of Tokyo Press and Minneapolis, University of Minnesota Press).

Hemmi, Kenzo. 1970. *Nogyo* (Agriculture) (Tokyo, Chikuma Shobo).

————. 1978. "The Future Role and Costs of the Agricultural Sector in Industrialized Countries," in Wolfgang Michalski, ed., *The Future of Industrialized Societies* (Alphen aan den Rijn, Netherlands, Sijthoff and Noordhoff) pp. 123–133.

Johnson, D. Gale. 1973. *World Agriculture in Disarray* (London, MacMillan and Fontana, and New York, St. Martin's Press).

MAFF. Ministry of Agriculture, Forestry and Fisheries. *Noka Keizai Chosa* (Farmhouse Economy Survey) (Tokyo, various issues).

————. Ministry of Agriculture, Forestry and Fisheries. *Nogyo Chosa* (Agricultural Survey) (Tokyo, various issues).

————. Ministry of Agriculture, Forestry and Fisheries. *Nogyo Census* (Agricultural Census) (Tokyo, various issues).

————. Ministry of Agriculture, Forestry and Fisheries. *Sakumotsu Tokei* (Crop Statistics) (Tokyo, various issues).

————. Ministry of Agriculture, Forestry and Fisheries. *Shokuryo Jikyu Hyo* (Food Balance Sheets) (Tokyo, various issues).

————. 1979. Ministry of Agriculture, Forestry and Fisheries. *Shokuryo no Antei Kyokyu to Nogyo no Yakuwari* (Stable Food Supplies and Agriculture's Role) (Tokyo).

Ministry of Finance. *Tsukan Tokei* (Customs Statistics) (Tokyo, various issues).

Organization for Economic Cooperation and Development. 1978. *Food Consumption Statistics 1970–1975* (Paris).

Prime Minister's Office, Bureau of Statistics. *Toshi Kakei Chosa* (Urban Household Economy Survey) (Tokyo, various issues).

————. *Kokusei Chosa* (National Census) (Tokyo, various issues).

————. *Rodoryoku Chosa* (Labor Survey) (Tokyo, various issues).

USDA. 1978. U.S. Department of Agriculture. *Agricultural Statistics 1978* (Washington, D.C.).

————. 1979. U.S. Department of Agriculture. *Foreign Agriculture* (Washington, D.C., October).

11

Managing Our Agricultural Interdependence

Fred H. Sanderson

Major Trends in Japan

The transformation of Japan's food system

As the previous chapters have documented in great detail, Japan's food system has undergone a major transformation since World War II. From a traditional, almost vegetarian pattern characteristic of a developing country, the Japanese diet has shifted toward a Western one that, given Japan's limited arable land, inevitably involves increasing dependence on imported livestock feed to sustain the production of animal products. As a result of this evolution, Japan's dependence on food and feed imports has risen from 20 to 50 percent of the primary food energy consumed. Well over half of these imports come from the United States (Sanderson, 1978, pp. 12–13).

At the heart of the process has been the stunning performance of the industrial sector, which grew tenfold. This unparalleled spurt in industrial development provided the basis for a fivefold increase in Japanese incomes and virtually closed the gap between Japan and other industrialized countries.

Fred H. Sanderson is a guest scholar at The Brookings Institution.

Japanese agriculture emerged from this transformation with a substantially reduced labor force but a level of prosperity unknown to
earlier generations. As in other developed countries, this was the result
of increased agricultural productivity and of the growth of farmers'
income from nonfarm sources.

In the process, however, Japan has largely avoided the mass exodus
of people from rural areas that has taken place elsewhere. Given the
country's compact size, the rural population found it relatively easy
to take advantage of nonfarm employment opportunities without having to leave the countryside. For this and other reasons, Japan has
not gone through the process of consolidation of land holdings that
has characterized U.S. and European agriculture, and this has stood
in the way of efforts to increase the economic efficiency of Japanese
agriculture (Hayami, 1980, p. 97; Tsuchiya, 1976). But this problem
has been overcome to some extent by cooperatives which provide
economies of scale in purchasing, processing, and marketing and, to
a lesser extent, in production.

The effect of policy

The effect of policy on this process is a matter of intense debate.
Japan's agriculture is one of the most highly protected in the world.
As of 1972, the resource cost[1] of this protection was put at $5.5 billion,
or 52 percent of Japan's gross agricultural output. Three-fourths of
this is for grains (mainly rice) (Sanderson, 1978, p. 24).[2] Defenders
of this policy have argued that a high level of protection of grain
production is necessary to (1) maintain farm incomes at levels comparable to those achieved in other sectors; (2) slow down the exodus
to the cities; (3) maintain a high level of food security. Economists
have criticized the policy on the ground that protection of uneconomic
production (primarily grains) is not only extremely costly for Japanese
society as a whole but tends to delay the process of adjustment—
toward high-value crops and livestock products and nonfarm employment—which has been the main source of income growth of Japan's rural population. Moreover, to diversify their sources of income
may be a more effective way to keep people in rural areas than the
maintenance of grain prices at four times world market levels. That

[1] Difference between gross agricultural output (excluding intermediate products) valued at producer prices and valued at world prices.

[2] This estimate is based on the assumption that a gradual liberalization of Japanese
imports would not lead to significant increases in world prices. For 1977–78, the resource cost of protection may be estimated at $15 billion or 120 percent—the result of
the 65 percent appreciation of the yen since 1972, and of increased real prices received
by Japanese producers.

the policy is making an important contribution to Japan's "food security" has also been questioned (Sanderson, 1978, chapters 6 and 9).

The economic case is less clear cut where new lines of agricultural production are concerned. Here, the "infant-industry" argument applies: it is possible that livestock and fruit production in Japan would not have grown as fast without a measure of government support and protection. The question then becomes one of degree, method, and timing. It is arguable, for example, that even more support should have been given, at least initially, to further the development of efficient dairy and meat production but that more emphasis should have been placed on investment, technical, and managerial assistance, and less on high price supports and import restrictions that hamper market development. There also is a tendency for infant-industry protection to be extended long after the need for it has passed.

Long-term prospects

It is reasonable to expect that for the foreseeable future—say the next two decades—domestic demand will continue to be the dominant influence on Japan's agricultural production and trade. As incomes rise—although probably at a slower pace than in the past twenty years—the per capita demand for rice will continue to decline and the demand for most livestock products will continue to grow. The speed of this adjustment will depend, first, on Japan's rate of economic growth and, second, on price developments and policies.

Despite rapid growth in the past twenty years, the proportion of calories derived from animal products (including fish) in the Japanese diet is far less than is true of other industrial countries (see figure 11-1 and table 4-A-7 in Kuroda's chapter).[3] This difference may be attributed to a number of factors, including (1) the usual time lag between changes in income and changes in food consumption habits; (2) competing claims of other expenditures (housing, automobiles, and the like) on the family budget; (3) the high level of food prices, particularly of livestock products.[4] The figure suggests that as incomes

[3] The lag is somewhat overstated because of two factors. The use of per capita GNP instead of disposable personal income fails to allow for differences in investment ratios (particularly high in Japan). Also, the use of exchange rates instead of purchasing power parities tends to overstate the GNP of Japan in relation to that of most other countries.

[4] According to the U.S. Foreign Agricultural Service survey of food prices in major world capitals, as of July 3, 1979, prices of livestock products in Tokyo had the following relation to median prices in seventeen other capitals: beef, 3.5 times; pork, 1.5 times; chicken, 1.5 times; whole milk, 1.8 times; butter, 1.5 times. Only eggs and natural cheese compared favorably with prices elsewhere (Phillips, 1979).

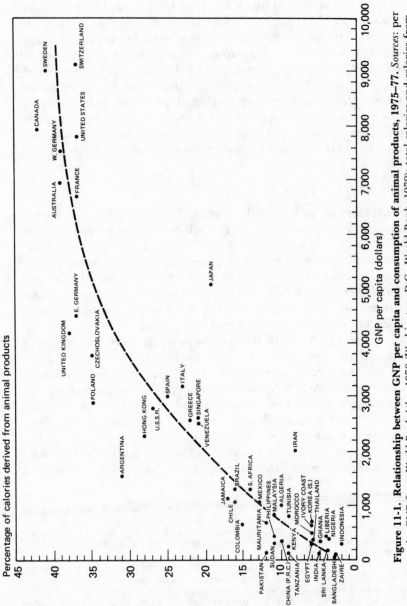

Figure 11-1. Relationship between GNP per capita and consumption of animal products, 1975–77. *Sources:* per capita GNP from *World Bank Atlas, 1978* (Washington, D.C., World Bank, 1979); total calories and calories from animal products from UN Food and Agriculture Organization, "Food Supply: Calories per Capita per Day," *Monthly Bulletin of Statistics* vol. 2 (November 1979).

rise, patterns of food consumption converge, and level off, at a point where approximately 40 percent of total calories consumed are derived from animal products.[5] It is likely that Japan will reach that level sometime in the remainder of this century (although price and trade policy will affect the timing).

Rough projections of food demand are shown in table 11-1. Per capita consumption in the base year 1977 was derived from the official food balance sheet of the Ministry of Agriculture, Forestry and Fisheries (MAFF 1979).[6] Calories derived from vegetable products and fish were converted into grain equivalents. Calories derived from livestock products (whether produced domestically or imported) were converted into the grain equivalent of feedstuffs required to produce them.[7] The resulting total per capita consumption of primary food energy, at 507 kilograms (kg) grain equivalent, is less than half that observed in Europe and North America and lower even than that estimated for countries with half Japan's current per capita income such as Greece, Hongkong, and Singapore. Japan's total consumption of primary food energy amounts to 56.8 million metric tons grain equivalent, of which about half is imported.

In projecting food demand to the end of the century, it was assumed that total per capita caloric intake in Japan, at 2,800 calories, would remain somewhat below that in Europe and North America. The proportion of calories derived from animal products is projected to approach the 40 percent figure characteristic of other high-income countries. All of the increase will have to come from livestock products; per capita fish consumption is expected to be maintained at the present (relatively high) level. Foodgrain consumption is projected to continue to decline, from 115 kg in 1977 to about 80 kg,[8] with rice accounting for nearly all of the decline. Meat consumption is projected to triple, to approximately the levels observed in the Scandinavian countries (which also consume much fish), but short of those pre-

[5] It is often asserted that this is a pattern peculiar to European societies and that Asian societies will never reach as high a level of consumption of animal products. However, experience in Hongkong, Singapore, and elsewhere seems to refute this contention.

[6] The MAFF data differ from those published by FAO and OECD because of differences in product definition and calorie conversion factors.

[7] The 6:1 energy conversion ratio is derived from data in University of California, 1974, table 4.4. The results for Japan shown here are consistent with a direct calculation of primary food energy consumption based on Japanese data on the consumption of food and feedstuffs.

[8] This estimate, which is higher than present foodgrain consumption in northwestern Europe and North America, allows for the greater role of rice and the lesser role of potatoes in the Japanese diet.

TABLE 11-1. JAPAN: PROJECTIONS OF FOOD DEMAND, 1977 TO 2000

Item	1977	2000
Total calories/capita/day:	2,490[a]	2,800
From vegetable products	2,060[a]	1,700
From animal products (incl. fish)	430[a]	1,100
From livestock products	329[a]	1,000
Annual per capita consumption of primary food energy (kg grain equiv., net):		
Vegetable products and fish[b]	265	221
Livestock products	242[c]	613[d]
Total	507	834
Population (millions)	112	130
Annual total consumption of primary food energy (million metric tons grain equiv.)	56.8	108.4
Per capita consumption of foodgrains (kg):	115.2	80
Rice	83.4	50
Wheat	31.8[a]	30
Per capita consumption of meat (kg)	20.3[a]	60
Per capita consumption of fish (kg)	34.1[a]	34
Total consumption (million metric tons):		
Foodgrains	13.0	10.4
Rice	9.4	6.5
Wheat	3.6	3.9
Meat	2.3	7.9
Fish	3.8	4.4
Livestock feed requirements (million metric tons grain equiv.):		
Total:	26.6[e]	
Imported (feedgrains and meal)	18.9[f]	
Domestic (mainly forage)	7.7[g]	

[a] From Ministry of Agriculture, Forestry and Fisheries, "Food Balance Sheet for FY1977," *Statistical Yearbook 1977–78* (Tokyo, 1979). (Note: consumption levels in Japanese statistics are lower than those estimated in UN Food and Agriculture Organization, "Food Balance Sheet, Japan. Average 1975–77," computer printout (New York, 1979).

[b] Calories converted to grain equivalent at the rate of 3,500 calories per kg, less 15 percent for seed and waste, equals 2,975 calories.

[c] Calories converted to grain equivalent at 2,975 calories per kg; then converted from livestock product to primary food energy basis by applying a food energy conversion factor of 6:1.

[d] Same as c except that energy conversion efficiency is assumed to increase, to 5:1.

[e] Estimated on basis of feed balance for 1972 as shown in Ministry of Agriculture and Forestry, *Long-Term Prospects of Production and Demand of Agricultural Products in Japan* (Tokyo, 1975), and changes in forage production and imports since 1972. Total digestive nutrients converted to grain equivalent using a factor of 1:0.8.

[f] Imports of feedgrains and meal, plus offals from imported wheat, less food and industrial uses. (U.S. Agricultural Counselor, Tokyo, "Commodity Statistics," July 1979).

[g] Residual.

vailing elsewhere in Northwestern Europe, and much lower than in the United States.

The projected changes in the food consumption pattern would lead to a 90 percent increase in total primary food energy requirements—even if a generous allowance is made for greater feeding efficiency.[9]

How much of this growth can be expected to come from domestic production? The historical record is not encouraging: production of primary food energy in Japan has virtually stagnated, at 28 million metric tons grain equivalent, since the mid-1950s, despite increasingly generous price incentives (Sanderson 1978, table 2-5 and chapter 3). The constraints on increased production have been both physical (limited land resources; an already high level of irrigation, fertilizer use, and crop yields) and socioeconomic (increasingly attractive nonfarm employment opportunities resulting, *inter alia*, in the decline of double-cropping). Assuming a continuation of present conditions and policies, the prospect is for a food energy deficit of 80 million tons, grain equivalent—about two and one-half times the present deficit.[10]

It is not easy to see what new factors or policies could change this prospect substantially. On the supply side, although there is room for yield increases for some crops (particularly forage crops), any significant growth in primary food energy output would require substantial increases in double-cropping. But even a return to the high cropping intensities of the mid-1950s (136 percent—a highly unlikely development) would raise Japan's primary food energy output by at most 10 million tons to 38 million tons, leaving a deficit of 70 million tons. Moreover, any increase in food energy output of this magnitude would require additional incentives that would be extremely costly to Japanese consumers and taxpayers.

The possibilities of reducing the deficit by restricting the demand for livestock products are also limited. Japanese policy makers will be faced with two basic trends that will stimulate demand: rising incomes and probable improvements in livestock production and in the efficiency of the distribution system that will reduce prices to the consumer. Only highly restrictive policies could offset these factors. Empirical evidence suggests that it would probably take a one-percent policy-induced increase in consumer prices to offset the demand-stimulating effect of a one percent increase in income.[11] It is ques-

[9] From 6:1 to 5:1.

[10] This estimate is consistent with the GOL projections by the U.S. Department of Agriculture (USDA, 1978c) which indicate Japanese imports of 61 million tons of grain and soybeans by 2000—about 2½ times present imports.

[11] See Sanderson, 1978, table 5-14, for estimates of income and price elasticities of demand for livestock products.

tionable whether the Japanese public, which is beginning to react to the present level of agricultural protection, would tolerate more restrictive policies.

Major Trends in the United States

America's second agricultural revolution

Following a period of slow growth during the first four decades of this century, American agriculture underwent a second[12] revolution during the next four decades. Farm output doubled during this period, with all of the growth attributable to productivity per unit of input. Crop production doubled, although no more land is cultivated today than forty years ago. Nor is there much evidence that productivity growth is slowing down, as the accompanying table shows.

Period	Percent increase in farm output per unit of input	Percent increase in crop production per acre	Percent increase in crop production per worker/ hour
1939–49	+20	+17	+66
1949–59	+24	+21	+85
1959–69	+15	+25	+77
1969–79	+20	+19	+92

The high rate of growth of factor productivity, averaging 1.8 percent annually, has been the result of economies of scale, factor substitution, changes in regional and commodity patterns of production, and technological advances (genetic improvements, pest control, and, generally, improved cultivating and feeding practices). Crop production more than doubled, using the same amount of land and one-fourth the labor, but three times the mechanical power and machinery, twelve times the fertilizer, and twenty-five times the nitrogen compared with forty years ago. The regional pattern of land use has changed, with declines in less productive regions such as the North-

[12] The first American agricultural revolution, marked by the transition from human power to horsepower, more effective machinery, and a general shift from self-sufficient agriculture to production for the market, occurred in the second half of the nineteenth century. See Rasmussen, 1974.

east, the Appalachians, the Southeast, and the Southern Plains offset
by increases in the Corn Belt and the Western states (USDA, 1976
and 1980a).[13]

Economies of scale were achieved through specialization and the
consolidation of farms. As the labor-intensive, diversified farm gave
way to the specialized, capital-intensive operation typical of American
farming today, the farm population shrank from 31 million in 1940
(23 percent of the total population) to 8 million (3.7 percent); the
number of farms declined from 6 million to 2.7 million; the average
farm size increased from 167 acres to 400 acres; the average net asset
value increased from $7,000 to $210,000. In 1977, the top 6 percent
of American farms, with sales over $100,000 and average net assets
over $1 million, accounted for 52 percent of all farm sales; the top
19 percent, with sales over $40,000 and average net assets of $575,000,
accounted for 78 percent of total sales (USDA 1978a and 1980a).

Farmers' incomes have been rising much faster than those of the
nonfarm population,[14] mainly because of the rapid growth of productivity per farm and per person employed in farming, and also
because of the increased importance of income from nonfarm sources.
(In recent years, from one-half to two-thirds of the average farmer's
total net income came from nonfarm sources; in the case of small
farmers, the proportion was about four-fifths.) This income growth
occurred despite the fact that real prices of most farm products have
tended to decline.[15]

Low food prices have favored domestic consumption and exports.
Per capita meat consumption, at 110 kgs (dressed carcass weight)
(OECD, 1980),[16] is among the highest in the world. Per capita grain
consumption for feed, at its peak level of 709 kgs in 1972, was three
times that in Western Europe and seven times that in Japan (USDA
1980b). There are indications, however, that per capita consumption
of meat, as well as feedgrains, has leveled off. In fact, the proportion
of calories derived from animal products declined, from 41 percent
in 1954–56 to 40 percent in 1966–68, and to 37 percent in 1975–77

[13] The recent upsurge of export demand has caused a comeback in some of the
declining regions, notably the Southeast and the Southern Plains.

[14] The real average disposable income per capita rose 5.5 times for the farm population
but only 2.3 times for the nonfarm population between 1939 and 1978 (see USDA,
1979b). (Nominal income deflated by Consumer Price Index.)

[15] The parity ratio (prices received over prices paid by farmers) declined from 81
percent in 1940 to 72 percent in 1970 and was only 67 percent in 1977. The trend is
overlaid by boom periods caused by strong export demand (1941–54, 1972–76, and
1978–79). See figure 11-2.

[16] On the same basis, Japanese consumption is about 25 kg.

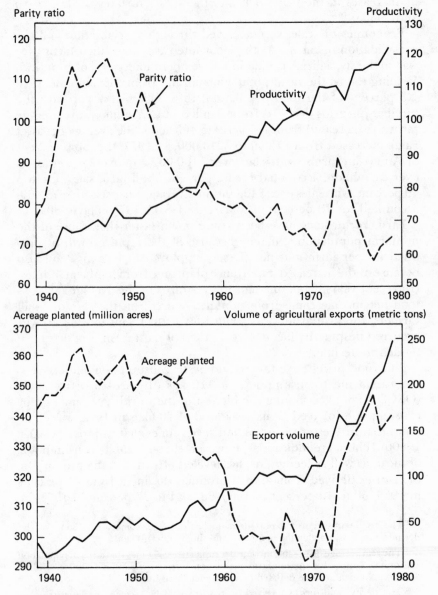

Figure 11-2. U.S. agriculture, 1939–79: productivity, parity ratio, export volume, and acreage planted. *Sources*: U.S. Department of Agriculture, *Agricultural Statistics* (Washington, D.C., 1972 and 1977); U.S. Department of Agriculture, *Changes in Farm Production and Efficiency* (Washington, D.C., 1978).

(FAO, 1960 and 1979a).[17] Thus domestic demand is no longer a dynamic factor: future growth in domestic food consumption probably will not exceed the rate of population growth.

As a consequence, American agriculture is becoming increasingly dependent on exports to absorb a large part of its productivity growth. Without a rapidly rising level of exports, and given the largely autonomous nature of productivity growth, the United States is faced with the need to reduce its cultivated acreage. This is, in fact, what happens in periods of slack foreign demand. It is only in periods of booming exports (for example, 1940–54 and 1973–to date) that the United States has been able to reactivate its "ready reserve" of idle cropland (see figure 11-2).

A widely quoted measure of this dependence is the fact that today one out of every three acres of U.S. land under crops produces for export (as compared with one out of five in 1960). Grains and soybeans alone account for two-thirds of the total value of U.S. agricultural exports. These crops have also accounted for virtually the entire export growth whereas some traditional exports such as cotton and tobacco have been stagnating or declining.

The effect of policy

In general, agricultural price and income policy has not impeded the process of transformation of American agriculture; in fact, it is likely that on balance it has accelerated it.

To the extent that American farm policy was successful in raising farm incomes, the benefits went primarily to large commercial farmers because they were linked to the volume of production (deficiency and other payments)[18] or to the size of a farmer's income or assets (various tax and loan privileges). One of its principal effects was the escalation of land values which, in turn, enabled efficient farmers to secure loans to purchase equipment and to buy out their neighbors. "The government programs were not designed to produce this outcome . . . [but in effect they] benefited the alert and the strong at the expense of the small and the weak" (W. Cochrane and Ryan, 1976).

The technique of production control has undoubtedly spurred productivity because it limited only acreage but left the producer free to

[17] Most of this decline is caused by the sharp drop in the consumption of animal fats (USDA, 1979c).

[18] The ceilings on deficiency payments per farm, introduced in the 1970s, "have had little impact either on reducing total payments to the larger producers or on slowing the transition to fewer and larger farms" (USDA 1978b).

increase other inputs to raise yields. Insofar as agricultural policy stabilized farm income, it encouraged investment. Traditional strong government support for agricultural research and extension services continued to play an important role in promoting productivity growth.

On the whole, American farm policy has not stood in the way of readjustments in the pattern of production in response to changes in demand. Rigidities in the commodity programs were progressively eliminated. (An example is the change from acreage restrictions for specific crops to set-asides applying to total cropland.) Protectionism was limited, in the main, to dairy products, sugar, and (in recent years) beef; but the level of protection, though rising, still is lower than in Europe or Japan. (In the case of beef, it is arguable that the protected prices received by American producers are no higher than those that would prevail in the world market under conditions of free trade.)

For export crops, the thrust of American policy has been aimed at stabilizing farm incomes while holding market prices at levels designed to maintain competitiveness in the world market. The policies for accomplishing these objectives evolved in several stages. In the 1950s the government attempted to prop up farm prices through high price supports and to cope with the resulting surpluses by export subsidies and surplus disposal programs. Inducements for idling acreage met with little success, and grain stocks reached a peak of 116 million tons in 1961—about eight months' consumption and exports, a level then considered "burdensome."

In the 1960s American policy shifted to a system of low support prices (nonrecourse loans at price levels deemed to be competitive in world markets), supplemented by direct subsidies (deficiency payments equal to the difference between market prices and a "target price"), which were, however, contingent on the farmer's cooperation with acreage limitations. The net effect of this system on grain production, market prices, and exports was essentially neutral, with acreage controls slightly more than offsetting the production-stimulating effects of the deficiency payments;[19] at the same time, the system did improve farm incomes in a period of slack demand.

However, the very success of the new approach in reducing "excess stocks" proved to be the source of a new and unexpected problem. As foreign demand for American grain soared in the wake of short crops in the USSR and South Asia, 1972 beginning stocks (73 million tons) were drawn down rapidly and grain prices tripled. Soybean

[19] Thus, Mayer, Heady and Madsen (Farm Programs for the 1970s) found that if all farm programs had been eliminated in 1966–67, U.S. grain production would have been only moderately (9 percent) greater than was actually the case. (Quoted in Johnson, 1974.)

prices also surged. Major crop shortfalls in North America in 1974 and in the USSR in 1975 compounded the problem.[20]

Did American food policy meet the test of the "food crisis"? Defenders of the policy would argue that the United States did perform its traditional role as a balance wheel in the world market. Except for the two-month embargo on soybean exports (necessitated by panic among foreign buyers), American supplies remained freely available, at world market prices, to domestic and foreign buyers alike. American consumers had to compete for the available supplies and accept reduced consumption. American grain producers rose to the challenge by increasing acreage by 27 percent; production caught up with demand, allowing prices of grains and soybeans to decline to levels roughly equivalent, in real terms, to those prevailing before the crisis. The critics would point to the tripling of grain and soybean prices which became a major factor in launching the worldwide inflation that was subsequently intensified by the energy price explosion; the sharp reduction in U.S. feedgrain consumption which was necessary to make an additional 90 million tons of grain available to the rest of the world; the massive liquidation of livestock which is at the root of the subsequent beef shortage; the damage done to the reputation of the United States as a reliable supplier of farm products at stable prices; and the fact that the crisis could have been avoided if it had not been for the excessive acreage restrictions in 1967–72. The lesson to be drawn from this experience was that American farmers cannot be counted upon to increase production quickly enough to avoid sharp price increases in the event of a series of major crop shortfalls; it took four years of very high prices before production caught up with demand. It was clear that substantial reserves would be required to meet such contingencies.

Drawing on this experience, the Carter administration introduced a farmer-held grain reserve of modest size to be built up by offering farmers incentives (storage payments and an interest-free loan after the first year) to hold grain off the market for three years or until prices reach a specified release level and to sell when that level is reached or exceeded. The objective was to stabilize grain prices within a band between the acquisition price (equal to the loan rate) and the release price (140 percent of the loan rate for wheat and 125 percent for feedgrains). The legislation also provided that as long as this program was in effect, government-held stocks could not be released at less than 150 percent of the loan rate (as compared with 115 percent

---

[20] Other factors contributing to the long-term growth of foreign demand, such as rising incomes and the depreciation of the dollar, played only a minor role in the 1972–75 upsurge of food prices (Sanderson, 1975).

in earlier legislation). The program did not obligate the farmer to release the reserve at any particular price: he could hold beyond the release point by assuming storage costs from that point on, and he could hold even beyond the point where the government loan is called (175 percent of the support price for wheat and 140 percent for feedgrains) by securing a commercial loan (USDA, 1979d).[21]

The farmer-held reserve has worked as expected. It reached its modest target of 33 million tons (11 million tons of wheat and 22 million tons of feedgrains) early in 1979 but subsequently declined to 23 million tons in October as market prices rose above the release levels. In early August 1980, the reserve was back to 30 million tons, of which 23 were feedgrains. After the 1980 drought, grain in the reserve declined again. Following the bountiful 1981 harvest, the reserves are being replenished.

More significant is the fact that the total U.S. grain carry-over, after recovering from a low of 27 million tons in 1975 to 73 million tons in 1978, failed to rise above that level—partly as a result of strong export demand and partly because of the acreage set-asides which were reintroduced in 1978 and 1979 in response to pressure for higher farm prices. As a result, U.S. carry-over stocks were not significantly greater in 1979 and 1980 than the stocks that proved inadequate in 1972.

Long-term prospects

Concerns about the future turn mainly around three kinds of questions:

1. Has there been a drastic change in the world supply–demand picture that will put increasing pressure on America's agricultural resources? If so, does the United States have the capacity to meet the rising demand? What are the implications for production costs?

2. Faced with a strong (and perhaps relatively inelastic) export demand, will the United States be tempted to lead an export cartel to raise world prices of grains and soybeans above competitive levels?

3. Will there be greater instability in world markets? If so, will U.S. policy be prepared, as in the past, to exert a stabilizing influence and to absorb market fluctuations?

[21] The grain reserve program continues, with some modifications, under the Reagan administration. The target has been raised to 45 million tons (19 million tons of wheat and 26 million tons of feedgrains). The secretary of agriculture is authorized to set loan rates for grain entering the reserve at higher levels than the regular loan rates and to set release prices at levels approximating the national average cost of production. The call price at which farmers were required to repay their loans was eliminated; the fact that storage payments cease and interest becomes payable when the release price is reached is considered sufficient to induce farmers to market their reserve stocks.

Demand projections

Demand projections for the United States to the year 2000 have been made by the U.S. Department of Agriculture (USDA, 1978c) and Resources for the Future (Crosson and Brubaker, 1982). The projections for total grains and soybeans are shown in figures 11-3 and 11-4, together with historical data on domestic use and exports from 1959/60 to 1979/80.

As indicated earlier, the domestic use of grain per capita, which increased from 770 kgs in 1960 to a peak of 860 kgs in 1972, is apparently leveling off. The present "normal" level is somewhat uncertain because of the sharp fluctuations in feed use during the past ten years. The sudden upsurge of export demand in 1972–75 cut sharply into domestic use so that per capita consumption declined to 660 to 700 kgs in 1974–76 and even now has recovered to only 800 kgs, a level which is still 7 percent short of the 1972 peak. After the expected rebuilding of cattle herds in the next few years, total grain utilization may regain the 1972 level but it is unlikely to exceed it for more than short periods. If it assumed that the trend level of per capita grain use will not exceed 860 kgs by the end of the century, total domestic demand may be projected at 200 to 214 million metric tons.[22]

United States grain exports have more than tripled during the past twenty years, from 30 million tons to over 114 million tons in 1981/82, most of the increase having occurred since 1971. Projections to 2000 range between 110 and 160 million tons, depending mainly on the assumptions one makes about the effective demand from developing countries.[23]

Adding the projections for domestic use and exports, it would appear that we can expect the total demand for U.S. grain to increase

[22] Based on U.S. census low and medium projections of U.S. population (234 and 248 million, respectively) (U.S. Department of Commerce, 1979). This projection is similar to the RFF projection but substantially lower than the GOL projection. It is roughly in line with the trend observed in 1960–80.

[23] The GOL and RFF projections shown in figure 11-3 represent a normal (trend) scenario, with the lower RFF projection (RFF 2) assuming a declining U.S. share in total grain exports. FAO projections (1979c) indicate total net grain import requirements by developing countries of about 150 million tons by 2000 (up from 32 million tons in 1975), on the trend assumption (table 3-2 in the FAO source). This would suggest a total import demand by food deficit countries (including Japan and the communist countries) of about 250 million tons. Assuming a constant U.S. share in total grain exports of net exporting countries (60 percent), U.S. exports would be about 150 million tons. (This is roughly in line with the trend observed in the past twenty years but much less than what would be indicated by the trend in the last ten years.) FAO's "normative assumption," based on accelerated agricultural development in the developing countries, would indicate a much lower trade volume (net LDC imports of 90 million tons, suggesting U.S. total grain exports of only 110 million tons).

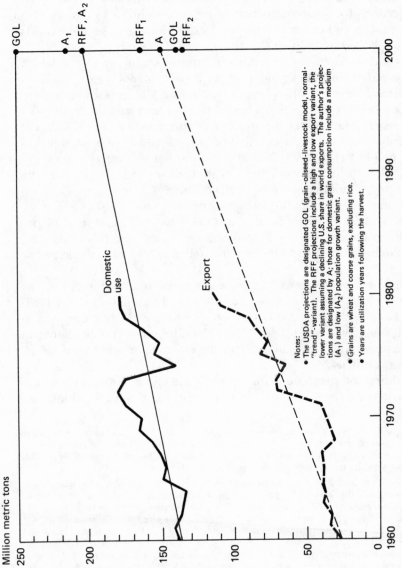

Figure 11-3. U.S. grain: domestic use and exports, 1960–80 and projections to 2000. *Sources:* U.S. Department of Agriculture, *Reference Tables on Wheat and Coarse Grain Supply-Distribution,* Foreign Agricultural Circular, Grains, April 1974 and *Reference Tables on Wheat, Corn, and Total Coarse Grain Supply—Distribution for Individual Countries,* Foreign Agricultural Circular, Grains, February 1980 (Washington, D.C.).

Million metric tons

250

200

150

100

50

0

1960   1970   1980   1990   2000

Domestic use

Export

GOL

A_1

RFF, A_2

RFF_1

A
GOL
RFF_2

Notes:
• The USDA projections are designated GOL (grain-oilseed-livestock model, normal-"trend" variant). The RFF projections include a high and low export variant, the lower variant assuming a declining U.S. share in world exports. The author's projections are designated by A; those for domestic grain consumption include a medium (A_1) and low (A_2) population growth variant.
• Grains are wheat and coarse grains, excluding rice.
• Years are utilization years following the harvest.

Million metric tons

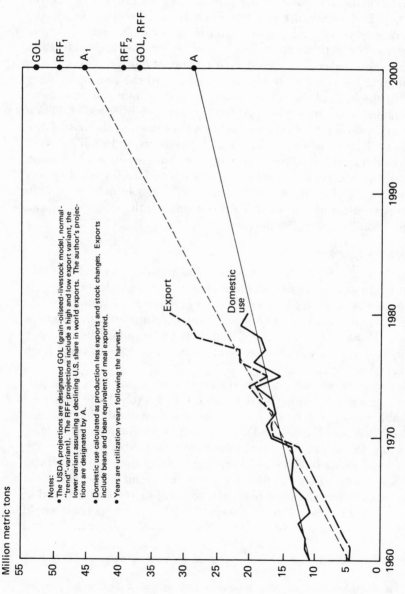

Figure 11-4. U.S. soybeans: domestic use and exports, 1960–80 and projections to 2000. *Sources:* U.S. Department of Agriculture, *Foreign Agricultural Circular, Oilseeds and Products,* various issues, and *Fats and Oils Situation,* various issues (Washington, D.C.).

Notes:
• The USDA projections are designated GOL (grain-oilseed-livestock model, normal-"trend" variant). The RFF projections include a high and low export variant, the lower variant assuming a declining U.S. share in world exports. The author's projections are designated by A.

• Domestic use calculated as production less exports and stock changes. Exports include beans and bean equivalent of meal exported.

• Years are utilization years following the harvest.

Export

Domestic use

GOL
RFF$_1$
A$_1$
RFF$_2$
GOL, RFF
A

from the 1980 "trend" level of about 280 million tons[24] to somewhere around 375 million tons. This would represent an increase of 95 million tons, or 34 percent.

The demand for soybeans has been rising even faster than that for grain: U.S. domestic use went up from 10 to 20 million tons in the past twenty years, and exports from 5 to 33 million tons, despite increased competition from Brazil (and, recently, Argentina). Both the grain-oilseed-livestock model (GOL) and RFF projections indicate a domestic use of 37 million tons by the end of the century—rather high in the light of the trend, which suggests a figure of only about 30 million tons. The export projections vary widely, from 39 million tons in the lower RFF estimate to 53 million tons in the basic GOL scenario. Extrapolation of the trend suggests about 46 million tons. Projected total demand thus varies between roughly 70 and 90 million tons, the trends suggesting about 75 million tons. The projected growth of total demand is, therefore, in a range of 20 to 40 million tons (40 to 80 percent), with the most likely outcome, in the writer's opinion, about 25 million tons (50 percent).[25]

Supply projections

Could the United States manage a 34 percent increase in grain production and a 50 percent increase in soybean production?

To answer this question, we make two alternative assumptions: (1) that yields per acre will continue to increase at the rates observed during the past twenty years; (2) that there will be no further increase in yields so that any additional production would have to come from increased acreage.

Grain yields per acre have increased by 60 percent during the past twenty years.[26] Assuming a continuation of this trend, the projec.ed 95 million ton (34 percent) increase in total demand during the next twenty years could be secured from increased productivity, while leaving some 45 million acres available for planting other crops.

Soybean yields have been increasing by only about 40 percent in the past twenty years. A continuation of this trend would be almost sufficient to meet the most likely (50 percent) increase in demand in the next twenty years, but the maximum (80 percent) increase would require the addition of 10 million acres. The total increase in demand

[24] 1980 "trend" demand consisting of 180 million tons for domestic use and 100 million tons for export.

[25] This projection does not allow for the possible effects of the gasohol program enacted in 1980, discussed below.

[26] Putting the 1980 "trend" yield at 1.6 tons per acre.

for grains and soybeans combined could be met on 35 million fewer acres than are currently planted to these crops.

If we assume no further increases in yields, the additional demand for 95 million tons of grain would require 60 million additional acres. For soybeans, the additional acreage requirement would range from 23 to 46 million acres, with the most likely increase requiring 30 million acres. The total additional acreage required to meet the increased demand for grains and soybeans combined would thus be between 83 and 106 million acres, with the most likely requirement around 90 million acres.

It is safe to predict that the actual outcome will be somewhere between these extremes. The rate of growth of yields is generally expected to slow down somewhat. The fate of similar predictions during the recent "food crisis" suggests, however, that we are still far from the end of the line: yields have resumed their upward trend despite increased energy costs and reduced fertilizer response ratios where fertilizer use is already high. It appears that considerable increases in average yields are still possible even in the absence of new technological breakthroughs, that is, through the more widespread application of the best technology presently available.

But even on the unlikely assumption of no further increases in yields, American agriculture could meet the projected demand by bringing additional land into cultivation. Although estimates of potential cropland vary widely, depending on the criteria for what constitutes acceptable quality, the most conservative of these estimates, the National Resources Inventory of 1977 (National Agricultural Lands Study, 1981), suggests that 127 million acres have high or medium potential for conversion to cropland (36 million acres with high potential and 91 million with medium potential).[27] The high potential acreage would present no significant development problems. The 127 million acres would add 31 percent to the 1977 cropland base of 413 million acres. However, because most of the potential acreage (90 million acres) is now in pasture and rangeland, its conversion to cropland would reduce the total pasture land by 16 percent and this would have a partially offsetting, adverse effect (of the order of 8 to 10

[27] Corresponding estimates by the U.S. Soil Conservation Service (USDA, 1977) show 78 million acres with high conversion potential and 33 million with medium potential. Other estimates of U.S. land resources are substantially higher. The President's Science Advisory Committee (PSAC, 1967) put the potentially arable land in North America at twice the land actually cultivated. The National Inventory of Soil and Water Conservation Needs, undertaken by the U.S. Soil Conservation Service in 1958 and 1967, put the additional land suitable for regular cultivation at 265 million acres, or 73 percent of the land actually used for crops (USDA, 1962 and 1975).

percent) on total livestock feed supply.[28] On the other hand, there is considerable scope for increased double-cropping (for example, winter grains followed by soybeans).

What are the implications of this outlook for production costs? Even those who agree that American agriculture has the capacity to meet prospective demand tend to assume that the demand can only be met at higher costs. This conclusion is not supported by experience, however: real prices of grains and soybeans have shown stable or declining trends until the recent food crisis and in 1977/78 they dropped back to within 15 percent of the 1971 level as production caught up with demand.[29] (The subsequent rise can be attributed to the combined effects of acreage set-asides, strong export demand, and the 1980 drought.) Thus far, therefore, any cost-raising effects of diminishing returns were offset, or more than offset, by the cost-reducing effects of economies of scale, factor substitution, improved cultivation practices, and other technological advances.

One reason often advanced to support the expectation of increased real prices of grains and soybeans is the sharp increase in energy prices. This new factor has, of course, increased production costs throughout the economy. But contrary to what one might expect, its effect on agricultural production costs, and particularly on those of basic crops, is less severe than in the economy generally. Despite its high degree of mechanization, American agriculture consumes less energy per unit of output than other sectors of the economy.[30] It follows that energy-related price increases should be less for agricultural products than for nonagricultural products and services, and "real prices" of grains and soybeans, in terms of the general producer price index, should actually decline.

The key to holding down real production costs is a rate of (all-factor) agricultural productivity growth which continues to match or exceed[31] that in the rest of the economy. The resources available to American agriculture—climate, soil, capital, technology, and managerial skills—favor such an outcome. The outcome does not depend on increased output being achieved exclusively by increasing yields per acre. Because a considerable amount of high quality land is avail-

[28] Concentrates and roughage, in grain equivalents.

[29] Prices received deflated by index of prices paid by farmers. At the same time, the "parity index" fell back to its trend level (see figure 11-2).

[30] Direct and indirect energy use by U.S. agriculture accounts for 2.9 percent of total U.S. energy use (FEA, 1976). This compares with a 5.5 percent share of agricultural deliveries to other sectors in total value produced (U.S. Department of Commerce, 1974).

[31] Productivity growth would have to be somewhat higher in agriculture than in the rest of the economy if it is assumed that input prices in agriculture will rise faster than input prices generally.

able, the most efficient way to accomplish it may well be through a combination of increased yields and expanded acreage.

Policy projections

The demand and supply projections presented here are based on the assumption that there will be no radical change in the agricultural production, utilization, and trade policies of the United States. Although this assumption is probably justified, it does call for some caveats.

With export markets seemingly assured in recent years, the need to remain competitive in world markets has lost some of its force in guiding U.S. policy. While resisting more extreme demands by some farm groups, the Carter administration shifted the emphasis of its farm support policy from deficiency payments toward higher market prices and used the available policy tools (acreage set-asides and diversion payments, increasingly attractive terms for farmers to store grain, and direct government purchases and subsidies for conversion of grain to alcohol) to maintain market prices above target prices. Nevertheless, corn and soybean prices in early 1980 were no higher in real terms than they were in 1971–72, and only wheat showed a significant (30 percent) gain. In fact, for countries such as Japan and Germany whose currencies have appreciated against the dollar, U.S. grains and soybeans are substantially cheaper than they were before the food crisis. The policy thrust of the Reagan administration has been to keep loan rates at levels competitive in world markets. Whether recourse to acreage set-asides will be avoided remains to be seen.

Although the notion of an export cartel may be attractive to some producers, the United States is unlikely to go very far in that direction, for several reasons. First, world grain markets are very different from the petroleum market: while OPEC controls two-thirds of world supplies, a would-be cartel of grain exporters would control a mere 10 percent. Grain can be grown almost anywhere; systematic price rigging would soon backfire against the exporters in that it would stimulate production elsewhere. Second, in the United States, most farmers are aware of the long-term adverse effects of high prices on exports and are, in any event, reluctant to comply with acreage restrictions except when prices are unusually depressed. Third, American consumers, who have become sensitized to the inflationary effects of high grain prices, may be expected to continue to resist a policy of high food prices.

Better founded are concerns about temporary export controls. We are not referring here to politically motivated export restrictions such as the recent partial grain embargo against the USSR: it is inconceivable that the "food weapon" would be used against Japan. What cannot be ruled out is a recurrence of temporary shortages requiring some form of rationing of exports. Assurances to the contrary notwithstanding, it is questionable whether public opinion in the United States would tolerate another run-up of grain and soybean prices of the dimensions experienced in 1973–75, without shifting more of the burden of adjustment to the importing countries. Indeed it is possible to conceive of circumstances in which political pressures could lead the United States to curtail exports rather severely so as to maintain stability in the domestic market. American policy has recognized the problem, but the grain stocks built up thus far under the farmer-held reserve program are not large enough to meet contingencies of the magnitude experienced in 1972–75. In effect, the farmer-owned reserves have merely replaced the stocks formerly held by the federal government, rather than contributing an addition to total stocks.

A major new factor affecting the future supply–demand balance for American grains and soybeans is the subsidized use of "biomass" for the production of fuel alcohol. Legislation passed in early 1980 provides, *inter alia*, for (1) the exemption (until 1992) of gasohol from the federal gasoline tax, worth 40 cents per gallon on the 10 percent ethanol content of gasohol; (2) special investment tax credits; and (3) government loans and loan guarantees up to $1.5 billion. Exemptions from state motor fuel taxes, now in effect in more than twenty states, add a subsidy amounting to another 40 cents to $1.00 per gallon of ethanol. The stated aim of these incentives is to encourage the production of 10 billion gallons of fuel alcohol a year by 1990 to replace about 10 percent of the gasoline consumed in the United States.

The effect of this legislation on the grain and soybean markets will depend on a number of factors, including (1) the comparative profitability of various feedstocks in the production of ethanol; (2) the future course of gasoline prices; (3) the speed with which distillers respond to the generous incentives that have been provided; (4) the supply and demand elasticities for grains and soybeans.

Enough is known about the economics of ethanol production from various biomass sources (Cecelski and Ramsay, 1980) to support the expectation that in the United States grains such as corn and grain sorghum will continue to be commercially more attractive for conversion into fuel alcohol than other biomass feedstocks until their real prices have been driven up to about twice their early 1980 levels. Because it would take about 100 million tons of corn to produce 10 billion gallons of ethanol, a doubling of U.S. feedgrain prices may well occur even before the 10 billion gallon target is reached. On the other hand, a substantially greater effect on grain prices is unlikely because at that price level other biomass materials, as well as unsubsidized coal-based synthetic fuel, may be expected to become competitive.

The effect on soybean prices and production is uncertain. Competition from distillers' dried grain (DDG) (a protein feed that is a by-product of the distilling process) might be expected to depress the market for soybeans. But this may be offset by increased demand as protein feeds are substituted for expensive grain in feed rations. In addition, the soybean market will be supported by the demand for oil.

On balance, the gasohol program as it stands could raise food prices in the United States substantially, since only about one-third of the feed value of the corn is returned to the food system in the form of DDG. The net additional burden on the U.S. food system would thus be on the order of 67 million tons, in terms of grain equivalent, by 1990. Coming on top of the expected increase in the demand for food—about 50 million tons of grain and 12.5 million tons of soybeans[32]—the demand for alcohol fuel would require a substantial increase in crop acreage. It would also require more fertilizer and pesticide per acre as land is shifted from other crops to corn. These increases would have to be accomplished in a space of a few years beginning around 1985; it is at that time that the gasohol program could be expected to exert strong upward pressure on grain prices (Sanderson, 1980 and 1981).

One cannot predict with certainty, of course, whether grain prices will actually double as a result of the gasohol program and if so, whether the increase will be permanent. The world energy situation may unexpectedly improve in the 1980s and petroleum prices may drop, in real terms, making gasohol less attractive commercially and politically. Construction of new distilling capacity may take longer than expected. Coal-based synthetic fuel may become economic sooner than expected. We may see a technological breakthrough in the conversion of cellulosic materials to alcohol. American taxpayers and consumers may become disenchanted with an extremely costly program that makes only a marginal contribution to American liquid fuel supplies.

There are indications that some of these factors are coming into play. Following an early spurt in 1980, planned investments in ethanol production appear to be slowing down. The slowdown can be attrib-

---

[32] Half the increases projected for 2000.

uted to several reasons, including the current petroleum "glut" and the high cost of borrowing. Probably more important, however, is the coolness displayed by the Reagan administration toward the subsidization of synthetic fuels, and specifically, its decision to terminate the loan guarantee program for ethanol projects. Although there is no indication, so far, that the administration will ask for the repeal of the federal tax exemption, modifications including a phase-out before 1992 are not inconceivable. Termination of the federal tax exemption would make crop-based ethanol production unprofitable under almost any foreseeable circumstances.

Transitional Problems of Japanese Agriculture

Not surprisingly, perhaps, the issues that make headlines in domestic as well as international discussions of agricultural policy are not the major historical trends but the problems of adjustment to these trends. In Japan, the most acute current adjustment problem concerns rice, but citrus and certain livestock products have also attracted attention.

Rice

Japanese rice policy has been guided by the principle that for this basic food, at least, Japan should remain self-sufficient. This objective has not been challenged by Japan's trading partners nor—despite its high costs—by domestic consumers and taxpayers. As it turned out, however, support prices were so high as to generate mounting surpluses. Attempts at surplus disposal are meeting with increasing opposition from taxpayers and also from American and other foreign rice exporters. There is a growing consensus in Japan that rice production will have to be cut back to match the declining domestic demand. Projections to 1990 by the Ministry of Agriculture, Forestry and Fisheries (U.S. Agricultural Counselor, Tokyo, 1979b) suggest that the area planted to rice, which declined by 570,000 hectares between 1969–71 and 1980, will have to be reduced by another 400,000 to 500,000 hectares so as to adjust production to a projected demand of only 9.3 to 10.0 million tons by 1990. Most of the diverted rice land is to be converted to the production of wheat, barley, and soybeans, with the remainder going to forage crops.

The rice diversion program, which relies mainly on incentive payments, is extremely costly: budgetary expenditures on the program now exceed $2 billion annually. From the point of view of the Japanese economy, the costs are actually higher than they would have been if rice production had been continued.[33]

But for various reasons, the most frequently discussed alternatives are even less palatable. A sharp reduction in rice support prices or sharp cuts in the acreage or quantities eligible for support seem to be ruled out by political considerations. Budgetary savings could be achieved by shifting the cost to the consumer—for example, by imposing a levy on imported grains to pay for the excess cost of domestically produced grain, or through the operation of a "blend" price system such as already exists for wheat and sugar. This solution is undesirable on several grounds. First, it would drive up the already high costs of livestock products. Second, the additional cost to the Japanese consumer would greatly exceed the budgetary savings. Third, this solution would be viewed by the United States and other foreign suppliers as a new barrier to imports (and in the case of soybeans, as an impairment of the zero duty bound in the General Agreement on Tariffs and Trade), and it could lead to retaliation against Japanese exports.

Given the strong desire to keep the diverted rice land in production, an incentive program for planting alternative crops is inevitable. The costs of the program could be reduced, however, by reducing the incentives for rice production. The Ministry of Agriculture, Forestry and Fisheries has already taken steps in this direction—for example, by limiting recent increases in rice support prices and by paying less for low-quality rice. Consideration might be given to increasing the incentives for growing forage, which is in short supply in Japan and cannot be imported as economically from abroad as feed concentrates.

Citrus

Japan is an efficient producer of citrus fruits. Current adjustment problems are caused by the leveling-off of demand for fresh *mikan*—

---

[33] In 1978, the farmer received $826 per ton for wheat, or $2,670 per hectare, plus a diversion payment of $3,000 per hectare (including the special subsidy for wheat), or a total of $5,670 per hectare. For brown rice, he would have received $1,370 per ton or $6,165 per hectare. Deducting the value of the output at world prices, the subsidy equivalent was $5,370 per hectare diverted to wheat, as compared with $4,365 per hectare planted to rice. The price of wheat planted on diverted rice land works out to $1,600 per ton—about ten times the world price (based on data supplied by the U.S. agricultural counselor, Tokyo).

the predominant orange variety grown in Japan—since 1972, while production resulting from earlier plantings continued to grow. Government policy has responded to the resulting pressure on producer prices by encouraging acreage cuts. Not surprisingly in this situation, Japanese growers have strongly resisted U.S. requests for import liberalization and have resented the modest quota increases (mainly for off-season imports) negotiated in the multilateral trade negotiations.

Japanese citrus growers point to the high level of fresh orange consumption in Japan (15 kgs per capita annually—about twice the U.S. level) as an indication that the saturation point may have been reached. But total per capita citrus consumption in Japan is only 25 kgs (including 4.5 kgs fresh fruit equivalent of processed fruits) as compared with 47 kgs (35 kgs in the form of processed fruit, mainly orange juice) in the United States. This, together with the evidently strong demand for imports, suggests that there still is considerable room for expansion of citrus consumption in Japan. This demand can be met by more diversified production and the development of a market for citrus juice. Although Japanese growers will not be easily persuaded of this proposition, experience suggests that imports can play a useful role in developing a market for a broader range of citrus products.

Livestock products

Japan's livestock producers have generally benefited from strong market demand resulting from high income elasticities for their products. But at times, the growth of demand has not been sufficient to absorb the domestic output at prevailing prices. Both producer and retail prices are high by international standards despite the low cost of imported feedstuffs. Although high land values (escalated by government crop supports) play a role here, particularly in dairy and beef production, the main reason for the high price level in the livestock sector lies in inefficiencies in production and distribution which can be remedied. Protection against imports is required so long as these inefficiencies persist, though on a decreasing scale as productivity catches up with that achieved elsewhere.

It is natural in this situation for producers to resist any liberalization of imports on the ground that it endangers the rationalization and growth of domestic production. But the "infant industry" argument can be carried too far: excessive protection removes the spur of foreign competition that can promote more efficient production and market expansion.

There is substantial evidence that Japan can become fully compet-itive in poultry[34] and pork and, at the same time, achieve a much higher level of efficiency in dairy and beef production. Further econo-mies of scale[35] and improved livestock housing and feeding practices will be required to accomplish these goals. A substantially expanded forage base for dairy and beef cattle will also be necessary. Production costs should decline as these problems are solved, and this should open the way for a further significant expansion of the domestic market. Although some of the increased demand should be met by increased imports, particularly of beef and manufactured dairy prod-ucts, there is little doubt that the bulk of it can be satisfied efficiently by domestic production.

Implications for U.S.–Japanese Agricultural Relations

Interdependence benefits both countries but causes uneasiness in Japan

Any realistic assessment of U.S.–Japanese agricultural relations must begin with the growing interdependence between the two economies. The United States has become Japan's most important single market, taking one-fourth of its exports. Japan is the market for one-tenth of American exports. Although Japanese exports consist mainly of in-dustrial products, more than one-third of U.S. exports to Japan are agricultural products. Japan's heavy dependence on food imports is a subject of perennial debate and concern in Japan. As indicated earlier, Japan now imports about half of its primary food energy, and half of the imports come from the United States.

The dependence is mutual, however. For the American farmer, the Japanese market is second only to that of the European Community. In 1980, American agricultural exports to Japan amounted to $6.1 billion, or 15 percent of total U.S. agricultural exports. Grains and soybeans alone accounted for $3.9 billion. Altogether about one out of twenty acres cultivated in the United States is producing agricul-tural products for Japan; and this acreage is greater than all the cropland in Japan. Five percent of all the grain produced by American farmers and 10 percent of all soybeans go to Japan.

[34] It is already competitive in egg production.

[35] For example, through cooperative production and marketing facilities.

That both countries benefit from this growing interdependence needs no elaboration. The benefits to American agriculture are equally obvious. But Japan's agriculture also benefits as it shifts toward high-value crops and livestock production based on imported feedstuffs. Yet, Japanese policy toward this transformation has been ambivalent. It has supported it by providing financial, technical, and administrative assistance. It has kept the door open for rising imports of feed-stuffs. But uneasy about this growing dependence on imports, government policy has also impeded change by protecting grain production at over four times the level of world prices. On balance, by far the greater effort has gone to preserving the old pattern rather than facilitating adjustments to changing conditions. The current campaign to increase the production of wheat and coarse grains, despite their high costs, is the most recent manifestation of the continuing effort to slow down and, if possible, arrest the decline in food self-sufficiency.

The food security issue

Americans tend to dismiss Japanese concerns about food security as irrational or a mere pretext to cover other motives. But it is not difficult to understand why the concept of "food security through self-sufficiency" has maintained such a strong hold on public opinion in Japan. Food supply has been a recurrent problem in the country's history. The older generation can still remember the acute food shortage in the years following World War II when famine was barely averted by emergency food imports arranged by the occupation authorities. The world food crisis of 1972–1975, the 1973 soybean embargo that is invariably invoked by Japanese discussing the matter, and developments in the world petroleum market have all contributed to keeping Japanese fears alive.

There is a growing awareness, on the other hand, that food self-sufficiency—or even potential self-sufficiency—is no longer a realistic goal for Japan and that ways must be found to ensure food security through dependable international arrangements.

One widely discussed type of arrangement would be an international buffer stock—or a system of national stocks managed according to common guidelines. Negotiations along these lines for wheat broke down in February 1979 because of differences with the developing countries that could not be overcome. Talks aiming at a less binding agreement are continuing in the International Wheat Council, but much larger stocks, including feedgrains and soybeans, would be required to meet likely contingencies of concern to Japan.

An alternative possibility, with better prospects for the near future, would be a bilateral agreement between the United States and Japan, similar to the Abe-Butz "gentleman's agreement" of August 1975, which was allowed to lapse in 1978. As it turned out, the quantities to be supplied by the United States and to be purchased by Japan (3 million tons of wheat, 8 million tons of corn and sorghum, and 3 million tons of soybeans annually in 1976 to 1978) were all exceeded. Because Japanese import demand is rather stable and predictable within narrow margins, it should be possible in a new agreement to provide for tighter commitments, for example, an import commitment by Japan at the level of current imports, and a supply guarantee by the United States at, say, one-third above that level. The agreement would, of course, have to be taken into account in domestic supply management decisions in both countries.

Although both sides will probably wish to limit the duration of a formal agreement to 3–5 years, it should be clearly understood that both parties expect to renew it periodically, taking account of the development of trade in the interim. It is only in this way that the agreement can be useful in facilitating long-term agricultural adjustments. Another possibility, suggested by the Forum for Policy Innovation in Japan, would be the acquisition by the Japanese government of a contingency grain reserve, possibly financed by foreign exchange reserves.

Beef, oranges, and other foods

Although American and Japanese agriculture are essentially complementary, with the United States supplying feedstuffs that cannot be produced economically in Japan, there are some products the United States is trying to export to Japan for which Japan can hope to become competitive. Is the United States justified in pressing Japan to admit such imports (as it did during the multilateral trade negotiations)?

As pointed out earlier, a case can be made for transitional protection of industries in the course of development (beef) or readjustment (oranges). On the other hand, excessive protection can be counterproductive, by removing the pressure for rationalization and readjustment of domestic production and by hampering the expansion of the domestic market. A gradual reduction of import barriers is, therefore, desirable.

Japan has removed or relaxed restrictions on some of these imports, either unilaterally or in the context of the General Agreement on Tariffs and Trade negotiations. Nevertheless, highly protective measures—ranging from import barriers such as quotas, duties, variable levies, tariff quotas, and import monopolies to domestic support measures—remain in place (Sanderson, 1978, chapter 3; Yoshioka, 1979). The volume of citrus fruits, dairy products, and meat that is trickling in over these barriers still is not large enough to have a significant effect on domestic prices.[36]

The MTN agreements and beyond

A pattern for further gradual liberalization of import quotas has now been set as a result of the multilateral trade negotiations (MTN) (USDA, 1979e). Specifically, Japan will increase its beef imports from 100,000 tons in 1978 to at least 135,000 tons in 1983 (about 30 percent of consumption). The quota for high-quality beef from the United States will be increased from 16,800 tons to 30,800 tons in Japanese fiscal year 1983. For oranges, Japan agreed to increase its import quotas progressively from 52,000 tons to 89,000 tons[37] (although over half of this is reserved for the "off-season," April to September, when domestic oranges are not available in the market). Imports of fresh oranges, rising from 1.5 percent of consumption to about 3 percent, will continue to be insignificant, however. Quotas for citrus juice have been increased by 8,500 tons (42,000 tons fresh fruit equivalent). Tariff reductions have been granted on a number of commodities including beef offals, turkeys, prepared and preserved poultry, chicken legs, vegetable oils, nuts, raisins, grapefruit, lemons and limes, and certain canned fruits. The fixed duty on pork has been cut in half but the trade value of this reduction is limited because of the continued existence of a variable levy designed to protect the domestic support price.[38] The binding of the duty-free treatment of soybeans is valuable to the United States mainly because it seems to close the door to future preferential treatment of competitors such as Brazil.

The total trade effect of these concessions will be exceedingly modest. Two estimates are available concerning their effects on Japanese

---

[36] The techniques of protection employed by Japan may have contributed to minimizing that effect. For both beef and oranges, sellers are expected not to undercut the prices of comparable domestic products. Large windfall profits accrue to the quota-holding importing firms (citrus) or to commodity groups such as the Livestock Industry Promotion Corporation acting as exclusive distributors. In the latter case, however, the profits are to be used, in principle, for the rationalization of the production and distribution systems, and this should reduce prices in the long run.

[37] Includes the special quota for Okinawa (7,000 tons).

[38] When supplies in the domestic market were short, the 10 percent fixed duty has often been waived in the past.

imports from the United States. In chapter 3 in this volume, Houck puts the gain from tariff reductions at $88 million[39] by 1987 and the gain from quota increases (mainly beef) at $123 million. Schnittker (1979) puts the total increase at $167 million. At this slow pace of trade liberalization, the effect on supplies and prices in Japan will be marginal.

Acceleration of the pace is desirable but difficult politically. To make it more acceptable to producers, direct government payments might be offered to offset, at least in part, any adverse price effects of increased imports. Such payments should be directed toward increasing productivity. Because of the high elasticity of demand and the relative importance of imports, the beef sector would seem to be a particularly promising candidate for a gradual shift from price supports to direct payments.[40]

Mechanisms for policy coordination and cooperation

A major problem in managing agricultural relations between the two countries has been the proclivity on the part of both governments to take policy decisions without adequate forewarning, let alone consultation, of the other partner. In the main, this has been caused by political considerations. Among often cited examples are the American soybean embargo in 1973; the unexpectedly hard line taken by the United States on beef and oranges in the MTN; Japanese rice disposal programs; and abrupt changes in Japanese import quotas, to name only a few. What most of these cases seem to have in common is an element of surprise and a lack of sensitivity to specific political problems in the partner country.

American officials have argued, for example, that frictions over beef and oranges could have been avoided if the Japanese side had taken adequate account of the American political need for spreading the benefits of the MTN among as many groups and areas as possible to maximize domestic support for the MTN; and of a similar need for minimizing the adverse effects of Japanese rice disposals upon American rice and feedgrain growers through an appropriately phased and diversified program. On the Japanese side, it was felt that American pressure for increased imports of oranges came at a particularly inappropriate time because it coincided with a massive acreage reduction program. In most such cases, the political arithmetic prevails

---

[39] Of which $35 million are accounted for by pork, a gain that is questionable.

[40] One proposal widely discussed in Japan, by the Forum for Policy Innovation, would use an import levy to finance payments to producers. (See also Takahashi, 1979.)

over the economic arithmetic, and the political arithmetic of one side may be in sharp conflict with that on the other.

Regular intergovernmental consultations, which began in 1979, can help to alleviate these sources of friction. But more is required than a mere exchange of technical information (which in any event is already supplied by the embassies). The main purpose of these meetings should be to give each side advance notice of possible policy changes and a better understanding of the economic and political considerations entering into the decision-making process. Confidential talks conducted in this fashion by responsible policy-making officials can help provide a broader perspective while ensuring, at the same time, that the interests of the trading partner are not ignored.

In Japan as in the United States, specific problems of agricultural adjustment will continue to arise from time to time. They invariably generate much heat when they impinge on agricultural trade. Strident demands by trading partners are not helpful in bringing about rational solutions in such situations. What is needed is a sense of proportion and some sensitivity to each other's political problems, but also a recognition that protectionist solutions are undesirable and should be phased out over a reasonable span of time.

References

Cecelski, Elizabeth, and William Ramsay. 1979. "Prospects for Fuel Alcohols from Biomass in Developing Countries," paper presented at the United Nations conference on Long-Term Energy Resources, Montreal (Washington, D.C., Resources for the Future).

Cochrane, Willard W., and Mary E. Ryan. 1976. *American Farm Policy, 1948–1973* (Minneapolis, University of Minnesota Press).

Crosson, Pierre, and Sterling Brubaker. 1982. "Resource and Environmental Effects of U.S. Agriculture" (Washington, D.C., Resources for the Future).

FAO. See U.N. Food and Agriculture Organization.

FEA. 1976. Federal Energy Administration. *Energy Use in the Food System* (Washington, D.C., May).

Hayami, Yujiro. 1980. *A Century of Agricultural Growth in Japan* (Tokyo, University of Tokyo Press).

Houck, James P. 1979. *The Tokyo-Geneva Round: Its Relation to U.S. Agriculture.* Committee Print 96-12, Senate Subcommittee on International Trade of the Committee on Finance, 96 Cong., 1 sess. MTN Studies No. 2 (June).

Johnson, D. Gale. 1974. "Where U.S. Agricultural Comparative Advantage Lies," in D. Gale Johnson and J. A. Schnittker, eds., *U.S. Agriculture in a World Context* (New York, Praeger for the Atlantic Council of the United States).

MAF. 1975. Ministry of Agriculture and Forestry. *Long-Term Prospects of Production and Demand of Agricultural Products in Japan* (Tokyo).

MAFF. 1979. Ministry of Agriculture, Forestry and Fisheries. *Statistical Yearbook, 1977–78* (Tokyo).

National Agricultural Lands Study. 1981. *Final Report* (Washington, D.C., GPO).

OECD. 1980. Organization for Economic Cooperation and Development. *Meat Balances in OECD Member Countries, 1973–1978* (Paris).

Phillips, Jane K. 1979. "Food Prices Still Climbing in Most Surveyed Countries," *Foreign Agriculture* (Washington, D.C., U.S. Department of Agriculture, August) pp. 18–19.

PSAC. 1967. President's Science Advisory Committee. *The World Food Problem, Volume II* (Washington, D.C., May).

Rasmussen, Wayne D. 1974. *American Agriculture, A Short History.* (Washington, D.C., U.S. Department of Agriculture).

Sanderson, Fred H. 1975. "The Great Food Fumble," *Science* vol. 188 (May 9, 1975).

———. 1978. *Japan's Food Prospects and Policies* (Washington, D.C., The Brookings Institution).

———. 1980. "Gasohol—Boon or Blunder?" *Brookings Bulletin* vol. 16, no. 3 (Washington, D.C., The Brookings Institution).

———. 1981. "Economic Benefits and Costs of the Gasohol Program," *Resources No. 68* (Washington, D.C., Resources for the Future).

Schnittker Associates. 1979. *Multilateral Trade Negotiations: Results for U.S. Agriculture.* Committee Print 96-11, Senate Subcommittee on International Trade of the Committee on Finance, 96 Cong., 1 sess. MTN Studies No. I (June).

Takahashi, Ishiro. 1979. "The Beef Price Stabilization and Import Policies in Japan, An Alternative Plan for Beef, Price and Import Policies," in Institute of Food Policy, *Food Policy Study* vol. 19, no. 3 (Tokyo).

Tsuchiya, Keizo. 1976. *Productivity and Technological Progress in Japanese Agriculture* (Tokyo, University of Tokyo Press).

U.N. Food and Agriculture Organization. 1960. *Food Supply, Time Series* (Rome).

———. 1979a. "Food Supply: Calories per Capita per Day," *Monthly Bulletin of Statistics* vol. 2 (November).

———. 1979b. "Food Balance Sheet, Japan, Average 1975–77," computer printout (Rome).

———. 1979c. "Agriculture: Toward 2000" (Rome).

University of California. 1974. *A Hungry World: The Challenge to Agriculture* (Davis, Calif.).

U.S. Agricultural Counselor, Tokyo. 1979a. "Commodity Statistics."

———. 1979b. "Agricultural Commodity Supply/Demand Projections to 1990 proposed by MAFF" (November 9).

USDA. 1962. U.S. Department of Agriculture. *Agricultural Land Resources*, Agriculture Information Bulletin no. 263 (Washington, D.C., May).

———. 1974. U.S. Department of Agriculture. *Reference Tables on Wheat and Coarse Grain Supply—Distribution*, Foreign Agricultural Circular, Grains (Washington, D.C., April).

———. 1975. U.S. Department of Agriculture. *Cropland for Today and Tomorrow*, Agriculture Economic Report No. 291 (Washington, D.C., July).

———. 1976. U.S. Department of Agriculture, *Changes in Farm Production and Efficiency*, Statistical Bulletin No. 561 (Washington, D.C., September).

———. 1977. U.S. Department of Agriculture, Soil Conservation Service. *Potential Cropland Study*, Statistical Bulletin No. 578 (Washington, D.C., October).

———. 1978a. U.S. Department of Agriculture. *Farm Financial Conditions, Perspectives and Projects*, table 7 (Washington, D.C., August).

———. 1978b. U.S. Department of Agriculture. *A Guide to Understanding the 1977 Food and Agriculture Legislation*, Agricultural Economics Report No. 411 (Washington, D.C., September).

———. 1978c. U.S. Department of Agriculture, Economics, Statistics and Cooperative Service. "The Grain-Oilseeds-Livestock Model, 2000 Base Run" (Washington, D.C., December 9).

———. 1979a. U.S. Department of Agriculture. *Handbook of Agricultural Charts* (Washington, D.C., October).

———. 1979b. U.S. Department of Agriculture. *Farm Income Statistics*, Statistical Bulletin No. 627 (October).

———. 1979c. U.S. Department of Agriculture. *National Food Review* (Washington, D.C., Fall).

———. 1979d. U.S. Department of Agriculture. *The Farmer-Owned Grain Reserve Program*, Issue Briefing Paper No. 18 (Washington, D.C., July 20).

———. 1979e. "US–Japan Pact," *Foreign Agriculture* (Washington, D.C., July).

———. 1980a. U.S. Department of Agriculture. *Changes in Farm Production and Efficiency*, Statistical Bulletin No. 638 (January).

———. 1980b. U.S. Department of Agriculture. *Reference Tables on Wheat, Corn and Total Coarse Grain Supply—Distribution for Individual Countries*, Foreign Agriculture Circular, Grains (February).

U.S. Department of Commerce. 1974. "The Input–Output Structure of the U.S. Economy, 1967," *Survey of Current Business* vol. 54 (February).

———. 1979. *Illustrative Projections of World Populations to the 21st Century* (Washington, D.C., Bureau of the Census, January).

Yoshioka, Yutaka. 1979. *Food and Agriculture in Japan*, About Japan Series (Tokyo, Foreign Press Center, March).

Index

427